Inquiry-Based Learning – Undergraduate Research

Harald A. Mieg
Editor

Inquiry-Based Learning – Undergraduate Research

The German Multidisciplinary Experience

 Springer Open

Editor
Harald A. Mieg, Prof. Dr.
Georg-Simmel Center for Metropolitan Studies
Humboldt-Universität zu Berlin
Berlin, Germany

ISBN 978-3-030-14222-3   ISBN 978-3-030-14223-0   (eBook)
https://doi.org/10.1007/978-3-030-14223-0

This Springer imprint is published by the registered company Springer Nature Switzerland AG.
The registered company address is: Gewerbestrasse 11, 6330 Cham, Switzerland

The book is a translation of
H. A. Mieg and J. Lehmann (Eds.) (2017). Forschendes Lernen: Wie die Lehre in Universität und Fachhochschule erneuert werden kann. Frankfurt/Main: Campus.

Funding
Translation: German Federal Ministry of Education and Research (BMBF)
Open access: University of Oldenburg

SPONSORED BY THE

Federal Ministry
of Education
and Research

Translation by: Tolingo GmbH, Hamburg

Foreword

If we take the Kuhnian view (Kuhn 1962), advances in science – or, indeed, in any discipline – take place as discrete paradigm shifts, presaged by a thorough synthesis of a community's or discipline's knowledge base. Often, those striving to integrate research into undergraduate degree programs hunger for connection to practitioners working in very different educational environments. For the paradigm shift from rote learning models to inquiry-driven, research-rich models is ascendant, but not yet established. Diverse perspectives and success stories are vital to accelerate the change process and strengthen shared confidence in the goal of combining research and teaching.

This is one reason why *Forschendes Lernen: Wie die Lehre in Universität und Fachhochschule erneuert werden kann* is such a welcome addition to the growing literature on the worldwide undergraduate research paradigm shift and why it is so valuable to have it translated into English to reach an even wider community. Edited by Drs. Harald Mieg and Judith Lehmann, this ambitious volume of essays provides a sweeping overview of the state of undergraduate research throughout German institutions and a vision of what baccalaureate education could be, given a wider embrace by faculty and institutions of a more student research-centered learning process. In some ways, the volume explores fairly well-trodden paths. The chapters that form the "Principles" section lay out background philosophies for re-centering education on the student experience, and their tenets will seem familiar to readers of publications produced by the Council on Undergraduate Research, as well as leading researchers and practitioners in the United Kingdom (e.g., Healey and Jenkins 2009) and Australasia (e.g., Brew 2010). Many other aspects of the publication are sui generis, portraying the two distinctive, complementary/competitive ecosystems operating within German higher education: the Universitäten and Fachhochschulen. Chapters on undergraduate research in diverse disciplines, ranging from sciences to highly applied arts (architecture) and social science (social work), illustrate both the breadth of German undergraduate research efforts and the growing sense of community among these disparate efforts. The final section of the book, "Perspectives," offers fascinating insights to the future of both German and European Union undergraduate education and connects the undergraduate research experience to economic development. As in the United States, the growing recognition in Germany that undergraduate students have the capacity, energy, and acumen to undertake sophisticated research projects is leading to an eagerness to invest in their entrepreneurial activities. Would enhancing and expanding undergraduate research lead to higher rates of transfer of research discoveries to the marketplace? To new industries and businesses led by undergraduate researchers? In a highly industrialized and sophisticated economy such as Germany's, greater investment in faculty-mentored undergraduate research is sure to yield significant economic dividends in the future. Social dividends, such as increased higher education success for students who are first in their families to attend university, are also tied to undergraduate research participation rates. Population segments that are socioeconomically and culturally marginalized may find their educational and career pathways significantly improved through participation in research-based coursework, particularly if it is tied to societal concerns, and projects that benefit the communities in which they live. There can surely be no better reason to shift the teaching practice to research-based curricula than the opportunity to reinvigorate and renew teaching, promote student success and acculturation, and spur economic development.

Executive Officer, Council on Undergraduate Research   Elizabeth L. Ambos
Washington, DC, USA
June 2018

References

Brew, A. (2010). Imperatives and challenges in integrating teaching and research. Higher Education Research and Development, 29 (2) 139-150.

Healey, M. and Jenkins, A. (2009). Developing Undergraduate Research and Inquiry. York: HE Academy. Available at: https://www.heacademy.ac.uk/sites/default/files/developingunder-graduate_final.pdf; accessed on December 5, 2015.

Kuhn, T. S. (1962). The Structure of Scientific Revolutions, 1st. ed., Chicago: Univ. of Chicago Press.

Preface

Why publish a book on German undergraduate research (UR)? Starting with the Boyer reform in the 1990s, there is more experience and discussion of UR in the United States than probably anywhere else in the world. It was Elizabeth Ambos, CEO of the Council on Undergraduate Research, who motivated us to translate our book into English. Her argument was there is a German tradition of inquiry-based learning (IBL), dating back to Wilhelm von Humboldt, that results in specific forms of research (e.g., community-based research) that might be of interest for advancing UR in the United States.

Wilhelm von Humboldt, a Prussian scholar and functionary, was the father of the German research university at the beginning of the nineteenth century and promoted the integration of research and teaching. Previously, universities all over Europe had focused on education – teaching the canons of philosophy, theology, medicine, and law. But in 1810, Berlin University was founded in accordance with Humboldt's new masterplan. There were already other pioneering, research-focused universities, such as at Göttingen. However, it was Humboldt who defined the model of the research university that still prevails throughout Europe, the United States, and elsewhere.

Since 2011, German universities have again faced reforms, this time by the Qualitätspakt Lehre, a nationwide initiative for advancing both study conditions and teaching quality at German universities. In this context, a community of about 50 universities and 300 individuals was formed to discuss IBL, with a specific aim of implementing more UR at German universities. Almost all of those universities are represented in this book. The original German edition sought a consented status quo on IBL and UR. The target group encompassed universities, politicians, and public administrations, with the aim of promoting UR.

This English version of our book is not only a translation but also an inversion: the original German edition contained some text windows showing more advanced international experiences of UR from outside Germany, in particular from the United States. That perspective is now inverted, providing a view into the German system of higher education. There are implicit specificities of the system that should be made explicit for international audiences:

- In general, higher education in Germany is public – there are no tuition fees. With some minor exceptions, German universities are run by the state.
- The system is highly differentiated, ranging from research universities to schools for vocational education (combining school-based education with work in an enterprise). Somewhere in between are Fachhochschulen, universities of applied sciences that try to find their own position and which are increasingly taking over more research functions.
- Almost all lecturers at German universities would consider their teaching as research-based. However, a profound assumption among German academics is, first, you have to study theory (as the condensed knowledge of a field); then, in a later phase of your studies, you can start your own research. That is why UR represents a cognitive and organizational challenge to the German system of higher education.

I hope that our glimpse into inquiry-based learning at German universities, and its role for UR, might inform the discussion of UR in its various contexts worldwide.

Berlin, Germany   Harald A. Mieg
July 2018

Acknowledgments

We thank the German Ministry of Education and Research (BMBF) for funding this translation of the book and the University of Oldenburg, host of the 2019 World Congress on Undergraduate Research (CUR), for funding the open access.

Contents

Focus: Curricula

Part II   Disciplines

Overview

Disciplines, class I

Life Sciences

STEM

Introduction: Inquiry-Based Learning - Initial Assessment

Harald A. Mieg

Inquiry-based learning is a didactic principle in higher education that relies on student independence: learning by conducting their own research. The principle of inquiry-based learning is part of the long tradition of education through scholarship (*Bilaung durch Wissenschaft*), which sees academic studies "as participation in scholarship as a never-ending process" (Huber 2009, p. 1, translated). Most institutions of higher learning use the definition of inquiry-based learning developed by Ludwig Huber (2009) as a working definition:

> In contrast to other learning methods, inquiry-based learning is characterized by the fact that learners shape, learn and deliberate on the process of a research project, which is aimed at obtaining insights that are of interest to third parties, doing so throughout all the essential phases of said project; from developing questions and hypotheses, selecting and implementing the methods, through testing and presenting the results, either by working independently or in active collaboration with an overarching project. (Huber 2009, p. 11, translated)[1]

This definition highlights three characteristics of inquiry-based learning: firstly, students should go through the entire research process; secondly, the results should have some degree of value in terms of novelty, and not just for the students themselves; thirdly,

---

[1] Huber and others used various English translations for "Forschendes Lernen." Besides "inquiry-based learning," we often find the terms "explorative learning" or "research-based learning." For the sake of clarity and consistency, we only use the translation "inquiry-based learning" in this book.

I would like to thank Ludwig Huber and Peter Tremp for their helpful comments on this introduction, which helped me to clarify my statements.

H. A. Mieg, Prof. Dr. (✉)
Humboldt-Universität zu Berlin, Georg-Simmel-Zentrum für Metropolenforschung,
Berlin, Germany
e-mail: harald.mieg@hu-berlin.de

© The Author(s) 2019
H. A. Mieg (ed.), *Inquiry-Based Learning – Undergraduate Research*,
https://doi.org/10.1007/978-3-030-14223-0_1

inquiry-based learning should be conducted independently. All of this raises broader questions, including: what role do professors or lecturers play? How does inquiry-based learning fit into a university education?

Numerous degree programs at German universities and universities of applied sciences have integrated inquiry-based learning into their program. The objective of this book is to provide an initial assessment of these efforts. To this end, we must examine the framework of higher education policy within which inquiry-based learning is currently being discussed. My introduction starts with the Bologna Process, a process which seeks to reform higher education at the European level, and which continues to shape the discussion regarding research today (presented in Sect. 1.1 of this introduction).

As we will see, inquiry-based learning has its own history, which extends back into the period of higher education reforms in the 1960s (presented in Sect. 1.2). Since that time, several variations have developed: there is increased focus on scholarship, as noted in Huber (2009), while at the same time, attention is placed on autonomous learning (Sect. 1.3). I conclude the introduction with an overview of the more than 30 chapters that comprise this book (Sect. 1.4). This will allow us to draw the conclusion that inquiry-based learning is advancing the notion of education through scholarship (*Bildung durch Wissenschaft*) by exploring the learning potential in conducting research or, respectively, in conducting independent research.

1.1 The Bologna Process

The Bologna Process implements the idea of harmonizing European standards at the level of postsecondary education. The objective was to create uniform European standards and thus to increase the mobility of students within Europe (cf. Hanft and Müskens 2005). To this end, the secretaries of education of 29 European countries signed a joint declaration in 1999. The name of the initiative and place where it was signed have immense symbolic significance: the first university was founded in Bologna in 1088.

1.1.1 Motivation, Content, Criticism

Anyone who studied in the 1980s could empathize with the fact that reform was needed. At the time, universities functioned like "educational authorities" where it was possible to stake a claim for a university education. The range of subjects offered at each university location was to be taught at the same level of quality. These were the days of the mass university. Mobility was not encouraged. Many students started in a course of studies at a university to which they had been admitted, and then switched to the city and the course of studies they had dreamed of later. The periods of study were extremely long. Anyone who left university early, after 3, 4 or 5 years, left without a degree in hand. Preliminary diplomas or interim certificates were of no value, if for no other reason than that they were never intended to serve as a terminal degree.

The Bologna Process is primarily associated with the introduction of the bachelor's/master's system. The bachelor's degree is intended to serve as a professional qualification in a field. The master's degree is a postgraduate degree intended to serve as an introduction to scholarship. The bachelor's/master's system was implemented very expediently in Switzerland. In Germany, fierce discussions ensued within seasoned programs that award a *Diplom*, in particular in the technical fields: a *Diplom-Ingenieur* (someone with a master's degree in engineering) had extensive training in an area, including all subsidiary studies that seemed relevant for potential professional activity. The German *Diplom* could and still can be considered certification for the quality of the academic education.

The primary critique of the Bologna reform, both on the part of the students and on the part of the educators, is the reduction of the degree program to the level of school instruction. While it was previously necessary for students to collect credit certificates for their Course Record Book over an extended period of time, i.e. proof of attendance for seminars or other courses, and then to complete exams, testing occurs at a much tighter pace in the bachelor's/master's system. The basis for this is the ECTS (European Credit Transfer System), a time-based system for recording academic achievements. A bachelor's degree, for example, comprises approximately 60 ECTS, whereby 1 ECTS point is equivalent to approximately 30 h of work. The time expenditure is assessed in such a way that it includes both attendance in seminars and work done at home. Instead of reflection and room for enthusiasm, the bachelor's degree is hectic and a source of exam stress.

1.1.2 And Inquiry-Based Learning?

How does the Bologna Process relate to inquiry-based learning? One of the criticisms is as follows: inquiry-based learning is nothing more than a "repair measure" that would not have been necessary had it not been for Bologna. Old, highly evolved degree programs (in particular those awarding the German *Diplom*) familiarized students with research and scholarship and, at the same time, offered them a great deal of leeway for personal initiative. This is no longer possible within the abridged bachelor's degree program. A likely response to this would be to note that the fact that old study programs that awarded a *Diplom* have simply been shoehorned into a new format has created problems with the bachelor's/master's system in Germany: the intermediate diploma program (*Vordiplomstudium*) became a bachelor's degree program and the primary course of study (*Hauptstudium*) became a master's degree program. As a result, the standard curricula are overloaded with material and there is only a limited likelihood that the degree program can be completed in the projected number of terms. It requires time and patience to get the bachelor's/master's system up and running.

It is often argued that there is simply no time for inquiry-based learning in bachelor's degree programs that have been reduced to the level of school instruction, with examination practice divided into small increments. In terms of the approach, the opposite is the case: the ECTS points system offers enormous potential to re-evaluate the time invested and in particular, to estimate and foster the value of the individual's own time that they have invested in a course of studies (cf. Sidler 2005). The individual's own time refers to self-organized learning. An ECTS point may comprise 15 h of attending a lecture, for example, as well as 15 h for research and preparation of a presentation (*Referat*). The ECTS system departs from the old system of semester hours per week, which only included the length of seminars or tutorials. The ECTS system makes it possible to create new areas of freedom. In this context, inquiry-based learning once again makes sense.

1.2   A Short History of Inquiry-Based Learning

The notion of inquiry-based learning was developed in conjunction with the higher education reforms of the 1960s. During that period, a series of new universities emerged – such as the Technical University of Dortmund and the University of Bielefeld – and there was a push for democratization, not least because of student unrest. Along with professors, students and student organizations acquired new co-determination rights. The original text on inquiry-based learning, "Inquiry-based learning – scholarly examination" ("Forschendes Lernen – Wissenschaftliches Prüfen"), published in 1970 by the Federal University Assistants' Conference (Bundesassistentenkonferenz), is both enlightening and at the same time, somewhat dismaying: enlightening because the educational issues and the task are depicted with great clarity; dismaying because there appears to have been so little change in the issues with the courses of study.

1.2.1   Reform Initiatives: Project-Based Studies

Project-based studies are a reform idea that is closely associated with inquiry-based learning. In the case of project-based studies, students must complete research projects. Historically, as Huber reports, project-based studies were "expressly brought up and advanced as a critical concept in opposition to inquiry-based learning" (2013, p. 25, translated). Project-based studies were less – or not solely – focused on scholarly understanding, but rather on the impact on social change. Project-based studies were introduced in the 1970s and 1980s in many degree programs, for example in sociology, and soon abandoned again. One reproach that was made by educational planners was that students were not learning enough theory. In sociology in particular, theoretical work is indispensable. It also became clear that many professors used the format of project-based studies to withdraw and actually reduce their teaching load. In project-based studies, it is the students who have to do the work. The University of Bremen has retained and transformed project-based studies; right from the beginning, inquiry-based learning was considered an essential element of project-based studies (Robben 2013).

Experience with project-based studies teaches us two things: Firstly, students cannot be left on their own, but instead require active support and regular feedback; secondly, students need a clear process structure which they can use to orient themselves There are degree programs and institutions of higher learning that have successfully developed the idea of project-based studies, for example workshops in the field of social work designed to introduce students to current research. What is essential is that such workshops be accompanied by courses that lead students further to their own research over the semesters (cf. Schmidt-Wenzel and Rubel, Chap. 13, in this volume).

1.2.2   The United States: Undergraduate Research

There was a university reform movement in the United States that led to the demand for inquiry-based learning; however, it originated under very different circumstances. The starting point was that the large research universities were receiving too little up-and-coming, research-oriented talent from their own bachelor's degree programs. Unlike the situation in Germany, undergraduate education in the United States is generally not linked to master's degree programs, and professors teach at the master's level, while bachelor's degree programs are organized by other lecturers. A bachelor's degree can be acquired in almost any field of study in the United States; the range of courses is driven not least by the wishes and expectations of the parents who are prepared to pay for the education.

In 1995, the Boyer Commission published a strategy paper regarding the transformation of bachelor's degree programs (1998). The primary and essential demand was: academic studies based on research should (once again) become the standard. The task of research universities should be neither to iron out the shortcomings of students' school education nor to attempt to comply with all of the educational ideas advanced by parents. The Boyer Commission introduced a new standard, one which parents have by now become willing to pay for: undergraduate research – in other words, bachelor's students working on their own research projects. To this end, programs referred to as UROP (Undergraduate Research Opportunities Programs) have been set up at many institutions of higher learning. Through these programs, educators, research facilities or even research-oriented companies can post project proposals for which students may apply. The intention is for research to become a matter of course in a degree program.

1.2.3   Education Through Scholarship and the Bologna Process

For the past 200 years, university education in Germany has been programmatically characterized by education through scholarship (*Bildung durch Wissenschaft*). Critics of the Bologna Process fear a departure from this underlying concept. They claim that the bachelor's/master's system is a frivolous replication of the American higher education system, which is based on different conditions than the German system. In particular, unlike in

England and the United States, German-speaking countries have a tradition of extra-occupational education at vocational schools. The main criticism is the bachelor's degree's explicit focus on employability: education is being made marketable.

Critics, and presumably some university administrators, consider employability to be specific vocational training. It is clear that a bachelor's degree neither can nor should provide this. Employability is better understood as a general employability: Students should be able to define problems and carry out projects, think analytically and present their proposals both orally and in writing. This makes university knowledge accessible in practice.

1.3 Approaches to Inquiry-Based Learning

The discussion surrounding inquiry-based learning is embedded in a broader didactic discussion on an international scale about the connection between research and teaching. As we will see, the emphasis here is on learning (Sect. 1.3.1). The discussion taking place in German-speaking countries focuses on research. Research in inquiry-based learning may refer to scholarship, as per Huber (Sect. 1.3.2) or the Zurich framework (Sect. 1.3.3). On the other hand, research may also refer to personal problem-solving; in this context, research is synonymous with learning from experience (Sect. 1.3.4).

1.3.1 International Discussion: Nexus

Since the 1990s, the motto characterizing the international discussion about instruction in higher education has been "From Teaching to Learning," which was influenced by the article of the same name by Barr and Tagg (1995). The two authors advocate a new didactic approach: move away from thinking in terms of defined courses and instead in terms of supporting and recording learning processes. Barr and Tagg focus on American colleges; however, they refer to higher education in general when they write: "In the Learning Paradigm… a college's purpose is not to transfer knowledge but to create environments and experiences that bring students to discover and construct knowledge for themselves, to make students members of communities of learners that make discoveries and solve problems." (Barr and Tagg 1995, p. 21). According to Barr and Tagg, a change in thinking is needed on all levels – from educators and students to curricula and institutional structures.

Participation in research is one way to shift the emphasis from instruction to learning. With regard to the connection between teaching and research, Healey and Jenkins (2009) made a proposal that has gained a great deal of currency in the international discussion. Essentially, they distinguish two dimensions that shape how to design research-related teaching. The first dimension concerns how actively students participate in a course. This dimension ranges from passive reception to active participation, for example in their own

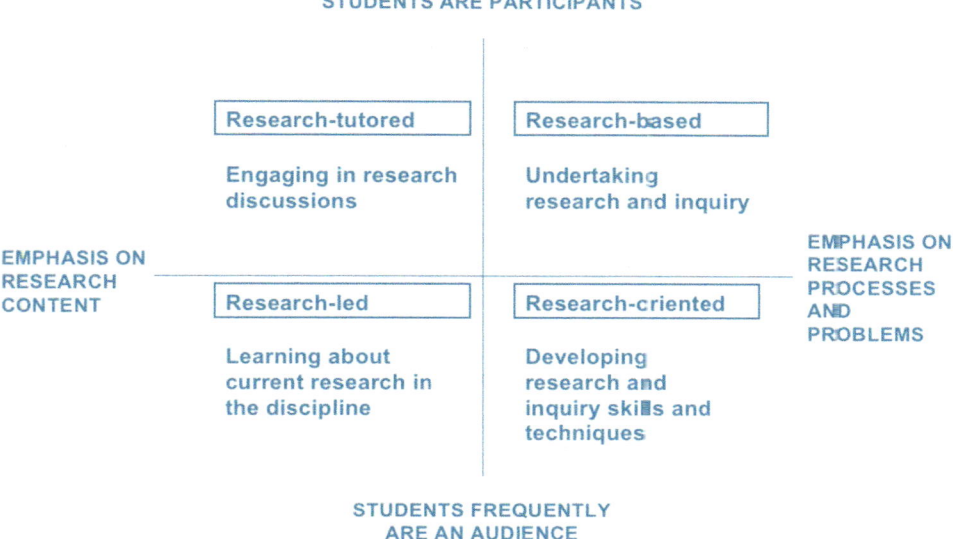

Fig. 1.1   The nexus between research and teaching according to Healey and Jenkins (2009, Fig. 1.1, p. 7). © 2009. Advance HE (formerly The Higher Education Academy). All rights reserved

research. The second dimension comprises the aspect of research on which the course should focus: is it more about obtaining research results, or is the purpose to present and practice the research process?

The intersection of these two dimensions yields a four-field matrix, which is shown in Fig. 1.1. Two fields represent the extremes of research-related teaching: Courses that focus on the introduction of research results, which are referred to as "research-led," are on one side. On the other, we find courses in which the students conduct their own research projects, referred to here as "research-based." These terms carry with them a great deal of potential for confusion: All educators at institutions of higher learning would claim that their teaching is research-based, i.e. based on scholarly research. The other two fields refer to the introduction to scholarly work and research methods ("research-oriented") as well as the subject-based discussion of current research ("research-tutored"). At the Humboldt University of Berlin, a study with a comparable typology has shown that all pure forms can be found in teaching (Rueß et al. 2016).

1.3.2   Research-Related Teaching and Learning According to Huber and Reinmann

Ludwig Huber (2014) illustrates the diversity and blurring of concepts in the field of research-related teaching and learning and proposes a restructuring. This is essentially a tripartite division that extends from "research-based" and "research-oriented" to "inquiry-based learning." Here, the space set up for students to participate in research is expanding.

1. *Research-based*: According to Huber, "research-based" means that "the teaching and learning is based or founded on research" (p. 24, translated). Regarded as a form of research-related teaching and learning, "research-based" does not simply mean information about research results (that would be "research-led," as seen in Fig. 1.1). Instead, instruction should "provide the student with the opportunity to follow the path of how a question is or, respectively, becomes research" (ibid., translated). This also includes reflecting on the "difference between social problems and the definition of scientific problems" (ibid., translated).
2. *Research-oriented*: Learning and teaching would be referred to as research-oriented if the research process is imparted in a sufficiently strong manner. This should "lead students as quickly as possible to current research or should enable them to begin doing research themselves" (ibid., translated).
3. *Inquiry-based learning*: Here, Huber refers to his definition of inquiry-based learning cited above, and emphasizes the distinguishing trait of independence: conducting one's own research. What is essential is "that the learners conduct research themselves; learning and research coincide in terms of the form of activity: the core of inquiry-based learning lies in the students' own actions" (ibid., p. 25, translated)

Gabi Reinmann used the Huber typology as a proposed model for research-related teaching and learning. As was the case with Healey and Jenkins (2009), the main dimension extends from "students receive" in the research-based mode to "students produce" in inquiry-based learning. Accordingly, the requirements for teaching are changing. According to Reinmann, research-based teaching is about teaching research, while research-oriented instruction is about empowering research and inquiry-based learning is about supporting students in their own research. Reinmann has developed corresponding suggestions for testing (Reinmann, Chap. 9, in this volume) (Table 1.1).

Table 1.1 Pragmatic definitions for the typology of inquiry-based learning according to Huber (2014), with explanations regarding the relevancy to teaching

	Research-based	Research-oriented	Inquiry-based learning
Definition	Learning to understand research	Conducting research	Conducting independent research
Learning	Reception		Production
Teaching	Imparting knowledge	Empowerment	Support

Source: author's illustration, based on Reinmann, Chap. 9, in this volume

Discussion of the possibilities of inquiry-based learning is kindled in particular when the subject is how to design the introductory phase of the course of study. Can and should one expect first-year students to begin their own research projects? In many disciplines, it is argued that students must first acquire a sufficient understanding of the technical basics. This line of reasoning avails itself of the metaphor of scholarship - or sciences - as a building. According to Huber (2009), in the case of inquiry-based learning, a more suitable metaphor for learning would be the growth of a tree:

> If we start thinking of education in the static nature of a building, then of course reliable foundations, et cetera, with sufficient width and depth would have to be laid as a 'basis'; at the same time, these would appear to be 'fixed,' 'unchangeable' 'able to be clearly delimitated'; only then can what is open, airy, diverse or different superstructures and expansions rest thereon. It is not conceivable, however, that education would be so static, especially nowadays. [...] Education – or, better, self-education – can more aptly be described as the growth of a tree that shoots up, extending its branches to different sides and, at the same time, driving its roots even deeper. (Huber 2009, p. 20, translated)

Figure 1.2 depicts the two alternative metaphors for teaching and learning. On the left, we see an image of sciences as a building. At the lowest level, we find basic knowledge. If we think of this as a basement-like foundation, a person would first have to descend to the bottom of the picture when starting university. In-depth specialist knowledge builds on basic knowledge (disciplinary knowledge). On the top floor we find sciences as an enterprise, illustrated here as an observatory. On the right, by contrast, we see the metaphor of the tree, which extends upwards while simultaneously deepening its roots. Applying the image to inquiry-based learning: Through our own research we are able to deepen our expertise and specialize in a meaningful way at any time.

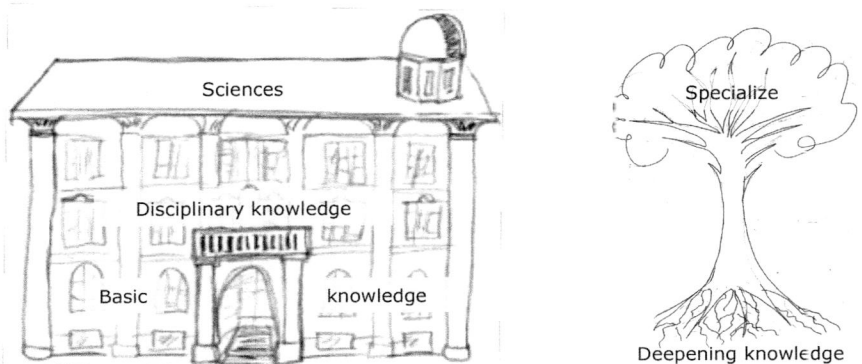

Fig. 1.2 House of sciences vs. tree metaphor for inquiry-based learning. (Source: author's illustration)

1.3.3 The Zurich Framework for Research-Oriented Instruction

The Zurich framework offers an approach for designing and revising curricula and degree programs so that they are research-oriented. The basis for the framework is a model of the research process, which is composed of research activities. Figure 1.3 depicts the research process with its stages in parentheses. The first stage or, respectively, the first research activity is "develop a question," and the second is "examine the state of research." A total of seven stages have been defined. The final stage is "present, explain and publish results." Various didactic issues in terms of proofs of performance, course formats or in conjunction with study programs must be dealt with in connection with a research orientation.

Proofs of Performance Possible proofs of performance are identified at each stage of the research process. These correspond to the products or, respectively, the intermediate products of research. For the first stage – the development of a question – this would be a research paper, for example; for the last stage, the presentation of the results, the proof of performance could be a conference poster. Examples of research products that can serve as proofs of performance are shown on the right in Fig. 1.3.

Course Formats The research activities are linked with course formats. In terms of the research activity, it is now possible to correlate course formats and proofs of performance such as a research paper as a proof of performance for the development of a question in a seminar. Thus even unusual course formats become gained increased significance, for example using a conference as a framework for teaching in order to practice presenting results using a poster. The course formats are listed to the left of the stages in Fig. 1.3.

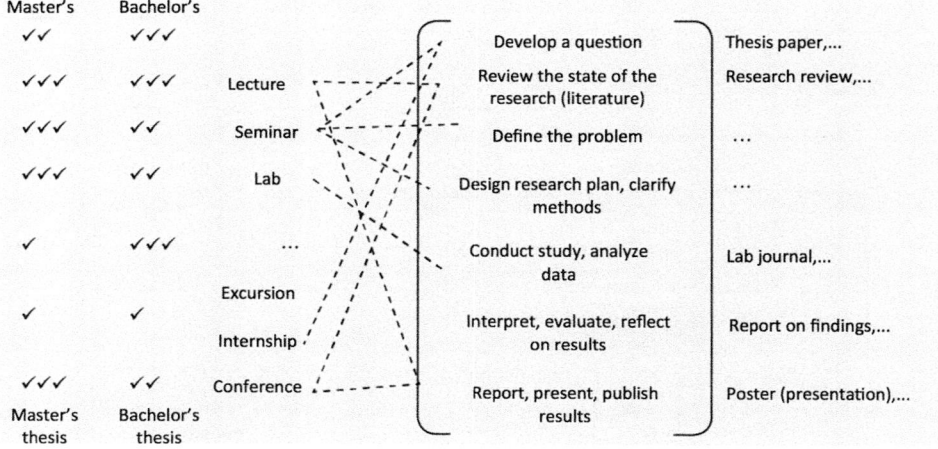

Fig. 1.3 Zurich framework for linking teaching and research (© Prof. Dr. Peter Tremp, Zurich; cf. Tremp and Hildbrand 2012)

Study Programs Curricular anchoring occurs through integration into study programs and study levels, for example in the bachelor's and master's degree. The University of Bremen implemented inquiry-based learning with the help of this model (cf. Schelhowe and Kaufmann, Chap. 33, in this volume).

1.3.4 Alternative Approaches: The Analogy of Research and Learning

In the German-language discussion of inquiry-based learning, the analogy of research and independent learning is sometimes used as an argument. Learning occurs when we perceive something as a problem and look for a solution. It thus depends more on the subjective interpretation of the problem and less on the scholarly derivation of a need for research. The approaches of Wildt (Wildt 2009; Schneider and Wildt 2009) and Ludwig (2011, 2014) are presented below by way of example.

Wildt (2009) or, respectively, Schneider and Wildt (2009) assume that the research cycle is to be understood by analogy with the learning cycle. They define the learning cycle based on Kolb (1984) as a sequence: experience, reflection, formation of a concept, experimentation and the formation of new experience. Accordingly, the research cycle begins with a question that is fostered by practical experience and topic identification. After passing through further stages of research planning and investigation, the research cycle leads to an application and "immersion in practice" (see Fig. 1.4), and then transitions to new research.

For students, the analogy of research and learning means that inquiry-based learning is to be understood as personal development (Schneider and Wildt 2009). An implementation of this approach can be found in art education at Folkwang University of the Arts: The goal and guideline of inquiry-based learning is personal development by means of "experience-based, cooperative and independent learning" (Spelsberg-Papazoglou et al. 2018, p. 5).

For Ludwig (2011, 2014), learning begins with subjective "action problems." Learning and research processes therefore resemble one another: "Because learning processes start with low-threshold action problems, but also with confusion that reaches a crisis (of realization), they are structurally identical to research processes" (Ludwig 2014, p. 12, translated). Learning is about "preserving or expanding our opportunities to participate in the world" (p. 11, translated). Here, Ludwig references Holzkamp (1993): We can only understand learning processes if we take into account the subjective reasons for learning.

Unlike Wildt, Ludwig is less concerned with personal development. Rather, according to Ludwig, the goal of university education is professionalism (Ludwig 2014, p. 8). Professionals "move between demands in practice on the one hand, and theoretical knowledge that their scholarly discipline makes available to them on the other" (ibid., translated). Accordingly, inquiry-based learning means participation in the professional community. Ludwig's approach has gained currency in social work (cf. Schmidt-Wenzel and Rubel, Chap. 13, in this volume).

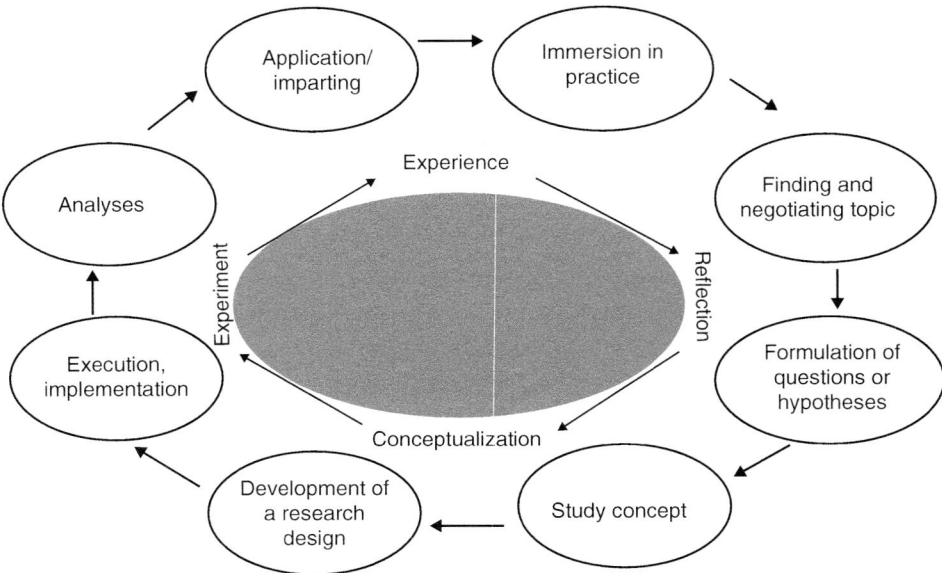

Fig. 1.4 Research cycle with embedded learning cycle. (Source: Wildt 2009, Fig. 4, p. 6, translated)

1.4   This Book, and the Discussion Regarding Institutions of Higher Learning

This book is based on experiences gathered at more than 20 institutions of higher learning. Access to and the implementation of inquiry-based learning is correspondingly diverse. We have structured the book according to three categories of questions.

1. The first is *principles*, which involves the following type of questions: What principles does inquiry-based learning follow?
2. Secondly, *disciplines*, concerning the following question: How is inquiry-based learning implemented in each discipline?
3. Thirdly, *perspectives*, which addresses the following question: What opportunities does inquiry-based learning offer for the development of institutions of higher learning and for society?

1.4.1   Principles

An examination of the principles of inquiry-based learning begins with an introduction from the perspective of higher education research (Pasternack, Chap. 2, in this volume). Peer Pasternack makes it clear that there are very different views on higher education within Europe, it being more instruction-oriented in France and more focused on general education in England. Pasternack points out the paradox that inquiry-based learning shares with schooling: the desire to foster student independence through a certain degree of compulsion. The subsequent chapters containing basic considerations are subdivided according to specific aspects:

- Learning in inquiry-based learning (e.g. independent learning, a "Shift from Teaching to Learning")
- Research in inquiry-based learning (e.g. developing skills, reflection)
- What does inquiry-based learning mean for the organization of study (e.g. exams, interdisciplinary nature)?

1.4.2 Disciplines

Organizing the section of the book on specific disciplines was somewhat challenging. An obvious solution would be alphabetical sequencing, from A as in architecture, to T as in theology. The presentation would thereby take on the quality of a handbook, and suggest that the user may choose their subjects. Another solution would be to use a traditional classification system of disciplines, for example with the natural sciences on one hand, and social sciences and liberal arts on the other. But this quickly results in numerous exceptions, e.g. teaching certifications, health sciences or design. All attempts at a complete classification system were unsatisfactory. This failure reveals how dynamic and how diverse subject development is today.

The solution, which we use here, is a hybrid comprising a classification system with sample disciplines, and an alphabetical listing of disciplines that fall outside of this classification system. Not least, the classification system takes this form due to the fact that we wish to take into consideration both universities and universities of applied sciences. We distinguish between four classes of disciplines:

1. Firstly, disciplines for which professional development is an issue and purpose (cf. Dick et al. 2016), e.g. social work.
2. Secondly, the STEM disciplines of science, information technology, engineering and mathematics (MINT in German-speaking countries), because these are the subject of an educational policy discussion of their own.
3. Thirdly, the "life sciences," from traditional medical studies to the newly created field of health sciences. Life sciences enjoy outstanding social significance and attract research funding that is not unsubstantial.
4. Fourthly, art and design, with the three disciplines of the arts, architecture and design by way of example, all three of which are grappling to reach an understanding of research.

The disciplines that are subsequently listed alphabetically include the sustainability sciences, for example. These implement transdisciplinary teaching as cooperation between university and society. Their example teaches us how inquiry-based teaching and learning can be implemented without explicitly referencing the concept of inquiry-based learning.

1.4.3   Perspectives

The final chapters deal with the prospects of inquiry-based learning for institutions of higher learning as well as for the economy and society. The main focus is on higher education development, an example of which being the University of Bremen (Huber et al. 2013; Schelhowe and Kaufmann, Chap. 33, in this volume), not least because of the correlation with the increasing level of heterogeneity among students (Satilmis, Chap. 36, in this volume), as well as new media that create completely new forms of teaching (cf. Hofhues, Chap. 35, in this volume). Unfortunately, what we failed to accomplish was a chapter on inquiry-based learning in continuing education. In general, the image provided by inquiry-based learning becomes blurred as soon as we leave the realm of university education. The question of how companies view inquiry-based learning remains crucial. Companies still appear to be largely unfamiliar with inquiry-based learning.

Finally, a word about inquiry-based learning at universities of applied sciences: Student surveys show that students at universities of applied sciences benefit more from inquiry-based learning than students at universities (cf. Multrus 2012). This may have something to do with the distance of universities of applied sciences to basic research. Critics even claim that universities of applied sciences are simply using the concept of inquiry-based learning to obtain university status. There are certainly quite divergent ideas at the universities of applied sciences themselves: While some believe the future of universities of applied sciences lies in more basic research and the right to award doctorates (much like the technical and artistic institutions of higher learning in the nineteenth century, which gradually developed into universities), others emphasize the special practical relevance, and the responsibility of the universities of applied sciences to teach with reference thereto. A function of universities of applied sciences in our knowledge-based society can certainly be sought in their proximity to the professional field (cf. Mieg 2016). This is because the processing of professional knowledge for the formation of scholarly theory benefits a great deal from practical relevance. In this sense, inquiry-based learning can also be a very helpful tool.

An initial assessment of inquiry-based learning could be summarized as follows: Inquiry-based learning is capable of enhancing the positive aspects of the Bologna Process: promoting independence, reflection and the use of one's own time; taking into account independent learning biographies and lifelong learning in general; as well as a reassessment of the relationship between higher education and forms of research in professional practice. This is accompanied by a redefinition of education through scholarship (*Bildung durch Wissenschaft*), with a university education as noted in Huber (2009) understood to be "participation in science as a never-ending process" (p. 1, translated).

References

Bundesassistentenkonferenz (BAK) (1970). Forschendes Lernen – Wissenschaftliches Prüfen. Ergebnisse der Arbeit des Ausschusses für Hochschuldidaktik, Bonn (Nachdruck 2009). Bielefeld: UniversitätsVerlagWebler.

Barr, R. B./Tagg, J. (1995). From Teaching to Learning – A New Paradigm for Undergraduate Education. *Change, Nov./Dec.*, 13–25.

Boyer Commission on Educating Undergraduates in the Research University (1998). *Reinventing undergraduate education: A blueprint for America's research universities.* Stony Brook: State University of New York at Stony Brook.

Dick, M./Marotzki, W./Mieg, H. A. (Hrsg.). (2016). *Handbuch Professionsentwicklung.* Bad Heilbrunn: Klinkhardt / UTB.

Hanft, A./Müskens, I. (Hrsg.). (2005). *Bologna und die Folgen für die Hochschulen.* Bielefeld: UniversitätsVerlagWebler.

Healey, M./Jenkins, A. (2009). *Developing undergraduate research and inquiry. Heslington: The Higher Education Academy.* Retrieved 28 April 2016 from https://www.heacademy.ac.uk/sites/default/files/developingundergraduate_final.pdf

Holzkamp, K. (1993). *Lernen. Subjektwissenschaftliche Grundlegung.* Frankfurt: Campus.

Huber, L. (2009). Warum Forschendes Lernen nötig und möglich ist. In L. Huber/J. Hellmer/F. Schneider (Hrsg.), *Forschendes Lernen im Studium. Aktuelle Konzepte und Erfahrungen* (S. 9–35). Bielefeld: UniversitätsVerlagWebler.

Huber, L. (2014). Forschungsbasiertes, Forschungsorientiertes, Forschendes Lernen: Alles dasselbe? Ein Plädoyer für eine Verständigung über Begriffe und Unterscheidungen im Feld forschungsnahen Lehrens und Lernens. *Das Hochschulwesen (HSW), 62*(1+2), 22–29.

Huber, L./Kröger, M./Schelhowe, H. (Hrsg.). (2013). *Forschendes Lernen als Profilmerkmal einer Universität. Beispiele aus der Universität Bremen.* Bielefeld: UniversitätsVerlagWebler.

Kolb, D. A. (1984). *Experiential learning: Experience as the source of learning and development.* Englewood Cliffs, NY: Prentice-Hall.

Ludwig, J. (2011). *Forschungsbasierte Lehre als Lehre im Format der Forschung* (Brandenburgische Beiträge zur Hochschuldidaktik 3). Potsdam: Universitätsverlag.

Ludwig, J. (2014). *Lehre im Format der Forschung* (Brandenburgische Beiträge zur Hochschuldidaktik 7). Potsdam: Universitätsverlag.

Mieg, H.A. (2016). Akademische Freiheit an Fachhochschulen: begrenzt und befördert durch Berufsorientierung. *Die Hochschule*, (2), 54–67.

Multrus, F. (2012). Forschung und Praxis im Studium: Befunde aus Studierendensurvey und Studienqualitätsmonitor. Berlin: Bundesministerium für Bildung und Forschung BMBF.

Robben, B. (2013). Projektstudium in Bremen. (K)Eine Entwicklungsgeschichte. In L. Huber, M. Kröger & H. Schelhowe, *Forschendes Lernen als Profilmerkmal einer Universität. Beispiele aus der Universität Bremen* (S. 37–55). Bielefeld: UniversitätsverlagWebler.

Rueß, J./Gess, C./Deicke, W. (2016). Forschendes Lernen und forschungsbezogene Lehre – Empirisch begründete Systematisierung des Forschungsbezugs hochschulischer Lehre. Zeitschrift Für Hochschulentwicklung, 11(2), 23–44.

Schneider, R./Wildt, J. (2009). Forschendes Lernen und Kompetenzentwicklung. In L. Huber/J. Hellmer/F. Schneider (Hrsg.), Forschendes Lernen im Studium (S. 53–58). Bielefeld: UniversitätsVerlagWebler.

Sidler, F. (2005). Studiengangsprofile: Die Konzeption »outcome-orientierter« Studiengänge. In A. Hanft/I. Müskens (Hrsg.), *Bologna und die Folgen für die Hochschulen* (S. 28–51). Bielefeld: UniversitätsVerlagWebler.

Spelsberg-Papazoglou, K./Wildt, B./Wildt, J. (2018). *Erprobungen von Elementen forschen-den Lernens in der künstlerischen Hochschulbildung im Rahmen eines fächerübergreifenden Projektes an der Folkwang Universität der Künste.* Unveröffentlichtes Manuskript. Essen: Folkwang Universität der Künste.

Tremp, P./Hildbrand, T. (2012). Forschungsorientiertes Studium – universitäre Lehre: Das »Zürcher Framework« zur Verknüpfung von Lehre und Forschung. In T. Brinker/P. Tremp (Hrsg.), *Einführung in die Studiengangentwicklung* (S. 101–116). Bielefeld: Bertelsmann.

Wildt, J. (2009). Forschendes Lernen: Lernen im »Format« der Forschung. *Journal Hochschuldidaktik, 20*(2), 4–7.

Overview

In the first part of the book, after an introductory chapter by Peer Pasternack, we will examine the principles of inquiry-based learning, which we will frequently reference over the course of the book. Here, we will introduce theoretical, didactic and methodical principles and basic conditions, as well as the current state of research in the principles of teaching research. In the case of the other basic texts in this section of the book, a tripartite division of the subject matter lent itself to the task, along with a distinct focus on (1) learning, (2) research, (3) curricula. These thematic blocks deal with the following nine fundamental questions in detail:

Focus: Learning

Independent learning: In the case of inquiry-based learning, students should initiate independent learning processes and self-organized learning. Educators are called upon to reinforce this process. Matthias Wiemer thereby makes it clear that, in so doing, both educators and students must learn to tolerate complexities and uncertainties.

Research orientation: Ever since the Bologna reforms, educators in particular are caught in the gap between the historically evolved notion of holistic student education and a greater focus on their employability. Karin Reiber shows, from a developmental perspective, how a professional qualification can be didactically achieved through scholarship.

From Teaching to Learning: The "Shift from Teaching to Learning" is based on a "constructivist" understanding of learning: Learning occurs when it is possible to connect to existing, individual constructs, interests and motivations. In her article, Carmen Wulf describes the difficulties that this paradigm shift poses for educators and students.

Focus: Research

Competence development: Accepting or even welcoming uncertainties is part of the affective-motivational component of the research competence being developed, which
Christopher Gess, Wolfgang Deicke and Insa Wessels examine in their article. Even after
graduation, one's own professional practice should be unbiased and inquisitively
questioned.

Enculturation: Job profiles are integrated into subject cultures with their own knowledge cultures, which have become established through long-term professionalization processes. According to Ines Langemeyer, a long-term goal of inquiry-based learning is the
enculturation of students, thus making them aware that they are part of a thought collective
(Denkkollektiv) and a scholarly community.

Reflection: Reflection on the process is frequently specified as the last step in the
research process, which has hitherto scarcely been addressed within the context of inquiry-
based learning. According to Ludwig Huber, it is necessary to reflect not only on the
applied methods and subjective learning process, but also on scholarship in relation to the
common good.

Focus: Curricula

Assessment: Despite the autonomous design of inquiry-based learning, students' achievements must remain testable and be translated into performance assessments ("proofs of
performance"). In her article, Gabi Reinmann creates a system of various suitable forms
of assessment based on the continuum between the poles of receptive learning and independent research (and the equivalents thereof in terms of teaching).

Peer-to-peer: According to Anke Spies, insofar as the higher education organization
allows it, consultation within the context of peer-to-peer reviews – e.g. through tutorials
held by a postgraduate student, or a student at the same stage of their education – provides
the opportunity to improve the benefits of research discussions. This time-consuming
exchange is often used in inquiry-based learning, but does not diminish the responsibilities
of the educators.

Interdisciplinarity: The implementation of interdisciplinary or transdisciplinary teaching-learning courses is especially resource-intensive. Michael Prytula, Tobias Schröder
and Harald A. Mieg demonstrate that institutions of higher learning must regard themselves as learning institutions beyond subject cultures if they are to remain viable in the
future on the basis of interdisciplinary projects at the University of Applied Sciences
Potsdam (FH Potsdam).

Concepts and Case Studies: The State of Higher Education Research on Inquiry-Based Learning

Peer Pasternack

First of all, the bad news: Higher education research has not yet precisely determined how widespread inquiry-based learning is at German institutions of higher learning. Empirical surveys of this issue are lacking. Nevertheless, there is extensive literature on the subject. The literature comprises two types of texts: conceptual clarifications and models of inquiry-based learning on the one hand, and exemplary case studies on the other.

2.1 The Historical

The notion of inquiry-based learning within a course of studies is not entirely new. Three authors of texts that date back to the beginning of the nineteenth century or, respectively, to 1970 are often cited. The ideal of education through scholarship (*Bildung durch Wissenschaft*) originates with Wilhelm von Humboldt (cf. Humboldt 1810/1993). Contrary to popular assumptions, however, this ideal did not take effect during the nineteenth century, since it was not yet known at the time: Humboldt's position paper "Über die innere und äußere Organisation der höheren wissenschaftlichen Anstalten in Berlin" ("On the internal and external organization of higher scholarly institutions in Berlin") was only discovered in 1896 and published in extracts (Paletschek 2001). In the twentieth century, however, the Humboldtian university ideal came to fruition, as it promoted permanent reference levels for higher education.

P. Pasternack, Prof. Dr. (✉)
Martin-Luther-Universität Halle-Wittenberg, Direktor des Instituts für Hochschulforschung an der Universität Halle-Wittenberg (HoF), Halle, Germany
e-mail: peer.pasternack@hof.uni-halle.de

© The Author(s) 2019
H. A. Mieg (ed.), *Inquiry-Based Learning – Undergraduate Research*,
https://doi.org/10.1007/978-3-030-14223-0_2

Traces of this can also be found in the influential memorandum from the Federal University Assistants' Conference (BAK) entitled "Forschendes Lernen – Wissenschaftliches Prüfen" ("Inquiry-based learning – scholarly examination"), which was published in 1970 (BAK 1970, p. 7). That memorandum defined the features of inquiry-based learning:

- independent selection of the topic;
- the independent strategy for processing the topic and finding a solution, with the corresponding risks and errors, detours and chance discoveries;
- checking the results in terms of the hypotheses and methods;
- and the public communication and representation of the result (ibid., p. 14 et seq.).

Ludwig Huber's essay on inquiry-based learning as a didactic principle in higher education has also been quoted time and again ("Forschendes Lernen als hochschuldidaktisches Prinzip", Huber 1970). Huber, who at the time was also the chairman of the BAK committee on higher education didactics, intensified the BAK memorandum therein and simultaneously added a liberal arts foundation.

However, despite the fact that inquiry-based learning had long since found a place on the agenda, it cannot be said that it has gained acceptance. The orientation of higher education toward the guiding principle of inquiry-based learning is also by no means self-evident. An international comparison is sufficient to show that the basic conditions for such a concept differ significantly, which also means that some national higher education systems do not necessarily provide for inquiry-based learning at certain levels of academic education.

In France and in French-inspired higher education systems, institutions of higher learning essentially serve the function of academically based vocational training. In Britain and in British-inspired higher education systems, the role of personal development is strongly emphasized. The Humboldtian type of university (ideally) primarily serves the function of conveying scholarship. Structurally, the American model manages to combine all three of these functions. It includes a bachelor's education serving the essential function of personal development, professional education focused on obtaining "professional master's degrees" and, in a narrower sense, a scholarly doctoral education (PhD).

2.2   The Conceptual

Conceptually, inquiry-based learning is classified within a broad field of concepts: experiential learning, exemplary learning, project-oriented learning, research-led teaching, problem-based or, respectively, problem-oriented learning and unity of research and teaching. The fact that early education also uses the term "inquiry-based learning," for example, demonstrates the wide range of ways in which the term is understood. On the one hand, early education claims that the term encompasses "discovery learning," in the sense of learning experiences that individually lead to surprises and that allow the individual to identify what was previously unknown, thereby making it known. In early education, inquiry-based learning begins "with questions that come from the everyday lives of children and adolescents: What color is water? What does home mean to me? How do you make the perfect free kick?" (DKJS 2015, translated).

On the other hand, inquiry-based learning must be understood as a didactic translation of the (notion of) unity of research and teaching in curricular arrangements in institutions of higher learning. In this case, this deals with student participation in the research process. But even that does not mean that students should move freely along the cutting edge of research – in other words, the results of inquiry-based learning do not need to be novel in the sense of "never before considered or discovered." It is sufficient that this learning method be "aimed at gaining insights that are of interest to third parties" (Huber 2015, translated). In contrast to discovery learning by children, the primary concern in institutions of higher learning is an approach that is guided by scholarly methods.

Ludwig Huber, who continues to be very committed to the issue, sought to make a conceptual distinction, and has suggested the following type differentiation (Huber 2014):

Research-based learning and teaching: This establishes or is based on research and should convey basic problems of research. In particular, it should generate an understanding of the distinction between everyday and scholarly knowledge, and between social and scholarly problems.

Research-oriented teaching and learning: This is focused on research. Students go through a process of knowledge acquisition, at the end of which they have arrived at the state of current research where they themselves could begin researching. In so doing scholarly working methods themselves become the focus of learning, the aim of which is methodological competence. One example is the preparation of a research proposal including a task list, schedule and cost projection.

Inquiry-based learning (and teaching, which is made possible thereby): Inquiry-based learning differs from other teaching-learning methods in that it is not so much an issue of imparting secured knowledge (research), but rather of the process of researching and the acquisition thereof, thus the active participation of the students in the process of obtaining knowledge. The learners conduct research themselves so that learning and research coincide (ibid., pp. 33–36).

There is a wide variety of conceivable and existing learning situations in each of the three types. There are differences in the weighting, but sharper distinctions do not appear to be meaningful since the commonalities outweigh the differences: a strong orientation towards students and the use of innovative teaching-learning methods such as cooperative learning or e-learning. Given this, Huber advocates using a common umbrella term: "research-related teaching and learning" (ibid., p. 38).

What is meant by inquiry-based learning in the narrower sense is that students experience the entire research process, learning and reflecting on it independently:

> Inquiry-based learning is understood to be a learning style that is characterized by inquisitive, problem-oriented and critical thinking, by autonomous and creative work, as well as by intellectually understanding a research process and direct participation in research projects. (Multrus 2012, p. 53, translated)

The conceptual basis is constructivist learning. It is assumed that each individual constructs a subjective image of their environment, that students independently construct new knowledge as part of an active process, and as such, that educators act not as instructors, but as moderators and coaches. The activity is on the part of the learners, who shape their own learning in a situated process. Educators support, advise and encourage this process, and create a situated learning environment for the learners. In conjunction with this situation, learners develop their knowledge themselves and (constructively) fit that knowledge into their individual knowledge structure. Only then, according to the corresponding concepts, does correctly apprehended knowledge emerge, and in a manner that is less sluggish than knowledge acquired through instruction (cf. Schelten 2000, p. 2).

Traditionally, the priority was (and is) the instruction itself: "The creative power of the human being should first be created through instruction. The constructivist concept of learning, on the other hand, assumes that people already possess creative power, and that this simply needs to be exposed and cultivated" (ibid., p. 5, translated).

In higher education didactics, this has been translated into the phrase "from teaching to learning." A precarious constraint in underfunded institutions of higher learning is that constructivist learning always requires more effort than teaching that is organized around instruction. Moreover, constructivist learning is difficult to adapt for mass lectures.

Two rationales are invoked for inquiry-based learning within higher education theory or, respectively, higher education policy: on the one hand, an idealistic rationale emulating Humboldt and, on the other hand, a functionalist one. The latter focuses on the function of the university education as what is primarily a non-scholarly employment system. It is certainly possible to build a bridge between these two rationales, however:

> If we take a closer look at the kind of core competencies that apparently decide employability (a critical and analytical intellectual capacity; reasoning abilities; capacity to work and learn independently; ability to solve problems and make decisions; planning, coordination and management ability; cooperative work behavior, etc.), it becomes clear that the traditional Humboldtian virtues of cross-fertilization between research and teaching are also astonishingly topical from today's perspective. It is surprising that the list of skills relevant to employability covers many of the competencies demanded by modern research (Bourgeois 2002, p. 41, translated)

The surprise essentially rests on the fact that there are increasing similarities between the research process on the one hand, and problem-solving professional action on the other. Anyone who studies today will very likely have to make decisions about complicated issues under pressure (e.g. time pressure) and handle complex, risky situations that are characterized by uncertainty in their professional life. In order to do so, he or she must be able to distinguish the essential from the nonessential, to select cause and effect bundles, to undertake societal contextualization and action impact assessments, to organize problem-solving arrangements, to select options for action and to control processes.

The career path is therefore completed via a university education (instead of other qualification paths) because university graduates often have to deal with situations that are not routine within their professional contexts of action. In order to be able to act confidently in the resulting professional situations, what is needed is a scholarship-based power of judgment, which is to say the ability to methodically manage and critically analyze and evaluate complex issues, as well as an ability to act that is explicitly based thereon. These abilities should also make it possible to solve problems that either cannot be taught during a course of study due to the quantity of material, or that could not have been known: "The learning objective is to develop intelligent knowledge that makes it possible to transfer solution strategies to new situations" (Schumacher 2009, p. 833, translated).

Because students are preparing to manage non-standard situations of knowledge application, successful career paths that originate in higher education must be both developmental and educational: Education teaches us how to survive, and development tells us why, as Hartmut von Hentig noted in a lecture. To this end, "infection through contact with scholarship" would be considered developmental (Daxner 2001, p. 74, translated). Inquiry-based learning is one of the most successful ways to achieve this: It promotes the recognition of correlations and thus the development of a knowledge of correlations; this fosters the ability to recognize the general in the specific.

2.3   The Empirical

As a rule, the empirical apprehension of a situation reveals discrepancies between an idea and the realization thereof. This is also true of inquiry-based learning; the idea and concept of institutions of higher learning, on which these are consistently based, do not typically coincide with the reality of higher education. As mentioned at the outset, there has been no survey on how widespread inquiry-based learning is. Nevertheless, it is still possible to establish how aware students are of the prevalence of research-based courses. Based on the data from the 11th and 12th student surveys and the Studierendenqualitätsmonitor (Student Quality Monitor), Multrus (2012) and Ramm et al. (2014) in particular arrive at a conclusion: not very aware. The results of the 12th student survey were as follows:

- 40 percent of students surveyed at universities and 39 percent of students at universities of applied sciences were unable to provide any information about the existence of research-related study programs.
- Up to a third of students indicated that there are no research-related courses in their degree program, with some differences between students at universities and universities of applied sciences. Twelve percent of students at universities and eight percent of students at universities of applied sciences indicate that they have a wide range of research-related study opportunities (ibid., p. 261 et seq.).

The broad literature on inquiry-based learning contains more descriptions and assessments of case studies than overall surveys (cf., instead of many: Reiber 2007; Huber et al. 2009; FH Potsdam n.d.). These regularly refer to the different and highly diverse forms of such learning: Teaching research project, research workshop, research seminar, project module, case study, practice project, intervention project, action research, or practice research. Recently, "service learning" – the integration of social engagement into the curriculum – has been added to this list. At the same time, this provides a new opportunity to work towards abolishing the (artificial) contradiction between research and practical relevance in a course of studies.

2.4   Conclusion

Unlike schools, institutions of higher learning depend on internal tensions that are what makes them institutions of higher learning in the first place. These tensions range between theory and practice, research and teaching, academic freedom and social responsibility, subjectivity and objectivity, natural sciences and liberal arts, basic and applied research, a specialist and generalist orientation, development and education, tradition and innovation, disciplinarity and interdisciplinarity, certainty and uncertainty.

The specific quality of a given institution of higher learning is not the product of the individual, opposite poles in this charged relationship, but instead in the way those poles are bridged. This gives rise to paradoxes. Immanuel Kant, for example, points out the so-called pedagogical paradox: Pupils are to be empowered to make use of their freedom, and yet must submit to the compulsion of education (Kant 1803/1964, p. 711). We should also mention the paradox in which the unity of research and teaching strives to unite the science that itself is fixated on the lack of knowledge (research) with the science that wishes to bypass ignorance as much as possible (education) (Baecker 1999, p. 64 et seq.).

The strength of institutions of higher learning is not in avoiding such paradoxes, but rather in consciously developing them in order to adequately prepare students to manage the conflict of norms that they will constantly encounter after their studies:

> Clergy deal with sinners and heretics, judges with lawbreakers and parties to a dispute, teachers with the deviant behavior of adolescence, psychologists with patients attached to their neurotic infantilisms, administrators with citizens and politicians who refuse to comply with the bureaucratic exigencies, architects with builders and their idiosyncrasies, engineers with business economists who counter their creative designs with cost arguments, etc. (Lenhardt 2005, p. 101, translated)

For this reason, as a rule, attempts at higher education reform likewise fail when, instead of cultivating the tensions, they seek to make one pole dominant, for example teaching rather than research, or practical application rather than a theoretical approach. Inquiry-based learning, on the other hand, is a paradigmatic example of how bridging one of the constitutive tensions on which institutions of higher learning depend can succeed.

References

Baecker, D. (1999). Die Universität als Algorithmus. Formen des Umgangs mit der Paradoxie der Erziehung. *Berliner Debatte Initial, 3/1999*, 63–75.

BAK – Bundesassistentenkonferenz (1970). *Forschendes Lernen – Wissenschaftliches Prüfen. Ergebnisse der Arbeit des Ausschusses für Hochschuldidaktik*. Bonn: Bundesassistentenkonferenz.

Bourgeois, E. (2002). *Zukunftsforschung zur Entwicklung der Beziehungen zwischen Hochschulausbildung und Forschung mit Blick auf den Europäischen Forschungsraum*. Luxemburg: Europäische Kommission/Generaldirektion Forschung.

Daxner, M. (2001). Qualitätssicherung. Die Steuerungsrelevanz von Qualitätsorientierung. In J.-H.Oltbertz/P. Pasternack/R. Kreckel (Hrsg.), *Qualität – Schlüsselfrage der Hochschulreform* (S. 71–75). Weinheim/Basel: Beltz Verlag.

DKJS – Deutsche Kinder- und Jugendstiftung (2015). *Forschendes Lernen*. Retrieved 22 April 2015 from http://www.forschendes-lernen.net

FH Potsdam (n.d.). *Formen Forschenden Lernens an der Fachhochschule Potsdam, Potsdam*. Retrieved 12 April 2015 from http://www.fh-potsdam.de/fileadmin/user_upload/fl2/Diverse/FL2_FoFoLe_Broschuere_WEB.pdf

Huber, L. (1970). Forschendes Lernen als hochschuldidaktisches Prinzip. *Neue Sammlung, 3/1970*, 227–244.

Huber, L. (2014). Forschungsbasiertes, forschungsorientiertes, Forschendes Lernen: Alles dasselbe? Ein Plädoyer für eine Verständigung über Begriffe und Unterscheidungen im Feld forschungsnahen Lehrens und Lernens. *Das Hochschulwesen, 1+2/2014*, 32–39.

Huber, L. (2015). *Forschendes Lernen: Begriff, Begründungen und Herausforderungen*. Retrieved 22 March 2015 from https://dbs-lin.rub.de/lehreladen/lehrformate-methoden/forschendes-lernen/begriff-begruendungen-und-herausforderungen/

Huber, L./Hellmer, J./Schneider, F. (2009). Forschendes Lernen im Studium. Aktuelle Konzepte und Erfahrungen. Bielefeld: UniversitätsverlagWebler.

Humboldt, W. v. (1810/1993). Über die innere und äußere Organisation der höheren wissenschaftlichen Anstalten in Berlin. In W. v. Humboldt, *Werke in fünf Bänden, Bd. IV*. Stuttgart: J. G. Cotta'sche Buchhandlung.

Kant, I. (1803/1964). Über Pädagogik. In I. Kant, *Werke, Bd. XII* (S. 691–761). Frankfurt a.M.: Suhrkamp Verlag.

Lenhardt, G. (2005). Hochschule, Fachmenschentum und Professionalisierung. *die hochschule, 1/2005*, 92–109.

Multrus, F. (2012). *Forschung und Praxis im Studium: Befunde aus Studierendensurvey und Studienqualitätsmonitor*, Bundesministerium für Bildung und Forschung. Retrieved 09 March 2015 von http://www.bmbf.de/pub/forschung_und_praxis_im_studium.pdf

Paletschek, S. (2001). Verbreitete sich ein ›Humboldt'sches Modell‹ an den deutschen Universitäten im 19. Jahrhundert? In R. C. Schwinges (Hrsg.), *Humboldt International. Der Export des deutschen Universitätsmodells im 19. und 20. Jahrhundert* (S. 75–104). Basel: Schwabe & Co. AG Verlag.

Ramm, M./Multrus, F./Bargel, T./Schmidt, M. (2014). *Studiensituation und studentische Orientierungen. 12. Studierendensurvey an Universitäten und Fachhochschulen*. Berlin: Bundesministerium für Bildung und Forschung.

Reiber, K. (2007). *Forschendes Lernen als hochschuldidaktisches Prinzip – Grundlegung und Beispiele*. Retrieved 13 April 2014 from https://www.uni-bielefeld.de/exzellenz/lehre/Research%20Oriented%20Teaching/dokumente/Forschendes_Lernen.pdf

Schelten, A. (2000). *Konstruktivistische Lernauffassung und Hochschullehre*. Retrieved 12 April 2015 von http://scheltenpublikationen.userweb.mwn.de/pdf/konleschelten2000prs.pdf

Schumacher, R. (2009). Was heißt es, etwas verstanden zu haben? Menschliches Lernen aus Sicht der Psychologie. *Forschung & Lehre, 12/2009*, 882–883.

van Wickevoort Crommelin, A. (o.J.). *Forschendes Lernen – Genese, Ansätze und geeignete Formate*. Retrieved 12 April 2015 von http://www.uni-greifswald.de/fileadmin/mp/1_studieren/ Qualitaetssicherung/interStudies/Forschendes-Lernen_Genese-Ansaetze-Formate.pdf

Focus: Learning

Learning through Research: Independent Learning. Self-Learning Processes and Self-Learning Abilities in Inquiry-Based Learning

3

Matthias Wiemer

3.1 Acting Independently: Learning Through Research

Upon raising the question of the possibilities and necessities of inquiry-based learning in a course of studies, three lines of reasoning can be identified: Inquiry-based learning

- is geared towards education *through scholarship* (*Bildung durch Wissenschaft*),
- (as part of the qualification process) is oriented towards the acquisition and (further) development of subject-related and interdisciplinary *competencies* and
- should enable sustainable and "deep" *learning processes* (cf. Huber 2009, pp. 12–18, translated).

These reasons overlap and complement each other at various points. Particularly noteworthy here is that each of these lines of reasoning emphasizes student independence, simultaneously requires self-organized action on the part of learners and is geared towards their further development. Learning processes are required that focus on more than the appropriation and accumulation of reproducible knowledge with their claim to self-organization, both from the perspective of the individual in the sense of personal development in the field of scholarship and forging an identity in the discipline, and from the perspective of social demands in the sense of acquiring and developing competencies. Such learning processes can only occur "when the learner organizes, elaborates on and critically reflects on his or her own knowledge. Beneficial are those situations in which independent decision-making and structuring has not been taken away, in which personal interests can be articulated and pursued in depth" (Huber 2009, p. 17 et seq., translated).

M. Wiemer (✉)

Georg-August-Universität Göttingen, Leitung Hochschuldidaktik, Göttingen, Germany

e-mail: Matthias.Wiemer@zvw.uni-goettingen.de

© The Author(s) 2019

H. A. Mieg (ed.), *Inquiry-Based Learning – Undergraduate Research*,

https://doi.org/10.1007/978-3-030-14223-0_3

29

Against this background, it is not surprising that even in the basic document by the Federal University Assistants' Conference (BAK) regarding inquiry- based learning, it is clear that the didactic implementation is characterized, in particular, by the design of open learning environments that typically involve a high degree of student independence (e.g. by selecting the methods and strategies, or the starting point in their own interests) (cf. BAK 1970/2009, p. 16).

This central role of independence and autonomy does not mean that students must develop their professional knowledge, acquire research-methodical action and practice scholarly attitudes and mindsets alone and without supervision, however. Supervision of inquiry-based learning processes by educators remains indispensable and is relevant on various levels, for example for initiating, advising on and supervising student research activities and learning processes with reference to the support of social processes such as group formation, integration into a scholarly community and reflection on their own learning and research. In this respect, with this strong emphasis on both independence and also the necessity of supervision by educators, inquiry-based learning can be described as a manifestation of *guided self-study*, or, in other words, as a teaching-learning method that generally provides students with a great deal of room for organizing, planning and carrying out their own learning, while at the same time being characterized by the activity of the educators who *initiate* learning activities through suitable inducements, who *support* students as they enact their goals, *screen* and *evaluate* the results, and *provide* students with *feedback* (cf. Landwehr and Müller 2008, pp. 58–73).

Besides looking at the independent and self-organized learning processes of the students, the focus is also on the development of a specific scholarly (research) conduct, which presupposes the learner's engagement with themselves, with their own interests and goals, and with the respective placement thereof relative to scholarship or the discipline with the goal of achieving *education through scholarship* (*Bildung durch Wissenschaft*). The article focuses on the significance and organization of self-organized learning for inquiry-based learning and argues the need to integrate suitable latitude and opportunities for self-reflection into the design of inquiry-based learning environments.

3.2   Independent Learning Formatted Through Research Activity

If *self-learning* merely indicated an individual who is learning, this would have little added value to learning, since it is true of every learning process that learners "always [decide] for themselves within the acquisition process what affects them and what [they] absorb. *Learning is always independent learning*" (Faulstich 2002, p. 63, translated, emphasis by author). The emphasis on self-learning abilities goes beyond the mere reference to self, underscoring the learning process as an actively self-organized "action-regulated process within the person who is nevertheless always part of a specific situation driven by external influences" (Reinmann 2010, p. 79, translated).

In order to make this process of self-organized learning activity productive for teaching, it is useful to distinguish between various phases and dimensions, which can be focused upon or at least differentiated during planning and implementation. A model for structuring self-regulatory processes that is widely prevalent in the literature is presented by Zimmerman (2000). This model focuses on those processes taking place within the person, which can be represented in cyclic phases (cf. Zimmerman 2000, p. 16 et seq.):

- The planning phase ("forethought phase") includes, inter alia, analyzing the respective (learning) task and setting the learning objectives as well as planning the learning and selecting suitable learning strategies. During this phase, there is also an analysis of one's own self-motivational beliefs (perceived self-efficacy and expected outcomes).
- During the action phase ("performance or volitional control phase"), the planned processes and selected strategies are implemented and the focus is directed towards one's own attention focusing, intentional control and emotional control. Self-observation and keeping records of learning is important so that the approach and learning behavior can be monitored and, if necessary, regulated.
- The self-reflection phase is used to evaluate and grade the learning processes (e.g. by comparing the goals with the results) and the reaction to the results obtained (self-satisfaction, emotional and affective reactions). The specific aim of the self-reflection phase is to optimize the design and planning of future learning processes.

With the cyclic phase model, the focus is on (meta-)cognitive, emotional and motivational processes that correlate with factors pertaining to the person, as well as with behavioral and environmental factors (Zimmerman 2000, p. 13 et seq.).

Against the background of the phases of self-regulated action presented above, some conclusions can be drawn regarding inquiry-based learning. Schneider and Wildt (2009) argue that both the teaching and learning processes in inquiry-based learning are formatted in a specific manner, that is as or through *research activity*. For clarification, according to Kolb, these processes synchronize the (empirical) research cycle with the cycle of experiential learning (ibid., p. 56 et seq., cf. Mieg in this volume). The educator's task is to design learning opportunities and occasions for students in such a way that these (must) be realized as research activity; the student's task is to adapt their learning processes and strategies to the research format.

In terms of Zimmerman's phases of self-regulated learning, it appears that this analogy continues, for example if

- the *planning phase* is synchronized with the processes of topic identification, specification of a research question, and the planning of research processes,
- the *action phase* is synchronized with the conducting and accompanying monitoring of the research, and
- the *self-reflection phase* is synchronized with the interpretation and evaluation of the research results.

The synchronization of the phases shows once again that research and learning processes have analogous logics and processes; however, it obscures the fact that all phases of learning process would also have to occur in every phase of the research cycle if the goal of inquiry-based learning also includes *learning how to conduct research*. This is because in order to learn how to conduct research and to learn by conducting research, it is not just the research process as a whole that must be planned, experienced, observed and reflected upon, etc., but the formulation of the question, laying out the research design and all other steps in the process as well; and this, in turn, in relation to the whole research process.

3.3   Self-Organized Learning: Self-Regulation – Self-Guidance – Self-Determination

In order to connect and break down the various aspects and levels of self-learning abilities with pre-structured and arranged learning environments, Reinmann (2010; following up on Sembill et al. 2007) distinguishes between various dimensions of self-organized learning. With a notion of learning as a process of self-organization, she proposes the terms self-regulation, self-guidance and self-determination therefore (cf. Reinmann 2010, p. 79 et seq.):

Self-regulation comprises the internal structuring of the learning processes. These include, above all, those cognitive metacognitive and emotional-motivational abilities also mentioned in Zimmerman's phase model, which make it possible to consciously examine (and monitor) one's own learning processes and learning behavior, to plan learning and to select suitable strategies, as well as to observe one's own learning processes and to adapt or adjust these as needed.

Self-guidance comes into focus as a second dimension with reference to the contextual environmental variables. Whether the learner learns in a self-guided manner, which "can have a serious and consequential effect on essential decisions as to whether, what, when, how, and toward what [they] learn" (Weinert 1982, p. 102), is always dependent on the external structure, on the (didactic) pre-structuring by educators and on environmental variables that constitute and influence the amount of leeway in selecting an activity and for decision-making.

Self-determination: Whether learning is actually experienced and perceived as self-organized, however, depends not only on the choice and design options provided by the learning environment, but above all on the extent to which the *self-determined learner* succeeds in "harmonizing *external* requirements and circumstances […] with *internal* goals and norms" (Reinmann 2010, p. 80, translated). *Self-determination* as a third dimension of self-organized learning means that the learner assumes responsibility for the internal and external structuring and is able to identify with external requirements or balance learning with the respective goals that exceed the learning task (e.g. career aspirations), for example. "Questions about the self, from identification to the ability to shape a 'good' life" (Sembill et al. 2007, p. 4, translated) are also integrated into the learning processes with this dimension.

> **Digression: "Self-Learning Architectures"**
>
> The ample leeway in selecting an activity, the learner's independent activity and the individualization of learning processes that open up the possibility of inquiry-based learning does not mean that learning now takes place independently and outside of external structures in a power-free learning space. Forneck (2005) points out that, in the discussion about self-guided learning, it is sometimes possible to detect an "emphasis on the self" (ibid., p. 7), which suggests that self-guided learning were learning without external guidance and influence. Here, however, instead of an absence of external control, we should assume "other forms of structuring and thus of the guidance of learning processes" (ibid., p. 17, translated). These other and changing forms of guidance implement "learning architecture" that, as an integrated concept of self-guided learning, connect or correlate (1) *highly structured learning materials* (known as "self-learning architectures"), (2) *learning guidance,* (3) *new, cooperative forms of teaching and learning* and (4) *new documentation, reflection and auditing practices associated with individual learning* with one another (Forneck 2005, 2006). In the case of all four elements, the focus is not just on the acquisition of learning techniques, but also the self-reflective development of learning practices that correlate the respective contents to the individual learning pathways, sensitivities and the learning environment.

3.4 Occasions for Self-Reflection in Inquiry-Based Learning Processes

Self-organized learning is not a *guaranteed success* and does not necessarily result from didactic design approaches that provide students with a great deal of leeway to decide their own activities and make their own decisions. In addition to this leeway, students need self-reflection processes in particular, which can be systematically integrated into the design of the self-learning architectures via topical occasions and triggers. Here, the self-organized learning in inquiry-based learning can be tied back to *education through scholarship* (*Bildung durch Wissenschaft*) and *skills development*: Huber points out that, without self-reflection, "it is not possible to speak of education" (Huber 2009, p. 13), and he specifies three dimensions that scholarship prescribes for reflection: "the self-reflection of scholarship as a mode of rational cognition, the self-reflection of the subject through scholarship, and the reflection on the common good to be promoted thereby" (Huber 2009, p. 13). These dimensions, in turn, can be associated with three areas of competency, which comprise the encounter with or dealing with the subject (professional competence), the subject's encounter with themselves (self-competence) as well as with others (social competence) (cf. Euler 2005, p. 260 et seq.).

With reference to these dimensions of reflection, it is possible to list some of the subject-related occasions that emerge from the specific format of inquiry-based learning, and that can be a trigger to self-reflection in inquiry-based learning and in self-learning architectures. Looking back on the dimensions of self-organized learning, these occasions thereby require that learners engage in adaptation processes within the meaning of self-determined learning, such as:

- balancing their own knowledge interest and the processes of the independent construction of knowledge with discipline-related research interests and processes of the collective construction of knowledge;
- practicing new, research-led patterns of information processing;
- conducting activities in environments with open outcomes and uncertain bodies of knowledge;
- individual motivation and enthusiasm for the chosen subject and its fundamental questions;
- "designing oneself into the future" as a scholar (thus not just the question of what constitutes an activity in scholarship and the selected discipline as such, but also a consideration of how the student imagines themselves as a researcher, whether the field of scholarship can be considered a possible career goal, and where, given the student's own strengths and weaknesses, etc.);
- making it possible to experience basic scholarly values and attitudes in a scholarly community as well as communication and interaction processes coded for the specific discipline;
- the transition from an ordinary perspective to a scholarly perspective, and the development of one's own justifiable and justified standpoint;
- the search for possible objections to this point of view, because the "'demands of scholarship' also include raising objections oneself or systematically searching for objections as an [...] operationalization" (Huber 2009, p. 10, translated).

With the learner's critical eye on themselves and on themselves as a participant in scholarship, the focus is likewise on the development of a specific scholarly (research) attitude, which is characterized, inter alia, by "distance from one's own prejudices and affects and [by the] independence of one's own judgment" (Honnefelder 2011, p. 25, translated). If learning always means "gaining an outsider's view of a subject and thus of oneself, challenging what is familiar, as well as abandoning self-assurance and forfeiting what is familiar" (Meyer-Drawe 2012, p. 15, translated), this applies to inquiry-based learning perhaps to an even greater degree. This is because, with the "transition from life-world experience to scholarly knowledge" (Meyer-Drawe 2012, p. 14), inquiry-based learning addresses a threshold, which virtually demands that one see the world *and one's self* with different eyes and from a different perspective.

3.5   Conclusion: Self-Education in Inquiry-Based Learning

Within the context of self-learning abilities and self-organized learning, the above-mentioned triggers and occasions thus make it possible to inquire as to the "subject" (i.e. the individual learner) of inquiry-based learning. This "subject" is generated by implementing and experiencing learning and research processes, and requires a "certain questioning *attitude* […], the disposition of someone who seeks knowledge" (Huber 1991, p. 194, translated). Thus, inquiry-based learning tasks students with "working on their own identity in a specific way" (Ludwig 2011, p. 10, translated). The acts of finding an identity in the field of scholarship and of developing scholarly research habits – both of which are indispensable for the preparation of independent research activities and which can also be decisive for the development of occupational competences – remain incomplete if they are not experienced through active participation in independent practice. Schneider and Wildt (2009) point out that the orientation of learning on research processes remains "[…] on a trivial level without dependence on or integration into a theoretical frame of reference" and does not necessarily yield "scientifically challenging learning processes" (ibid., p. 59, translated). It can likewise be stated that the implementation of inquiry-based learning will remain impeded if there is no reflection on the self or the relationship of the self to the object and other learners and educators. In that case, the confrontation with oneself as a person conducting research, the clarification of one's own standpoint with respect to the subject being researched, and one's activity in a research and learning community would thus be left to chance.

References

Bundesassistentenkonferenz (BAK). (1970/2009). *Forschendes Lernen. Wissenschaftliches Prüfen.* Neuauflage nach der 2. Aufl. Bielefeld: UniversitätsVerlagWebler.

Euler, D. (2005). Forschendes Lernen. In S. Spoun/W. Wunderlich (Hrsg.), *Studienziel Persönlichkeit. Beiträge zum Bildungsauftrag der Universität heute* (S. 253–272). Frankfurt/Main: Campus Verlag.

Faulstich, P. (2002). Vom selbstorganisierten zum selbstbestimmten Lernen. In P. Faulstich/ D. Gnahs/S. Seidel/M. Bayer (Hrsg.), *Praxishandbuch selbstbestimmtes Lernen. Konzepte, Perspektiven und Instrumente für die berufliche Aus- und Weiterbildung* (S. 61–98). Weinheim, München: Beltz Juventa.

Forneck, H.-J. (2005). Selbstsorge und Lernen – Umrisse eines integrativen Konzepts selbstgesteuerten Lernens. In H.-J. Forneck/U. Klingovsky/P. Kossack (Hrsg.), *Selbstlernumgebungen. Zur Didaktik des selbstsorgenden Lernens und ihrer Praxis.*(S. 6–48). Baltmannsweiler: Schneider Hohengehren.

Forneck, H.-J. (2006). *Selbstlernarchitekturen. Lernen und Selbstsorge.* Baltmannsweiler: Schneider Hohengehren.

Honnefelder, L. (2011). Bildung durch Wissenschaft? In L. Honnefelder/G. Rager (Hrsg.), *Bildung durch Wissenschaft?* (S. 11–30). Freiburg, München: Alber.

Huber, L. (1991). Bildung durch Wissenschaft – Wissenschaft durch Bildung. Hochschuldidaktische Anmerkungen zu einem großen Thema. *Pädagogik und Schule in Ost und West, 39*(4), 193–200.

Huber, L. (2009). Warum Forschendes Lernen nötig und möglich ist. In L. Huber/J. Hellmer/F. Schneider (Hrsg.), *Forschendes Lernen im Studium. Aktuelle Konzepte und Erfahrungen.* (S. 9–35). Bielefeld: UniversitätsVerlagWebler.

Landwehr, N./Müller, E. (2008). *Begleitetes Selbststudium. Didaktische Grundlagen und Umsetzungshilfen* (2., korr. Aufl.). Bern: hep verlag.

Ludwig, J. (2011). *Forschungsbasierte Lehre als Lehre im Format der Forschung* (Brandenburgische Beiträge zur Hochschuldidaktik 3). Potsdam: Universitätsverlag.

Meyer-Drawe, K. (2012). *Diskurse des Lernens* (2., durchges. und korr. Aufl.). München: Wilhelm Fink.

Reinmann, G. (2010). Selbstorganisation auf dem Prüfstand: Das Web 2.0 und seine Grenzen(losigkeit). In K.-U. Hugger/M. Walber (Hrsg.), *Digitale Lernwelten. Konzepte, Beispiele und Perspektiven* (S. 75–89). Wiesbaden: VS Verlag für Sozialwissenschaften.

Schneider, R./Wildt, J. (2009). Forschendes Lernen und Kompetenzentwicklung. In L. Huber/J. Hellmer/F. Schneider (Hrsg.), *Forschendes Lernen im Studium. Aktuelle Konzepte und Erfahrungen* (S. 53–68). Bielefeld: UniversitätsVerlagWebler.

Sembill, D./Wuttke, E./Seifried, J./Egloffstein, M./Rausch, A. (2007). *Selbstorganisiertes Lernen in der beruflichen Bildung – Abgrenzungen, Befunde und Konsequenzen.* Berufs- und Wirtschaftspädagogik online, Ausgabe 13. Retrieved 28 April 2015 from www.bwpat.de/ausgabe13/sembill_etal_bwpat13.pdf

Weinert, F.E. (1982). Selbstgesteuertes Lernen als Voraussetzung, Methode und Ziel des Unterrichts. *Unterrichtswissenschaft, 2/1982*, 99–110.

Zimmerman, B. (2000). Attaining Self-Regulation. A Social Cognitive Perspective. In M. Boekaerts/P.R. Pintrich/M. Zeidner (Hrsg.), *Handbook of self-regulation* (pp. 13–39). San Diego: Academic Press Inc.

Research-Oriented Learning and Teaching from a Didactic Perspective

4

Karin Reiber

The following article explains the didactic challenges of inquiry-based learning in light of the current, in part paradigmatic, shift in university education. To this end, I will outline the charged relationship between the traditional ideal of education and contemporary societal and educational policy expectations for academic studies, in which the teaching and learning at institutions of higher learning are currently situated. In order to counteract the oft-lamented conceptual blurring of inquiry-based learning I have undertaken to limit and delineate the use of the term. The classification of the approach within the context of the history of ideas serves to make clear the complex historical social causal network within which university education must be interpreted and shaped. Furthermore, I undertake an internal differentiation of inquiry-based learning in order to be able to systematize various degrees of expression and forms. The next step is to develop research-oriented learning and teaching in an evolutionary way by structuring these progressively along a course of studies based on this development-oriented approach. Manifestations of inquiry-based learning are ordered and classified by differentiating between various dimensions of understanding and knowledge, and taking into account different course formats. Finally, not only the opportunities and scope of inquiry-based learning, but also limitations and risks are outlined in order to avoid an overly euphoric stylization of the approach, while ignoring specific structural and curricular deficits.

K. Reiber, Prof. Dr. (✉)
Hochschule Esslingen, Professur für Erziehungswissenschaft/Didaktik,
Esslingen am Neckar, Germany
e-mail: Karin.Reiber@hs-esslingen.de

© The Author(s) 2019
H. A. Mieg (ed.), *Inquiry-Based Learning – Undergraduate Research*,
https://doi.org/10.1007/978-3-030-14223-0_4

4.1   Research and Teaching Caught Between Innovation and Tradition

The historical ideal of university education is based on an understanding of education, the mainstay of which is scholarship and research. Here three basic postulates are combined (cf. Euler 2005):

- research and teaching constitute an inseparable unit;
- teaching and learning are closely related to one another as a form of research communication;
- despite its differentiation into different disciplines, scholarship constitutes an entity unto itself.

This educational ideal goes back to the Humboldtian university reform and has become the normative concept for university education, even if it was never realized in its full manifestation (cf. Aepkers 2002).

Today, the historical concept of university education is in conflict with higher education teaching, which has been shaped by the Bologna Process and which is dedicated to the stated goal of *"employability."* Its external characteristics are, to name but a few of the most prominent ones, highly regulated degree programs with a precisely calculated workload, examinations that accompany the course of study rather than the previous central final examinations as well as an overall focus on the expected results in the form of competencies ("outcome orientation") in contrast to the conventional focus on the discipline's constitutive content ("input orientation"). The associated opportunities and risks are now well known due to widespread discussion, both amongst higher education policymakers and also publicly: On the one hand, the degree programs are becoming more predictable and calculable both for students and for the institutions of higher learning, and those programs are gaining legitimacy due to their transparent and labor market-related goals; on the other hand, students and educators are losing much of their freedom to determine their own focus, and the perceived workload has increased significantly for both (cf. Reiber 2012).

While the intention of the Bologna reform is to increase the number of academically qualified persons, global research competition also brings with it demands that research be conducted at a high level of excellence (cf. Reiber and Tremp 2007). This creates an additional charged relationship for institutions of higher learning: To put it succinctly, they are becoming mass institutions of education on the one hand, and with their research, they are involved in a national and international competition for money and reputation on the other (cf. Huber 2004).

The original concept behind a university education which entails the development of the entire person – meaning not just their cognitive abilities – so that they are able to act responsibly in a manner that is self-determined and ethical, but which also entails a professional qualification as a side effect (as it were) (cf. Webler 2008), can be adapted for the

Bologna philosophy with its primacy of employability (cf Horn 2007). Contemporary concepts of university education are likewise based on a comprehensive educational goal, which considers cognitive and personal skills development to be as important as the ethical power of judgment (for Leuphana University of Lüneburg cf. e.g. Spoun 2007).

The orientation of higher education instruction towards *clearly definable results* is closely related to the key objective of employability. However, this is by no means new, nor an invention of the Bologna reform: The postulate of outcome orientation has already been discussed in higher education didactics using the slogan of "*the shift from teaching to learning*" (cf. Wildt 2003). The teaching-related perspective, which focuses on the selection of content and options for imparting that content, should be transformed into a learning-related perspective: What is important are the learning outcomes, i.e. what is actually acquired by students, their knowledge, skills and their mindset.

In recent discourse pertaining to higher education didactics as well, this "learning-outcome perspective" is the standpoint from which teaching-learning processes can be analyzed and balanced. This opens up significantly more design leeway than an attitude towards teaching that believes students can be classified as either "good" or "bad" in order to henceforth focus on the good students (*"blame-the-students perspective"*). With respect to the equally one-sided attitude of educators who see learning success solely in terms of their own abilities as an educator (*"blame-the-teacher perspective"*), the outcome orientation has the advantage: Certainly "bad" educators can improve as a result of appropriate training and techniques; however, in so doing they become even more focused on themselves, and often from a perspective that has been narrowed down to methodical "tricks," than they are on the learning processes of the students (cf. Biggs and Tang 2011). A differentiated analysis of the teaching-learning process and an improvement of the teaching quality is only possible when the mutual influence of teaching and learning, and their respective strengths and development potential, are perceived.

4.2   Conceptual Distinctions and Limitations

To begin with, we define inquiry-based learning as a target for research-oriented teaching in such a way that both learning and teaching follow the problem-solving process of research and reproduce its individual work steps as learning phases, as it were. Ultimately, the aim of this teaching and learning is to give rise to recognizable added value in terms of knowledge with innovative content, which can, in turn, serve as the starting point and reference point for further research and learning processes. This teaching and learning is tied to the form of research communication, which serves to facilitate the integration of processes and results into the discipline (cf. Reiber and Tremp 2007).

If one now attempts to classify inquiry-based learning in terms of the history of ideas, the objectives and function of this approach become more apparent, and it becomes clear that this is more than just one didactic variety among many. While the topic of inquiry-based learning initiated by the Federal University Assistants' Conference (BAK) in the

1970s was widely discussed, this was followed by a phase in which the approach was addressed, in particular in works on teacher education (cf. for example Wildt 2005). Inquiry-based learning is dealt with here, in particular within the context of practical studies, with the objective of didactically making practical experience the starting point for the "initiation or founding of skills in scholarly reflection […] [and] the development of a metacognitive capacity for reflection" (Weyland 2010, p. 246), while at the same time providing insight into the contingency of pedagogical action and its theoretical attempts at explanation and justification.

It is only in the course of the Bologna reform that a broad discussion concerning inquiry-based learning was again rekindled and that this old and self-evident principle of university education was rediscovered for many disciplines (cf. Huber 2009; Hofhues et al. 2014). For the first time, this implicit principle of inquiry-based learning became a consciously postulated guiding principle when it came to the democratization of university relations by developing the Humboldtian educational ideal. A return to the core of university education was a reflexive response to the Bologna reform: The transition to bachelor's and master's degree programs was and is tied to the fear that academic education processes might be reduced to vocational qualification. Within the context of contemporary history and the history of ideas, inquiry-based learning has become a central concept in efforts concerning the maintenance, renaissance, and also the contemporary development of the notion of a university education.

The focus in the recent discussion of inquiry-based learning has therefore been on maintaining a comprehensive educational goal within the context of higher educational studies that encompasses cognitive and personal development as well as the development of an ethical power of judgment, even under changed basic conditions. To this end, leeway in terms of content is possible and necessary in order to accommodate individual prioritization, even in degree programs having a regulated curriculum (cf. Spoun 2007).

A further and more detailed definition of the "inquiry-based teaching and learning" format can be made by distinguishing it from those educational processes that occur in other sub-segments of the education system. Ideally speaking, these are the following fundamental differentiating features:

- In contrast to the learning processes that take place in schools, in particular at the upper secondary level, a university education includes the cognitive process itself to a much greater degree (cf. Webler 2007). Knowledge is discussed more in connection with the formation of the insights, reflected upon, and therefore received more critically than is the case in schools.
- While knowledge and insight are brought into focus with greater emphasis on the (professional) functional perspectives during a vocational education, inquiry-based learning as a principle of academic study correlates this with a critical reflection on the application context (cf. Kossek 2009).
- In no other educational sector does research serve as intensely as the basic mode of teaching and learning than in higher education (cf. Tremp and Futter 2012).

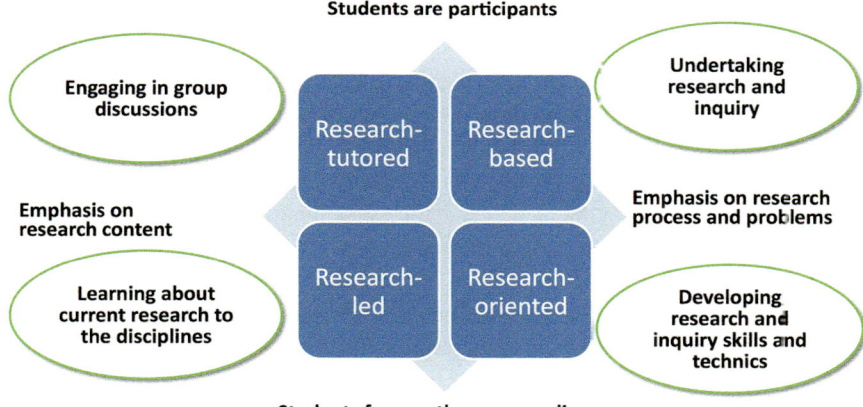

Fig. 4.1 Various degrees of expression of research-related learning; author's representation according to Jenkins and Healey (2011, p. 38)

It is possible to differentiate between various degrees of expression by tracing the two charged relationships in inquiry-based learning (see Fig. 4.1): It can be classified between the poles of participatory and receptive student roles, and can be defined along the continuum of a clearer focus on the research results and research content or research problem and process (cf. Jenkins and Healey 2011).

In the discourse on research-related teaching, the pure form of inquiry-based learning is now frequently, and usually implicitly, assumed; it entails the idea, already anchored in the curriculum, that students largely learn through their own research activities and has an increased emphasis on the process itself (right upper quadrant in the diagram: research-based).

From this perspective, learning is conceptualized in steps analogous to the phases of the research process (cf. e.g. Wildt 2009). However, one can object that there are also constitutive differences between the two basic operations of *research* and *learning*: In research, as a rule, self-organization and determination are generally greater than in learning processes (especially if these are associated with academic performance/test performance). The research process is characterized by even greater uncertainty and potentially also harbors the possibility of failure; learning processes imply stronger hierarchical relationships between the agents than is commonly the case in a research community (cf. Hofhues et al. 2014). Overall, there is a fundamental difference between the claim to scholarship and to education at institutions of higher learning (cf. Huber 2009).

From a developmental perspective, the next step is to conceptualize the research-related learning from the perspective of teaching.

4.3 Research-Related Learning from a Development-Oriented Perspective

If, from a didactic perspective, one considers the entire course of study as a development process, inquiry-based learning ultimately involves the gradual acquisition of the necessary sub-competences, whereby all the sub-steps have both their own intrinsic logic and their intrinsic value, and the goal of which is the "systematic development of an approach that has a scholarly basis and that is committed to scholarly values" (Tremp and Hildbrand 2012, p. 109).

From this developmental perspective, the acquisition of research-related competency can be described using the taxonomy provided by Anderson and Krathwohl (2001). The horizontal axis of this matrix maps the various quality levels of learning processes as goal dimensions (see Fig. 4.2). The vertical axis differentiates between various knowledge dimensions. The horizontal goal dimensions are a progressive gradation which extends from "remember" to "create," and which thus represents different levels of learning. In terms of knowledge dimensions, Anderson and Krathwohl (2001) distinguish between factual knowledge, abstract conceptual knowledge, process-oriented procedural knowledge and metacognitive knowledge.

Competency development can be planned using this matrix for the various degrees of expression of research-related learning by combining differing yet mutually complementary teaching-learning formats (e.g. lecture, seminar or tutorial) and by combining cognitive dimensions of different scope with different types of knowledge within these courses. If one now places one phase model on top of the other (Jenkins and Healey 2011; Anderson and Krathwohl 2001), inquiry-based learning can be anchored as a study objective in the curricular sequence, and can be didactically operationalized and designed over modules and with different teaching and examination formats. Thus, for example, up-to-date research results could be imparted as fundamental knowledge within the context of a lecture. In addition to this, students would apply this factual knowledge by preparing their

	Remember	Understand	Apply	Analyze	Evaluate	Create
Factual Knowledge		e.g. Lecture: **research-led**	e.g. Presentation: **research-oriented**			
Conceptual Knowledge				e.g. Case Study: **research-tutored**		e.g. Research Project: **research-based**
Procedural Knowledge						
Metacognitive Knowledge						

Fig. 4.2 Research-related learning from a development-oriented perspective; on the basis of Anderson and Krathwohl (2001); source: author's representation

own presentations while accompanying the research. Building on this, the dimension of process-oriented procedural knowledge is added and, within the context of case studies, the learning levels of analysis and evaluation are addressed within the context of research-oriented learning. Finally, research-based learning can occur in the form of projects within a tutorial, in which new knowledge or, respectively, new solutions for a clearly defined practical problem can be developed; at the latest, this learning method also implicates the knowledge dimension of metacognitive knowledge, since projects also always include reflection on one's own learning and working processes (see Fig. 4.2).

As such, the individual cognitive steps, knowledge dimensions and various degrees of expression relating to the extent of the students' participation, as well as the focus on the research process and result, have their time and place in the course of study – and their respective justifications. This is because, in the synopsis of all of the components and the way in which these complement one another, research-related learning can also be didactically grasped and developed more precisely.

4.4   Consequences and Conclusions

From this perspective of university education, which is as much developmentally oriented as enabling oriented, in the conflict of objectives between research and employability outlined above, it is possible to describe the overriding goal of university education as "professionalism through scholarship" (Brinckman et al. 2002, p. 29). As such, a research-based and responsible attitude is defined as a specific feature of university education, which refers to a dynamic concept of knowledge. As such, learning is a continuous, reflective process of cognition and the construction of knowledge; it can only be performed in a manner that is active, engaged and critical (cf. Kossek 2009). Within this understanding, professional employability means a general vocational orientation which adequately addresses the "growing complexity and uncertainty" (Kossek 2009, p. 5) of our society.

Pursuant to the Humboldtian concept of a university education, it is the task of university educators to generate new knowledge themselves, or to test new knowledge and to make this accessible to others. In the spirit of a contemporaneous, vocationally oriented university education, this claim can be turned around in terms of higher education didactics: University instructors can stage teaching-learning processes as small research projects of varying scope and make these transparent. In so doing, it is important to reflect on the process and developmental nature of a course of study with a view to acceptance on the part of the students. Since inquiry-based learning may always be accompanied by phases of uncertainty on the part of students, appropriate support offers must be provided to guide the teaching-learning process if needed; however, at least one exchange forum for this process must be offered. In any case, university instructors are role models for the approach of inquiry-based learning, independent of whether they teach in a specific field, in which they themselves conduct research, or in which they are at least active in a research capacity.

Thus for all involved, inquiry-based learning is an ambitious form of education through scholarship (*Bildung durch Wissenschaft*). It requires didactic planning, design and evaluation. At the same time, like any other serious didactic approach, inquiry-based learning must not be misunderstood as a "smoothing and acceleration of learning pathways" (Rumpf 2007, p. 50), but rather as a deceleration caused by the fact that the "initial attentiveness" (ibid.) is reestablished as a starting point for subjectively meaningful learning.

References

Anderson, L. W./Krathwohl, D. R. (2001). A Taxonomy for Learning, Teaching and Assessing. A Revision of Bloom's Taxonomie of Educational Objectives. New York u. a.: Longman.

Aepkers, M. (2002). Forschendes Lernen – Einem Begriff auf der Spur. In M. Aepkers/S. Liebig (Hrsg.), *Entdeckendes, forschendes und genetisches Lernen* (S. 69–87). Baltmannsweiler: Schneider-Verlag Hohengehren.

Biggs, J./Tang, C. (2011). *Teaching for Quality Learning at University.* New York: Open University Press.

Brinckman, H./Garcia, O./Gruschka, A./Lenhardt, G./ZurLippe, R. (2002). *Die Einheit von Forschung und Lehre: Über die Zukunft der Universität.* Wetzlar: Büchse der Pandorra.

Euler, D. (2005). Forschendes Lernen. In W. Wunderlich/S. Spoun (Hrsg.), *Studienziel Persönlichkeit. Beiträge zum Bildungsauftrag der Universität heute* (S. 253–272). Frankfurt/New York: Campus-Verlag.

Hofhues, S./Reinmann, G./Schiefner-Rohs, M. (2014). Lernen und Medienhandeln im Format der Forschung. In O. Zawacki-Richter/D. Kergel/N. Kleinefeld/P. Muckel/J. Stöter/K. Brinkmann (Hrsg.), *Teaching Trends 2014* (S. 19–36). Münster: Waxmann.

Horn, K.-P. (2007). Lehren und Lernen an Hochschulen – Historisches Erbe und Zukunftsauftrag. In K. Reiber/R. Richter (Hrsg.), *Entwicklungslinien der Hochschuldidaktik – Ein Blick zurück nach vorn. Dokumentation der gleichnamigen Tagung vom 29.11. bis 1.12. 2006 in Tübingen* (S. 27–41). Berlin: Logos.

Huber, L. (2004). Forschendes Lernen: 10 Thesen zum Verhältnis von Forschung und Lehre aus der Perspektive des Studiums. *die hochschule, 13*(2), 29–49.

Huber, L. (2009). Warum Forschendes Lernen nötig und möglich ist. In L. Huber/J. Hellmer/ F. Schneider (Hrsg.), *Forschendes Lernen im Studium* (S. 9–35). Bielefeld: Universitätsverlag Webler.

Jenkins, A./Healey, A. (2011). Research based learning – a collection of case studies in different disciplines. In I. Jahnke/J. Wildt (Hrsg.), *Fachbezogene und fachübergreifende Hochschuldidaktik* (S. 37–46). Bielefeld: W. Bertelsmann Verlag.

Kossek, B. (2009). *Survey: Die forschungsgeleitete Lehre in der internationalen Diskussion.* Retrieved 31 March 2015 from https://ctl.univie.ac.at/fileadmin/user_upload/elearning/ Forschungsgeleitete_Lehre_International_090414.pdf

Reiber, K. (2012). Forschendes Lernen im Zeichen von Bologna. In B. Kossek/C. Zwiauer (Hrsg.), *Universität in Zeiten von Bologna. Zur Theorie und Praxis von Lehr- und Lernkulturen* (S. 111_119). Wien: V&R unipress.

Reiber, K./Tremp, P. (2007). Eulen nach Athen! Forschendes Lernen als Bildungsprinzip. In B. Behrendt/H.-P. Voss/J. Wildt (Hrsg.), *Neues Handbuch Hochschullehre. 30. Ergänzungslieferung. A 3.6* (S. 1–14). Berlin: Raabe.

Rumpf, H. (2007). Anfängliche Aufmerksamkeiten und ihre Verdrängung – Über bleibende Probleme, Wissenschaft zu lehren. In K. Reiber/R. Richter (Hrsg.), *Entwicklungslinien der Hochschuldidaktik – Ein Blick zurück nach vorn. Dokumentation der gleichnamigen Tagung vom 29.11. bis 1.12. 2006 in Tübingen* (S. 43–55). Berlin: Logos.

Spoun, S. (2007). Universität hat Zukunft - Gestaltungsperspektiven am Beispiel der Universität Lüneburg. In A. Dudeck & B. Jansen-Schulz (Hrsg.), *Zukunft Bologna!?: Gender und Nachhaltigkeit als Leitideen für eine neue Hochschulkultur* (S. 33–43). Frankfurt am Main: Lang Verlag.

Tremp, P./Futter, K. (2012). Forschungsorientierung in der Lehre: Curriculare Leitlinie und studentische Wahrnehmungen. In T. Brinker/P. Tremp (Hrsg.), *Einführung in die Studiengangentwicklung* (S. 69–79). Bielefeld: W. Bertelsmann Verlag.

Tremp, P./Hildbrand, T. (2012). Forschungsorientiertes Studium – universitäre Lehre: das »Züricher Framework« zur Verknüpfung von Lehre und Forschung. In T. Brinker/P. Tremp (Hrsg.), *Einführung in die Studiengangentwicklung* (S. 101–116). Bielefeld: W. Bertelsmann Verlag.

Webler, W.-D. (2007). Geben wir mit der Akkreditierung das Hochschulniveau unserer Studiengänge preis? Zur Differenz von Schule und Hochschule. *Das Hochschulwesen, 55*(1), 15–20.

Webler, W. D. (2008). *Zur Entstehung der Humboldtschen Universitätskonzeption: Statik und Dynamik der Hochschulentwicklung in Deutschland–ein historisches Beispiel.* Bielefeld: UVW.

Weyland, U. (2010). *Zur Intentionalität Schulpraktischer Studien im Kontext universitärer Lehrausbildung.* Paderborn: Eusl.

Wildt, J. (2003). »The Shift from Teaching to Learning« – Thesen zum Wandel der Lernkultur in modularisierten Studiengängen. In Fraktion Bündnis 90 / die Grünen Landtag NRW (Hrsg.), *Unterwegs zu einem europäischen Bildungssystem. Reform von Studium und Lehre an den nordrhein-westfälischen Hochschulen im internationalen Kontext* (S. 14–18). Düsseldorf.

Wildt, J. (2005). Auf dem Weg zu einer Didaktik der Lehrerbildung? *Beiträge zur Lehrerbildung, 23*(2), 183–190.

Wildt, J. (2009). Forschendes Lernen: Lernen im »Format« der Forschung. *Journal Hochschuldidaktik, 20*(2), 4–7.

"From Teaching to Learning": Characteristics and Challenges of a Student-Centered Learning Culture

Carmen Wulf

Inquiry-based learning is part of the tradition of the much-discussed "shift from teaching to learning" (Barr and Tagg 1995), which calls for the learning culture to be oriented towards a student-centered view. This transition is not a new phenomenon. However, it has gained popularity, particularly since the start of the Bologna Process and discussions of higher education didactics at European institutions of higher learning. As such, learning culture, as a concept, should be examined and defined from various perspectives (Schüßler and Thurnes 2005). In the following article, I will present a holistic view of learning processes using the term "learning culture."

In a knowledge-based society, current specialist knowledge quickly becomes outdated, and so it is important for university education to impart abilities and skills to students which will allow them to acquire knowledge autonomously and learn to manage uncertainties. In this context, the importance of conveying merely content-based knowledge decreases; the focus is increasingly on conveying key competencies. Formats in the sense of student-centered learning culture, for example inquiry-based learning, are considered especially suitable for fostering key competencies such as self-guided learning.

In order to present a student-centered learning culture, I will first examine the theoretical approach of learning as a construct, subsequently explain the characteristics of this learning culture and then discuss the challenges inherent in a transition in the learning culture.

C. Wulf, Dr., Dipl.-Psych. (✉)
Carl von Ossietzky Universität Oldenburg, Institut für Pädagogik, Fachgruppe
Forschungsmethoden in den Erziehungs- und Bildungswissenschaften, Oldenburg, Germany
e-mail: carmen.wulf@uni-oldenburg.de

© The Author(s) 2019
H. A. Mieg (ed.), *Inquiry-Based Learning – Undergraduate Research*,
https://doi.org/10.1007/978-3-030-14223-0_5

5.1 Constructivist Learning Approaches as a Theoretical Background to a Student-Centered Learning Culture

A student-centered learning culture is oriented towards a "constructivist" view of learning, without ignoring the fact that this is not an autonomous learning theory, but rather an epistemological position that is applied to different contexts. Constructivist perspectives on learning are closely related to the progressive educational remarks by John Dewey (1859–1952), the humanistic psychology of Carl Rogers (1902–1987) or the developmental psychology research of Piaget (1896–1980) and unify assumptions about teaching, learning and the resulting learning environments. In summary, constructivist approaches consider *the acquisition of knowledge to be a constructive, active, self-guided, social and situational process* (cf. Reinmann-Rothmeier and Mandl 1997; Reinmann and Mandl 2006). Some of the principles of a student-centered learning culture will be presented below.

Learning as a constructive process: Learning processes take place in the individual interpretation and construction of meaning, and occur either as a result of connecting new experiences with existing constructs or by expanding existing constructs (in the sense of an assimilation and accommodation according to Piaget). New information must be related to already acquired impressions and elements. Since each individual draws on different experiences and different prior knowledge in order to process new information, knowledge structures represent individual interpretations of reality.

Learning as an active processing of content: Cognitive learning theories focus on the way new knowledge is cognitively processed (Ausubel 1968). While these theories primarily regard learning as a way to process information to be assimilated and stored by learners, constructivist approaches assume that knowledge cannot be transmitted; instead, every learner must recreate knowledge. When perceptions and knowledge do not represent a subject-independent reality, but are rather individual constructs, these have a personal, private character that cannot be transferred from one person to another. Thus it is not possible to learn by passively taking in information – instead, learning can only be achieved by engaging in an active examination of learning content and integrating individual experiences and knowledge backgrounds.

Learning is self-regulated: Learning is initiated and fostered when it is self-regulated, i.e. when learners are able to decide for themselves when, what and how they learn. From a constructivist perspective, learners should determine their learning process independently to the greatest extent possible, coordinated with their own interests and previous knowledge, just that an active process of construction can be initiated.

Learning as a cooperative process: In constructivist theories, social interactions are a core element, since learning occurs in a communicative form through engagement with others: In every learning process, not only is content exchanged, but expectations, attitudes and moods are also transmitted as indirect messages. Students and teachers, as well as students among themselves, have reciprocal effects on one another so that "learning in relationships" represents an essential part of conceptions about learning.

Learning content is situational: Instruction-oriented, traditional transfer of knowledge often results in the phenomenon known as "sluggish knowledge" (Reinmann-Rothmeier and Mandl 1997, p. 364), meaning the inadequate transfer of theoretical knowledge to other contexts. One explanation for this phenomenon is the situatedness of the knowledge acquired: Learning always occurs within a specific context and is therefore linked with this context. Accordingly, the difficulty of transferring knowledge to other contexts is regarded as a "normal" problem in learning processes and should be resolved by designing the learning environments appropriately. In order to minimize the discrepancy between knowledge and behavior, learning should always occur in contexts that are oriented as much as possible towards later application contexts in terms of content and structure. Didactic formats that take this into consideration are conceptually grouped together as "situated cognition" approaches (Reinmann and Mandl 2006).

These aspects are generally of decisive importance for any learning process, but they are weighted even more heavily in adult education, since aspects such as independent activity, taking one's own interests into account and prior experience, as well as reference to concrete situations, are especially important (Reinmann-Rothmeier and Mandl 1997, p. 356). Moreover, in contrast to learning environments in school, learning environments in higher education are characterized by a greater heterogeneity of learner types in terms of individual previous knowledge, cognitive prerequisites, learning strategies, motivation, attitudes and expectations (Viebahn 2008). Constructivist learning approaches provide the opportunity to consider this diversity and to support the learning process for all students.

5.2   Characteristics of a Student-Centered Learning Culture

A student-centered learning culture involves a paradigm shift that is characterized by a *constructivist perception of learning processes* and that distinguishes itself from a more instruction-centered learning culture in terms of the design of *learning objectives and* associated *performance assessment* and *learning structures*, as well as the *role designs for educators and learners* (Barr and Tagg 1995). Based on various observations of the transition in learning culture and of student-centered learning, in which the focus of each is emphasized (Barr and Tagg 1995; Lea et al. 2003; O'Neill and McMahon 2005; Taylor 2013), it is possible to derive the following definition:

A student-centered learning culture is oriented on constructivist findings, considering the activity of learners in the process of knowledge acquisition; emphasizes self-regulated and autonomous learning processes that take place in social interaction; takes into account social, emotional and motivational aspects of the learning process in addition to cognitive factors; is responsive to varying prior knowledge and experiences; and involves an emancipated relationship between educators and learners in an open and flexible, competence-oriented learning environment.

From a constructivist perspective, learning is always an active process, meaning a direct transmission of knowledge from teacher to learner is not possible. The focus, when considering learning processes, must therefore be on the learners and their learning activities, rather than (as is the case in an instruction-centered learning culture) on the educators and the structuring of content. Specific learning objectives within the context of a student-centered learning culture are associated with this focus: Kowledge transfer—in the sense of providing students with "correct" answers to questions—takes a back seat; instead, it becomes more about teaching students how to proceed in order to obtain answers to questions autonomously. Imparting learning strategies, techniques and attitudes that foster learning are most important. Thus, the core focus of a student-centered learning culture is to promote key competencies such as self-regulated learning, critical thinking or teamwork.

In addition, one aim of student-centered learning culture is to foster deep learning and understanding (deep approaches to learning) and intrinsic learning motivation (Baeten et al. 2013; Lea et al. 2003). Deep approaches to learning involve intensive study of the subject matter with a focus on understanding the content as opposed to just memorizing the learning material. Deep approaches of this kind require learning strategies by which new information can be related to the knowledge that learners already possess. Motivational components are positively related to the application of deep approaches to learning, and indirectly influence the learning process by moderating the selection of tasks or the effort invested (Baeten et al. 2010). Self-determined motivation—in the meaning of Deci and Ryan (1993)—appears to be especially encouraging for learning processes.

Since, in a student-centered learning culture, learning is considered as an active, individual construction, it is also implicitly assumed that heterogeneity among students could be better taken into account and that it will thus be possible to better enhance their learning (Barr and Tagg 1995)—an aspect that is of great significance in terms of higher education policy. Building on constructivist learning approaches, this involves coordinating teaching and learning formats with the needs, previous knowledge and experiences of the students.

Moreover, with its orientation toward student activities, a student-centered learning culture focuses on competence-orientation as a learning outcome (Attard et al. 2010; Barr and Tagg 1995). The essential outcome is not what is taught (i.e. which and how many courses are provided by educators), but what the student learns. As such, the objectives are more closely oriented toward the learning outcomes at the end of the course (e.g. students are able to classify basic procedures) and less toward the transmission of specific content (e.g. students will be imparted basic procedures).

With regard to concrete learning formats in a student-centered learning culture, enormous methodological diversity is possible. Although student-centered learning is often mentioned with reference to learning formats such as inquiry-based learning, problem-based learning or discovery learning, it is not possible to deduce the individual didactic formats directly from the characteristics or to avoid instruction-oriented formats such as lectures. The recommendations of the moderate constructivist view of learning are oriented towards uniting instruction and construction (Reinmann and Mandl 2005).

The orientation towards a student-centered learning culture is accompanied by the design of specific roles for educators and learners. In a more instruction-centered learning culture, the role of educators is to present and explain new information, to guide learners and to monitor and evaluate the learning progress. According to this view, learners are assigned a rather passive position, in which external control and monitoring are required for successful learning. In a student-centered learning culture, students are allocated a much more active role. Students are part of a community of learners and educators, independently helping to shape their learning process and take ownership of their own learning progress. As a result, in this approach, autonomous and self-regulated learning is of great importance.

The role of educators is to provide learners with encouragement, support and advice. Educators must recognize learners' individual needs, provide appropriate "tools" for the learning processes and encourage engagement with other learners. In a student-centered learning culture, educators are learning guides. In this sense they are conceived primarily as experts for designing and adjusting learning environments to students' experiences and previous knowledge, thereby enhancing self-regulated learning. Actions are guided less by questions such as "How can I convey the material and present it in a well-structured manner?" and more by questions such as "How can I facilitate learning and encourage learning activities, and thus make it possible for students to engage in independent learning?" The role of educators is thus conceived as much more restrained than in a primarily instruction-oriented learning culture, since the focus is less on the educator's well-structured and professionally competent lecture than on the educator as role model, facilitator, and advisor to the learning processes. Barr and Tagg (1995) describe this change in roles using the analogy of the soccer coach, who not only gives the players instructions as to how they should play, but also designs training concepts and strategies and actively supports them during the game, for example with technical decisions. In a similar sense, educators should shape learning environments and use their skills to create the best possible learning atmosphere.

5.3 Challenges of a Student-Centered Learning Culture

A student-centered transition in the learning culture is a clear goal of the Bologna Process. The format, including its objectives, is particularly suitable for adult learners, is geared to the needs of lifelong learning, and should replace what has previously been an excessively instruction-oriented and insufficiently student-oriented learning culture. A number of studies indicate a positive effect in terms of promoting deep approaches to learning, self-motivation and student diversity (cf. Lea et al. 2003 for an overview). However, student-centered learning approaches have been viewed critically in recent years (O'Neill and McMahon 2005; Taylor 2013, amongst others) because it seems that such approaches are not equally appropriate for all students; the demands on educators and structural factors are very stringent; and the findings on the desired effects are contradictory. For example, students are very accustomed to "traditional" forms of teaching and often prefer reproductive, instruction-oriented learning (Reinmann-Rothmeier and Mandl 1997). Even by adapting the learning environment, it is only possible to change this orientation slightly (Baeten et al. 2013). In their study, Brahm and Gebhardt (2011) also found that students rely heavily on the guidance, control and supervision of an instructor. Such an attitude inhibits the implementation and success of a student-centered learning culture.

The ability and willingness to engage in self-regulated learning, which is of particular importance in student-centered contexts, is influenced by cognitive, metacognitive and motivational components (Boekaerts 1996), while how pronounced these are varies from student to student (Viebahn 2008). It appears that particular students who already display appropriate attributes at the beginning of their academic studies—i.e. good cognitive abilities, high level of self-motivation and pronounced use of deep approaches to learning—benefit from a student-centered learning culture (Baeten et al. 2010). If the attempt to secure and activate basic (preliminary) knowledge is unsuccessful, there is a risk that a student-centered learning culture will be regarded as lacking structure and will overwhelm students. Similarly, evidence on the effects of student-centered learning environments demonstrates that the original learning orientation—surface learning or deep learning—impacts the efficacy of learning, and students who originally have a surface learning orientation are less likely to engage in deep learning (Baeten et al. 2010).

With regard to motivational components, self-motivation is ascribed great importance within the context of self-regulated learning (Deci and Ryan 1993). On average, students tend toward self-guided motivation (Wulf 2013); however, some students have a more extrinsic learning orientation and thus lack an essential prerequisite for self-guided learning. Furthermore, differences in self-determined motivation can be identified: For example, in a study comparing various subjects, students of social work or special-needs education showed significantly greater self-motivation than those engaged in teaching certification programs or social sciences (Wulf 2013).

An additional challenge in a student-centered learning culture is to what extent self-study activities are prioritized. With the Bologna reform, the envisioned time expenditure for reaching learning objectives has been identified as a workload comprised of time allotments for active class attendance and self-study. In addition to time spent in active class attendance, intensive, individual learning is expected of students in their role as active learners. Findings from various studies indicate a low overall incidence of self-study, however, which frequently occurs only during exam times (Schulmeister and Metzger 2011). Initial results of our own longitudinal survey over the course of the semester regarding a module in the format of inquiry-based learning likewise point to a low proportion of self-study, which is on average about 2 h per week with a high degree of individual variability.

Another problem appears to be that student-centered learning formats are perceived as more complex and this perception can lead to a negative attitude among students (Baeten et al. 2010).

5.4   Conclusion

Various consequences can be derived from the characteristics of student-centered learning and the challenges for learners and educators.

With regard to the role of students, it seems particularly necessary to make the expectations and requirements for autonomy and self-guidance of learning transparent. Since student-centered learning formats are perceived as more complex and since this perception can lead to a negative attitude that prevents deep learning, the paradigm shift (including its goals) and the didactic structure must be made transparent if it is to be accepted by all students. In order to balance differences in previous knowledge, there will be a continued need for additional courses related to certain modules and the learning objectives thereof, but which are not obligatory for all students. The phases of independent learning should be clearly stated in the curriculum and discussed with the students at the beginning of the courses, as the time expenditure for self-study would otherwise only be utilized to a small extent, which, instead of contributing to the deep understanding of the content, may instead promote strategies associated with surface learning.

Due to the focus on student learning activities as well as the competence orientation, it is necessary for a student-centered learning culture to readjust concepts regarding evaluation. Here, it would be possible to orient ourselves on evaluation models such as those that have been used in the United States for more than a decade in the National Survey of Student Engagement (Kuh 2001). All student activities serve as indicators of competence orientation, i.e. it is assumed that students' academic competence and thus their learning success are reflected in the extent to which students practice and carry out study-related activities (Messner et al. 2009; Winteler and Forster 2008).

In terms of the role requirements for educators, a high degree of teaching-related engagement, a generally student-centered attitude as well as a high level of technical and didactic competence appear to be necessary requirements for promoting a transition in the learning culture. Since the amount of preparation and support required in student-centered forms of learning is significantly higher and less tied to the time spent in active class attendance, this must be taken into account when calculating teaching capacities. The existing calculation using the number of courses provided clearly corresponds to an instruction-oriented paradigm and does not take into account the various degrees of effort associated with the individual learning formats or generally associated with a student-centered learning culture.

Furthermore, courses in higher education didactics should be extended to those status groups that have not only been excluded from such by the university culture, but for whom such activities also carry little weight for university career paths. Although teaching engagement is taken into account more clearly in job placement decisions, at least in individual disciplines (e.g. teaching portfolios, evaluation records, sample teaching, teaching awards, etc.), the primary focus is still on research activities.

References

Attard, A./Di Ioio, E./Geven, K./Santa, R. (2010). *Student Centered Learning. An Insight into Theory and Practice*. Bukarest: Education International, European Students Union.

Ausubel, D. P. (1968). *Educational Psychology: A Cognitive View*. New York: Holt.

Baeten, M./Dochy, F./Struyven, K. (2013). The effects of different learning environments on students' motivation for learning and their achievement. *British Journal of Educational Psychology, 83*(3), 484–501.

Baeten, M./Kyndt, E./Struyven, K./Dochy, F. (2010). Using student-centred learning environments to stimulate deep approaches to learning: Factors encouraging or discouraging their effectiveness. *Educational Research Review, 5*, 243–260.

Barr, R. B./Tagg, J. (1995). From Teaching to Learning – A New Paradigm for Undergraduate Education, *Change, Nov./Dec.*, 13–25.

Boekaerts, M. (1996). Self-regulated Learning at the Junction of Cognition and Motivation. *European Psychologist, 1*(2), 100–112.

Brahm, T./Gebhardt, A. (2011). Motivation deutschsprachiger Studierender in der »Bologna-Ära«. *Zeitschrift für Hochschulentwicklung, 6*(2), 15–29.

Deci, E. L./Ryan, R. M. (1993). Die Selbstbestimmungstheorie der Motivation und ihre Bedeutung für die Pädagogik. *Zeitschrift für Pädagogik, 39*(2), 223–238.

Kuh, G. D. (2001). Assessing what really matters to student learning. *Change, May/June*, 10–17.

Lea, S./Stephenson, D./Troy, J. (2003). Higher education students' attitudes to student centred learning: beyond 'educational bulimia'. *Studies in Higher Education, 28*(3), 321–334.

Messner, H./Niggli, A./Reusser, K. (2009). Hochschule als Ort des Selbststudiums – Spielräume für selbstgesteuertes Lernen. *Beiträge zur Lehrerbildung, 27*(2), 149–162.

O'Neill, G./McMahon, T. (2005). Student-centred learning: What does it mean for students and lecturers? In G. O'Neill/S. Moore/B. Mc Mullin (Hrsg.), *Emerging issues in the practice of university learning and teaching* (pp. 27–36). Dublin: AISHE.

Reinmann-Rothmeier, G./Mandl, H. (1997). Lehren im Erwachsenenalter: Auffassungen vom Lehren und Lernen, Prinzipien und Methoden. In F. E. Weinert/H. Mandl (Hrsg.), *Enzyklopädie der Psychologie: Psychologie der Erwachsenenbildung.* (S. 355–390). Göttingen: Hogrefe.

Reinmann, G./Mandl, H. (2006). Unterrichten und Lernumgebungen gestalten. In A. Krapp/B. Weidenmann (Hrsg.), *Pädagogische Psychologie - Ein Lehrbuch* (S. 613–658). Weinheim: Beltz PVU.

Schulmeister, R./Metzger, C. (Hrsg.). (2011). *Die Workload im Bachelor: Zeitbudget und Studierverhalten. Eine empirische Studie.* Münster: Waxmann.

Schüßler, I./Thurnes, C. M. (2005). *Lernkulturen in der Weiterbildung*. Bielefeld: Bertelsmann.

Taylor, J. (2013). What is student-centredness and is it enough? *The International Journal of the First Year in Higher Education, 4*(2), 39–48.

Viebahn, P. (2008). *Lernerverschiedenheit und soziale Vielfalt im Studium. Differentielle Hochschuldidaktik aus psychologischer Sicht.* Bielefeld: Webler.

Winteler, A./Forster, P. (2008). Lern-Engagement der Studierenden. Indikator für die Qualität und Effektivität von Lehre und Studium. *Das Hochschulwesen, 56*(6), 162–170.

Wulf, C. (2013). *Motivationale Voraussetzungen Studierender für Forschendes Lernen*. Vortrag im Rahmen der Tagung »Forschendes Lernen: Forum für gute Lehre«, Fachhochschule Potsdam (02.–03.09.2013).

Focus: Research

Competence Development Through Inquiry-Based Learning

6

Insa Wessels, Christopher Gess, and Wolfgang Deicke

One basic principle of inquiry-based learning that hitherto has received too little reflection is its potential to allow for a focus on competence goals rather than on discipline- or course-specific educational contents (e.g. disciplinary knowledge). Although a broad potential for fostering a wide array of competences is attributed to inquiry-based learning, this has yet to be systematically researched and demonstrated. This chapter outlines which competences can be fostered by inquiry-based learning and how these competences are to be understood. So far, the competence goals of inquiry-based learning have only been abstractly specified. This is insufficient for competence-oriented teaching, since it remains unclear which particular competences are to be fostered and how these may be actively promoted. Drawing on concepts and findings from current research projects, this chapter will operationalize these abstract competence goals and discuss ways to address these during higher education teaching.

6.1   Competence Goals

In looking at the module catalogs or course descriptions for inquiry-based learning (Rueß et al. 2016), educators primarily associate significant discipline- and even topic-specific goals with these formats. Inquiry-based learning in these cases is employed to help students deepen and develop their knowledge of topics independently. Such topic-related goals necessarily need to be differentiated for each individual purpose of inquiry-based learning and cannot be examined from a cross-curricular perspective at this point. Instead,

I. Wessels (✉) · C. Gess · W. Deicke
Humboldt-Universität zu Berlin, bologna.lab, Berlin, Germany
e-mail: insa.wessels@hu-berlin.de; christopher.gess@gmail.com; wolfgang.deicke@ hu-berlin.de

© The Author(s) 2019
H. A. Mieg (ed.), *Inquiry-Based Learning – Undergraduate Research*,
https://doi.org/10.1007/978-3-030-14223-0_6

the focus of this chapter will be on overarching, supra-disciplinary competence goals. These fall within three principal categories: the promotion of research competence, the development of a researcher's mindset and the promotion of what are known as metacognitive competences.

- The most frequent references in the literature credit inquiry-based learning with the promotion of students' *research competence*. The German Science Council (Wissenschaftsrat 2006) recommends inquiry-based learning so that students can learn how to develop questions, solve problems, acquire insights methodically and reflect critically on questions of principle.
- Secondly, inquiry-based learning is associated with the goal of teaching students a *researcher's mindset*. Such mindset should not only make it possible for them to utilize largely theoretical knowledge acquired during their studies in order to analyze the professional field, but will also support them in their own professional activity in a critical reflexive manner that fosters development through inquiry. This goal is formulated for teacher training especially often (Fichten 2013; Wildt 2009; Wissenschaftsrat 2001).
- Finally, inquiry-based learning should foster *metacognitive competences* (Huber 2004). This includes those processes and experiences that deal with knowledge and the control of students' own cognitive functions (Flavell 1979). The metacognitive competences are considered higher-level competences that are acquired throughout the course of study, but not in individual courses.

This quick look at competence goals summarizes the literature on inquiry-based learning. Descriptions of competence goals, however, comprise scarcely more than mere naming of goals. Such general goal formulations are suitable neither for empirical analysis nor for designing teaching in a competence-oriented manner. Simply specifying goals leaves unresolved the question of how these competencies are to be understood. In the following, we therefore attempt to further differentiate the first two goals, namely the acquisition of research competence (Sect. 6.2) and the acquisition of a researcher's mindset (Sect. 6.3), and thus make these applicable to both research and teaching. Figure 6.1 specifies the different components of the first two competence goals, which we will explain below.

6.2   Research Competence

The description of research competence draws on the results of current research projects, including, inter alia, from the German scientific transfer project "Modeling and Measuring Competencies in Higher Education – Validation and Methodological Innovations" ("Kompetenzmodellierung und Kompetenzerfassung im Hochschulsektor"), which has coordinated national and international research projects in this area since 2011. Based on the concept of competence developed by Koeppen et al. (2008), this projects understands

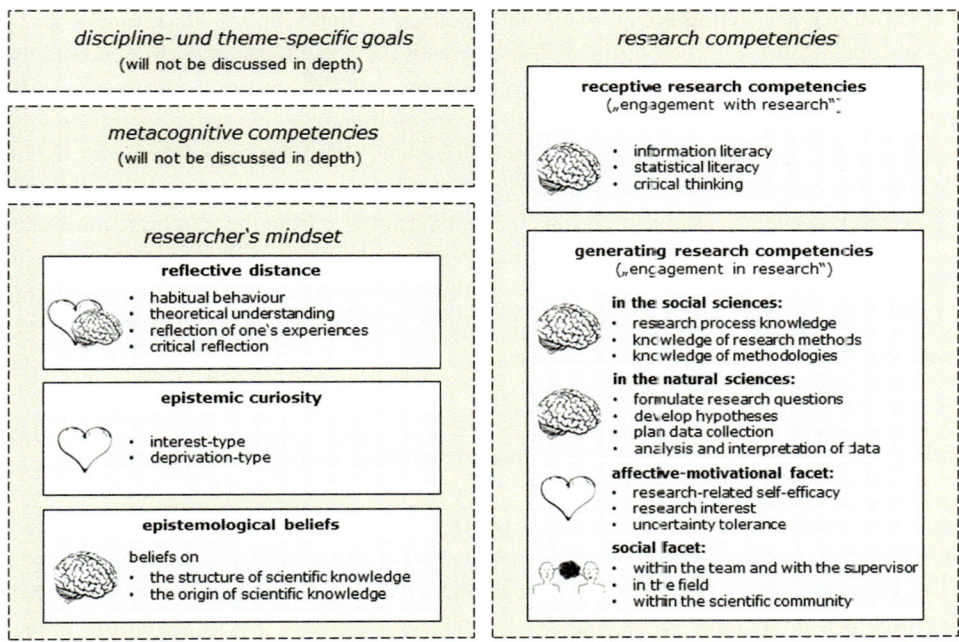

Fig. 6.1 Overview of the potential competence goals in inquiry-based learning. (Source: author's representation)

competences as context-specific cognitive dispositions relating to performance; the emphasis is therefore largely placed on cognition (Blömeke et al. 2013).

In addition, a distinction must be made between two approaches to modelling research competence: *receptive research competence* and *actively generating research competence*. The difference between the two approaches lies in how they understand research competence. First, receptive research competence refers to the understanding and application of existing research results. Borg (2010) describes this as *"engagement with research."* Second, the term "actively generating research competence" may refer to the *active generation* of research findings, which – in contrast to the reception of research findings – can be understood as *"engagement in research"* (Borg 2010). This second understanding of research competence tends to originate in teaching practice and is conveyed by the goals formulated in study regulations: Students should be enabled to conduct independent research.

6.2.1   Cognitive Facets of the Receptive Research Competence

An exemplary approach to the operationalization of research competence in understanding "engagement with research" can be found in the project 'Learning the Science of

Education" (Groß Ophoff et al. 2015), where research competence in educational science is conceptualized by an emphasis on working with the scientific literature. Accordingly, students must first be able to ask suitable questions, and then to find and assess specific information regarding this question, usually research literature. This requires information competence ("information literacy"). The subsequent interpretation of this information requires the competent handling of data ("statistical literacy"). Finally, the evidence that is identified must be assessed and conclusions must be drawn from the interpreted information. This, according to the conceptual framework, requires critical thinking. According to this model, competence-oriented inquiry-based learning would mean conducting less empirical work oneself and instead working on an application-oriented research question with the available literature.

6.2.2   Cognitive Facets of the Generating Research Competence

In understanding research competence as referring to "engagement in research," it cannot be understood to be a generic or supra-disciplinary construct. Due differing research methodologies between disciplines, it must be assumed that the required tendencies relating to performance differ between the larger disciplinary traditions. Accordingly, discipline-specific models for social and natural sciences are available for the operationalization of this competence.

6.2.2.1 Social Sciences

An empirically sound model for research competence exists for disciplines employing research methods from the social sciences (Gess et al. 2017). The model was developed on the basis of interviews and surveys with experts (namely professors). It consists of linking three *competence dimensions* and three *research activities*. According to the model, competence dimensions include: (1) research process knowledge; (2) knowledge of research methods; and (3) knowledge of methodologies, which includes an awareness of the basic methodological concepts and principles. Research activities include: (a) identification of a research problem, (b) planning a research project and (c) analyzing and interpreting data. According to this model, competency-oriented inquiry-based learning would mean that students conduct an empirical study that involves acquiring and applying knowledge of research methods. This corresponds to a type of inquiry-based learning in which students proceed through the entire research process (Rueß et al. 2016).

6.2.2.2 Natural Sciences

Research competence in the natural sciences was examined in the German cross-university project "Competence Modeling and Assessment regarding the Understanding of Science with regard to Natural-Science-Related Methods of Working and Thinking in Teaching-Students in the Three Disciplines Biology, Chemistry and Physics". Based on Mayer (2007), the competence model makes distinctions between the sub-competences "formulating a research question," "developing hypotheses," "planning studies" and "analyzing and interpreting data" (Hartmann et al. 2015). Competency-oriented inquiry-based learning pursuant to this model would mean that students would conduct open-ended experiments and reflect on the inquiry process. This corresponds to the type of inquiry-based learning in which research questions are pursued for the purposes of learning research methods (Rueß et al. 2016).

6.2.3   Affective-Motivational Facets of the Generating Research Competence

The models of research competence that have hitherto been presented all limit themselves to the cognitive facet. This is generally the case for most of the current projects in competence measurement and is, among other things, based on the priorities of the research funding programs. Other facets, such as the affective-motivational, are often not taken into account due to pragmatic issues of conducting research (Fleischer et al. 2013). Even when these facets are considered, efforts to define and model them lag far behind those of the cognitive facet. Based on Kunter et al. (2013) who looked at the professional competence of instructors, the following sections will examine: (1) research-related expectations of self-efficacy, (2) intrinsic motivation or research interest and (3) the tolerance of uncertainty in the research process.

6.2.3.1 Research-Related Self-Efficacy

Expectations of self-efficacy are a person's subjective belief in their own ability to successfully perform certain tasks, even under difficult circumstances (Bandura 1977). Research-related expectations of self-efficacy thus refer to challenging research tasks. This disposition has already been studied a number of times and is often operationalized pertaining to the steps in the research process (Forester et al. 2004; Gess et al. in review). Based on Forester et al. (2004), four areas of self-efficacy can be identified: self-efficacy in data collection, self-efficacy in data analysis, self-efficacy in the analysis of the state of research and in merging findings with the state of research and self-efficacy in the creation of a written research report. According to theory, self-efficacy expectations can be fostered when people have a sense of achievement, can learn by example, are encouraged verbally or experience an emotional response (Bandura 1977).

6.2.3.2 Research Interest

A distinction can be made between two types of research interest: thematic research interests, which relate to concrete objects or discipline-related topics, and activity-related research interests, which relate to classes of activity. The *thematic* research interest is often the impetus for especially ambitious student research projects. However, the practical benefit of promoting thematic research interest is questionable, since a thematic interest is unlikely to be transferable to other topics. Therefore, for practical purposes, it appears that *activity-related* research interest is better suited to such investigation. Here, the research interest is operationalized via the interest in the steps of the research process (Bishop & Bieschke 1994; Gess et al. 2014). Individuals who are interested in research will conduct research because they enjoy the activity itself and regard this as subjectively important. Empirically, two factors of activity-related research interests emerge: firstly, working with literature and the communication of results, and secondly, interest in collecting and evaluating data (Gess et al., in review). The more research steps students take in exploratory learning, the more intensely interest is fostered (Gess et al. 2014).

6.2.3.3 Tolerance of Uncertainty in the Research Process

The research process, which is per se open, frequently leads to contradictory or complicated results or situations for which there is no "right" or "wrong" decision. This can be daunting and demotivating if students are not able to deal positively with these uncertainties. Accordingly, the *tolerance of uncertainty* in the research process should play a significant role (Wessels et al. 2018). It refers to a person's tendency to view unclear decision-making situations and contradictory findings in the research process as a positive challenge and thus the ability to successfully handle these situations. Intolerance of uncertainty would be expressed as anxiety or discomfort. In our interviews, experienced educators in particular mentioned students' anxieties about making decisions in critical research situations, which frequently result in students failing to make necessary decisions or else avoiding these situations.

6.2.4 Social Facets of the Generating Research Competence

Like affective-motivational facets, social facets of competences are rarely examined. For this reason, it is only possible to provide an initial, preliminary list of social sub-competences associated with research competence based on the literature and our interviews with experienced educators (Wessels et al. 2018). In so doing, the focus is on students' communication skills, which can be examined from three perspectives, concerning students': (1) capacity for internal communication, i.e. with their research team and supervisor, (2) ability to adequately communicate externally, in the field of research, and (3) ability to comunicate with the scientifically engaged public.

6.2.4.1 Communication in the Research Team and with Supervising Instructors

Inquiry-based learning is often conducted in teams. Students need to acquire skills such as setting common goals, sharing tasks among themselves and providing feedback. This falls within the capacity for internal communication. In addition, there is communication with the supervisor. Students should acquire both the ability to seek help and to accept assistance and criticism, as well as to convince supervising instructors of the merit of their own ideas. In order to align inquiry-based learning with this competence goal, these communication processes should be explicitly addressed. For instance, supervising faculty could provide suggestions for improving communication that go beyond the technical feedback.

6.2.4.2 Communication in the Field of Research

Communication in the field of research is particularly necessary in the case of qualitative social research since this accounts for a large proportion of a researcher's time. In the natural sciences, communication with others in the research lab, e.g. with technical assistants, is necessary. Communication in the field itself could be made the subject matter of the research, in order to implement inquiry-based learning pertaining to this competence goal. Conversation partners could be asked for feedback regarding communication in interviews or students could reflect on communication in the field in research journals. Even in laboratory situations, contact with colleagues and technical personnel can be recorded and reflected upon.

6.2.4.3 Communication with the Scientific Public

In communication with the scientific public, it is important that students are able to empathize with the recipient's perspective so that they can describe their research projects and results appropriately. Experienced educators emphasize that this ability is also needed in conversation with other researchers so that common interests and opportunities for collaboration can be identified. In order to align inquiry-based learning with this competence goal, exchange with outside collaborators should be integrated into the course. This typically takes the form of final poster presentations.

6.3   Researcher's Mindset

Especially in the case of students aiming to achieve teaching certification, the goal is often formulated as promoting an "attitude of inquiry-based learning" (Wissenschaftsrat 2001), a "researching stance" (Fichten 2010) or an "investigative habitus" (Reitinger 2013) through inquiry-based learning. This often refers to a reflective approach to one's own professional practice. In professions other than teaching, such an attitude is also required, as one's own practice must be reflected upon in nearly every field. In the following, we will postulate that the constructs of (1) reflective distance, (2) epistemic curiosity and (3) epistemological beliefs are components of a researcher's mindset.

6.3.1   Reflective Distance

An objective, unbiased attitude towards practice is the basis for improving practice. Taking a reflective distance enables critical questioning and an empirically based change to one's own professional practice. In the literature, this ideal of the critical-reflective professional is referred to as a "reflective practitioner" (Schön 1983) and "reflective thinking" is looked at empirically (Kember et al. 2000). Inquiry-based learning aiming to foster a reflective distance would mean to primarily pursue practice-relevant research topics. Practical problems that students identify while observing their future occupational field of activity would be especially suitable. The reflective distance can then be tested by consciously checking the students' own presuppositions and beliefs and then questioning them during seminars.

6.3.2 Epistemic Curiosity

In addition to a distance from the professional field, curiosity that motivates students to find out more about an issue is also important—termed epistemic curiosity in the literature. A distinction is made between two dimensions of curiosity (Litman and Mussel 2013): firstly, there is a search for knowledge that is driven by interest or enjoyment ("I-type"), and secondly, there is a search for information that is driven by a sense that knowledge is missing ("D-type"). As yet, little is known about how epistemic curiosity can be fostered. Inquiry-based learning that aims to promote I-type epistemic curiosity should probably involve an extended phase, to allow students to identify their own topics and research questions. In order to promote D-type curiosity, educators could point out the consequences of a lack of knowledge for the research process, but at the same time be available as counselors to fill in any knowledge gaps when asked for information.

6.3.3 Epistemological Beliefs

Epistemological beliefs are beliefs regarding the structure and formation of scientific knowledge in a domain (Stahl and Bromme 2007). It is to be assumed that individuals who regard knowledge as flexible, changeable and useful in practice would be more likely than others to wish to generate new knowledge or change the practice. In inquiry-based learning, students can gain experience with the formation of knowledge and thus receive an impetus that could lead to a change in their own beliefs. Epistemological beliefs can be fostered in a course of academic study by explicitly addressing them and having students reflect upon them (Elby 2001), by discussing the various methods of arriving at the construction of knowledge and the quality of scientific findings (Lahtinen and Pehkonen 2012) and by confronting students with controversially discussed scientific topics, in which conflicting studies trigger epistemic doubt (Ferguson et al. 2012).

6.4   Outlook

There are various competence goals associated with inquiry-based learning. In addition to imparting disciplinary knowledge, competence goals can be classified according to three levels: the promotion of research competence, conveying a researcher's mindset and the development of general metacognitive competences. While general metacognitive competences have already been defined in detail elsewhere and are only partially suitable as competence goals of individual courses due to their breadth, research competence and a researcher's mindset must be comprehensively operationalized in order to be usable for competence-oriented courses and competence-oriented teaching evaluation.

Educators can refer to these competence goals when designing their courses. It is thereby essential to consciously choose from the competence goals presented here, since it is not possible to address all goals in a single course. Depending on the competence goal, different priorities should be set: For example, if the goal is to foster the receptive research competence and reflective distance among students, then students should pursue practice-relevant research questions about which they already have emotionally charged assumptions (for example, regarding homework assignments in teacher training). If, on the other hand, the goal is to develop the *generating* research competence, then the course will have to be designed differently from the ground up. The focus should then be on the research process, which the students should go through as completely as possible and upon which they should repeatedly reflect.

For the design of degree programs, this implies the use of multiple forms of inquiry-based learning within the course of studies, either in order to leave students free to decide which competences they would like to acquire, or in order to allow development of a broad range of competences in the course of study. Naturally, these goals would have to be combined with discipline-specific and topic-specific competence goals, which were not discussed in detail in this chapter.

References

Bandura, A. (1977). Self-efficacy: toward a unifying theory of behavioral change. *Psychological Review, 84*(2), 191–215.

Bishop, R. M./Bieschke, K. J. (1994). *Interest in Research Questionnaire*. Unpublished scale, The Pennsylvania State University.

Blömeke, S./Zlatkin-Troitschanskaia, O./Kuhn, C./Fege, J. (2013). Modeling and measuring competencies in higher education. In *Modeling and measuring competencies in higher education* (pp. 1–10). Sensepublishers, Rotterdam.

Borg, S. (2010). Language teacher research engagement. *Language Teaching, 43*(04), 391–429. doi:https://doi.org/10.1017/S0261444810000170

Elby, A. (2001). Helping physics students learn how to learn. *American Journal of Physics, Physics Education Research Supplement, 69*(7), 54–64.

Ferguson, L. E./Bråten, I./Strømsø, H. I. (2012). Epistemic cognition when students read multiple documents containing conflicting scientific evidence: A think-aloud study. *Learning and Instruction*, *22*, 103–120.

Fichten, W. (2010). Forschendes Lernen in der Lehrerbildung. In U. Eberhardt (Hrsg.), *Neue Impulse in der Hochschuldidaktik – Sprach- und Literaturwissenschaften* (S. 127–182). Wiesbaden: VS Verlag für Sozialwissenschaften.

Fichten, W. (2013). Über die Umsetzung und Gestaltung Forschenden Lernens im Lehramtsstudium. In Didaktisches Zentrum diz (Hrsg.), *Modelle Forschenden Lernens*. Oldenburg: Didaktisches Zentrum diz.

Flavell, J. H. (1979). Metacognition and cognitive monitoring. *American Psychologist*, *34*, 906–911.

Fleischer, J./Koeppen, K./Kenk, M./Klieme, E./Leutner, D. (2013). Kompetenzmodellierung: Struktur, Konzepte und Forschungszugänge des DFG- Schwerpunktprogramms. *Zeitschrift für Erziehungswissenschaft*, *16*(5), 5–22. doi:https://doi.org/10.1007/s11618-013-0379-z

Forester, M./Kahn, J. H./Hesson-McInnis, M. S. (2004). Factor Structures of Three Measures of Research Self-Efficacy. *Journal of Career Assessment*, *12*(1), 3–16. doi:https://doi.org/10.1177/1069072703257719

Gess, C./Wessels, I./Blömeke, S. (2017). Domain-specificity of research competencies in the social sciences: Evidence from differential item functioning. *Journal for Educational Research Online/ Journal für Bildungsforschung Online*, *9*(2), 11–36.

Gess, C./Rueß, J./Deicke, W. (2014). Design-based Research zur Verbesserung der Lehre an Hochschulen: Einführung und Praxisbeispiel. *Qualität in der Wissenschaft*, *1/2014*, 10–16.

Gess, C./Rueß, J./Deicke, W. (in review). The development of the affective-motivational aspect of students' research competencies through research-based learning.

Groß Ophoff, J./Schladitz, S./Leuders, J./Leuders, T./Wirtz, M. A. (2015). Assessing the development of educational research literacy: The effect of courses on research methods in studies of educational science. *Peabody Journal of Education*, *90*(4), 560–573.

Hartmann, S./Upmeier zu Belzen, A./Krüger, D./Pant, H. A. (2015). Scientific Reasoning in Higher Education. *Zeitschrift für Psychologie*, *223(1)*, 47–53. doi:https://doi.org/10.1027/2151-2604/a000199

Huber, L. (2004). Forschendes Lernen: 10 Thesen zum Verhältnis von Forschung und Lehre aus der Perspektive des Studiums. *die hochschule*, *2*, 29–49.

Kember, D., Leung, D. Y. P., Jones, A., Loke, A. Y., McKay, J., Sinclair, K., Tse, H., Webb, C., Wong, F. K.-Y., Wong, M.,Yeung, E. (2000). Development of a Questionnaire to Measure the Level of Reflective Thinking. *Assessment & Evaluation in Higher Education*, *25*(4), 381–395. doi:https://doi.org/10.1080/713611442

Koeppen, K., Hartig, J., Klieme, E., & Leutner, D. (2008). Current issues in competence modeling and assessment. *Zeitschrift für Psychologie/Journal of Psychology*, *216*(2), 61–73.

Kunter, M./Klusmann, U./Baumert, J./Richter, D./Voss, T./Hachfeld, A. (2013). Professional competence of teachers: Effects on instructional quality and student development. *Journal of Educational Psychology*, *105*(3), 805.

Lahtinen, A.-M./Pehkonen, L. (2012). »Seeing things in a new light«: conditions for changes in the epistemological beliefs of university students. *Journal of Further and Higher Education*, *37(3)*, 1–19.

Litman, J. A./Mussel, P. (2013). Validity of the Interest-and Deprivation-Type Epistemic Curiosity Model in Germany. *Journal of Individual Differences*, *34*(2), 59–68. doi:https://doi.org/10.1027/1614-0001/a000100

Mayer, J. (2007). Erkenntnisgewinnung als wissenschaftliches Problemlösen. In D. Krüger/H. Vogt (Hrsg.), *Theorien in der biologiedidaktischen Forschung* (S. 177–18). Springer Berlin Heidelberg. doi:https://doi.org/10.1007/978-3-540-68166-3_16

Reitinger, J. (2013). *Forschendes Lernen. Theorie, Evaluation und Praxis in naturwissenschaftlichen Lernarrangements*. Immenhausen: Prolog.

Rueß, J./Gess, C./Deicke, W. (2016). Forschendes Lernen und forschungsbezogene Lehre – Empirisch gestützte Systematisierung des Forschungsbezugs hochschulischer Lehre. *Zeitschrift für Hochschulentwicklung*, *11*(2), 23–44.

Schön, D. A. (1983). *The Reflective Practitioner - how Professionals Think in Action* New York: Basic Books.

Stahl, E./Bromme, R. (2007). The CAEB: An instrument for measuring connotative aspects of epistemological beliefs. *Learning and Instruction*, *17*, 773–785.

Wessels, I., Rueß, J., Jenßen, L., Gess, C., & Deicke, W. (2018). Beyond cognition: Experts' views on affective-motivational research dispositions in the social sciences. *Frontiers in Psychology*, 9.

Weldt, J. (2009). Forschendes Lernen: Lernen im »Format« der Forschung. *Journal Hochschuldidaktik*, *20*(2), 4–6.

Wissenschaftsrat. (2001). *Empfehlungen zur künftigen Struktur der Lehrerbildung*. Berlin.

Wissenschaftsrat. (2006). *Empfehlungen zur künftigen Rolle der Universitäten im Wissenschaftssystem*. Berlin.

Research-Related Teaching and Learning as an Enculturation into Science

Ines Langemeyer

Does pedagogy need models? Although the question may cause astonishment, models are an integral part of scientific and professional practice. They are used in architecture to visualize building site plans, in economics for the reconstruction (and if possible the forecasting) of complex economic developments, and in physics to explain certain laws, especially where observation is no longer able to accomplish anything (at an atomic level, for example). But what is the purpose of models in teaching-learning research? Is their purpose to illustrate, reconstruct or explain teaching and learning?

The model for undergraduate research and inquiry developed by Healey and Jenkins (2009) has become well known. It depicts a polarization along two orthogonal axes (see figures in Mieg or Reiber, in this volume) between the active and receptive role of students on the one hand, and between the research process and the results of research as teaching content on the other, making it possible to identify four different teaching practices.

What is the purpose of this model? Does it illustrate real practice? Probably not, because it abstracts the many concrete phenomena of the multifaceted teaching-learning process. Not taken into consideration, for example, are which learning challenges are involved in research-driven activity – whether a fresh topic will be introduced or whether students will transfer and/or reinforce what they already know by applying it in a research project (or a portion thereof). In general, the intentions of the educators remain rather unclear. It is not specified, for example, whether their goal consists of developing students' capacity to think, or to help them to become more independent by engaging in research activities.

I. Langemeyer, Prof. Dr. (✉)
Karlsruher Institut für Technologie, Institut für Berufspädagogik und Allgemeine Pädagogik/
House of Competence, Professur für Lehr-Lernforschung, Karlsruhe, Germany
e-mail: ines.langemeyer@kit.edu

H. A. Mieg (ed.), *Inquiry-Based Learning – Undergraduate Research*,
https://doi.org/10.1007/978-3-030-14223-0_7

7.1 Empirically Founded Modeling of Research-Related Teaching and Learning in Higher Education

In three online surveys conducted among educators (at the Karlsruhe Institute of Technology in 2013 and 2016, and at the University of Tübingen in 2014), investigated research-driven teaching, hot on the heels, as it were, of the model of Healey and Jenkins (Langemeyer and Rohrdantz-Herrmann 2014). Explorative factor analyses have shown that, from a subjective perspective, a distinction can actually be made between two approaches to research-related teaching for all data sets: In the first approach, teaching is process-oriented and students conduct experiments, projects, research, etc. largely independently. In the second approach, the focus is on the transfer of knowledge, in which students give talks or presentations, demonstrate their experiments, but also search independently (e.g. information, literature). We could thereby consider both the vertical axis of the Healey-Jenkins model, and also the horizontal axis, to have been confirmed. Nevertheless, the empirical findings can also be interpreted differently.

The following way of modeling practice places *long-term and short-term objectives* in the foreground as structuring features. Short-term goals can be modified as the situation demands while maintaining the long-term goal. Each short-term goal specifies the long-term goal. Thus this analytic view also takes into consideration the subjective premises of behavior and does not necessarily regard these forms of teaching as opposites. The analysis of the 2016 survey conducted among educators confirms that this would be misleading (Langemeyer 2017). It would be more correct to arrange the forms of teaching in parallel, since educators observe students and then decide whether to first organize learning more as *understanding* or more as *independent development*. It is possible to switch between the two modes, however. The choice is made by assessing whether it makes more sense to teach students the basics, to show, explain to and discuss research with them, or whether to enable them to do independent research. Both modes can be realized in all phases of research, roughly stated in (1) problem identification (understanding or finding a research question), (2) acquiring an understanding of or conducting a study, in which theory and empiricism or different theories are related to one another and (3) when reviewing, providing evidence for, and forming a judgment about the findings of the investigation (see Fig. 7.1). Realistically, educators will not strictly choose one mode or the other, but switch back and forth between them so that students know why they can research something and how they can draw a conclusion.

In both cases of the research-related acquisition of experience, the teacher tries to work towards an *enculturation process* in their long-term goal: They attempt to teach students the distinction in scientific thinking and to certain scientific ethos and the rigor of a particular discipline. At this point, it should be stressed that the *short-term goals* of the instructor can – and indeed must – vary within the long-term goal of enculturation. These short-term goals are specified under various, alterable premises, for example study phases or course requirements. The structuring of teaching behavior does not always correlate with the implementation of a didactic plan on a one-to-one basis; under no circumstances

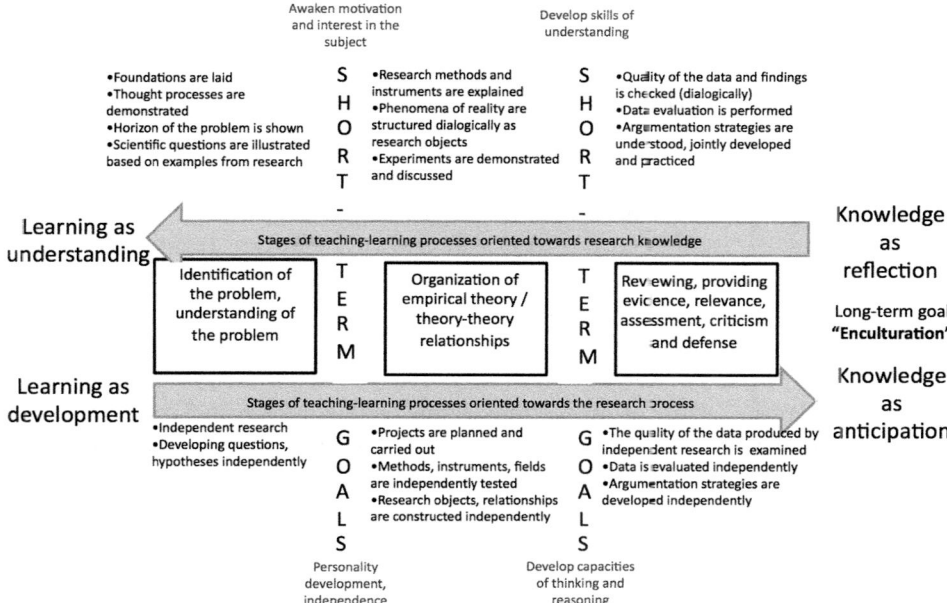

Fig. 7.1 Research-related academic studies as an enculturaticn process. (Source: author's representation)

is it a mere either/or decision made between "receptive" versus "active" (in the case of student roles). This is because it is not just development, but also the processes of understanding that requires a mode of learning activity. The essential structuring of teaching-learning processes is at the relationship level and must be understood psychodynamically.

7.2   Enculturation as a Guiding Principle

As a concept, *enculturation* can be developed theoretically with the help of a number of sources. In the following, I will first draw on gestalt psychology and the reception thereof by the philosopher Michael Polanyi, secondly on the work of the biologist and science theorist Ludwik Fleck, and thirdly on the work of the psychologist Lev S. Vygotsky. Although these sources have many intersections, the authors listed here are not directly connected in a historical context.

Enculturation (independent of the specific scientific orientation) is becoming important because science exists in the form of *epistemic cultures* (Knorr Cetina and Reichmann 2015). Research processes and the teaching-learning process based thereon are partly similar to professionalization processes. Both (at least partially) open themselves up to the problematic, the unforeseeable, to what is not yet known, or to the coincidental (Langemeyer and Rohrdantz-Herrmann 2015), which is intended to prompt questioning and research-oriented behavior in learners (Huber 2009, p. 9).

Learning how to pursue scholarship is a long, never-ending self-teaching process that transcends a well-defined and didactically predictable teaching-learning process. For this reason, research-related instruction aims to show students the possibilities of thinking and acting with which they can continue to work in an area autonomously and independently, since it is only in this way that subjectively meaningful connections arise between individual learning processes.

Thus, from the point of view of the educators, the research-related instruction is less about optimal preparation for exams or about forms of individualized instruction. As was noted in the comment fields of the survey, research-related teaching is regarded as important because it "helps to introduce students to reflection on the subject's research questions" and because it thus promotes "analytical skills and transfer skills." Nevertheless, the notion that such skills could be formed directly through teaching is viewed critically. It is sometimes even negated: "Skills such as analytic thinking, the transfer of ideas as well as a deeper understanding of a subject, etc. unto themselves have nothing to do with the content of teaching." One participant interpreted the "educator's role in implementing results-oriented study projects" via the "need [to support the] open research process in terms of content and group dynamics until a presentable result suitable for the general public without direct intervention (pursuant to the motto: prepare and point in the right direction, then stay calm and wait, but also steer and push in the right place)". All quotes in the comments fields have been taken from the survey conducted among educators at the University of Tübingen in 2014.

In addition to the independent acquisition of experience, students should also familiarize themselves with a state of research by presenting research findings and learn to grasp differences in the development of various theories by demonstrating possibilities of thinking. By showing and demonstrating certain solutions to problems, they should be inspired by one or another methodological approach and actively engage in research questions by discussing together. The long-term goal of *enculturation* thus essentially *overarches* the respective didactic preparation of the material in courses. It does not merge with it, however.

Research-related teaching always includes a number of short-term goals, some of which are pursued in parallel at different levels. As such, a guiding idea is to broaden the students' thinking, so that the latter can go beyond what is known and understood and think independently. This long-term goal is neither the sum of the short-term goals nor compatible with the concept of a modularized acquisition of competences.

7.3 Theoretical Foundations of the Concept of Enculturation

These assumptions are further substantiated below by drawing on Michael Polanyi, Ludwik Fleck and Lev Vygotsky. All three approaches, which were developed in the first half of the twentieth century, share a specific understanding of thought, knowledge and science (for details, see Langemeyer 2015). Gestalt psychology, the holistic core idea of which states that cognitive percepts are global wholes that have more significance than the sum of their parts, had a significant impact on this. In the case of Polanyi, this idea is applied directly to the process of thought; Fleck links thought to the collective process of recognizing and the emergence (not just the discovery!) of facts. Vygotsky adopts this basic assumption in his methodological work on the relationship between general and individual science.

Even before Polanyi, gestalt psychologists explain the ability to recognize a percept through the figure-ground organization: Elements arrange themselves in the process of perception as a figure or as a percept when they come together in the foreground. Analogously, every realization can be understood as a holistic perception of elements in which there is a movement *from* the details *to* the whole – to the gestalt figure. Recognizing a face, for example, means recognizing its elements (especially the eyes, nose and mouth) as a whole. One is not focused on the elements themselves, but instead, one looks through them to see the entire face. Polanyi (1959) uses the term *subsidiary* for that, which is consciously in the background, thus temporary consciousness: Being aware of something subsidiary means that we are not aware of unto itself, but are aware of it as a clue or instrument that points beyond itself (cf. Neuweg 1999, p. 189).

Thinking therefore always completes a movement from a *proximal* to a *distal* term, e.g. from the eyes, nose, mouth, etc. to the face (cf. ibid; cf. Polanyi 1966). What is surprising about intellectual activity is that the *integration* between the proximal and the distal term is experienced as both active and passive. "On the one hand, [the integration is] induced by the subject, while on the other hand, it happens to the subject" (Neuweg 1999, p. 206, translated), as can be seen in the example of a scientific discovery: "We *make* it, and yet it *surprises* us" (ibid.). This is what constitutes the sometimes elusive nature of learning and research processes, but which also gives them the power to elicit enthusiasm and motivation in those who experience them.

Therefore, let us transfer Polanyis' fundamental ideas to learning experiences in scholarship! Scholarly communities have the power to organize a specific way of thinking and perceiving. If such a community (further) develops theories, it thereby actively clears away specific orders of perception in order to consciously restore them in a changed relationship. This new relationship is guided by a certain new *theoretical* organization of seeing and thinking. What people in day to day life often do not realize is that, since everyday theories also structure perceptions, students must first learn to reflect on the premises of their thinking. Every scientifically driven reorganization of thought is based on the experiences of previous generations and scholarly communities, however. The laboriousness of the work of questioning and revising forms of perception is illustrated by Vygotsy's commentary on the realizations about the "earth rotating around the sun" and the "vision of ants":

> How much critical work on our perceptions and, thus, on the concepts linked with them, how much direct study of these concepts – visibility, invisibility, apparent movement –, how much creation of new concepts, of new links between concepts, how much modification of the very concepts of vision, light, movement etc. was needed to establish these facts! (Vygotsky 1997, p. 251)

Fleck also shows that the questioning concepts and forms of perception are not just a learning process of an individual person. Scientific experiences are therefore more than just personal experiences. They must be situated within the context of historical-social experiences. Fleck therefore speaks of *thought collectives*. Communities alone would muster up the strength to reshape the disorder of all real correlations in a system of knowledge: "Between the subject and the object there exists a third thing, the community. It is creative like the subject, refractory like the object, and dogmatic like an elemental power" (Fleck 1960/2011, p. 470, translated).

Historically, the cultural framework in which facts are seen and interpreted arises in relation to the common way of life and forms the background for the way to ask and to research. That framework determines the "moodiness of the researcher," which, in turn, decides "whether he perceives the new percept as a symbolic glaring vision, or as a feeble aviso of resistance, which slows the unbounded, almost arbitrary choice from among the alternating images," for example (Fleck 1935/2011, p. 232, translated). This is why researchers and learners in science face the challenge of breaking with some culturally learned everyday forms of thinking in order to be able to understand the experiences of previous generations and scientific communities.

In addition, Fleck observed what happens when people wish to engage in science *without* the enculturation process, and *without* being familiar with the specific thinking styles and forms of perception. The insight into this need came to him in several bacteriological laboratories. One experience in particular was crucial to him: When he (1945/2011, p. 492 et seq.; 1948/2011, p. 538 et seq.) arrived at Buchenwald concentration camp as a prisoner in 1943, he worked there as a specialist in the typhus vaccine. There was already a working group there, also made up of prisoners; however, they had no expertise in this field. Thus for more than two years, Fleck had the opportunity "to observe the scientific work of a collective comprised entirely of laymen" (1935/1983, p. 135 et seq., translated). The group believed that it had found typhus pathogens, which Fleck was in fact able to identify as granules of stain from white blood cells from the laboratory animals being used for the research. The group was correspondingly far from developing a viable vaccine for the Nazis, which Fleck did not reveal, however. They had simply learned about the appearance of the pathogen from the scientific literature. The reason they were convinced of their own discovery can be explained as mutual reinforcement, the buildup of expectation of seeing specific effects, the desire for recognition, competitiveness, and the desire to satisfy the group leader (ibid.). In epistemological terms, Fleck comments on this (ibid., translated): "The elements of the mood were, in principle, identical to those normally encountered. I observed a situation of this kind – the birth of the discovery." Against this background, he concludes that "the social mechanism that gives rise to an error [is] the same as the mechanism that gives rise to true knowledge" (Fleck 1946/1983, p. 140, translated).

By supporting the notion of enculturation with these theses, we can identify several key aspects of learning processes in a research-oriented course of study. It becomes obvious that a scholarly course of study in a field means more than knowledge of the technical literature and access to research equipment and methods. In particular, the absolutely necessary process of independently learning science and the requirements of science is not possible without the prerequisite of having been part of a thought collective. It is only by participating in a scientific community and its special style of thinking that students can meaningfully and adequately deal with the opportunities for thought and action offered hereby and learn to recognize errors. Important experiences arise during the enculturation process within the frame of reference of a discipline, in that research questions or "facts" are theoretically interpreted and questioned. As with Polanyi, empirical experiences and theoretical considerations organize themselves in a certain way "in the background" as a result of participation in a collective style of thinking. This creates a "system of knowledge" of how something becomes a subject of research, what subject matter may or must be made the object of empirical study, and what cannot be considered as such.

This cultural-historical view of the history of science can be supplemented by further insights by Vygotsky. He examines how the acquisition of scientific concepts restructures intellectual activity. For him, every concept is a theory (or form of perception) that *performs* a different task for scientific thinking. In his view, ideas do not express themselves in language, but are rather born and completed within it. Thus, for Vygotsky, a purely empirical science without philosophical work on one's own concepts is not possible. Concepts have always had a problematic relationship with empirical facts. This is because, "if concepts, as tools, were set aside for the facts of experience in advance, all of science would be superfluous" (Vygotsky, 1927/2003, p. 93, translated; cf. 1997, p. 325). In general and special science, philosophical work differs only in terms of its function within concrete cognitive activity in a scientific field. Thus, he draws a comparison between scientific work, which is done within the limits of a single study (or special science), and the "function of a funnel," where the object being examined "condenses theories into hypotheses" (Vygotsky, 1927/2003, p. 97). However this same function is likewise fulfilled by "general science with the same procedures and the same goals for multiple special sciences" (ibid.).

This results in a reciprocal, dialectical relationship between two types of experience: One focuses on the aspect of how a research subject has been theoretically conceptualized and changed in the research process. The other proceeds indirectly along the same process by reflecting on the theoretical concepts. It examines how perceptions were initially organized, how a certain theoretical classification was made, and how it can be systematically evaluated on the basis of individual empirical observations.

7.4   What Are the Implications?

As has been shown, the concept of enculturation can be used to describe the process of inquiry-based learning as the appropriation of scientific practice in the mode of self-education, but also of participation. Moreover, research-related teaching as a specification of this process is made clear by short-term goals. This more complex understanding goes far beyond the need to systematize manifestations of the teaching-learning process that have only been considered superficially. It leads to the level where interactions occur between the actions of educators and the actions of students; these interactions repeatedly undergo reflection within the research-oriented course of study. The central issue for educators, which is currently the most pressing issue for students as well, can be decided through the orientation towards the long-term goal of *enculturation*. Without this long view, it would be necessary either to proclaim the option of inquiry-based learning impossible, or to curtail the research itself, for example by limiting it to simply repeating experiments that have already been performed. However, this would simply sweep under the carpet the challenges of research questions that are as yet unresolved, and the difficulties of conducting, reviewing and defending one's own steps in research. If the objectives of higher education policy, such as anchoring inquiry-based learning in modularized degree programs, are to be achieved, it seems necessary to obtain deeper insight into the dynamic of the teaching-learning process and to not be guided by supposed opposites that are, in fact, not oppositional.

References

Fleck, L. (1983). *Erfahrung und Tatsache. Gesammelte Aufsätze*. Frankfurt/M.: Suhrkamp.

Fleck, L. (1935/1979). *Genesis and development of a scientific fact*. Chicago: The University of Chicago Press. (Original work in German, published 1935)

Fleck, L. (2011). *Denkstile und Tatsachen: gesammelte Schriften und Zeugnisse*. (hrsg. v. Werner, S./Zittel, C./Stahnisch, F.). Frankfurt/M.: Suhrkamp.

Healey, M./Jenkins, A. (2009). *Developing undergraduate research and inquiry*. York: Higher Education Academy.

Huber, L. (2009). Warum forschendes Lernen nötig und möglich ist. In L. Huber/J. Hellmer/F. Schneider (Hrsg.), *Forschendes Lernen im Studium* (S. 9–35). Bielefeld: UniversitätsverlagWebler.

Knorr Cetina, K./Reichmann, W. (2015). Professional Epistemic Cultures. In I. Langemeyer, M. Fischer/M. Pfadenhauer (Hrsg.), *Epistemic and Learning Cultures – Wohin sich Universitäten entwickeln* (S. 18–33). Weinheim: Beltz Juventa.

Langemeyer, I. (2015). *Das Wissen der Achtsamkeit. Kooperative Kompetenz in komplexen Arbeitsprozessen*. Münster: Waxmann.

Langemeyer, I. (2017). *Forschungsorientiert Lehren und Studieren Empirische Untersuchungen zu Lehr-Lernformen, Gründen, Erwartungen und Einstellungen am KIT*. Karlsruhe: KIT.

Langemeyer, I./Rohrdantz-Herrmann, I. (2014). Forschungsorientiertes Lehren. Eine Bestandsaufnahme am KIT. A + B Forschungsberichte. Retrieved 1 July 2015 from http://www.ibap.kit.edu/berufspaedagogik/download/AB_Forschungsbericht_Lehrendenbefragung_20140723.pdf

Langemeyer, I./Rohrdantz-Herrmann, I. (2015). Wozu braucht eine Universität Lehr-Lernforschung? – lädoyer für eine entwickelnde Forschung. In I. Langemeyer, M. Fischer/ M. Pfadenhauer (Hrsg.), *Epistemic and Learning Cultures – Wohin sich Universitäten entwickeln* (S. 211–227). Weinheim: Beltz Juventa.

Neuweg, G. H. (1999). Könnerschaft und implizites Wissen. *Zur lehr- und lerntheoretischen Bedeutung der Erkenntnis- und Wissenstheorie Michael Polanyis*. Münster: Waxmann.

Polanyi, M. (1959). *The study of man*. Chicago: The University of Schicago Press.

Polanyi, M. (1966). *The tacit dimension*. Chicago: The University of Schicago Press.

Vygotsky, L. S. (1997). The historical meaning of the crisis in psychology: A methodological investigation. In Rieber, R. W., & Wollock, J. (eds.), The collected works of LS Vygotsky (pp. 233–343). Springer US. (Russion original in 1927)

Reflection

8

Ludwig Huber

8.1 Reflection – A Genuine Element of Inquiry-Based Learning?

It is "self-evident" that reflection is a part of inquiry-based learning. One is given this impression as soon as one looks into descriptions of the concept: In the first list detailing the features of inquiry-based learning, which was created by the Federal University Assistants' Conference (BAK) (1970, paragraph 4.21), we already find the following: "self-critical examination of the outcome in terms of its dependence on hypotheses and methods." The term is included in definitions, for example in the oft-cited definition from Huber (2009, p. 10, translated):

> In contrast to other learning methods, inquiry-based learning is characterized by the fact that learners shape, experience and reflect on the process of a research project, which is aimed at obtaining insights that are of interest to third parties, doing so throughout all the essential phases of said project: from developing questions and hypotheses, selecting and implementing the methods, through testing and presenting the results, either by working independently or in active collaboration with an overarching project.

This same impression is created by models of the phase cycle that inquiry-based learning should ideally undergo, not only as described by Huber (2009, also in the definition provided above), but also, for example, by Joachim Ludwig (2011): In each of the three types of "teaching in the format of research" distinguished by Ludwig (research-based, research-oriented, community), which accentuate different parts of such a cycle, reflection appears to be a central aspect. Schneider and Wildt (2009) formulate their "process model of inquiry-based learning" in a manner that is explicitly analogous to Kolb's experiential

8

L. Huber, Prof. em. Dr. Dr. h.c. (✉)
Fakultät für Erziehungswissenschaft, Universität Bielefeld, Bielefeld, Germany
e-mail: lwhuber@gmx.de

© The Author(s) 2019
H. A. Mieg (ed.), *Inquiry-Based Learning – Undergraduate Research*,
https://doi.org/10.1007/978-3-030-14223-0_8

learning, in which reflection of experiences gained acts as the starting point for new questions and hypotheses. Accordingly they define phase VII (after the phases of carrying through the research and evaluating the research results) as "interpretation of the data, reflection on the research process." The words "reflection" and "to reflect" are also frequently found in reports on inquiry-based learning projects that have been conducted (cf. Huber et al. 2009, 2013; Lepp and Niederdrenke-Felgner 2014).

But perhaps, as is so often the case, there is an issue with the self-evident way in which the word is used: specifically the problem that it is in no way self-evident what is meant when these words are used. Therefore, in the following, I will attempt to develop what can and should be theoretically understood and to classify, or at least assume, what actually happens in practice.

8.2   Concept and Tasks of Reflection

8.2.1   Reflection from a Philosophical and an Educational-Theoretical Perspective

The word "reflection" has a long history in the philosophical tradition. In the course of this, the meaning of the word, which derives from optics, has gradually shifted from considering (originally: mirroring) a matter and reconsidering an idea to thinking about cognitive achievements, in accordance with Descartes' "redirection of the knowledge interest from the subject matter to the act of knowing itself" (Schmidt and Gessmann 2009; cf. also Zahn 1992). The focus is thus placed on the "explicit raising of awareness and becoming aware of the subject and the activity of an act of knowing or act of will" (Brugger and Schöndorf 2010, p. 400). In the philosophical theory of cognition, in the case of Kant, in German idealism and even in phenomenology and existentialism, reflection acquires a changing but increasingly central significance. It is not our task here to refine this (cf. however Zahn 1992).

In everyday language following the usage in French or English, "reflection" or "to reflect" is frequently used to simply mean "to consider, or regard in a contemplative manner." In addition, reflection can mean integrating the respective facts within a wider context or considering them from another perspective.

In scientific activity, the role of reflection also includes: Raising awareness of the activity and experience, of the decisions that have been made more or less unconsciously, of the cognitive process and the factors that influenced that process. Similarly this is its role in inquiry-based learning insofar as, like every course of study according to Humboldt, such learning refers to the beginning participation in the work and community of those pursuing science by teachers and learners (cf. Humboldt 1810/1964, p. 256).

At the same time, inquiry-based learning can be regarded as that form of study in which "education through scholarship" (*Bildung durch Wissenschaft*) is most likely (possible), because "knowledge is always treated as a problem that is not yet completely resolved" and therefore "one always continues to research" (ibid.). The concept of education (*Bildung*) is also associated with reflection (or also "reflectiveness"; cf. e.g. Hentig 1980, p. 180 et seq.). In Humboldt's considerations on the matter – to draw on him once again – the word reflection does not appear, but the meaning of the concept does indeed: It is constitutive of his concept of the education (*Bildung*) of mankind that said individual "seeks [   ] to grasp as much world as possible and bind it as tightly as he can to himself" (1794/1960, p. 235, translated), but not to lose himself too fully in one thing or in the diversity of objects itself, but rather to place everything "in relation to our inner education". This is why he seeks "allness" (*Allheit*), coherence (an "overseeable circle"), a "final purpose" (*letzter Zweck*) in his thinking. This "process of our mind [...] can only be fathomed by profound reflection and constant observation of oneself" (ibid., pp. 237–239; cf. also 1810/1964, p. 258, translated). Elsewhere, Humboldt makes clear that individuals cannot acquire this education on their own: The problem of the difference between the universality of thought and the particularity of practical decisions must "be resolved in such a way that his [the individual's] own advance toward the goal simultaneously promotes the universal approach thereto, and indeed directly and immediately [...]" (1797/1960, p. 508; cf. also p. 511 et seq., translated).

The "science" (*Wissenschaft*) that Humboldt had in mind, however, was philosophical and included the humanities, in contrast to the "collecting sciences," which were separated from it. Reflection on the process of cognition itself is therefore inextricably linked with "science." According to Humboldt's understanding of "science," its continued reference to the universal must per se overcome all ties to particular perspectives and purposes (Humboldt 1810/1964, pp. 258, 261). Since it is no longer self-evident, if indeed it ever was, that this can be expected of the particularized disciplines of today, this raises the question as to what supplementation is required for the study of said disciplines. Clearly the postulation that, for any knowledge one discipline must supplement the other, is no longer sufficient (cf. also Schleiermacher 1810/1956, p. 223 et seq., as well as Brüggen 1988, p. 310 et seq.), and what is instead at issue is confronting overarching questions, the problems of society, even of humanity, which exceed the segments of problems addressed by individual disciplines, but which nevertheless need to be dealt with by the sciences together.

This is because, in the meantime, the sciences have become a problem in a completely different sense. They have produced the possibility of means for the total destruction of the world (nuclear physics), irreversible changes to life (molecular genetics), the permanent pollution of the natural environment, the control of information and the manipulation of individuals, groups and entire societies: Simple harmony is no longer possible between this version of science as a technical disposition and regulation of the world, and the view of education as a "reflective self-understanding of man" (cf. Benner 1990, p. 598 et seq.). Even "reflection" must be comprehended in a more complex way: Specifically in the confrontation with the key problems mentioned above, in particular the destruction of the environment and the global, universal and irreversible risks which are produced simultaneously when technological advances are made, science encounters its own actions and their consequences, and in turn has to invent new means to combat said consequences. Similarly, industry is expanding with products that are needed to offset the damage caused by previous ones. As Beck (1986) understood in his fruitful analysis of these developments, this is the sciences becoming reflexive (reflecting back on themselves) in the sense of a confrontation with the consequences of their own actions. Although one might contend that modern science does not think (philosophically) while in action, scientists should, in fact, reflect in this way when reviewing their actions. The reflection intended in the educational ideal, at any rate, is self-reflection by those engaged in science with regard to the process.

Benner (1990, p. 609 et seq.) combines both the traditional and the present understanding of this demand for self-reflection in a model of "the four levels of an educational interpretation of modern science": Completion of knowledge acquisition in discourse (message, dispute, understanding); transcendental philosophical reflection on limitations in the validity claims of scientific statements; epistemological reflection on its historical-social origin and new applications; and questioning the scientific statements in terms of their meaning in and for reality while reflecting on the situational context of dealing with them.

Thus if education through scholarship (*Bildung durch Wissenschaft*) is still possible at all and if inquiry-based learning is to serve this purpose, then it will only be through the power of reflection: "education through scholarship requires the intensive active examination of how science is conducted" (cf. Brinckmann et al. 2002, p. 29; Brunkhorst 2002, p. 246). On the other hand, while certainly also a goal and component of "education through scholarship" (*Bildung durch Wissenschaft*), "critical thinking" has an even greater significance insofar as it generally questions social relationships and processes and the justifications thereof. Summarizing the considerations so far, there are three dimensions to reflection as defined here: the self-reflection of scholarship as a mode of rational cognition, the self-reflection of the subject through scholarship, and the reflection on the common good to be promoted thereby. Autonomy and social responsibility both belong here as goals (cf. Euler 2005, pp. 255, 263 et seq.).

8.2.2 Reflection from the Perspective of Experiential Learning and Professional Practice

The reasoning for reflection presented so far has been based on its importance to scholarship, in particular to the goal of education through scholarship (*Bildung durch Wissenschaft*), which, in turn, is especially bound to the concept of inquiry-based learning. Another line of reasoning could be derived from the importance of reflection for continued learning by individuals and organizations in a concept of learning based on reflective experience. It would go beyond the scope of this project to present the development of this from Dewey and Lewin to Kolb. In any event, it has also become important in understanding the practice and justification of professions that cannot simply apply laws or technologies to the complexities of the problems and situations they face, but that also cannot continue to develop if they only cope with unexpected problems more or less successfully within a given situation itself ("reflection *in* action"; cf. Schön 1983): Instead, they must develop orientations and justifications for future action based on the subsequent reflection on such actions and experiences ("reflection *on* action") (Schön 1987. p. 31). In this sense, "reflective practice" is the motto of many writings and discussions regarding professions such as health and education. In view of the dissolution of many hitherto stable boundaries, this could also be the case in academic life and in science as a profession. Following the lead of Gibbons et al. (1994), in "mode 2," modern science is increasingly project-oriented, transdisciplinary, contextualized and thus confronted with structuring problems that change based on the situation, while "mode 1" describes the traditional production of knowledge in accordance with disciplinary paradigms.

From this perspective, it is necessary to conclude that reflection is also highly significant for professional education, in terms of both studies and training (for example, in dealing with initial practical experiences). Curricula should be measured by the degree to which they create space and opportunity for this purpose. As far as I can see, the most advanced are degree programs in medicine, in which elements such as early practical experiences and reflective seminars on ethics or health policy hold a notable place. In many instances this also applies to teacher education. Here, the compulsory internships are often the subject of explicit exercises in reflection, for example in the writing of practical reports or the evaluation of portfolios, sometimes also connected with access to this practice in the form of inquiry-based learning (cf., only by way of example, the anthology by Schüssler et al. 2014, and in particular the article by Valdorf et al. (2014) in that anthology).

With these considerations, however, one enters a new, much wider field, actually that of study itself; while many issues also arise from the concept of inquiry-based learning in general, in the following I shall again limit myself to the discussion within the context of education through scholarship (*Bildung durch Wissenschaft*).

8.2.3 Reflection Within the Context of Inquiry-Based Learning

From the above, it will also be possible to develop questions for reflection within the context of inquiry-based learning. These go in three directions:

- science as a mode of rational cognition, i.e. the research which is pursued in the respective project considered from an epistemological viewpoint: cognition-inducing interests; explicit and implicit premises, the decisions made regarding the question, choice of method, etc. in terms of where the focus is placed and what is dismissed, the scientific status of the results and their dependence on the design and methods of the study;
- science in its relationship to the common good: the social relevance of such research as currently experienced, the relationship of general and particular interest, especially in contract research or the use of research to provide consulting and, associated therewith,

the problems of publicness and confidentiality, issues of research ethics (in the forms of the study) and scientific ethics (integrity, etc.);

- science as a subjective learning process and experience in the course of the project: in terms of content (learning problems, stages, aporia, insights…) and social aspects (relationships and collaboration in the group, with the educators/supervisors, etc.).

It hardly needs to be emphasized that each of these directions of reflection is important, demanding and facilitative, especially in projects related to inquiry-based learning. In view of the unavoidable limitations on student projects, e.g. the consequences of limited methodologies and the scope and validity of the results are particularly important in the first of these directions. In the second direction, for example animal experiments and the implications thereof or – as is the case in many of the possible and popular projects at many universities of applied sciences – the particular interests of the party commissioning the study in their charged relationship with the young researchers' advanced perspectives on the problem provide a great deal of material for discussions about research ethics. Finally, in the third direction, there may be an intense connection with the level of meta-learning which is so important to the entire course of study.

Since, in our context, inquiry-based learning does not simply deal with individual education through scholarship (*Bildung durch Wissenschaft*), but also with a didactic format in higher education, as with other teaching and learning methods, reflection on the course (or, respectively, the project) comes up as an additional direction that reflection can take: facilities, organization, equipment, etc. In the case of topic forums, for example, the organization, coordination and supervision support are reflected upon. Questions and answers from the process typically referred to as *evaluation* can also be used for such reflection.

Summarizing the previous considerations, we can say: If reflection is an element of professional scientific work for ethical as well as functional reasons, it must also be an element of inquiry-based learning. This reflection is therefore involved in setting goals for this learning and, as such, as a means to an end. Undoubtedly, however, the capacity for reflection is a competence unto itself, can be described as such and can be transferred to other forms of professional action; in this regard, reflection can also be regarded as a goal unto itself and as one of the competences that can be further developed through inquiry-based learning.

8.3 Forms of and Situations for Reflection in Inquiry-Based Learning

There is no question that reflection can be combined with any activity in inquiry-based learning: potentially every step offers an occasion to pause, to be aware of what you are doing and why, the purpose thereof and what you feel.

Nevertheless, it is possible to single out special opportunities for reflection. Such situations include those where there is a transition from one phase of the process to another.

In many project reports, it can be seen that stages are already set up at caesuras, at which otherwise independent project teams involved in the research come together in the plenary session provided by the class in order to mutually report to one another about the project and their plans for the next phase. It only takes one additional step and a little time, also, to reflect on experiences and intentions. Reflection can become a primary topic in the introductory and final phase: at the beginning because there are immediate questions regarding the interest, topicality, relevance, and possibly even the ethics of the research under consideration, and at the end because not only the significance of the findings and their possible consequences, but also the process through which those findings have been reached must be assessed and conclusions drawn for future work.

The situation is similar for the forms and media of reflection beyond quiet individual reflection. The natural and most obvious of these is oral communication among those involved or other interested parties, for example in the situations mentioned above. However, given the time intervals between these situations as well as the variety and rapid succession of tasks and impressions, it is advisable to record reflections during the process, in particular by writing them down so that they may be introduced in the midst of that exchange. Means for doing so include field notes, work journals, interim reports, learning journals or portfolios; this may also comprise drawings or images. The act of writing things down itself holds the potential for a reflective process (cf. Bräuer 2003; Lahm 2015). In larger rounds of discussions, for example in plenary session for a project or, respectively, a course, short phases of note-taking in the form of *one-minute papers* or cards help all those involved to be sure of their thoughts and see that these are factored in. *Peer reviews* could also provide students with another entry point, if created and recorded appropriately.

So far, little is known about what use participants in courses using inquiry-based learning make of these options. Published reports, for example in anthologies that have appeared in recent years – examples of which include those from Huber et al. (2013) and Lepp and Niederdrenk-Felgner (2014) – have thus far scarcely been productive regarding the question how to deal with reflection. This does not mean that it does not exist, but for the time being it only confirms, as already stated, that reflection is rarely discussed. Many activities are reported that can smoothly lead to reflection, and that perhaps have already done so; one example is scrutinizing central concepts that determine a problem (example: The students "scrutinize [...] the current inflationary and in particular often abusive use of the concepts of 'sustainability'" in a course entitled "Innovation for Sustainability," see Arndt 2014, p. 102), or they sometimes scrutinize the assurance "in specific places" that the path they have taken is correct (Lepp 2014, p. 37), or, frequently, scrutinize the critical assessment of (intermediate) results (Gervers 2014, p. 135; Schmidt et al. 2013, p. 180). Evaluation questions that require self-assessment, such as one's own participation or acquisition of competencies, can act as a step into self-reflection.

Guidelines for learning reports or portfolios often include sections for reflection (mentioned, for example, by Lorenzen et al. 2013, p. 154 et seq.; or Kaufmann 2013, p. 133; in "Reflection texts on the research process and teamwork" ("Reflexionstexte zum

Forschungsverlauf und zur Teamarbeit") as material for the final overall interpretation, ibid., p. 137). Reflection is rarely (and the competence of reflecting) explicitly named among the learning objectives (if any), almost as though one need not or could not learn it. To summarize, even where reflecting or reflection are mentioned, nothing more is said about what was reflected upon, how extensive or how deep this reflection was and in what forms it was communicated and discussed.

In a short working phase which was dedicated to our topic during the meeting of the working group for inquiry-based learning of the Deutsche Gesellschaft für Hochschuldidaktik (DGHD) (German Society for Higher Education Didactics) within the context of the annual meeting of the DGHD in Paderborn on March 4, 2015, most of the situations and forms of reflection mentioned above were mentioned once or twice as possibly occurring. There were additional suggestions made that could also serve the purpose of promoting reflection such as tutorials or mentoring sessions, team meetings or fireside chats, research workshops or special interviews. However, the predominant impression was that at least those higher education didactic experts who must support or evaluate inquiry-based learning projects thus know far too little about what actually happens in the process of such projects in order to facilitate and promote reflection. A significant task of future supporting research looms here.

The picture was clearer for continuing education of educators in a higher education setting insofar as that staff development is offered by higher education didactic experts. In any case, according to the oral reports at this gathering, such education is frequently designed in such a way that fruitful occasions exist for professional and scientific self-reflection by educators, which are in fact utilized: joint curriculum planning, co-teaching and collegial advice in terms of self-understanding as educators, setting goals, choice of methods, etc. An interdisciplinary composition of the groups is also seen as an opportunity for changing perspectives and questioning the self-evidence of one's own disciplinary culture, evaluating one's own teaching or even researching it. How much of the kind of reflective activity that they experience in such settings educators subsequently transfer to their courses and practice there with students remains an open question, however, and one that calls for investigation.

Ultimately, this is true of inquiry-based learning in general. A reflection on reflection itself and reassurance about its practice in inquiry-based learning projects is essential.

References

Arndt, C.(2014). Innovation for Sustainability (IfS): Eine interkulturelle und interdisziplinäre Sommerschule im Format des Forschenden Lernens. In S. Lepp/C. Niederdrenk-Felgner (Hrsg.), *Forschendes Lernen initiieren, umsetzen und reflektieren* (S. 99–116). Bielefeld: Universitätsverlag Webler.

Beck, U. (1986). *Risikogesellschaft. Auf dem Weg in eine andere Moderne.* Frankfurt: Suhrkamp.

Benner, D. (1990). Wissenschaft und Bildung. Überlegungen zu einem problematischen Verhältnis und zur Aufgabe einer bildenden Interpretation neuzeitlicher Wissenschaft. *Zeitschrift für Pädagogik, 36*(4), 597–620.

Bräuer, G. (2003). Schreiben als reflexive Praxis. Tagebuch, Arbeitsjournal, Portfolio. Freiburg im Breisgau: Fillibach Verlag.

Brinckman, H./Garcia, O./Gruschka, A./Lenhardt, G./ZurLippe, R. (2002). Die Einheit von Forschung und Lehre: Über die Zukunft der Universität. Wetzlar: Büchse der Pandorra.

Brüggen, F. (1988). Lernen – Erfahrung – Bildung. Oder: Über Kontinuität und Diskontinuität im Lernprozeß. Zeitschrift für Pädagogik, 34(3), 299–314.

Brugger, W./Schöndorf, H. (Hrsg.). (2010). Philosophisches Wörterbuch. Freiburg: Alber.

Brunkhorst, H. (2002). Die Universität der Demokratie. *Blätter für deutsche und internationale Politik, 47*(2), 237–247.

Bundesassistentenkonferenz (1970/2009). *Forschendes Lernen – Wissenschaftliches Prüfen. Bd. 5. Schriften der BAK*. Bonn. Neudruck Bielefeld: UniversitätsverlagWebler.

Euler, D. (2005). Forschendes Lernen. In S. Spoun/W. Wunderlich (Hrsg.), *Studienziel Persönlichkeit. Beiträge zum Bildungsauftrag der Universität heute* (S. 253–272). Frankfurt, New York: Campus.

Gervers, S. (2014). Destinationsmarketing im Bachelorstudiengang Gesundheits- und Tourismusmanagement. In S. Lepp/C. Niederdrenk-Felgner (Hrsg.), *Forschendes Lernen initiieren, umsetzen und reflektieren* (S. 134–154). Bielefeld: Universitätsverlag Webler.

Gibbons, M./Limoges, C./Nowotny, H./Schwartzman, S./Scott, P./Trow, M. (1994). *The New Production of Knowledge. The Dynamics of Science and Research in Contemporary Societies*. London: SAGE Publications.

Huber, L. (2009). Warum Forschendes lernen nötig und möglich ist. In L. Huber/J. Hellmer/ F. Schneider (Hrsg.), *Forschendes Lernen im Studium. Aktuelle Konzepte und Erfahrungen* (S. 9–35). Bielefeld: UniversitätsverlagWebler.

Huber, L./Hellmer, J./Schneider, F. (Hrsg.). (2009). *Forschendes Lernen im Studium. Aktuelle Konzepte und Erfahrungen*. Bielefeld: UniversitätsverlagWebler.

Huber, L./Kröger, M./Schelhowe, H. (Hrsg.). (2013). *Forschendes Lernen als Profilmerkmal einer Universität. Beispiele aus der Universität Bremen*. Bielefeld: UniversitätsverlagWebler.

Humboldt, W. v. (1794/1956). Theorie der Bildung des Menschen. Bruchstück. In Ders. (hrsg. von A. Flitner/K. Giel), *Werke. Bd. I* (S. 234–240). Stuttgart: Cotta.

Humboldt, W. v. (1797/1960). Über den Geist der Menschheit. In Ders. (hrsg. von A. Flitner/K. Giel), *Werke. Bd. I* (S. 506–518). Stuttgart: Cotta.

Humboldt, W. v. (1809/10/1964). Über die innere und äußere Organisation der höheren wissenschaftlichen Anstalten in Berlin. In Ders. (hrsg. von A. Flitner/K. Giel), *Werke. Bd. IV.* (S. 255–266). Stuttgart: Cotta.

Kaufmann, M. E. (2013). »Wir haben selbst neue Wissenszusammenhänge geschaffen!« Forschendes Lernen zu »Diversity« in der Kulturwissenschaft. In L. Huber, M. Kröger/H. Schelhowe (Hrsg.), *Forschendes Lernen als Profilmerkmal einer Universität. Beispiele aus der Universität Bremen* (S. 123–142). Bielefeld: UniversitätsverlagWebler.

Lahm, S. (2015). *Schreiben als spreche man selbst. Lernen durch reflektierendes Schreiben in Lehrveranstaltungen*. Bielefeld: Typoskript.

Lepp, S. (2014). Wissenschaftliches Arbeiten im Bachelorstudiengang Automobilwirtschaft. In S. Lepp/C. Niederdrenk-Felgner (Hrsg.), *Forschendes Lernen initiieren, umsetzen und reflektieren* (S. 30–53). Bielefeld: Universitätsverlag Webler.

Lepp, S./Niederdrenk-Felgner, C. (Hrsg.). (2014). *Forschendes Lernen initiieren, umsetzen und reflektieren*. Bielefeld: Universitätsverlag Webler.

Lorenzen, S./Stützle, H./Unger, A. (2013). Wie funktioniert ein Betrieb? BWL- und Psychologiestudierende erkunden Bremer Betriebe. In L. Huber/M. Kröger/H. Schelhowe

(Hrsg.), *Forschendes Lernen als Profilmerkmal einer Universität. Beispiele aus der Universität Bremen* (S. 143–164). Bielefeld: UniversitätsverlagWebler.

Ludwig, J. (2011). *Forschungsbasierte Lehre als Lehre im Format der Forschung Potsdam. Brandenburger Beiträge zur Hochschuldidaktik, 3*. Potsdam: Universitätsverlag.

Schmidt, H./Gessmann, M. (2009). *Philosophisches Wörterbuch* (23., vollst. neu bearb. Auflage). Stuttgart: Kröner.

Schleiermacher, F. (1808/1956). Gelegentliche Gedanken über Universitäten im deutschen Sinn. In E. Anrich (Hrsg.), *Die Idee der deutschen Universität* (S. 219–308). Darmstadt: Wiss. Buchgesellschaft.

Schmidt, T./Sebald, K./Gutowski, J. (2013). Forschendes Lernen im Bachelor-Wahlpflichtfach Festkörperphysik – Ein Pilotprojekt am Fachbereich Physik/Elektrotechnik. In L. Huber, M. Kröger/H. Schelhowe (Hrsg.), *Forschendes Lernen als Profilmerkmal einer Universität. Beispiele aus der Universität Bremen* (S. 179–194). Bielefeld: UniversitätsverlagWebler.

Schneider, R./Wildt, J. (2009). Forschendes Lernen und Kompetenzentwicklung. In L. Huber, J. Hellmer/F. Schneider (Hrsg.), *Forschendes Lernen im Studium. Aktuelle Konzepte und Erfahrungen* (S. 53–68). Bielefeld: UniversitätsverlagWebler.

Schön, D. A. (1983). *The reflective practitioner: How professionals think in action*. New York: Basic Books.

Schön, D. A. (1987). *Educating the reflective practitioner*. San Francisco: Jossey Bass.

Schüssler, R./Schwier, V./Klewin, G./Schicht, S./Schöning, A./Weyland, U. (Hrsg.). (2014). *Das Praxissemester im Lehramtsstudium: Forschen, Unterrichten, Reflektieren*. Bad Heilbrunn: Klinkhardt.

Valdorf, N./Schwier, V./Schüssler, R. (2014). You'll never walk alone – Unterstützung und Reflexion im Praxissemester. In R. Schüssler/V. Schwier/G. Klewin/S. Schicht/A. Schöning/U. Weyland (Hrsg.), *Das Praxissemester im Lehramtsstudium: Forschen, Unterrichten, Reflektieren* (S. 89–100). Bad Heilbrunn: Klinkhardt.

Zahn, L. (1992). Reflexion. In J. Ritter und K. Gründer (Hrsg.), *Historisches Wörterbuch der Philosophie, Bd. 8* (S. 396–405). Darmstadt: Wissenschaftliche Buchgesellschaft.

Focus: Curricula

Assessment and Inquiry-Based Learning

9

Gabi Reinmann

Assessments within the context of inquiry-based learning pose a special challenge: On the one hand, in the "Bologna degree programs," the practice of academic assessment is generally lagging behind in the requirement that not just teaching and learning be done in a competency-oriented manner, but assessment as well; this has an especially grave impact on issues of performance recording relating to inquiry-based learning. On the other hand, the concept of inquiry-based learning allows teaching, learning and research to be combined in multiple formats and therefore needs to be differentiated – with corresponding consequences for research-related assessment. In the face of such challenges, the first step taken in this article is to propose a model of the possible combinations of teaching, learning and research, which suggests that a distinction can be made between at least three types of inquiry-based learning: learning to understand research, practicing research and conducting independent research. In a second step, the proposed model is expanded to include assessment.

9.1 Competence-Oriented Assessment: Claim and Reality

Competence orientation has been a guiding idea for the design of degree programs since the beginning of the Bologna Process (Schaper 2012): Bachelor's and master's degree programs are modularized. A module should be designed in such a way that, in a best-case scenario, multiple courses jointly foster subject-specific and/or interdisciplinary competences, which can be covered in one final exam at the end of the module, and which can be

G. Reinmann, Prof. Dr. (✉)
Universität Hamburg, Hamburger Zentrum für Universitäres Lehren und Lernen (HUL), Hamburg, Germany
e-mail: gabi.reinmann@uni-hamburg.de

© The Author(s) 2019
H. A. Mieg (ed.), *Inquiry-Based Learning – Undergraduate Research*,
https://doi.org/10.1007/978-3-030-14223-0_9

assessed in terms of quality and level. Lurking behind the seemingly clear concept of competence, however, are different versions and models (Reinmann 2011; Tenberg 2014, p. 19 et seq.). At most, there is consensus that competences encompass several components, namely abilities & skills and attitudes (e.g. values, motives) in addition to knowledge. Although generally recognized, it is often forgotten that competences are dispositions relating to performance and, by definition, cannot be directly measured. Rather, one concludes that there is an (invisible) underlying competence based on a performance, in other words a visible achievement (Wilbers 2013, p. 302). Therefore, the common term proof of performance is quite appropriate for assessment within a higher-education context, especially as it draws attention to the non-trivial challenge that, strictly speaking, the conclusion about *competence* based on performance is still pending when the proof of performance is provided.

Precisely what competence-oriented assessments actually are remains largely undetermined: "Instead of testing on the content that has been taught, it is now necessary to test and assess what the learner is capable of in terms of competences at a given point of time during his/her academic studies or, respectively, at the end of study modules" (Schaper and Hilkenmeier 2013, p. 7). This description is not very enlightening, especially since even before the Bologna Process, "contents" were not "tested on assessments" in exams, but rather those assessments simply measured what content students *command*, thus what they *know* or how they can apply their knowledge to solve a task. An *ability* is likewise tied to the content, meaning that any discussions of competence which suggest that content no longer plays a role are, ultimately, misleading (Ladenthin 2011). If, despite the critique of competence orientation, one goes along with (and there are good reasons for doing so) the request for assessments that – in addition to knowledge, also measure the flexible application thereof as well as abilities, and possibly even attitudes – then another question arises, namely: When do these components constitute a special *academic* competence that students should be expected to acquire in and from a course of study at a university? According to the much-cited suggestion, academic competence (a) is reflective, (b) can be expatiated on (as a prerequisite for reflexivity) and (c) is based on knowledge acquired through theory and empiricism; while it is (d) not developed exclusively, it is developed primarily from the perspective of the selected discipline, (e) it is geared towards mastering novel and complex situations and problems and (f) it contributes to flexible employability in a field of activity that is near to the chosen discipline (Wick 2011, p. 5 et seq.; cf. also Schaper 2012, p. 22 et seq.).

A further requirement in the course of competence orientation is to base the *design of assessments* as much as possible on the expected learning outcomes that have been described as precisely as possible, and from there, to create assessment situations, tasks and forms (e.g. Bachmann 2011). Assessments must thus be coordinated with the courses in the sense of the "constructive alignment" (Biggs and Tang 2011) in such a way that, together with the goals (learning outcomes), they result as far as possible in a coherent whole. From an *organizational* point of view, it is expected that assessments take place at the end of each module in order to continuously monitor and evaluate knowledge and skills, and possibly attitudes, during the course of studies.

Continuous, competence-oriented and accurate assessment may sound desirable at first: It promises to relieve students of a few, all-important periods of time in which summative examinations are held (with legal consequences); it can be expected that it will widen the scope of assessment objectives, which will no longer be limited to merely querying students about fact-based knowledge; and it sounds like multiple forms of examination that will do justice to the various facets of academic competence.

However, current assessment practice within German institutions of higher learning is far from meeting these expectations. One of the big problems is the *quantity* of exams. Module exams certainly do remedy problems inherent in fewer exam periods (such as the *Zwischenprüfung* and *Abschlussprüfung*) (interim exam and leaving exam before graduation). Still, conversely, module exams mean that assessments are distributed throughout a course of study and thus constitute a concomitant and continuous burden as a result of the large number of these assessments. In addition, according to Bologna, one theoretically presumes that, as a general rule, module exams – by virtue of being *integrated assessments* – measure competences that are acquired in multiple courses. In practice, however, the types of assessment that are given are more often *additive* assessments, in which tasks from various courses are strung together (as in the case of written assessments); or *submodule exams*, in which *every* course ends with an exam (Pietzonka 2014). It is therefore not uncommon for students to complete 50 to 60 assessments in the form of small final examinations during their bachelor's degree, for example, all of which have legal consequences in that they are incorporated into the student's overall grade.

The quantity of assessments is a burden not only on students, but also on instructors, and naturally influences the *quality* of assessments. The more assessments that must be planned, carried out and evaluated, the more efficient the forms of assessment must be in order to be able to cope with the high number of assessments (Franke and Handke 2012, p. 155). Especially efficient are those assessments that work with closed questions and are implemented electronically before being automatically evaluated. These forms of assessment can assess knowledge, but are not well suited – in their usual and widespread form – for measuring the required *competences*. In addition to assessments, the assessment practice also includes term papers and presentations, depending on the disciplines there are sometimes also oral and practical exams. How these forms of assessment live up to the claim of measuring academic competence in particular remains an open question. Overall, the theoretically possible diversity faces the risk of practical impoverishment given the problems in terms of the quantity and quality of assessments.

9.2   Learning, Teaching, Researching – More Than *one* Connection

Certainly, assessments within the context of inquiry-based learning cannot be decoupled from the existing assessment situation with reference to the requirements and problems as outlined above. They can serve as a special impetus for assessment practice, however, because it is specifically inquiry-based learning or, respectively, various connections between learning, teaching and research – or as summarized by Huber (2014, p. 28), "research related" – that make *academic* skills development possible in the first place. To put it another way: "Towards what should a university education be oriented if not research?" (Gerdenitsch 2015, p. 89). An understanding of the diversity of these connections from the perspective of both learning and teaching is, in my view, a prerequisite for designing assessments that are suitable for measuring genuine academic achievements and assessing compentence.

9.2.1   Diversity from the Perspective of Learning and Teaching

It has often been lamented that inquiry-based learning is losing its contours due to its frequent and varied use in higher education instruction (cf. Huber 2009, 2014). Literally speaking, it only makes sense to talk about *inquiry-based* learning when students do their own research and learning. This means that all phases of research, from formulating a question and researching the associated state of research, to planning a methodical design and the implementation thereof, to describing and presenting the findings, are implemented by students alone or collaboratively in a team (observable for all parties involved). Inquiry-based learning (learning by performing one's own research) means that students learn by scrutinizing the matter and posing independently substantiated questions (*asking*), selecting from among various methodical options in order to answer their questions (*deciding*), and implementing the goals and plans that arise as a result (*acting*). The learning processes being activated here are *productive* in the sense that they not only lead to new mental structures for the learners, but also prompt those learners to produce knowledge in the form of visible artifacts (summaries of existing findings, research plans, survey instruments, presentations of results, etc.).

As early as the 1970s – the first heyday of inquiry-based learning (cf. BAK 1970) – "genetic learning" was mentioned and legitimized in addition to learning by performing one's own research. Learning within the context of research is genetic when a research process is intellectually reconstructed and subsequently understood without producing any visible artifacts. This learning method is by no means passive, because it is absolutely inconceivable how learning can occur when students are not at least mentally active. It makes more sense to call this learning method *receptive* (Prange 2005, p. 95), a label which implies mental activity. As a rule, receptive learning requires that one *observes what one wishes to learn,* insofar as someone is able to demonstrate the material, by *listening,* insofar as someone can orally present the material, and/or by reading if the knowledge that one wishes to acquire is in written form. Here, the connection between research and learning is that students learn to understand research by being taught *how* research is possible and accomplished, what Huber (2014, p. 24) refers to as "research-oriented."

Receptive and productive learning cannot be clearly differentiated from one another. Rather, reception and production constitute the poles of a learning continuum and are thus orientation markers showing the direction in which a learning method goes. It is possible to classify all forms of *practicing* learning in the middle of this continuum. Various phases of research require knowledge and skills that can be practiced, even without implementing an entire research cycle oneself or as part of a team. This knowledge and these skills are, in part, very specific to academic thinking and activity; however, they are also applicable to non-academic areas. Practice may involve how to find, read and excerpt scholarly texts and how to classify them into the landscape of academic genres. It is also possible to practice methods in the respective chosen discipline: empirical methods, or hermeneutic, historical and other methods. Even writing scholarly texts, visualizing findings or presenting scholarly content can be practiced. Practicing means that students *imitate* what they are shown, *try out* what they have just learned about and *develop routines* that will become part of an approach. Practicing research – and this may be heading in the direction that Huber (2014, p. 24 et seq.) referred to as "research-oriented" – is more than, and different from, learning to understand research and may (but does not have to) be a prerequisite to performing one's own research.

If we make a distinction between three types of connections between research and learning (specifically, learning to understand research, practicing research and performing research oneself), this would require different forms of teaching or, respectively, different forms of stimulating and supporting these learning methods along the continuum between reception and production.

From the perspective of teaching, receptive learning requires that students be *taught* how to conduct research. This may be done *directly*, in that instructors explicitly present, explain and clarify – using words and pictures or multimedia – or *indirectly*, in that the opportunity is used to draw attention to the logic, phases and specifics of research, for example. Teaching as a means of communication is a teaching method that is mainly pursued in lectures and seminars with a high proportion of mediating activities. This teaching method is, in fact, widespread and does not have a good reputation. Nevertheless, we must distinguish between the teaching method (receptive learning) and its potential (imparting knowledge) on the one hand, and the prevalence (dominance of imparting information through too many lectures) and implementation (poor imparting of information in the form of lectures that fail to promote learning) on the other.

From the perspective of educators, by contrast, productive learning requires encouraging students in their research activities, instructing them as needed, creating contexts and resources, and *supporting* the process of learning through research through these (or other) means. The *degree of support* thereby provided may vary: Needs-based, more intensive instruction in individual phases does not necessarily mean that the character of self-research is lost, as long as the goal is maintained. Students also learn independent research by experiencing research and actively (assisting in) shaping it. Teaching as a means of supporting inquiry-based learning is common in project seminars, in (independent) projects, and possibly also in colloquia, if these are arranged along the lines of research activity.

From the teaching perspective, it is particularly clear that learning through practice has both receptive and productive aspects. In order to practice research, one needs learning environments that allow students to imitate something, which requires that something be demonstrated and thus conveyed, while at the same time students must be allowed to try things out and sometimes build up routines; this requires support and feedback. In the broadest sense, teaching activities are required here that *empower* students to practice research. The type of empowerment largely depends upon the phase of research being practiced. Tutorials, seminars with a high proportion of tutorials and seminars held by postgraduates are the course formats that are suited for this and already established.

9.2.2   Interim Conclusion: A Suggested Model

The following proposed model serves to systematize the diversity that is possible when learning, teaching and research are combined. The starting point is therefore learning and the continuum between the poles of reception and production, on which it is possible to arrange receptive, practicing and productive learning. This means that students at the institution of higher learning should be able to (a) learn to understand research, (b) practice research and (c) and conduct research themselves in connection with research. These forms of academic learning are by no means distinct; rather, they serve as orientation markers, not just for students, but for educators and their teaching activities as well. Academic teaching involves varying combinations of (a) conveying scholarship, (b) empowering the students to engage with scholarship and (c) supporting students' scholarly activities (Reinmann 2013). These forms of teaching largely correspond to the three forms of connections between research and learning, whereby this distinction is also to be understood as merely *accentuating* (see Fig. 9.1).

9.3   Learning, Teaching, Researching, Assessment – More Than *one* Possibility

According to the conclusion in the first section of this article, academic assessment must measure whether students have knowledge of the material and methods, can apply them in complex situations, and can reflect critically upon and utilize them for many activities. However, the question of whether currently established exams are suitable for conducting such an academic assessment has scarcely been explored. To the best of my knowledge, not even a theory of assessment exists. While there are various taxonomies for teaching/

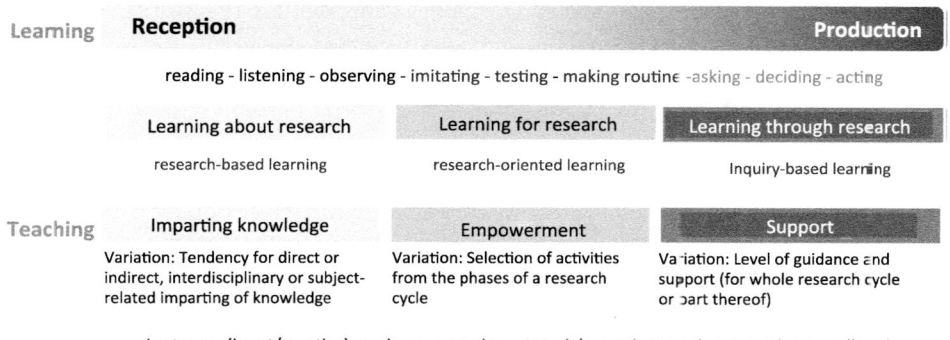

Fig. 9.1 Proposed model: Learning – teaching – researching. (Source: author's representation)

learning methods, for example (cf. Baumgartner, 2011), one searches in vain for a theory-based taxonomy for assessment at institutions of higher learning. Usually, various forms of assessment are merely listed without being systematically comparable. While the following sections cannot fill that gap, they nonetheless address the deficit and zero-in on a well-founded system of various forms of assessment that is simultaneously oriented towards practice.

9.3.1   The (Missing) System of Various Forms of Assessment

If we start with the frequency and degree of familiarity of assessment at institutions of higher learning, then exams, term papers, presentations and oral exams rank first; in application-related disciplines, proof of practical achievements also ranks highly. Using the modes of representation developed by Jerome Bruner (1966), it is clear that a large percentage of university assessments are of a *symbolic nature*, i.e. based on language; pictorial forms of representation (iconic) may be integrated therein. It is relatively easy to classify symbolic forms of assessment into oral and written exams. *Oral* exams are either dialogues in the sense that questions are asked and must be answered (akin to "surveys" which may transition into oral examinations); or they are *monological* in the sense that students report on their knowledge (i.e. "present" it). *Written* exams, on the other hand, are best classified into those that require the person's actual presence and those that can be written away from the university (in absentia). Written exams taken *in person* (exams) are fixed in terms of time, duration and location; as a rule, written exams taken *in absentia* (term papers) are usually fixed only in terms of the time period and the scope.

Symbolic forms of assessment primarily assess knowledge (and the application thereof). With reference to research, one could state that, above all, it examines what knowledge students have regarding the research (assessment on research). Less frequently (depending on the subject), forms of assessment are used that can be referred to as *enactive* because they require action in situations arranged for them. These types of assessments tend to assess skills and abilities. Thus with reference to research, they assess what students are able to do in their research (assessment in research).

Enactive forms of assessment can be classified according to whether students show their abilities by acting, or whether they do so through action sequences in the form of artifacts. The former comes down to demonstrating a skill in a situation, and therefore I have chosen the term situated for this type of assessment. The second of these means that one deduces a skill from something that was produced, which is why I refer to this form of assessment as materialized. The lack of common designations alone, as compared to symbolic forms of assessment, shows to some extent how much less familiar these forms of assessment are (in part) in the assessment practice at institutions of higher learning.

If we utilize the *symbolic – enactive determination* on the one hand and *forms of examination* established in practice on the other, we can construe the following possible system (see Fig. 9.2):

A system of this sort with only a few basic forms of assessment can have practical advantages, for example when it comes to the design of assessment rules, but also in terms of the technical modeling in current campus management systems. A wide variety of assessment variants can be designed using these basic forms of assessment as a foundation. *Design criteria* may include, for example:

- purpose (knowledge reproduction, knowledge application, knowledge creation),
- social form (individually, in groups),
- media use (with or without media, online or offline, text or multimedia etc.),
- resources (none, limited, open),
- conditions (e.g. field or laboratory conditions).

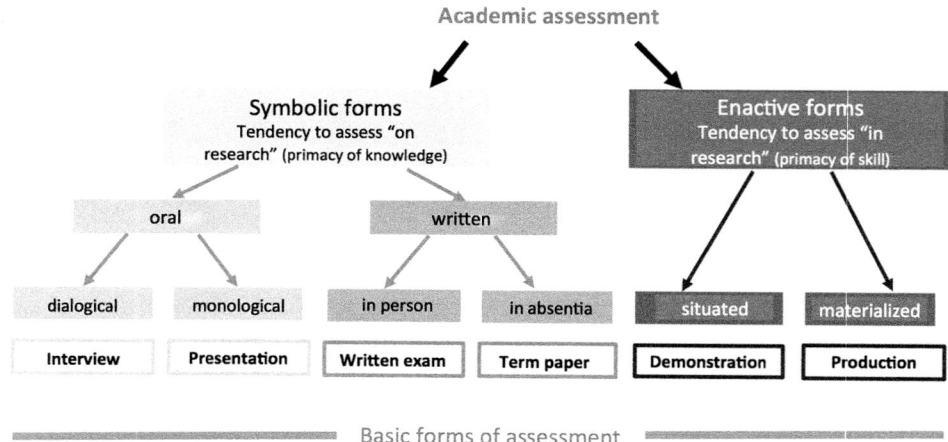

Fig. 9.2 Attempt to establish a system of forms of academic assessment. (Source: author's representation)

Interview	Presentation	Written exam	Term paper	Demonstration	Production
• One-on-one conversation based on a research paper • Group conversation regarding the given subject • Conversation regarding artifacts that have been brought • Conversation in a video conference • Group conversation regarding one's own project • Case study discussion	• Individual presentation with research paper • Group presentation regarding the group's own project • Presentation in reference to a poster • Lecture in an audio/video conference • Recorded presentation (audio, video) • Ad hoc presentation in a team of two	• Multiple choice exam • Written exam with open-ended questions • Open-book written exam • Electronic written exam with multimedia application tasks • Debate with choice of given topics	• Individual work on a self-selected topic • Team work on a given topic • Essay without using literature • Book or article review • Collaborative homework with the help of a wiki • Collection and reflection of own texts (portfolio)	• Role-playing regarding a topic • Displaying a skill (including in a video) • Simulation or simulation game • Participation in a conference as a speaker • Moderation of a scholarly discussion • Performance of a task in the field	• Article in a professional journal • Own wiki entry • Media products (audio, video) for a professional audience • Development of research instruments • Collection of artifacts from a research process (portfolio)

Fig. 9.3 Example forms of assessment and variants within the context of research-related assessment. (Source: author's representation)

Without being able to go into greater detail here, the following figure provides an exemplary view of the variety of possibilities for assessment relating to the basic forms proposed here (Fig. 9.3).

Enactive forms of assessment, in which students demonstrate their abilities in research situations (e.g. conducting an interview, evaluating data) or produce research artifacts (e.g. visualizing a research design; research journal with field notes) clearly fall within the context of assessment in research. In contrast, symbolic forms of assessment, such as written exams and oral exams in the form of interviews, are generally designed in such a way that they can be relatively easily categorized as assessment on research. Term papers and presentations are also usually used in the assessment practice in such a way that it is possible to test *about* research if need be. In principle, however, they can be expanded into forms of assessment *within* research: Within the context of scientific courses, for example, presentations are also a research artifact, and a term paper can be further developed into a scientific article that is published (see Fig. 9.4).

9.3.2 Conclusion: An Expanded Proposed Model

The model proposed above for a system of the possible diverse connections between learning, teaching and research distinguishes between (a) the goal that students learn to understand research, which requires the mediation of scholarship by educators, (b) the goal that students practice research, which requires that teaching empowers the students to engage with scholarship, and (c) the goal that students perform research themselves, which requires that teaching activities be scheduled that support students' scholarly activities. If

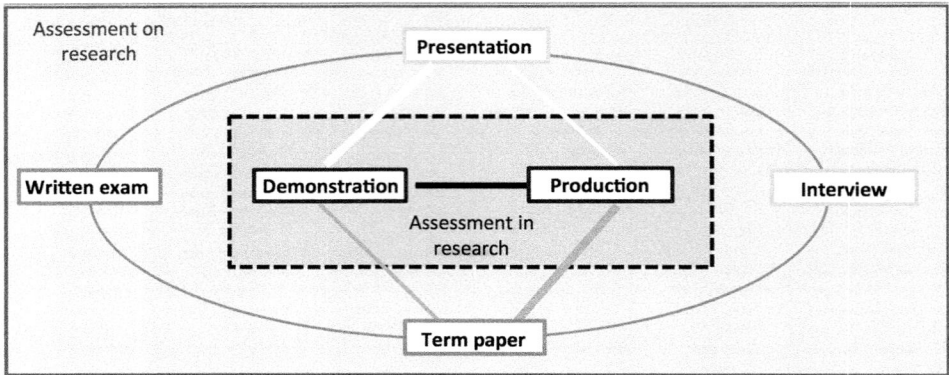

Fig. 9.4 Assessment on research and assessment in research. (Source: author's representation)

one wishes to extend this proposed model to include assessment, the first question to arise is whether one needs summative examinations (receptive, practicing, productive) with legal consequences for all research-related learning methods. If one takes the concept of practicing learning seriously, this prohibits summative assessment because the purpose of practicing is precisely to help students reach a level where they are prepared for exams. If courses and modules pursue the goal that students practice research, one could record achievements exclusively in a formative manner and provide feedback *without* giving grades (formative assessment). The second question is whether there is any usefulness in linking the above system of different forms of assessment with the two other forms of research-related learning and teaching. The following figure (Fig. 9.5) makes it clear that, in theory, assessment on research and receptive forms of learning on the one hand, and assessment in research and productive learning methods on the other correspond well. In practice, however, it is difficult to unambiguously classify common forms of assessment including options for their design (cf. Fig. 9.3).

9.4 Research-Related Assessment: Opportunities and Limits

In principle, combining learning methods with teaching methods and course formats in education, as well as possible forms of assessment, falls within the concept of "constructive alignment." In the meantime, it has become common knowledge that the didactic design of assessments presents a great opportunity to introduce changes in learning and teaching; this is because, above all, students learn in the manner in which they are assessed. To conclude that educators should teach as they assess and vice versa, however, also carries risks: fixation on the assessment process, a compartmentalized operationalization of learning outcomes in favor of a high practicability of assessments and a loss of education options (cf. Tremp and Eugster 2006). This is especially true when trying to coordinate

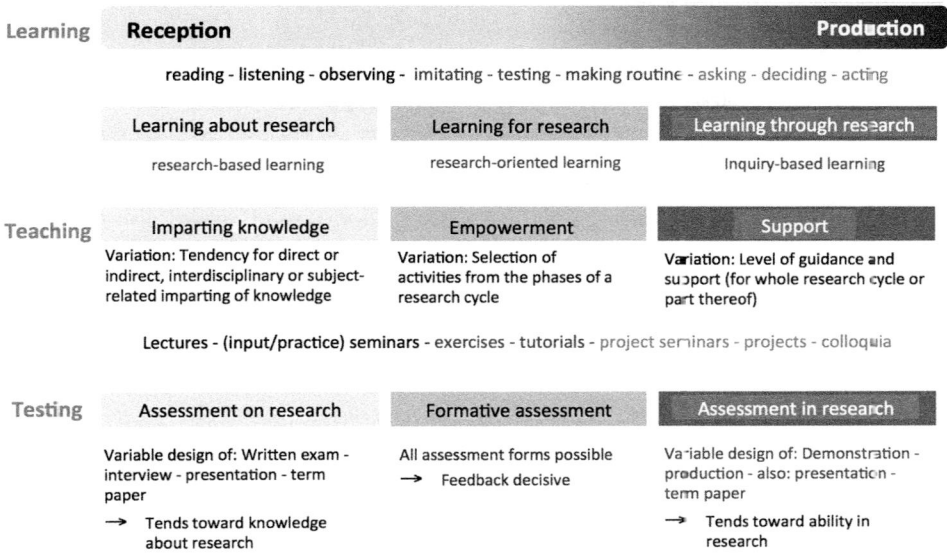

Fig. 9.5 Proposed model: Learning – teaching – researching – assessing. (Source: author's representation)

learning, teaching, assessment *and research*, i.e. when research becomes the focus as a constitutive element of academic learning and teaching.

The present text attempts to elucidate theoretically based classification criteria on the one hand, and conditions in teaching and assessment practice (current teaching formats, basic forms of assessment) on the other in order to relate learning, teaching, research and assessment with one another. It appears necessary to me that practical conditions be taken into account in order to increase the chances that the model will be implemented. Similar attempts have already been made in the Zurich model for inquiry-based learning in the narrower sense (cf. Tremp and Hildbrand 2012), however without taking into account the different variations in research-related learning. In this context, however, one has to conclude that, in comparison to research-related learning, there has as yet been insufficient theoretical discussion regarding research-related assessment at the micro-level of didactic design (one exception: BAK 1970). The preceding explanations address this deficiency and provide a starting point for further development. The didactic design of assessments cannot solve the problem concerning the number of exams, however. Here, changes must be made to the degree program design and formulation of assessment rules (e.g. a reduction in the number of exams that have legal consequences, consciously keeping courses or modules free of exams).

References

Bachmann, H. (2011). Formulieren von Lernergebnissen – learning outcomes. In H. Bachmann (Hrsg.), *Kompetenzorientierte Hochschullehre* (S. 34–49). Bern: Hep-Verlag.

Baumgartner, P. (2011). *Taxonomie von Unterrichtsmethoden. Ein Plädoyer für didaktische Vielfalt*. Münster: Waxmann.

Biggs, J./Tang, C. (2011). *Teaching for quality learning at university*. Glasgow: McGraw Hill.

Bruner, J. S. (1966). *Toward a theory of instruction*. Cambridge. Mass.: Harvard University Press.

Bundesassistentenkonferenz (BAK) (1970/2009). *Forschendes Lernen – Wissenschaftliches Prüfen*. Bielefeld: UniversitätsVerlagWebler.

Franke, P./Handke, J. (2012). E-Assessment. In J. Handke/A. M. Schäfer (Hrsg.), *E-Learning, E-Teaching und E-Assessment in der Hochschullehre* (S. 147–208). München: Oldenbourg.

Gerdentisch, C. (2015). Unterricht an Universitäten? Systematische Überlegungen zum intradisziplinären Transfer. In R. Egger/C. Wustmann/A. Karber (Hrsg.), *Forschungsgeleitete Lehre in einem Massenstudium. Bedingungen und Möglichkeiten in den Erziehungs- und Bildungswissenschaften* (S. 77–92). Berlin: Springer VS.

Huber, L. (2009). Warum Forschendes Lernen nötig und möglich ist. In L. Huber/J. Hellmer/F. Schneider (Hrsg.), *Forschendes Lernen im Studium. Aktuelle Konzepte und Erfahrungen* (S. 9–35). Bielefeld: UniversitätsVerlagWebler.

Huber, L. (2014). Forschungsbasiertes, Forschungsorientiertes, Forschendes Lernen: Alles dasselbe? *Hochschulforschung, 1+2*, 22–29.

Ladenthin, V. (2011). Kompetenzorientierung als Indiz pädagogischer Orientierungslosigkeit. *Profil* (Mitgliederzeitung des Deutschen Philologenverbandes), *09*, 1–6.

Pietzonka, M. (2014). Die Umsetzung der Modularisierung in Bachelor-und Masterstudiengängen. *Zeitschrift für Hochschulentwicklung, 9*(2), 78–90.

Prange, K. (2005). *Die Zeigestruktur der Erziehung. Grundriss der Operativen Pädagogik*. München: Schöningh.

Reinmann, G. (2011). Kompetenz – Qualität – Assessment: Hintergrundfolie für das technologiebasierte Lernen. In M. Mühlhäuser/W. Sesink/A. Kaminski/J. Steimle (Hrsg.), *Interdisziplinäre Zugänge zum technologiegestützten Lernen* (S. 467–493). Münster: Waxmann.

Reinmann, G. (2013). Studientext Didaktisches Design. Retrieved 28 January 2016 from http://gabireinmann.de/wp-content/uploads/2013/05/Studientext_DD_Fassung2013.pdf

Schaper, N./Hilkenmeier, F. (2013). *Umsetzungshilfen für kompetenzorientiertes Prüfen. HRK-Zusatzgutachten. Hochschulrektorenkonferenz Projekt nexus*. Retrieved 28 January 2016 from http://www.hrk-nexus.de/fileadmin/redaktion/hrk-nexus/07-Downloads/07-03-Material/zusatzgutachten.pdf

Schaper, N. (2012). *Fachgutachten zur Kompetenzorientierung in Studium und Lehre. Hochschulrektorenkonferenz*. Retrieved 28 January 2016 from http://www.hrk-nexus.de/fileadmin/redaktion/hrk-nexus/07-Downloads/07-02-Publikationen/fachgutachten_kompetenzorientierung.pdf

Tenberg, R. (2014). Kompetenzorientiert studieren – didaktische Hochschulreform oder Bologna-Rhetorik? *Journal of Technical Education, 1*, 16–30.

Tremp, P./Eugster, B. (2006). Universitäre Bildung und Prüfungssystem – Thesen zu Leistungsnachweisen in modularisierten Studiengängen. *Das Hochschulwesen, 5*, 163–165.

Tremp, P./Hildbrand, T. (2012). Forschungsorientiertes Studium – universitäre Lehre: Das »Zürcher Framework« zur Verknüpfung von Lehre und Forschung. In T. Brinker/P. Tremp (Hrsg.), *Einführung in die Studiengangentwicklung* (S. 101–116). Bielefeld: Bertelsmann.

Wick, A. (2011). *Akademisch geprägte Kompetenzentwicklung: Kompetenzorientierung in Hochschulstudiengängen*. Heidelberg: HeiDOK. Retrieved 28 January 2016 from http://archiv. ub.uni-heidelberg.de/volltextserver/12001/1/Wick_Akademisch_gepraegte_Kompetenzen.pdf

Wilbers, K. (2013). Kompetenzmessung: Motor der Theorie- und Praxisentwicklung in der Berufsbildung? In S. Seufert und C. Metzger (Hrsg.), *Kompetenzentwicklung in unterschiedlichen Kulturen* (S. 298–321). Paderborn: Eusl.

The Peer-to-Peer Principle of Inquiry-Based Learning

10

Anke Spies

The interconnecting peer-to-peer principle appears to be a motivationally beneficial yet demanding component of inquiry-based learning. The principle is the maxim behind the implementation of participatory *and* inquiry-based learning settings that should stimulate their own professionalization in the context of their studies. After briefly situating the peer-to-peer principle, this article will first explain the ideal of low-threshold network formation in research-related teaching formats based on the tutorial variant and will then discuss the peer-to-peer principle from a group-dynamic point of view. Afterwards, I will outline a model of a moderated peer-to-peer orientation. Finally, I will present a brief look at the inconsistencies inherent in linking the peer-to-peer principle with further maxims of inquiry-based learning.

10.1 The Ideal in Higher Education Didactics of the Low-Threshold Network

To begin with, the peer-to-peer principle is a facet of *networking* and, as such, an attempt at optimization in order to facilitate the sustainable use of resources: Regardless of whether it concerns correlations in information science, the economy, or in an ethnographic view of groups of young people, this principle pursues the notion of optimizing the benefits of the work as a whole through the interaction of close parts of a whole. In the academic

A. Spies, Prof. Dr. (✉)
Carl von Ossietzky Universität Oldenburg, Fakultät Bildungs- und Sozialwissenschaften, Institut für Pädagogik, Professur für Erziehungswissenschaft, Oldenburg, Germany
e-mail: anke.spies@uni-oldenburg.de

© The Author(s) 2019
H. A. Mieg (ed.), *Inquiry-Based Learning – Undergraduate Research*,
https://doi.org/10.1007/978-3-030-14223-0_10

didactic setting of inquiry-based learning, students work together as peers in order to improve the benefits of the explorative engagement with the subject matter of their academic studies. The strategy refers to the networking of students of equal educational levels whose learning process should benefit from the different levels of knowledge available within the student body (*peers*) and from the collaboration. The instructive function of the educator, hereinafter referred to as "principal investigators," recedes into the background. It is replaced by mentoring functions which support the peer-to-peer principle during the process (cf. Pita et al. 2013). The shared research process of the peers benefits from the exchange of existing knowledge, which is bundled and shared. The self-reinforcing contacts optimize the benefits of the student research process (cf. ibid.). Edgcomb et al. (2010) described an additional, possible peer-to-peer relationship: collaborative mentoring as a networking strategy between students who have not yet graduated and doctoral students.

The tutorial peer-to-peer understanding in an academic didactic tradition is based on different degrees of knowledge and, in part, on different degrees of qualification as well and will be examined in greater detail below. At the same time, students in the master's degree who have already provided proof of qualification are nevertheless still counted among the peers in the bachelor's degree program in a discipline. Peer status is acquired by belonging to the same or a similar cohort of a common professional orientation or context.

10.2 Peer-To-Peer in Tutorials

Tutorials serve as supplemental courses to regular courses, where the material is reviewed and expanded upon. As an expansion on the learning material that is designed to be largely receptive (and, depending on the subject culture, also discursive), it is primarily new students who are introduced to academic engagement with content and issues in a subject-related context, whereby (as a rule) trained students who are professionally supervised by principal investigators and want low-threshold teaching experience pass on the knowledge they have hitherto acquired to subsequent students, thereby simultaneously deepening and thus expanding their professional qualifications.

In tutorial settings of inquiry-based learning, on the other hand, the focus is on the learning process of the students involved: the low-threshold format is intended to facilitate access to an examination of research results and research practices, whereby it is assumed that the approach via peer-mediated content and interactions will increase the willingness to actively engage and will reduce "learning resistances" (Grell 2006, p. 10). Since learning takes place and is initiated within the context of social activities, "when routines do not work, when discrepancies arise between the action problem and solution potential" (Faulstich 1999, p. 32) and learning only then occurs "when individuals encounter obstacles and resistances in their actions" (ibid.), it must nevertheless be expected that "action problems that cannot be overcome with existing competencies" (ibid.) will be encountered along the way towards this goal, which can then become "learning difficulties" (ibid.).

Students in the expansive learning situation of an inquiry-based learning setting are also engaged at the level of the learning process in overcoming their learning behavior, which tends to be resistant. As long as they are accustomed to defensive learning in particular (ibid., p. 24), the *socialization process* into research-oriented behavior will be reduced to a "learning imposition" (ibid., p. 25), which should be reduced by situational proximity to the tutorial peers. The guidance of peers who have already overcome their resistance to inquiry-based learning should encourage productive learning processes and the elimination of learning resistance from peers who have begun their studies more recently.

Tutorials for new students as peer-to-peer formats in the receptive as well as the interactive research must be situated within the classification system for inquiry-based learning presented by Rueß et al. (2016): In the exchange between the instructing tutors and their participating peers, a learning gain is expected for both sides of the peer relationship out of their shared engagement with research results and research methods. The same applies to explanations of research processes, which in (small) tutorial group formats should lead to in-depth understanding and competence gains for both peer positions. This is based on the pedagogic premise that not only does the explanation lead to sustained learning processes, the low-threshold setting of the tutorial also leads to explanations that promote the learning processes and that encourage engagement.

Depending on the technical-methodical requirement, the requirement for guidance of the peers who are employed as tutors also increases: Insofar as the support in a tutorial setting is also intended to increase the level of activity of the explicitly researching students, their introduction into higher education didactics requires further intensification since both the independent review of literature in a field of research and applying methods make stringent demands on quality assurance measures, while the head start of the tutors in their capacity as peer may be limited.

In explaining the strategies for guiding and supporting student research, Fita et al. (2013) emphasize that the needs for accompanying support advising be provided from the perspective of the students, who simultaneously advise classmates as peer mentors, so that the positive effects of inquiry-based learning can be realized: "Mentoring undergraduates is distinct from the process of mentoring graduate students. Unique challenges stem from, for example, differences in the students' general level of experience and stage of career development" (ibid., p. 11). The authors point out that enthusiasm, expertise, engagement and a sense of responsibility are crucial for the quality of the work results and cannot be presupposed, but rather require systematic support so that an increase in professionalism can be achieved over the course of the relatively short phase of collaboration.

10.3   Peer-To-Peer with the Help of Instructing Moderation

Moderating support of student research along the peer-to-peer principle thus by no means implies easing the burden on the principal investigators postulated by Edgccmb et al. (2010). Rather, according to Pita et al. (2013), the autonomy concept of inquiry-based learning requires reliable and closely moderating, protective and encouraging principal investigators, who can reconcile the aspirations, ideals and student possibilities of inquiry-based learning. In the peer-to-peer process, which is supported and moderated by principal investigators, students are assisted by a research-experienced person, who pre-structures the group formation process and processes within peer-communication in such a way that the specifics of the group-dynamics can be used didactically or, respectively, such that assistance is available to the group during critical phases in the group-dynamic process (see Box 10.1).

For a professionally and methodically guided, moderated student research group, the orientation phase (forming) is the introduction to the research process, which is followed by the power struggle phase (storming), during which the individual or group research question is clarified. Both phases require guidance or space, or moderation for the negotiation processes and bring with them a potential for conflict that can place the successful

---

Box 10.1: Group Dynamics

Since the work of Kurt Lewin (1890–1947), who first researched group processes in the 1930s, the terms "group dynamics" and "team formation" usually draw a distinction between five phases of group formation, which regularly recur in a wide variety of group constellations or on a variety of occasions (cf., inter alia, König and Schattenhofer 2006).

(1) During the orientation phase (forming), the group members come together under similar conditions or on similar occasions, behave cautiously while getting to know one another, follow leadership and have not yet developed a sense of community.

(2) During the confrontation or power struggle phase (storming), which is characterized by negotiation of control, all group participants are engaged in finding and defining their position and role within the group.

(3) The clarifying phase of the confrontation is followed by the familiarization phase (norming). Now cooperation and rule-based collaboration determine the common process, as the strengths and weaknesses of the participants are known and tolerated. A sense of togetherness provides stability. The common rules facilitate a productive collaboration.

(4) On this basis, the group can go into the differentiation phase (performing), during which it is capable of significant achievements. It is at the peak of its working and group process and can distinguish itself from other groups, but also establish contact with them.

(5) During the separation phase (adjourning), these connections are once again severed: The task is done, and interest ebbs or differentiates individually. Reaching the group goal requires that this conclusion be marked.

course of the research process at risk. Because the group is initially guided in the moderated peer-to-peer setting and only gradually assumes process responsibility for the *joint* research over the course of the working process, it is able to coordinate its data collection, data analysis and securing of the findings in the research report (largely) autonomously during the familiarization phase (norming) and the differentiation phase (performing). In so doing, the group can analogously "grow together" as a group structure along the peer-to-peer principle because process moderation provides a relatively secure framework, in which academic success is not jeopardized by the unsettling forming phase or by the conflict-sparking storming phase. As a component of an expanded peer-to-peer understanding, "adjourning" can be staged as a separation phase, whereby the work results of the current group's research process is passed on to one or more subsequent student groups.

In this setting, the student research group profits from the support provided by the moderating instructor because group principles can be taken into account and made transparent to the group members. In the moderated, research-based student group, the encouragement and development of the individual is the focus of the group process; for the latter to be successful, the professional *and* dynamic status of the group must be determined before moderating guidance can be progressively reduced or withdrawn over the course of the collaboration.

In my practice of this variant of inquiry-based learning, the following method of working has proven itself: the primary orientation of the higher education didactic setting should facilitate student learning processes in the mode of research that corresponds to currently relevant or, respectively, professionally "significant" (see above) issues, embedded within the context of a *long-term* project. In addition, structuring aids as well as offers of professional and methodical support are provided. The free choice of topic and method is made by selecting the course (forming). On the one hand, the respective focus is on the findings of previous research groups, which have been transferred to the subsequent group; on the other, this focus is part of the storming, because the new group will continue to modify the content and methods in accordance with their perspectives and interests. Students in a newly beginning research group receive the previous research of their peers (over several semesters) and subsequently situate their own research approaches relative to the existing intermediate results (norming and performing). At the end of their own working process, these peers also formulate further research assignments for subsequent peers, who, in the engagement of their study group, differentiate these assignments/research questions/methodical guidelines and implement them in accordance with their own priorities (adjourning), until they can formulate new assignments themselves.

The respectively active student research groups use both the research reports and excerpts from empirical master's theses by their classmates, which can be written in the research group as a follow-up to research, as a basis for their own research processes. In this receptive format, the peer-to-peer principle may be indirect; however, in this way, the networking of student resources can be utilized well beyond graduation. Here, the peer-to-peer principle refers to the work results, which are used again as a starting point for the working processes of subsequent peers, which can diffuse both the forming and the storming phases, and which can underpin the norming and performing phases. In this way, the resource of the available student research products continues to steadily grow.

10.4   Inconsistencies

Although the method outlined here contradicts the fundamental maxims that have been applied to the most unstructured beginning phase of group processes since Lewin's work, its structural specifications nevertheless meet the requirements of study under the conditions of the Bologna reform. The latter is neither designed for the peer-to-peer principle nor for group processes that follow Lewin's thesis that uncertainty is necessary for the initiation of learning opportunities. The observations of Pita et al. (2013) demonstrate that the thesis of uncertainty as a prerequisite for acquiring new behaviors and attitudes should not be transferred to the student setting of inquiry-based learning, since this can place the positive learning processes at risk.

As a setting that reflects the group dynamic, the alignment with the peer-to-peer principle on the one hand and goal-oriented research on the other should be weighed against one another and the peer-to-peer principle should be distanced from the goals of group-dynamic trainings with claims of promoting self-awareness, since character-forming benefits cannot be measured in credit points. Only the research result – in the sense of the correct methodology and stringent reasoning – can be assessed. Group-dynamic interactions cannot be assessed with credit points and measurable evaluation, which ultimately must be considered in relation to the group-dynamic interventions. In the higher education didactic setting of moderated peer-to-peer research groups, however, group processes are committed to the acquisition of scientific competence and are bound to professional insights into the findings that are produced. Thus, they are part of a systematic professionalization process. *In this respect, the peer-to-peer principle must be subordinated to the learning outcomes of inquiry-based learning.*

In inquiry-based learning, the peer-to-peer principle demonstrates a series of additional inconsistencies, which likewise arise from the field of tension between the ideals of inquiry-based learning and the current requirements for student learning:

- Peer-to-peer follows the economic intent of generating sustainability in work and networking. However, students are only able to obtain the sustainability benefits during the working process, however, since cooperative and collaborative forms of work require a (group-dynamic) learning process, which leads from possibly different attitudes among the researchers to a common interest in the results.
- The initial learning situation of the students, who are learning through research or, respectively, researching through learning in line with the peer-to-peer principle (cf. Rueß et al. 2016), is heterogeneous in terms of the students' existing professional background knowledge and in terms of the methodical application competence, depending

on the degree program, phase of study and the composition of the student group, and structured higher education didactic considerations are required so that the heterogeneity of the initial situation in the process can become a resource.

- The postulate of freedom is also opposed by the demand that the findings be of interest to third parties (Huber 2014): Student research should be based on the subject and should by no means be random or incidental, but rather based on *significant* (cf. Clark 1997) issues, the development of which can provide insight into existing, subject-related bodies of knowledge on the one hand and can generate new insights in the sense of scholarship on the other.

With the peer-to-peer principle, the fundamental intention of the higher education didactic setting in inquiry-based learning, which seeks to promote independence and thus personal responsibility in the learning process, appears to multiply: If inquiry-based learning per se is to expand and encourage the motivation to actively and autonomously shape the learning process, the same would be expected of the principle of learning from and through classmates (peers). It is questionable, however, whether such "multiplication" of the motivational postulate acts to underpin the entire format and to what degree the principle can dispense with instruction and supervision by principal investigators. Which framework secures the professional content in the sense of methodical and discursive research accuracy? What risks (of failure) are associated with group-dynamic processes and which structural prerequisites are required pursuant to the measures of the Bologna reform?

It is questionable whether inquiry-based learning along the peer-to-peer principle can dispense with the portion of *teaching* that provides support and guidance. Peer-to-peer does not absolve educators from the responsibility of securing the learning setting in such a way that certificate-relevant benefits are actually obtained, and the risk of failure is (or can be) minimized. The higher education didactic price for this is technically and methodically justifiable restrictions or relativizations of the freedom to select topics and methods. The benefit, on the other hand, can be the increase in the quality of final theses and the optimization of the theory-practice ratio.

References

Clark, B. (1997). The modern integration of research activities with teaching and learning. *Journal of Higher Education, 68*(3), 241–255.

Edgcomb, M. R./Crowe, H. A./Rice, J. D./Morris, S. J./Wolffe, R. J./McConnaughay, K. D. (2010). Peer and near-peer mentoring: Enhancing learning in Summer Research Programs. *Council of Undergraduate Research Quarterly, 31*(2), 18–25.

Faulstich, P. (1999). Einige Grundfragen zur Diskussion um selbstgesteuertes Lernen. In S. Dietrich, E. Fuchs-Brüninghoff (Hrsg.), *Selbstgesteuertes Lernen – Auf dem Weg zu einer neuen Lernkultur* (S. 24–39). Frankfurt/M.: DIE.

Grell, P. (2006). *Forschende Lernwerkstatt: Eine qualitative Untersuchung zu Lernwiderständen in der Weiterbildung.* Münster: Waxmann.

Huber, L. (2014). Forschungsbasiertes, Forschungsorientiertes, Forschendes Lernen: Alles das-
    selbe? *Das Hochschulwesen, 62*(1+2), 22–29.
König, O./Schattenhofer, K. (2006). *Einführung in die Gruppendynamik.* Heidelberg: Auer.
Pita, M./Ramirez, C./Joacin, N./Prentice, S./Clarke, C. (2013). Five effective strategies for men-
    toring undergraduates: Students' perspectives. *Council of Undergraduate Research Quarterly,
    33*(3), 11–15.
Rueß, J./Gess, C./Deicke, W. (2016). (2016). Forschendes Lernen und forschungsbezogene Lehre -
    empirisch gestützte Systematisierung des Forschungsbezugs hochschulischer Lehre. *Zeitschrift
    für Hochschulentwicklung, 11*(2), 23–44.

Inter- and Transdisciplinarity

Michael Prytula, Tobias Schröder, and Harald A. Mieg

How does inquiry-based learning work in interdisciplinary, practical teaching contexts? This chapter presents examples of interdisciplinary inquiry-based learning and the associated basic conditions. The conclusion is comprised of three theses. We claim that inter- and transdisciplinarity require a new unity of teaching and research.

11.1 Social Transformation Processes and Their Consequences for Scholarship and Higher Education

Global development is characterized by many challenges that elude categorization by academic discipline. Examples include not only climate change and increasing urbanization, but also terrorism, ensuring food security and the integration of the Internet into industry and society. The processes of change are mutually interdependent and have an impact in a global, regional and local context, e.g. in day-to-day issues of urban development and urban management.

Social transformation processes are characterized by what have been referred to as "wicked problems," which cannot be described by clearly speciñable actual and target states, and the solutions to which always contain normative valuaticns ("what should we do

M. Prytula, Prof. Dr.-Ing. (✉) · T. Schröder, Prof. Dr. Dipl.-Psych.
Fachhochschule Potsdam, Institut für angewandte Forschung Urbane Zukunft,
Potsdam, Germany
e-mail: prytula@fh-potsdam.de; schroeder@fh-potsdam.de

H. A. Mieg, Prof. Dr.
Humboldt-Universität zu Berlin, Georg-Simmel-Zentrum für Metropolenforschung,
Berlin, Germany
e-mail: harald.mieg@hu-berlin.de

© The Author(s) 2019
H. A. Mieg (ed.), *Inquiry-Based Learning – Undergraduate Research*,
https://doi.org/10.1007/978-3-030-14223-0_11

and what do we want to do?"). We often find ourselves dealing with contradictory goals and heterogeneous bodies of knowledge (Wissenschaftsrat 2015, p. 16). Urban district development and efforts to achieve social peace in cities provide much-discussed examples.

Given these challenges, time and again, scholarship requires rethinking that goes beyond disciplinary boundaries. Approaches to this take different names (cf. Schneidewind and Singer-Brodowski 2014), e.g. "Mode 2," "transdisciplinarity" or the "co-production of knowledge." What all of these approaches have in common is that (1) interdisciplinary collaboration is regarded as necessary and (2) dialogue with society is sought.

11.2   Challenges in Inter- and Transdisciplinarity in Inquiry-Based Learning

Interdisciplinarity is not a new requirement. It comes to the forefront again and again – because working within disciplines has become established over the centuries as the "operating condition" of sciences (Mieg and Evetts 2019). Collaboration across the disciplines can take various forms:

- *Multidisciplinary* refers to the collaboration that occurs when different disciplines work alongside each other on a project. This can be considered the normal case for research projects that span multiple disciplines.
- Project work is *interdisciplinary* when the disciplines are essentially dependent on the mutual exchange of methods or results. Interdisciplinary work is more commonly found in practice than in scholarship, e.g. large construction projects require the integration of technical, architectural, infrastructural and landscape planning aspects.
- *Transdisciplinary* refers to collaboration that goes beyond disciplines. Sometimes the term is used to denote increased interdisciplinarity, i.e. finding a common language and superordinate approach. Other times, the term is interpreted as the inclusion of social groups outside the university. Hereinafter, we will assume the latter definition of transdisciplinarity.

The concept of transdisciplinary teaching includes a determination of types of knowledge, towards which inquiry-based learning must be oriented. Corresponding teaching projects were developed in Switzerland in the 1990s (cf. Mieg et al. 2001; Scholz and Tietje 2002). It makes sense to distinguish between three types of knowledge (cf. Schneidewind and Singer-Brodowski 2014):

- *Systems knowledge*, which describes knowledge about complex systemic connections (knowledge about what is);
- *Target knowledge or knowledge about evaluation,* which asks how normative assumptions can be justified (knowledge about what should and should not be);
- *Transformation knowledge*, which is needed in order to reach new goals and intentions (knowing how to get from the actual state to the desired state).

11.3   Case Study: InterFlex Seminar, "Visionen Urbaner Zukünfte" ("Visions of Urban Futures") at the University of Applied Sciences Potsdam

In the following, we will take a specific course as an example in order to illustrate our ideas about mediating interdisciplinary and transdisciplinary competencies within the context of urban transformation, utilizing methods of inquiry-based learning.

The project seminar, "Visionen Urbaner Zukünfte – Leitbildprozess Potsdam" ("Visions of Urban Futures – Urban Development Guidelines for Potsdam"), which is presented here in detail, was held within the context of the "InterFlex" teaching format (see Box 11.1). The project seminar serves as a model for the interdisciplinary and transdisciplinary master's degree program "Urbane Zukunft" ("Urban Future"), which was then being

---

Box 11.1: *What Is InterFlex?* (Diemut Bartl)

InterFlex is a regular teaching format that is open to all students at the University of Applied Sciences Potsdam, which connects interdisciplinary teaching with research. It allows students to come into contact with real fields of research even before completing their studies and, in so doing, to investigate their own questions, often in interdisciplinary teamwork with the help of inquiry-based learning. Participants are intermixed in terms of discipline due to the interdisciplinary course, and are supported by an equally interdisciplinary teaching tandem team consisting of at least two educators.

An example of an InterFlex course is "People – Migration – Memories. What historical migratory movements lie buried in family history?" ("Menschen – Migration – Memorien. Welche historischen Migrationsbewegungen verbergen sich hinter der Geschichte von Familien?"). The project, on which the disciplines of archive studies and social studies cooperated, ran for two semesters from 2010 to 2011 and struck a nerve with many students, who devoted themselves with research and scientific work to the ever-present phenomenon of flight, migration and displacement and, in doing so, grappled with their own family histories. The result was an interactive digital map that documented the migratory movements and the various reasons for leaving home with the help of official and private documents.

InterFlex is based on the "Exzellente Lehre" ("Excellent Teaching") competition tender for 2009 and was financed from 2010 until the end of 2013 by funding from the Stifterverband der Deutschen Wissenschaft (German Association of Donors for the Promotion of Sciences and Humanities) and the Ministry for Science, Research, and Culture of the State of Brandenburg. The university has continued to fund the project since 2014. To date, more than 80 teaching-research courses have been created within the context of InterFlex and 50 percent of educators and more than 1500 students have been involved (cf. Ammann et al., 2013).

developed at the University of Applied Sciences Potsdam (FHP). The course was attended by students in FHP degree programs in architecture and urban development, cultural advancement, design, and information science. The two educators represented the disciplines of architecture and social psychology, respectively, and introduced actively ongoing research (Prytula 2011; Schröder et al. 2011; Wolf et al. 2015). The project seminar took place in cooperation with the participatory process of developing policy guidelines for the city of Potsdam (Landeshauptstadt Potsdam 2015). In the course, the students examined visions and models of future urban development from the perspective of architecture and urban planning on the one hand, and from the perspective of social psychology in terms of the processes and mechanisms of action on the other. By visions we refer to the mental representations of future conditions shared by agents in a social system, which are emotionally appealing and cognitively persuasive. If they inspire the agents in a social system and motivate them to coordinate their activity towards a common goal for the future, visions can serve as powerful building blocks in processes of change (cf. Nanus 1992).

A central component of the seminar was the cooperation with the regional capital of Potsdam and the simultaneously occurring process of developing new policy guidelines, "Rethinking the Future of Potsdam" ("Potsdam weiterdenken," cf. Landeshauptstadt Potsdam 2015). The citizens of Potsdam were involved in the discussion about the strategic goals for the future development of Potsdam in an inductive participatory process. The goal of the process was, in particular, to make urban changes and growth processes sustainable, to coordinate the multitude of sub-strategies and concepts in regional capital, and to ensure its long-term financial performance. The task of the students was to develop and prepare their own project ideas based on the topics specified by the citizens. The student projects were discussed with representatives of the city administration and finally presented as poster presentations and in a final report (see Fig. 11.1 for examples).

While the project work carried out in small groups was a central thread for students throughout the semester, we supported the working process purposefully with methodological and theoretical basic knowledge in four consecutive thematic fields:

1. *Basic principles of visioning*: To begin with, we asked: based on the current state of social psychological research, what are visions, how and when do they exert an effect, and what distinguishes successful visionary processes from failing ones? Inter alia, the basic principles with regard to values, milieus and lifestyles, power and influence processes, as well as concepts of transformational leadership in a management context, were developed and discussed with students.

2. *Architecture of a vision process*: The students were then instructed to think through their own chosen project topic systematically with the help of a structured vision process. In so doing, they were to fall back on a process model of visionary leadership known within the context of organizational change management (Nanus 1992), which the two course instructors had adapted to the context of urban transformation processes.

3. *Methods of futurology*: In the third thematic block, basic principles concerning complex systems were taught and some methods of futurology were presented by way of example such as

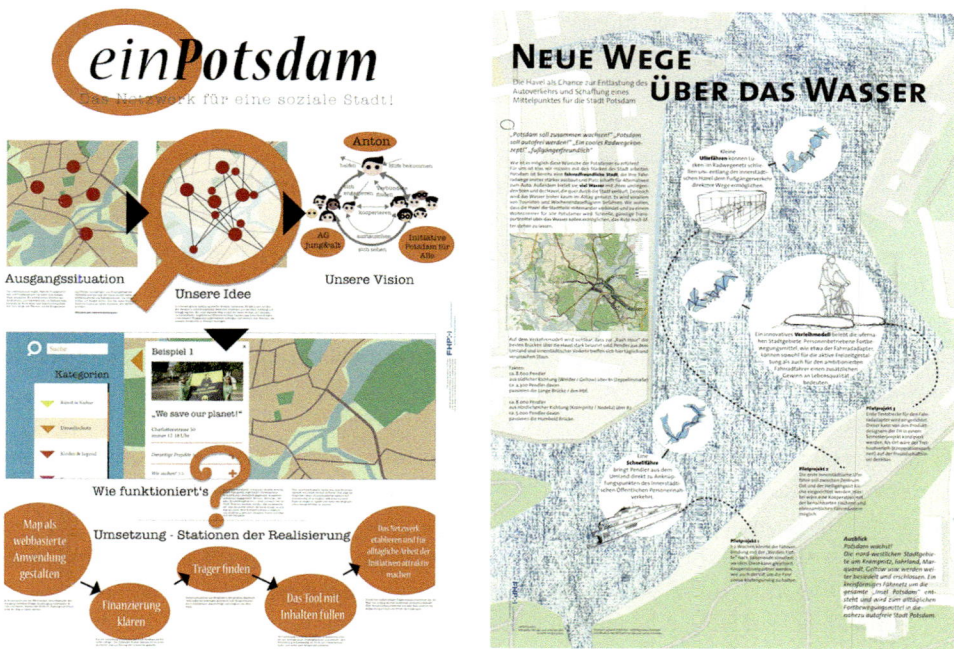

Fig. 11.1 Poster presentations of the results of the seminar. The task of the visualization was to develop a self-explanatory and inspiring project presentation formatted on an A0-size poster containing all of the important information regarding the understanding of the "vision," as well as its implementation. (Source: representation by students at FH Potsdam; left: Manuela Goschy, Lucas Horn, Paulina Kietzell and Stefan Pudellek; right: Johanna Olm and Sebastian Witzke)

- SWOT analyses (a tool for assessing the strengths, weaknesses, opportunities and threats associated with a project),
- Delphi studies (multi-stage expert interview; e.g. Schröder et al. 2011),
- scenario analysis (software-assisted generation of consistent, plausible development paths; e.g. Scholz and Tietje 2002),
- system dynamics models (mathematical description of the variable relationships; e.g. Prytula 2011) or
- agent-based simulation (modeling of agent behavior in the social system; e.g. Wolf et al. 2015).

Students were familiarized with the approach associated with the methods, and for what purposes they are used.

4. *Communicating visions*: Last but not least, the effective use of suitable media (figures, diagrams, texts and other media) and the empowerment of different perceptual channels of the target groups contribute to the understanding and acceptance of a project. Among other things, there was discussion of the experimental studies through which

the effectiveness of different ways of communicating a vision for the future within the context of urban development processes was examined (e.g., Shipley and Michela 2006).

11.4   Didactic, Methodological and Organizational Challenges

The project course "Visionen Urbaner Zukünfte – Leitbildprozess Potsdam" ("Visions of Urban Futures – Process of Developing a Model for Potsdam") serves as an example of the challenges that accompany inter- and transdisciplinary inquiry-based learning. In our experience, the following organizational and methodological principles have been shown to work (cf. also Mieg et al. 1996; Stauffacher 2001):

(1) *Project work in interdisciplinary groups* makes results-oriented work possible and does not overwhelm the students with subject-specific detailed knowledge. The project forms the "common thread" in the seminar, along which specialist knowledge, professional and personal competencies, interdisciplinary and complementary perspectives can be imparted. In the above example, the added value of interdisciplinary work lay in particular in studying urban development tasks (strategies for growth or shrinkage processes, demographic change, etc.) both from a planning perspective (spatial structures, building structures and infrastructures) and from a socio-psychological perspective (values, leadership models) using methods associated with futurology.

(2) *Good preparation, coordination of learning objectives and working methodology* are essential prerequisites for a successful course, in particular when multiple instructors are involved, as is the case with "InterFlex" courses. It is useful to have an elaborated schedule for the respective courses with exact assignments of responsibilities, methods and media used, as well as defined learning and intermediate goals (milestones). It is advantageous if the instructors already coordinate their subject-related perspectives with one another during the preparation and then focus the discussion during the course on concrete questions pertaining to the project work.

(3) Early *involvement of practice partners* in the design of the seminar and in implementing the course itself has proven to be successful, e.g. through lectures or guest reviews. Practice partners can present real problems from a mostly non-academic perspective. The involvement of practice partners requires a degree of coordination and preparation time that should not be underestimated. Here, binding appointments and a clarification of the respective expectations and roles are helpful.

(4) *Field visits or excursions* have proven to be very beneficial for the learning process. In addition to a practical view, these offer in particular the opportunity for students to meet each other amongst themselves, as well as for students and instructors to interact with one another in an informal way. An excursion allows the group to have shared, holistic experiences and fosters communication within the group since its activities include concrete organizational tasks must be solved. The shared experiences can be referenced in later discussions.

(5) Finally, one should not have unfulfillable *expectations of the results of the seminar.* Frequently, only limited relevant research results can be obtained within the framework of a university course, in particular due to students' limited time resources.

"Failure" also sometimes provides useful learning outcomes. Any experience can be considered a useful one if it prompts new insights and actions. Often, however, new incentives and ideas emerge in inter- and transdisciplinary teaching contexts that can then inspire the instructors' research program. In addition, teaching in the InterFlex format offers the opportunity to try new research ideas in a low-threshold way.

11.5   Theses on Inquiry-Based Learning in the Context of Inter- and Transdisciplinarity

Finally, we would like to present our experiences and our reflections on inquiry-based learning within the context of inter- and transdisciplinarity in the form of three theses.

Thesis 1: Inter- and transdisciplinarity require a new unity of teaching and research.

Classifying courses as non-research-oriented "compulsory or basic subjects" (usually with a focus on lecturing-centered teaching methods) and "inquiry-based learning" is not (or no longer) up-to-date in terms of a successful transfer of knowledge and preparation for professional practice according to the common thesis of the present volume. This especially applies to inter- and transdisciplinary research and teaching topics. In a society that is permeated with "wicked problems" (see above), in practice, every problem solution constitutes a research process. As such, the integration of interdisciplinary knowledge and the reduction of uncertainty with respect to the pure application of secured disciplinary knowledge are the central challenges. It is therefore very important to confront students with uncertain knowledge, or different or deviating knowledge and positions, so that they can practice the ability to independently assess complex issues.

Therefore, the development and training of competencies for problem-solving strategies as well as knowledge, project and group management should be a priority in inter- and transdisciplinary teaching. It is more expedient to confront students with complex problems and issues derived from those problems, the solution to which then requires that content and methodology be learned. Here, educators provide support, but there is a certain dissolution of the traditional role relationship. Although educators may have a head start in terms of experience, they are fundamentally faced with the same challenge as the students when faced with complex "wicked problems" and the limitations of their own knowledge. Interdisciplinary and transdisciplinary educators and researchers are also constantly in the position of having to acquire new, unfamiliar knowledge and thus are able to serve as "somewhat more advanced" role models for students instead of as authoritative mediators of knowledge.

Thesis 2: Inquiry-based learning can serve as a testing ground for larger innovation processes.

As a learning institution, a university as a whole must be able to transform itself and adapt to changing technological, ecological, and socio-economic challenges. To this end, inquiry-based teaching offers a suitable testing ground and learning arena in order to develop innovations in a manageable learning context. At the same time, by involving practice partners, requirements from society, the economy, and the development of technology can be brought directly into the university. In the long run, ideas for new content concepts or organizational forms for bachelor's and master's degree programs may be created as a result, for example with networked, interdisciplinary courses, which help to secure the quality and innovative capacity of the university.

Course-immanent and inter-semester tools for quality control and improvement must be implemented in the courses themselves. These include, inter alia, appropriate forms of teaching evaluation or peer feedback, both between students and between educators. Thus, the adaptability of the teaching concepts can be facilitated within the seminar itself as well as across semesters. Inquiry-based teaching can be represented by the image of a developmental spiral, where both individual and organizational-structural development continues to occur. "Errors" and "failure" cannot be ruled out in innovation processes and must also be allowed in innovative teaching formats.

Thesis 3: Inquiry-based learning can act as a catalyst on the development of application-oriented research collaborations.

Inquiry-based teaching can serve as a building block in the strategic development of research projects, when courses are used either as a starting point for, in support of, or as a complement to research projects. Interdisciplinary courses can be used as a basis for identifying additional research activities or to support such activities by adding depth.

Inquiry-based teaching can be excellent for initiating practice collaborations and for exploring research topics. Ideally, this creates win-win situations for the practice partners, who can benefit directly from the results of practice-oriented project work, and who are therefore motivated to engage in further collaboration, but also for the students, due to the practical instruction.

References

Ammann, B./Bartl, D./Cartes, S./Klose, B. (Hrsg.). (2013). *InterFlex – Querdenken erwünscht: Interdisziplinär und forschend lernen.* Fachhochschule Potsdam.

Landeshauptstadt Potsdam (2015). Potsdam weiterdenken. Leitbildprozess der Landeshauptstadt Potsdam. Retrieved 30 October 2015 from https://www.potsdam-weiterdenken.de/

Mieg, H. A./Evetts, J. (2019). *Professionalism, science, and expert roles.* In K. A. Ericsson/R. R. Hoffman/ A. Kozbelt/A. M. Williams (Hrsg.), *The Cambridge handbook on expertise and expert performance* (2nd ed., pp. 127–148). New York: Cambridge University Press.

Mieg, H. A./Hübner, P./Stauffacher, M./Bösch, S./Balmer, M. (Hrsg.). (2001). *Zukunft Schiene Schweiz II: Ökologisches Potenzial des Schienengüterverkehrs am Beispiel der Region Zugersee, Fallstudie 2000.* Zürich: Rüegger.

Mieg, H. A./Scholz, R. W./Stünzi, J. (1996). Das Prinzip der modularen Integration: Neue Wege von Führung und Wissensintegration im Management von Umweltprojekten. *Organisationsentwicklung, 15*(2), 4–15.

Nanus, B. (1992). Visionary leadership: Creating a compelling sense of direction for your organization. San Francisco: Jossey-Bass.

Prytula, M. (2011). Ein integrales Energie- und Stoffstrommodell als Grundlage zur Bewertung einer nachhaltigen Entwicklung urbaner Systeme. Dissertation an der TU Berlin, Universitätsverlag der TU Berlin. Retrieved 30 October 2015 from https://depositonce.tu-berlin.de/handle/11303/3425

Schneidewind, U./Singer-Brodowski, M. (2014). *Transformative Wissenschaft. Klimawandel im deutschen Wissenschafts- und Hochschulsystem* (2. verbesserte und aktualisierte Auflage). Marburg: Metropolis-Verlag.

Scholz, R. W./Tietje, O. (2002). *Embedded case study methods: Integrating quantitative and qualitative knowledge.* Thousand Oaks: Sage.

Schröder, T./Huck, J./de Haan, G. (2011). *Transfer sozialer Innovationen. Eine zukunftsorientierte Fallstudie zur nachhaltigen Siedlungsentwicklung.* Wiesbaden: Springer VS.

Shipley, R./Michela, J. L. (2006). Can vision motivate planning action? *Planning, Practice, & Research, 21,* 223–244.

Stauffacher, M. (2001). Fallstudiendidaktik: Die Steuerung von gruppendynamischen Prozessen in einem transdisziplinären Lehrprojekt. In H. A. Mieg, P. Hübner, M. Stauffacher, S. Bösch/ M. Balmer (Hrsg.), *Zukunft Schiene II: Ökologisches Potenzial des Schienengüterverkehrs am Beispiel der Region Zugersee, Fallstudie 2000* (S. 217–228). Zürich: Rüegger.

Wissenschaftsrat (2015). *Zum wissenschaftspolitischen Diskurs über Große gesellschaftliche Herausforderungen. Positionspapier.* Retrieved 15 October 2015 from http://www.wissenschaftsrat.de/download/archiv/4594-15.pdf

Wolf, I./Schröder, T./Neumann, J./de Haan, G. (2015). Changing minds about electric cars: An empirically grounded agent-based modeling approach. *Technological Forecasting and Social Change, 94,* 269–285.

Overview: Disciplines

Our overview of inquiry-based learning in teaching encompasses 21 disciplines, including traditional disciplines such as philosophy and medicine as well as newer disciplines such as design and sustainability sciences. For this presentation, we will forego an attempt to create a complete discipline classification system. Instead, we introduce four classes based on three typical disciplines in each class. All additional disciplines will be dealt with in alphabetical order, although some of these could also be categorized as one of the four classes.

The first class comprises disciplines for which *professional development* is an issue and purpose, e.g. social work. In these disciplines, inquiry-based learning is seen in conjunction with training in a specific type of professionalism. Teacher education is also included among the selected disciplines. Here, there is a long tradition of inquiry-based learning. Inquiry-based learning is new in information science, the third discipline presented.

The second class is defined by the *life sciences*, which extend from medicine to the health sciences that are currently being developed in contrast or as a supplement to medicine. Here, inquiry-based learning has different functions. In medical education, inquiry-based learning is largely unknown; in any case, an education in natural science-related life sciences is research-oriented and inquiry-based learning is an option. In the health sciences, inquiry-based learning is used for professional development in a manner similar to the disciplines in the first class.

The third class comprises the *STEM disciplines*: natural sciences, information technology, engineering and mathematics. The STEM disciplines are the subject of an educational policy discussion of their own, on the one hand because of their relevance to innovation activities in a country, and on the other because of the low proportion of women in these degree programs. The disciplines are inherently research-intensive; the general question that arises is: Which formal and methodological basic knowledge would allow students to begin their own research?

The fourth class comprises the arts and design, with the three disciplines of the arts, architecture and design presented by way of example. Education in these disciplines is mostly project-based and characterized by design exercises. Some lecturers already consider the act of designing to be research. Overall, the role of methods and the understanding of research are rather unclear and the subject of critical controversy. Therefore, the chapter on design consists of a discussion among design professors.

The remaining disciplines, which were assigned to none of the four classes, are highly diverse. The series spans business administration on the one hand – where we would anticipate inquiry-based learning, but rarely find it – and theology on the other, where we would not expect inquiry-based learning, but do find successful examples thereof. Inquiry-based learning is often introduced via *teacher education*, where inquiry-based learning is already the standard (cf. Fichten, in this volume) and is now blazing a trail, for example in theology or history, and most recently in business administration as well.

The nine disciplines presented individually reveal a further field of activity for inquiry-based learning: in *interdisciplinary* instruction (cf. Prytula et al., in this volume). Disciplines such as sustainability science or movement sciences (sports) depend on an exchange with other disciplines. Inquiry-based learning helps students to quickly become familiar with interdisciplinarity. The same applies to geography and cultural studies. Traditional disciplines such as legal studies, which are not subject to interdisciplinary pressure nor need to take care of teaching certification, could benefit from inquiry-based learning, but are only showing initial approaches to it.

Disciplines, class I

Inquiry-Based Learning in Teacher Training

12

Wolfgang Fichten

In recent years, inquiry-based learning has become an integral part of teacher training as a guiding principle of a contemporary university education. The background to this is the development of new educational and study concepts on the one hand, and the structural changes resulting from the implementation of the Bologna Process on the other. This article examines the experiences and research findings on inquiry-based learning in the teaching certification program and discusses perspectives on this.

12.1 Teacher Training as a Context for Inquiry-Based Learning

In recent years, inquiry-based learning has become broadly established in university teacher education and has virtually become a guiding principle. In the course of the discussion about reforming teacher education, inquiry-based learning gained special significance. The reasons for the "career" of this higher education didactic concept within the context of reflective, research-oriented or research-focused teacher education are complex and can only be outlined here.

Scholarly Orientation – Skills Orientation – Practice Orientation The Bologna process requires institutions of higher learning to align themselves with the goals of "employability" and skills development, i.e. the student's ability to pursue a professional activity based on scholarly work (cf. in addition BAK 1970, p. 9). From this perspective, how the university will contribute to the qualification of future teachers must be specified. According to

W. Fichten, Prof. Dr. (✉)
Carl von Ossietzky Universität Oldenburg – Leiter der „Forschungswerkstatt Schule und LehrerInnenbildung" im Didaktischen Zentrum, Oldenburg, Germany
e-mail: forschungswerkstatt@uni-oldenburg.de

© The Author(s) 2019
H. A. Mieg (ed.), *Inquiry-Based Learning – Undergraduate Research*,
https://doi.org/10.1007/978-3-030-14223-0_12

the consensus, scholarship can provide a basis for professional action by providing and imparting scholarly theoretical and foundational knowledge. Students should be taught theoretical knowledge and methodological skills for the analysis of and reflection on practices. If scholarship is to have any significance for later professional activity, it must not remain unknown to students; instead, they must take part in the process of acquiring scholarly knowledge. Such "participation in scholarship" (BAK 1970, p. 9) has its educational-theoretical basis: "if scholarship educates, then only scholarship that one 'works through' oneself as unconcluded; not scholarship that is merely imparted as concluded" (Huber 2009, p. 13, translated).

An Explorative Attitude as a Prerequisite for Dealing with Uncertainties Regarding the scholarly nature of the education and, in consequence, scholarship-based professional activity, the German Science Council (*Wissenschaftsrat* 2001, p. 41, translated) determined the following: "A university education should teach and promote the attitude of inquiry-based learning in order to enable future teachers to use their theoretical knowledge for analyzing and shaping the professional field, and in this way, should not teach in a manner that is distanced from scholarship, but instead, should teach with an investigative attitude." Research into professionalization has examined the complexity of teaching in greater detail: Teaching activities are accompanied by an irresolvable element of insecurity. Although recourse to routines that have been developed over time is possible on a limited basis, these routines fail in novel situational constellations, which therefore require a reflective type of action ("reflection on action," see also Huber, in this volume). In dealing with the complexity typical of a given occupation, a type of "researching within the context of practice" (forming hypotheses, creating, testing and evaluating alternative actions) or an experimental attitude is required, which can be acquired and developed through inquiry-based learning.

Developing an Investigative Habit The model of the professional derived from research findings was used to delineate an ideal image of an instructor who is capable of constantly critically examining their own goals, of generating alternative interpretations of practical conditions and of developing new perspectives. In order to succeed productively, the instructor must not only have an inventory of suitable methods available to them but above all must have a critical reflexive attitude towards the practice that fosters development through inquiry. In the discourse on inquiry-based learning, "a habit developed through the issues and methods of scholarly activity" (Terhart 2000, p. 69, translated) or an "investigative habit" is an essential target component. What is meant here is the internalization of a curious, skeptical view of the practice, which adopts the mode of scholarly inquiry, making certainties consistently available. Such an attitude makes it possible to question pedagogic activities as well as the understanding of school and teaching, in order to gain orientation for future action. It is aimed both at mastering practice by generating one's own solutions to problems and at fostering the professional development of the instructor.

12.2   Contours of Inquiry-Based Learning

The slogan "professionalization through inquiry-based learning" has become a commonplace in academic discourse. Ludwig Huber (2009) criticizes the "inflationary" use of the term, which threatens to blur the contours of the concept. Koch-Priewe and Thiele (2009, p. 271) state that the concept has "innumerable facets" and allows for numerous variants. A common feature of the realization approaches documented in Roters, Schneider, Koch-Priewe, Thiele and Wildt (2009) is that inquiry-based learning is primarily directed "at different forms of reflectivity and participation in scholarly, methodological discourse" (ibid., p. 279, translated). Wischer, Katenbrink and Nakamura (2014, p. 12 et seq.) attribute the diversity to the "context-specific basic conditions and formal structures that allow inquiry-based learning [...] to be developed in the respective degree programs in the first place" as well as the absence of a definition on which a consensus can be reached. There is no consensus on the question as to "what inquiry-based learning is even supposed to achieve and what conditions must exist so that the respective goals can be reached" (ibid., p. 15, translated).

The following definition clarifies the concept: "Within the context of teacher training, inquiry-based learning is understood to be the acquisition of experience, knowledge and competencies based on a self-reflective and theory-based confrontation with school as an area of activity" (Ministerium für Schule, Jugend und Kinder des Landes Nordrhein-Westfalen, cited in Wilde and Stiller 2011, p. 171, translated).

While Huber's definition (see, for example, Mieg, in this volume) places the research process in the foreground and emphasizes the aspect of independence, the goal and result of inquiry-based learning are addressed in the quoted definition: The component of reflection can be situated in the discourse on professionalization, while the reference to theory can be justified by the academic nature of a university education. Both components are mutually dependent, since it is indispensable for reflection intended to question one's own subjective theories to reference scholarly theories.

Accordingly, inquiry-based learning exhibits three central characteristics: independence, relation to theory, and reflection. It is not easy to implement these characteristics, as the descriptions of various course formats show (Roters et al. 2009; Huber et al. 2009; Katenbrink et al. 2014). Ideally, seminar concepts should be geared towards meeting all three criteria. This shows that the realization of inquiry-based learning is a didactically demanding task that may not be mastered right away, which – in a manner analogous to that of school instruction – suggests an experimental approach to one's own higher education instruction.

12.2.1 Approaches and Formats of Inquiry-Based Learning

As noted, inquiry-based learning in teacher training encompasses a wide spectrum that ranges from its inclusion in practical studies, compulsory elective modules in the educational sciences and its establishment in internships requiring intense supervision. The variety has forced attempts at classification, which can be based, inter alia, on the aspects of participation (cf. Fichten 2010, p. 149) and dimensioning. The spectrum extends from limited observation tasks in a general school internship/job orientation internship to comprehensive projects within the context of research modules based on educational science and of the practical semester. In the course of implementing inquiry-based learning in teacher training, consequential determinations were arrived at. Very little attention has been paid to the approach developed by Huber (2009, p. 18), who mentions various implementation options that allow students a high degree of independent activity in complex task formats, taking into account discipline-related conditions (researching, excursions, simulations, etc.).

The "internship solution" is currently the most common form of inquiry-based learning – in many places, it's the only form. One of its positive aspects is that it allows the individual's own practice can be taken into consideration. Academic studies' increased orientation towards practice and the subsequent expansion of the practical part of those studies do not guarantee unto themselves that prospective instructors will later work professionally in that occupation, however, since there is a risk that the practices observed will be adopted without reflection. Inquiry-based learning is intended to counteract this and contribute to a perception and analysis of the practice at a distance, from a position of observation associated with research.

Linking student research with internships has far-reaching consequences for students as well as for supervising instructors, because it makes inquiry-based learning a compulsory study component for all. This corresponds to the position of the Federal University Assistants' Conference (BAK 1970): "participation in scholarship" for all, and right from the start. Inquiry-based learning is an element of academic studies that requires intensive supervision; instructors' limited capacities must be distributed among larger groups. In addition, academic achievement must be certified and assessed. The inquiry-based learning that was established in the old degree programs took the form of an elective course that was used by particularly interested and motivated students. If inquiry-based learning is obligatory for all, it can no longer be assumed that one is only dealing with motivated students, meaning the issue of motivation must be raised in an entirely different way (cf. Huber 2009).

12.2.2 Realization Approaches

Inquiry-based learning that is not linked to internships has been increasingly used in teacher training since the end of the 1990s. As such, the focus is placed less on individual professionalization, and more on the benefits for school and teaching development.

Oldenburg team research is an example of this (Fichten and Meyer 2009). Instructors participate in seminar sessions and actively participate in research based on two-hour blocks of time. Teams comprised of instructors and students research issues that arise from within a school context. Research projects are oriented towards action research; their aim is to generate solutions or a framework of action for school and teaching-related problems. The team research program, which has existed since 1996, was carried out as a one- to two-semester seminar within the scope of a pedagogic portion of academic studies. Comparable courses exist at other locations (e.g. Bielefeld, Hamburg, Osnabrück).

Evaluation results concerning team research show that students take away a changed view of the problem from their involvement in the research, i.e. personal assumptions are relativized or changed (cf. Fichten and Moschner 2009, p. 251 et seq.). The intensive engagement with school-related issues (the relevance of which to one's own qualification becomes clear) contributes to students frequently pursuing the contents more deeply and more extensively (for example in state examination (*Staatsexamen*) theses or masters' theses). Students acquire interdisciplinary competencies (e.g. a capacity for teamwork or collaboration) as well as research competence. In their own estimation, they are better able to evaluate published research reports and have a more differentiated and critical view of scholarship. In view of the limited theoretical framing of the projects, the increased appreciation of scholarly theory by some students is somewhat surprising.

The concept at RWTH Aachen (Boelhauve 2009) presents an example of an "internship solution" which provides one gradation of inquiry-based learning. The first element of inquiry-based learning is linked to the introductory school internship during the basic studies (*Grundstudium*). In the preparatory seminar, central tasks of the teaching profession are developed; these provide a "structuring instrument" for the focal points of the observation task to be performed during the internship. The educational science and the teaching methodologies of two subjects are involved in the "field studies" module during the primary studies (*Hauptstudium*). During the internship, students carry out previously agreed-upon "investigative tasks" that have been framed in terms of educational and didactic theory. They may select the subject on which the content of the project will focus from among the disciplines involved in the module.

The introduction of the practical semester – which has been completed in some federal states of Germany, and is pending in others – creates further possibilities for implementing inquiry-based learning. The practical semester in Lower Saxony, which was introduced for the degree programs for elementary, secondary and junior high school education, includes what is known as a "practical block," during which the students themselves teach up to 40 hours. In addition, this block also includes the *Projektband* or project phase (in other federal states: study project, research task), in which an empirical study relating to school or instruction must be conducted; a number of variations for this study are specified (cf. Klewin and Schüssler 2012: Varianten der Studienprojekte in NRW). There is adequate time for student research projects due to the length of the practical semester. However, in addition to the observed lessons, the interns involved in the program must also prepare and teach their own lessons and so they cannot focus exclusively on their research project.

An example from biology didactics at the University of Bielefeld shows how inquiry-based learning can be shaped during the practical semester (Wilde and Stiller 2011). In the *preparatory seminar*, theories that are relevant to biology didactics and their possible applications are presented in class, along with lesson-planning methods. After the theoretical portion of each seminar session, an attempt should be made to integrate the respective theory into concrete lesson plans (presentation of different lesson designs and assessment of the same against the backdrop of theory). The methodological foundations for student study projects will be imparted in the *supervision seminar* and linked with issues that are based on theories relating to biology didactics. Students will then create a lesson plan and a questionnaire for class evaluation, taking into account the selected theory. The lesson is held and evaluated with regard to the respective issue, and the results are presented in a project report or as a poster.

Experiences with inquiry-based learning in teacher training are as varied as the formats. There are nevertheless some convergences:

- Inquiry-based learning succeeds when the seminar is designed with a balance of guidance and independence. In the case of Oldenburg team research, the percentage of direct instruction alternates with extensive phases of self-regulated teamwork and additionally required individual work.
- Inquiry-based learning focuses on students' learning gains. As newcomers to research, students must be taught research competence so that they can carry out an empirical investigation to their own satisfaction and mark it down as a success. If this does not happen, it will hinder the development of an investigative habit.
- Depending on the format, the student projects are determined by the needs and problems expressed by schools, or by contents imparted in the preparatory seminar, the practical relevance of which is to be examined.
- Teaching both research methods and disciplinary content in a *single* seminar results in an overload. A combination of courses belonging to a module with primarily research-related and content-oriented seminars appears to be a suitable system.

12.2.3 Perspectives on Inquiry-Based Learning in Teacher Training

Given its widespread establishment in university teacher education, it is not particularly daring to predict that, in the future, inquiry-based learning will continue to play a role as an element of academic studies and will be significant in the training of prospective teachers. The extent to which it will sustain its position, however, depends on the processing of questions that have arisen over the years regarding site-specific implementation.

In its implementation in teacher education, inquiry-based learning has become associated with a number of goals, requirements and effects that must be implemented due to the inclusion of various discourses (professionalization, competence and practice orientation, etc.), and thus the original approach and the intention associated therewith are scarcely recognizable. For example, the educational-theoretical reasoning set forth in the BAK paper (1970) has receded into the background these days, where the focus is not so much on personal development as it is on professional qualification. In view of what is, in principle, welcome diversity in the available interpretations and approaches to implementation, which can also lead to arbitrariness, it is necessary to understand fundamental features of inquiry-based learning, as well as to clarify and contour the concept.

A further problem area stands out with regard to positioning the curriculum of inquiry-based learning. Katenbrink and Wischer (2014, p. 122) have noted a tendency for inquiry-based learning "to be added, as it were, to other targeted competencies and concepts of teacher education." Imparting research competence, for example, is "simply added to the already diverse goals, standards and competence profiles for teacher training" (ibid., p. 123). The lack of or insufficient integration of student research into the overall curriculum means, inter alia, that when inquiry-based learning is situated later in the course of study, students have very little knowledge on which to build. The positioning of the curriculum must not be limited to the module level, but must instead be based on the entire course of studies and lead to the construction of a spiral curriculum that allows connections to be made within.

Attention is paid to the various institutional relationships and constellations of agents associated with the implementation of the concept. Since student projects are established at the school, the school's expectations, interests and requirements also come into play. There is a need for coordination and clarification (e.g. with reference to the participation of study groups in research studies, contact persons at the school, etc.). As such, obligations and responsibilities must also be specified and defined. One problem, among several, is that the timing of events at the university and at school differ, and therefore there is usually only a limited timeframe for student projects, with the exception of the practical semester.

What should be decisive for the prospects of inquiry-based learning in teacher education is whether – and the degree to which – the intended goals are reached and the postulated effects occur. Available evaluation results indicate that some target components have been reached (see above). The validity of the findings is limited, however, since it is not possible to determine which effects are attributable to the respective settings and contexts, and which are genuinely attributable to inquiry-based learning. Among other things, the question arises as to the level of reflection students achieve through the practical semester and inquiry-based learning. The "bulky" construct of reflective competence has already been operationalized for studies in this regard (cf. Leonhard et al. 2010).

In the case of inquiry-based learning, it is repeatedly emphasized that the process is more important than the results, and the development of research-oriented behavior is more decisive than the acquisition of knowledge. If one admits that inquiry-based learning primarily depends on the formation and internalization of certain dispositions and attitudes towards practice, and if one assumes that this is actually achieved, the question remains whether students will take this attitude from the university learning situation and transfer it to other situational contexts, and how stable that attitude will be (transfer and stability hypothesis; cf. Fichten 2010, p. 159). This means that, ultimately, it will only be possible to assess the effectiveness of inquiry-based learning more precisely by basing that assessment on comprehensive longitudinal studies, which currently have yet to be performed. If it should turn out that the envisaged research-oriented behavior is a short-lived, fleeting phenomenon, this would likely have repercussions for the extent to which the concept is used in teacher education.

A "scenario" of this kind is not too farfetched. The three phases of teacher education (university education phase, internship, further teacher education) should be considered as a single entity (Terhart 2000). The second phase is still centered on social integration into the profession and on "teaching classes." An explorative-developing, critical reflective attitude, which students have acquired via the first phase of inquiry-based learning, seems to be hardly in demand in internships and will therefore possibly be abandoned. Such an attitude is more likely to be permanent and to be included in the student's professional activity when all phases of teacher education include elements of inquiry-based learning. While the second phase has a deficit in this regard, there are isolated approaches and projects in further teacher training (e.g. Andreitz et al. 2014).

Klewin and Kneuper (2009, p. 84, translated) state: "Overall, it seems to be [...] necessary to first differentiate the precise description of students' learning processes in inquiry-based learning processes in greater detail. Only then can the competencies (that can be) acquired within this process be grasped theoretically and then studied empirically." Some publications exist for this first step of the indicated pragmatic-inductive path, and it would be decisive for the prospects of inquiry-based learning in teacher education if we were to take the second step now.

References

Andreitz, I./Müller, F./Dirninger, E./Mayr, J. (2014). Bedingungen und Wirkungen forschenden Lernens in der Lehrer_innenfortbildung. Ergebnisse aus der Begleitforschung der Lehrgänge Pädagogik und Fachdidaktik für Lehrer_innen (PFL). In E. Feyerer/K. Hirschenhauser/K. Soukup-Altrichter (Hrsg.), *Last oder Lust? Forschung und Lehrer_innenbildung* (S. 189–204). Münster: Waxmann.

Bundesassistentenkonferenz (BAK) (1970). *Forschendes Lernen – Wissenschaftliches Prüfen.* Schriften der BAK 5: Bonn.

Boelhauve, U. (2009). Forschendes Lernen im Rahmen von Praxisstudien im erziehungswissen-schaftlichen Studium der Lehramtsausbildung an der RWTH Aachen. In B. Roters/R. Schneider, B/Koch-Priewe, J./Thiele/J. Wildt (Hrsg.), *Forschendes Lernen im Lehramtsstudium* (S. 37–62). Bad Heilbrunn: Klinkhardt.

Fichten, W. (2010). Forschendes Lernen in der Lehrerbildung. In U. Eberhardt (Hrsg.), *Neue Impulse in der Hochschuldidaktik* (S. 127–182). Wiesbaden: VS-Verlag.

Fichten, W./Meyer, H. (2009). Forschendes Lernen in der Lehrerbildung – das Oldenburger Modell. In N. Hollenbach/K.-J. Tillmann (Hrsg.), *Die Schule forschend verändern. Praxisforschung aus nationaler und internationaler Perspektive* (S. 119–145). Bad Heilbrunn: Klinkhardt.

Fichten, W./Moschner, B. (2009). Forschendes Lernen in der Oldenburger Lehrerbildung. In B. Roters/R. Schneider/B. Koch-Priewe/J. Thiele/J. Wildt (Hrsg.), *Forschendes Lernen im Lehramtsstudium* (S. 242–270). Bad Heilbrunn: Klinkhardt.

Huber, L. (2009). Warum Forschendes Lernen nötig und möglich ist. In L. Huber/J. Hellmer/
F. Schneider (Hrsg.), *Forschendes Lernen im Studium. Aktuelle Konzepte und Erfahrungen* (S.
9–35). Bielefeld: UniversitätsVerlagWebler.

Huber, L./Hellmer, J./Schneider, F. (Hrsg.). (2009). Forschendes Lernen im Studium. Aktuelle
Konzepte und Erfahrungen. Bielefeld: UniversitätsVerlagWebler.

Katenbrink, N./Wischer, B. (2014). Konzepte forschenden Lernens in der Osnabrücker
Lehrerbildung. Versuch einer Einordnung und Reflexion. In N. Katenbrink/B. Wischer/Y. Naka
mura (Hrsg.), *Forschendes Lernen in der Osnabrücker Lehrerausbildung* (S. 109–131). Münster:
MV Wissenschaft.

Katenbrink, N./Wischer, B./Nakamura, Y. (Hrsg.). (2014). Forschendes Lernen in der Osnabrücker
Lehrerausbildung. Münster: MV Wissenschaft.

Klewin, G./Kneuper, D. (2009). Forschend lernen in der Bielefelder Fallstudienwerkstatt
Schulentwicklung. In B. Roters/R. Schneider/B. Koch-Priewe/J. Thiele/J. Wildt (Hrsg.),
Forschendes Lernen im Lehramtsstudium (S. 63–85). Bad Heilbrunn: Klinkhardt.

Klewin, G./Schüssler, R. (2012). Forschendes Lernen im Bielefelder Praxissemester. In C. Freitag/I.
von Bargen (Hrsg.), *Praxisforschung in der Lehrerbildung* (S. 75–84). Berlin, Münster: LiT.

Koch-Priewe, B./Thiele, J. (2009). Versuch einer Systematisierung der hochschuldidaktischen
Konzepte zum Forschenden Lernen. In B. Roters/R. Schneider/B. Koch-Priewe/J. Thiele/J. Wildt
(Hrsg.), Forschendes Lernen im Lehramtsstudium (S. 271–292). Bad Heilbrunn: Klinkhardt.

Leonhard, T./Nagel, N./Rihm, T./Strittmatter-Haubold, V./Wengert-Richter, P. (2010).
Zur Entwicklung von Reflexionskompetenz bei Lehramtsstudierenden. In A. Gehrmann/
U. Hericks/M. Lüders (Hrsg.), *Bildungsstandards und Kompetenzmodelle* (S. 111–127). Bad
Heilbrunn: Klinkhardt.

Roters, B./Schneider, R./Koch-Priewe, B./Thiele, J./Wildt, J. (Hrsg.). (2009). Forschendes Lernen
im Lehramtsstudium. Bad Heilbrunn: Klinkhardt.

Terhart, E. (2000). Perspektiven der Lehrerbildung in Deutschland. Abschlussbericht der von der
Kultusministerkonferenz eingesetzten Kommission. Weinheim, Basel: Beltz.

Wilde, M./Stiller, C. (2011). Ansätze Forschenden Lernens in der Biologiedidaktik an der Uni
Bielefeld. *TRiOS, 6*(2), 171–183.

Wischer, B./Katenbrink, N./Nakumura, Y. (2014). Forschendes Lernen in der (Osnabrücker)
Lehrerbildung – eine einführende Problemskizze. In dies. (Hrsg.), *Forschendes Lernen in der
Osnabrücker Lehrerausbildung* (S. 5–26). Münster: MV Wissenschaft.

Wissenschaftsrat (2001). Empfehlungen zur künftigen Struktur der Lehrerbildung. Drs. 5065/01.
Berlin.

Inquiry-Based Learning in Social Work

13

Alexandra Schmidt-Wenzel and Katrin Rubel

Research-led teaching is designed to give students the opportunity to engage with their learning process and develop the skills needed to build their professional identity through active participation in the scientific cognitive process. Here in particular, social workers need *research-oriented behavior*, hermeneutic competencies and reflexivity in order to master the imminent requirements of case comprehension and case processing in a professional way.

13.1 Research-led Teaching – Central Aspects

From a *subject-scientific* perspective, learning is understood to be a social, subjectively justified action, embedded in the respective social relations. Learning processes are therefore not extrinsically available and, at best, can be supported by others. Perceived action problems that are to be overcome in order to secure or expand the individual capacity to act represent the starting points of learning processes (Holzkamp 1995). Elaborating on this, Joachim Ludwig (2014) assumes that, in addition to learning processes, research activities also begin with the perception of current action problems and – in the event that this is accompanied by the development of knowledge – ideally results in an expansion in

A. Schmidt-Wenzel, Prof. Dr. (✉)
Fachhochschule Potsdam, Fachbereich Sozial- und Bildungswissenschaften, Professur für Soziale Arbeit mit dem Schwerpunkt Pädagogik der Lebensalter, Potsdam, Germany
e-mail: schmidt-wenzel@fh-potsdam.de

K. Rubel, M.A.
Fachhochschule Potsdam, Fachbereich Sozial- und Bildungswissenschaften, Potsdam, Germany
e-mail: rubel@fh-potsdam.de

© The Author(s) 2019
H. A. Mieg (ed.), *Inquiry-Based Learning – Undergraduate Research*,
https://doi.org/10.1007/978-3-030-14223-0_13

social participation. He therefore argues in favor of designing a "teaching in the format of research" (Ludwig 2014, p. 12), in which the teaching content can be linked with students' action problems in order to develop behavior-influencing questions, in the course of which students can participate in scientific cognitive processes.

According to Wolfgang Fichten and Hilbert Meyer (2014), student research is only realized if the collection and evaluation of the data has been done in a methodologically controlled manner in accordance with scientific standards. Learning processes that are intended to go beyond a mechanical practice of data collection and evaluation require consistent reference to the subject, as well as critical engagement with the researchers' (own) research practice (Fichten and Meyer 2014). Against this background, the present article will summarize, as *research-led teaching*, all of the teaching settings that seek to link research and teaching, and that invite students to actively engage in the process of generating scientific knowledge. The range extends from courses in which it is possible to integrate student learning (and research) questions into the discursive debate on epistemo-logical foundations and research methodologies to the formats of students' direct involve-ment in real research projects, for example within the context of teaching research projects.

Research-led teaching should, in principle, address all students, not just those who see their future career path in science. By critically considering and applying specialist and methodical knowledge, it is possible to acquire key occupational qualifications. The focus will be on skills required for method-based action – for the analysis and critical classifica-tion of the resulting findings – in each case with the goal of being able to form one's own position, including in relationship with the professional community. Reflecting on one's (own) cognitive process simultaneously promotes conscious responsibility for one's own learning processes. For the introductory phase of the course of study, Ludwig (2012) emphasizes the goal of accompanying students from the learning culture that characterizes school into the scientific research culture as well as of introducing them to the specific subject culture. Associated therewith is the challenge that students learn to differentiate between everyday knowledge and scientific knowledge in the future, and ideally be able to use both forms of knowledge productively.

13.2 Social Work – Reflexivity and Hermeneutic Competence as Central Developmental Goals

The central task of the bachelor's degree in social work is to prepare students for very heterogeneous and complex fields of work, which are characterized by ambiguity and inconsistency. The professional actors face the challenge of having to grasp the specific problems of the addressees of social work in a differentiated and contextualized manner and to open up scientifically justified options for action on the basis of a professional working alliance (Oevermann 2013).

Despite available planning strategies and methods of action, social workers cannot handle life praxes that have become critical in a standardized way if they wish to be professionally active. Rather, they must fundamentally consider each individual case unto itself, but also grasp that case in terms of its situatedness in the social milieu in order to be able to make appropriate recommendations for action in accordance with the specific life praxis. At the same time, they are called upon to tolerate recurrent antinomies and uncertainties, and to process these by relating them to one another (Oevermann 2013; Becker-Lenz and Müller-Hermann 2013). The development of a professional identity therefore requires a highly reflective approach to the knowledge acquired (Dewe and Otto 2012) and also includes the capacity for critical reflection on existing power structures and embeddedness in the form of societal disciplinary measures (Oevermann 2013).

At its core, professional action in social work practice is based on a complex process of *understanding the case* based on the inductive-deductive interplay of a case analysis; over the course of this analysis – however it may be organized – processes for providing assistance must be kept dynamic. Those who are professionally active must therefore always reassure themselves of the appropriateness of the options once selected. Both the primary case information and the subsequent (self-)reflection process about the course of the case are based on the same professional approach, as outlined by Ulrich Oevermann (ibid.).

Thus it is initially an issue of recognizing and understanding the idiosyncrasy, the agents' inherent, subjective horizons of meaning. It is only in the next step, the reconstruction of the case structure, that the challenge becomes to identify the generalizable patterns hidden within it and to make them accessible to methodologically motivated processing, while recognizing the realized inner logic. The necessary central capability can be understood as a capacity for self-reflection and enables the specific relation of scientific knowledge and professional action strategy in socio-pedagogical practice (Schmidt-Wenzel 2012). Consequently, the practice alone can become the venue for professional activity that must constantly be rearranged.

13.3   Research-Led Teaching in the Study of Social Work – An Overview

Although research in social work has a long tradition (Miethe and Schneider 2010), Thomas Rauschenbach and Werner Thole (1998) critically scrutinized the research culture of social pedagogy in 1998. They call for stronger profiling as well as a scholarly debate on research in the subject as well as for supportive basic conditions for expanding research, with an eye towards the relevance of research to formation, stabilization and recognition as a scientific discipline. In the meantime, a social-pedagogical research landscape has established itself. It has a variety of research approaches (Schefold 2012), as well as a lively discourse on its own research practice, which grapples with the requirements for social-pedagogical issues, for example (Oelerich and Otto 2011). These developments have and still do influence the academic education for the professional field of social work.

Thus, research-led teaching has long since played a role in shaping higher education instruction for degree programs in social work and is echoed in various teaching formats. *Teaching research projects*, which allow students to work on research questions independently by incorporating their previously acquired knowledge and methodological knowledge, are very popular. They are supervised in this learning and research process by instructors. The structure and configuration of the project's contents are very heterogeneous (e.g. Schimpf and Göbel 2015; Pichler 2009; Schmitt 2007). However, *internships* are also used to carry out student research projects, which are then flanked by research-methodological seminars (e.g. Griesenhop and Hanses 2005). *Research workshops*, on the other hand, are places where students should be supported with mutual critical exchanges, especially during data analysis (e.g. Reim and Riemann 1997). In addition to these teaching formats, which allow students to conduct research themselves, there are courses in which students grapple with the research methodology of research projects that have already been carried out in critical-reflective discussions (e.g. Riemann 2010).

Three essential goals are pursued when incorporating social-pedagogical research in the study of social work, according to Gisela Jakob (2005). Firstly, students become familiar with relevant research methods that will enable them to critically classify future scientific studies in terms of their cognitive value. Secondly, collaboration in (student) research projects allows students to become familiar with and take on the role of researcher, and to thereby reflect on potential correlations between their own biographical experience and their subjective actions in the research process. Thirdly, by implementing qualitative-reconstructive research methods in particular, students can further develop their capacities for analysis and self-reflection, which are important competencies for future professional practice in the field of social work. Here, this must not result in a shortened transfer of research methods to action methods. At issue instead is preserving the open, self-reflective mode of knowing developed over the course of qualitative research for future professional practice (ibid.).

The focus on qualitative-reconstructive research methods in the study of social work (Jakob 2005; Kricheldorff 2010) is due, inter alia, to the tenets and principles of these methods. In the tradition of qualitative research, complex life situations must be grasped from the perspective of those who have been researched in order to subsequently reconstruct the subjective contexts in the course of the assessment and analysis, taking into account their social interconnection. In teaching research projects in which qualitative research methods are applied, students already have direct access to potentially unfamiliar living environments within the context of their data collection. This insight can mean a broadening of perspectives for them with reference to the existing diversity of social reality. The reconstruction and analysis of those living environments is done from a reflective distance within the context of the assessment (Hanses 2012). The dominance of qualitative research methods in the study of social work is also reflected in the literature, which presents examples of teaching formats utilizing research-led teaching (e.g. Schimpf and Göbel 2015; Schmitt 2007; Griesenhop and Hanses 2005).

In addition to the generally emphasized importance of action and reflective competencies, Ingrid Miehte and Johannes Steher (2007) stress that participation in teaching research projects fosters the independence of students, who (must) plan and perform the research process autonomously. While freely selecting the research question may be perceived as especially inspiring and supports the development of an intractable research attitude, commissioned research is faced with the challenge that the differing interests of clients, researchers and subjects must be taken into consideration in the research design (ibid.). In research-led teaching settings, instructors should primarily function as advisors who support students, especially when faced with difficult situations, so that errors and problems can be perceived as possible learning approaches.

13.4 Practical Example: Core Format of Research-led Teaching in the Bachelor's Degree Program in Social Work at the University of Applied Sciences Potsdam

A comprehensive concept for research-led teaching was developed at the University of Applied Sciences Potsdam (FH Potsdam) for the bachelor's degree program in social work, which allows all students to approach the subject matter being learned from an explorative perspective throughout the entire course of studies in teaching formats that are anchored in the curriculum. All students take part in the two-semester workshop at the beginning of their academic studies. In the fourth semester, students complete a supervised internship. In the last two semesters of study, they choose between an instructor project and a student project.

13.4.1 Core Format of Workshop

Since the winter semester of 1996/1997, the two-semester workshop has been implemented as a mode of a structured degree program phase in the module system for the degree program in social work at FH Potsdam, and thereby connects three foundational perspectives that can scarcely be discussed independently of one another. For the sake of clarity, however, this separation is temporarily carried out here.

Firstly, the module supports student socialization in the general *research and learning culture at an institution of higher learning*, which, as a rule, clearly stands out among previous learning experiences within the context of the institutional acquisition of knowledge. The group, which meets once a week for a full day (known as the "workshop day"), forms at the start of the semester based on the individual decision in favor of one of six available framework topics.

The core goal in the second concern of the workshop module is to allow students direct access to the *subject culture of social work*. How does one speak in theory and how does one speak in practice about the societal problems inherent in social work? How does one behave and with what professional justifications? Where do those who practice the profession see themselves?

And thus the third concern of the workshop module has already been formulated: *direct work with the subject matter in a research-led teaching mode*. After a theoretical and methodical introduction, students work on a self-chosen issue. They approach the subject matter in an interest-led exploratory movement and test their methodological and subject-related knowledge for the first time. Students not infrequently come up against unexpected obstacles in research practice and are confronted with the current limits of their own abilities in the course thereof as well. A central teaching task of instructors is to help students learn to acknowledge failures and wrong turns as unavoidable, even logical stages on the way to occupational professionalism and that these can be used as opportunities for development.

13.4.2 Core Format of Internship

The fourth semester is the practical semester within the degree program in social work. Students must go about finding an internship placement that is suitable for their (learning) interests early in the process. "University day" takes place once a week, during which students leave their institutions to participate in supervision classes and practical supervision seminars in alternation. Both courses complement one another as spaces for exchanging opinions with other students, as a podium for clarifying current problems in which – committed to its original intention – the focus of supervision is on advising in case-specific action problems and the involvement of the individual.

Practical supervision seminars, on the other hand, seek to clarify structural and subject-related methodological questions. During these consultations, the student practice projects in particular are on the horizon. This is because students are required to initiate, carry out and, ultimately, evaluate an action or a research project. Students can freely select the topic and method for these projects, however. If the focus of these research projects is on empirically researching a subject from the current field of practice, action projects deal more significantly with the implementation of concrete project ideas in the respective institution, for example organizing an exhibit, a theme day, etc., while the research orientation is only indirect.

13.4.3 Core Format of an Instructor/Student Project

At the end of their studies, students have the opportunity to pursue their current learning and research interests for two semesters. The theory-practice module offers two different modes for this, which allow a possible tie-in to students' interests, to some extent to varying degrees. On the one hand, there is the chance to carry out what is known as a "student project" in relative autonomy, in collaboration with other students. On the other hand, it is possible to work on an "instructor project," which, as the name already suggests, is based on the notion of a corresponding initiative of the respective instructor.

We will first outline the model for the student project here; the model allows self-determined learning in accordance with one's own interests like no other didactic concept in the course of studies so far. Thus, within the context of the student projects, which start in the fifth semester, it is possible to engage intensively with a topic identified as a problem in a student working group and work on that topic from a scientific perspective. In this context, students work independently with a free time schedule and with minimal instructor support, which becomes an issue when an actual need for advising arises. As a general rule, such needs are of a methodological or conceptual nature.

Within the context of so-called instructor projects, students become part of a scholarly cognitive process under the guidance of an instructor, said project either focusing on an action problem that must be solved in practice, or that pursues a specific research question within the context of empirical social research. In contrast to the student projects, there is a significantly more intensive collaboration between students and instructors in the case of the instructor project, since both are directly involved in the same working process, working cooperatively on a single project.

The findings and benefits of the work and research processes completed in the course of the student or instructor projects are presented for discussion at the end of the sixth semester both in the form of detailed written reports, and in the form of presentations that are often accessible to the entire university (e.g. as exhibitions or at conferences that are based on the project).

13.5   Conclusion

The exemplary depiction of teaching formats and the mediation contexts on which they are based show that research-led teaching has the potential to allow students to be exposed to knowledge that is oriented towards their interests right at the start of their studies. A series of general requirements both for the basic conditions and for the agents involved can be formulated for the design of these teaching settings. In principle, all of those involved, both instructors and students, face the challenge of engaging in an open, uncertain learning and research process. While the students actively contribute to the project, formulate their questions and ideas, and work autonomously on the jointly coordinated steps in the research team, it is the task of the instructors to assist the students and tolerate their potential self-will, and not prematurely provide their own expertise and methodological knowledge (cf., for example, Miethe and Stehr 2007).

The presented teaching formats from FH Potsdam provide all of these creative spaces and give students the opportunity to participate in scientific cognitive processes via a reflective engagement with relevant bodies of knowledge and research methods, thereby creating the foundation for the development of their own professional identity. Against this backdrop, the formats for research-led teaching in the bachelor's degree program in social work that are established in the curriculum actually serve an orienting function, even for other disciplines. Utilizing this potential, including in the sense of interdisciplinary work has currently led to the idea at FH Potsdam of allowing students in various disciplines to conduct research on a current social problem that they select themselves over the course of the first and second semester.

References

Becker-Lenz, R./Müller-Hermann, S. (2013). Die Notwendigkeit von wissenschaftlichem Wissen und die Bedeutung eines professionellen Habitus für die Berufspraxis der Sozialen Arbeit. In R. Becker-Lenz/S. Busse/G. Ehlert/S. Müller-Hermann (Hrsg.), *Professionalität in der Sozialen Arbeit. Standpunkte, Kontroversen, Perspektiven* (3. Auflage) (S. 203–228). Wiesbaden: Springer VS.

Dewe, B./Otto, H.-U. (2012). Reflexive Sozialpädagogik. Grundstrukturen eines neuen Typs dienstleistungsorientierten Professionshandelns. In W. Thole (Hrsg.), *Grundriss Soziale Arbeit: Ein einführendes Handbuch* (4. Auflage) (S. 197–217). Wiesbaden: Springer VS.

Fichten, W./Meyer, H. (2014). Skizze einer Theorie forschenden Lernens in der Lehrer_innenbildung. In E. Feyerer/K. Hirschenhauser/K. Soukup-Altrichter (Hrsg.), *Last oder Lust? Forschung und Lehrer_innenbildung* (S. 11–42). Münster: Waxmann.

Griesenhop, H. R./Hanses, A. (2005). Forschungspraktika im Studium der Sozialen Arbeit – Über die Bedeutung sozialer Lernprozesse hinsichtlich Aneignung rekonstruktiver Methoden und Perspektiven. In C. Thon/D. Rothe/P. Mecheril/B. Dausien (Hrsg.), *Qualitative Forschungsmethoden im erziehungswissenschaftlichen Studium*. Bielefeld. Retrieved 02 April 2016 from https://pub.uni-bielefeld.de/download/2302143/2302152

Hanses, A. (2012). Forschende Praxis als Professionalisierung. Herstellung von Reflexivität durch forschendes Lernen im Studium Sozialer Arbeit. In R. Becker-Lenz/S. Busse/G. Ehlert/S. Müller-Hermann (Hrsg.), *Professionalität Sozialer Arbeit und Hochschule: Wissen, Kompetenz, Habitus und Identität im Studium Sozialer Arbeit* (S. 187–200). Wiesbaden: Springer VS.

Holzkamp, K. (1995). *Lernen. Subjektwissenschaftliche Grundlegung* (Studienausg.). Frankfurt am Main [u. a.]: Campus-Verlag.

Jakob, G. (2005). Forschung in der Ausbildung zur Sozialen Arbeit. In W. Thole (Hrsg.), *Grundriss Soziale Arbeit: Ein einführendes Handbuch* (2. überarbeitete und aktualisierte Auflage) (S. 929–941). Wiesbaden: VS Verlag für Sozialwissenschaften.

Kricheldorff, C. (2010). Das Kerncurriculum Forschung in der Sozialen Arbeit. Von der normativen Handlungsorientierung zur empirisch fundierten Intervention. In K. Bock/I. Miethe (Hrsg.), *Handbuch Qualitative Methoden in der Sozialen Arbeit* (S. 566–572). Opladen [u. a.]: Barbara Budrich.

Ludwig, J. (2012). Studieneingangsphasen als Professionalitätsproblem. In P. Kossack, U. Lehmann/J. Ludwig (Hrsg.), *Die Studieneingangsphase - Analyse, Gestaltung und Entwicklung* (S. 45–56). Bielefeld: UniversitätsVerlagWebler.

Ludwig, J. (2014). Lehre im Format der Forschung. *BBHD (Brandenburgische Beiträge zur Hochschuldidaktik)*, (7). Retrieved 09 March 2015 from https://publishup.uni-potsdam.de/opus4-ubp/files/6860/bbhd07.pdf

Miethe, I./Schneider, A. (2010). Sozialarbeitsforschung – Forschung in der Sozialen Arbeit. Traditionslinien – Kontroversen – Gegenstände. In S. B. Gahleitner, H. Effinger, B. Kraus, I. Miethe, S. Stövesand/J. Sagebiel (Hrsg.), *Disziplin und Profession Sozialer Arbeit. Entwicklungen und Perspektiven* (S. 61–74). Opladen [u. a.]: Barbara Budrich.

Miethe, I./Stehr, J. (2007). Modularisierung und Forschendes Lernen. Erfahrungen und hochschuldidaktische Konsequenzen. *neue praxis*, 37(3), 250–264.

Oelerich, G./Otto, H.-U. (2011). Empirische Forschung und Soziale Arbeit – Einführung. In G. Oelerich/H.-U. Otto (Hrsg.), *Empirische Forschung und Soziale Arbeit. Ein Studienbuch* (S. 9–22). Wiesbaden: Springer VS.

Oevermann, U. (2013). Die Problematik der Strukturlogik des Arbeitsbündnisses und der Dynamik von Übertragung und Gegenübertragung in einer professionalisierten Praxis von Sozialarbeit. In R. Becker-Lenz/S. Busse/G. Ehlert/S. Müller-Hermann (Hrsg.), *Professionalität in der Sozialen Arbeit. Standpunkte, Kontroversen, Perspektiven* (S. 119–147). Wiesbaden: Springer VS.

Pichler, M. (2009). Theorie-Praxis-Bezug in der Forschungs- und Projektarbeit an Fachhochschulen am Beispiel des Forschungsprojektes Schulsozialarbeit. In A. Riegler, S. Hojnik/K. Posch (Hrsg.), *Soziale Arbeit zwischen Profession und Wissenschaft. Vermittlungsmöglichkeiten in der Fachhochschulausbildung* (S. 169–184). Wiesbaden: VS Verlag für Sozialwissenschaften.

Rauschenbach, T./Thole, W. (1998). Sozialpädagogik – ein Fach ohne Forschungskultur? Einleitende Beobachtungen. In T. Rauschenbach/W. Thole (Hrsg.), *Sozialpädagogische Forschung: Gegenstand und Funktion, Bereiche und Methoden* (S. 9–28). Weinheim: Juventa.

Reim, T./Riemann, G. (1997). Die Forschungswerkstatt. Erfahrungen aus der Arbeit mit Studentinnen und Studenten der Sozialarbeit/Sozialpädagogik und der Supervision. In G. Jakob/H.-J. von Wensierski (Hrsg.), *Rekonstruktive Sozialpädagogik. Konzepte und Methoden sozialpädagogischen Verstehens in Forschung und Praxis* (S. 223–238). Weinheim: Juventa.

Riemann, G. (2010). Formen der Vermittlung fallanalytischer Forschungskompetenz im Studium der Sozialen Arbeit. In K. Bock/I. Miethe (Hrsg.), *Handbuch Qualitative Methoden in der Sozialen Arbeit* (S. 550–560). Opladen: Barbara Budrich.

Schefold, W. (2012). Sozialpädagogische Forschung. Stand und Perspektiven. In W. Thole (Hrsg.), *Grundriss Soziale Arbeit: Ein einführendes Handbuch* (4. Auflage) (S. 1123–1144). Wiesbaden: Springer VS.

Schimpf, E./Göbel, A. (2015). Forschendes Lernen als Möglichkeit der Auseinandersetzung mit gesellschaftlichen Macht- und Konfliktverhältnissen. In A. Schneider/M. Kötting/D. Molnar (Hrsg.), *Forschung in der Sozialen Arbeit. Grundlagen – Konzepte – Perspektiven* (S. 113–127). Opladen [u. a.]: Barbara Budrich.

Schmidt-Wenzel, A. (2012). Pädagogische Professionalität als Entwicklungsaufgabe. Eine empirische Analyse von Transformationsprozessen in einer Selbstlernarchitektur. In D. Wrana/C. Maier Reinhard (Hrsg.), *Professionalisierung in Lernberatungsgesprächen. Theoretische Grundlegungen und Empirische Untersuchungen* (S. 287–300). Opladen [u. a.]: Barbara Budrich.

Schmitt, R. (2007). Die Lehre qualitativer Forschung im Studium der Sozialen Arbeit: Ein Erfahrungsbericht von Nebenschauplätzen. Diskussionsbeitrag zur FQS-Debatte »Lehren und Lernen der Methoden qualitativer Sozialforschung«. *Forum Qualitative Sozialforschung / Forum Qualitative Social Research*, 8(1). Retrieved 10 March 2015 from http://www.qualitative-research.net/index.php/fqs/article/view/219/484

Inquiry-Based Learning in Information Science

Inquiry-Based Learning in Information Science

14

Antje Michel and Hans-Christoph Hobohm

Inquiry-based learning has selectively found its way into the teaching of information science – not as a didactic guiding principle, however. In the following article, the basic conditions for research in information science and the application of methods in the discipline will be used to work out the opportunities provided by using inquiry-based learning formats in information science.[1]

14.1 Basic Conditions for Information Science Research

Information science is a relatively new discipline within the scientific landscape. The increasing production of scientific information as well as its integration into mechanisms of economic exploitation and political utilization – which, for example, became apparent in 1957 as a result of what became known as the "Sputnik crisis" – required that the process of conveying information be professionalized to the same degree as the process of generating information in research and development (Kuhlen 2013). A major impetus for

---

[1] This article focuses on the didactic potential of inquiry-based learning in German information science. Determining the extent to which the presented inventory is also of international relevance would require closer consideration.

A. Michel, Prof. Dr. (✉)
Fachhochschule Potsdam, Fachbereich Informationswissenschaften,
Professur für Informationsdidaktik und Wissenstransfer, Potsdam, Germany
e-mail: michel@fh-potsdam.de

H.-C. Hobohm, Prof. Dr.
Fachhochschule Potsdam, Fachbereich Informationswissenschaften,
Professur für Bibliothekswissenschaft, Potsdam, Germany
e-mail: hobohm@fh-potsdam.de

© The Author(s) 2019
H. A. Mieg (ed.), *Inquiry-Based Learning – Undergraduate Research*,
https://doi.org/10.1007/978-3-030-14223-0_14

149

the development of academic information science in the Western world came in the wake of the social and scientific-political discourse as a result of the Weinberg report, as "information," understood as the meritorious good and common good, drew increasing attention (Weinberg et al. 1963).

In Germany, information science was developed as a concept based on the documentation science founded in approximately 1895 by Paul Odlet. In terms of content, these days they are an integration of documentation science, library science and archival science and focus on the social concepts of "information" and "knowledge" from the perspectives of information processing, of the representation of knowledge, of "information retrieval" (thus the computer-aided search for complex content), of information behavior and of information transfer (Umlauf 2011). In the international context, they have always been associated with the provision of information as "library and information science" (abbreviated as LIS).

Although information science is more or less extensively anchored at a total of 12 institutions of higher learning in Germany and information science research activities occur at a pace commensurate with this number, Germany lacks a genuine information science research culture. There are three essential reasons for this:

First, a large proportion of scientists in information science and research in Germany also belong to other disciplines. This is the result of the fact that a high proportion of information science education takes place at universities of applied sciences. Since these institutions do not possess an independent right to award doctorates, German information science has a small number of highly talented junior researchers. In the Anglo-American and Scandinavian countries, information science is established in postgraduate studies (Bawden and Robinson 2012).

Secondly, despite the attention in terms of scientific policy paid to the central concepts of information science, there is no institutionalized funding structure for research in information science in Germany. This is reflected especially prominently in Germany in the absence of a continuous funding line in the German Research Foundation (DFG). The lack of a funding structure makes it difficult to develop a longer-term epistemological and research-related discourse for the further development of the discipline of information science.

Thirdly, the training of junior scientists is primarily practice-oriented. This is due, on the one hand, to the highly profession-related design of the curricula in the corresponding bachelor's degree programs at the universities of applied sciences, which is highly focused on the professions, and on the study interests of students on the other, which are highly focused on professional training, and finally on the prevalence of practice orientation in existing research. The result of the high practical relevance of education results is that it is only occasionally possible for students to develop a scientific identity that is characterized by information science. The perception that a familiarity with scientific methods and working methods is an essential qualification for a later occupational or academic career is simply less pronounced (Booth and Brice 2004).

14.2   Research Methodology in Information Science and Opportunities Through the Use of Inquiry-Based Learning

According to Hider and Pymm (2008), research in information science is characterized by:

1. an overall broad quantitative and qualitative range of methods,
2. a focus on the application of quantitative research methods,
3. the dominance of surveys and experiments as methods,
4. a high proportion of publications without reference to a research method.

Bawden and Robinson (2012) expound on the problems related to the sample sizes, which are frequently small, and the result thereof, which is that information science research is insufficiently generalizable. An analysis of big data, which would be expected due to the technical roots of information science in documentation science and the consequent obvious methodical approaches such as logfile analyses, could not yet be entirely demonstrated in the study by Hider and Pymm with their dataset from 2005. Insofar as it is possible to take the more recent findings from Greifeneder (2014) – which focused on information behavior research and concluded that the use of big data analyses has thus far been low, but is ever increasing – and transfer those findings to the entire discipline, such analyses seem to be slowly finding their way into information science.

A transfer of the data collected by Hider and Pymm to the situation facing German information science should be treated with caution, however. To begin with, the data of Hider and Pymm focuses on Anglosphere publications and, as already mentioned above, the establishment of information science academia is significantly more advanced in the United States and in Great Britain than it is in Germany. In addition, the authors have focused explicitly on basic research and the analysis of practice-oriented research and its methods. However, as already described, this makes up the majority of German-language research in information science. A cautious thesis as to the methodological situation in German information science could be that, due to the basic conditions that are implemented, it can be assumed that the application of methods will be based more on small-scaled quantitative and on more or less theory-saturated qualitative studies than was determined for the Anglosphere research area.

That methodological reflection in German information science tends to still be in its infancy can also be deduced from the fact that the first German-language manual for information science methodologies was only published in 2013. Even in this manual, information science is referred to as an empirical discipline characterized by a low proportion of epistemological meta-reflection and a range of methods largely derived from the social sciences, ethnology and information science (Umlauf et al. 2013). Historically rooted between technology and social science, information science offers a diverse range of methods that, in Germany, is extended into research and teaching in information science due to the integration of scientists originating in other disciplines. The challenge for research in information science is in competently applying this range of methods in research and teaching. It is desirable for information science to have a shared body of methods and the classification thereof as canon for teaching, as Hider and Pymm also explain in their article.

In addition to the wide range of methods that characterizes research in information science, the discipline has an additional special characteristic, which is relevant in terms of its use in inquiry-based teaching-learning methods: In practice, the central field of activity for "information professionals" lies in the collection, development and provision of information *for* a specific target group and in determining competencies for dealing with existing information resources and their carrier media. In terms of methodology, information professionals must not only to be able to organize their own information needs, but must also be able to take on roles in order to anticipate and serve the information needs of other target groups. This requires a capacity for reflection, understood as meta-competence, which involves reflecting one's own position in relation to the situation of another person and the parameters of the relevant social environment (Hobohm et al. 2015). Therefore, practitioners must be especially capable of researching the need for information as well as the specific handling of information for their target groups, and of developing creative concepts in order to adequately satisfy them. Even in professional practice, research-oriented behavior is effective and should therefore be the subject of teaching in information science.

The following goals for the use of concepts and methods of inquiry-based learning in information science can be derived from the previous explanations: To begin with, students should be familiarized with the process of scientific work in a discipline with a very heterogeneous range of methods, and should be given the ability to work with the methods in a research-oriented manner. Moreover, students should be socialized so that they develop research-oriented thinking and activity, giving them the ability to objectively apply the instruments of information science research appropriately, both within the context of a later academic career and, in particular, when starting a career in an information science profession.

14.3 Concept and Implementation of Inquiry-Based Learning in Information Science

To date (i.e., at the time of writing the original German version of this article in February 2016), inquiry-based learning has only occasionally been implemented in individual courses of the various information science degree programs in Germany, if at all. It is only seldom applied as a guiding didactic concept for an academic education in information science. Comparing the curricula for information science bachelor's degree programs in the German-speaking area shows that project work is implemented as an element of inquiry-based learning at almost all institutions of higher learning; however, the percentage of such work in the workload of the overall curriculums is frequently low or cannot be precisely determined. The research orientation of teaching and the use of research-based teaching-learning methods as a didactic guiding principle in teaching are only explicitly emphasized in the study documentation at HTW Chur and FH Potsdam.

To date, there have been very few meta-reflective publications regarding a research orientation in information science. One such publication describes the situation at HTW Chur (Schuldt and Mumenthaler 2015). Although there are differences between German and Swiss academic information science, the situation is quite comparable in terms of its strong focus and location at a university of applied sciences. As part of a curriculum revision in the fall of 2015, HTW Chur has begun to expand the already-selective incorporation of scientific methodology in its information science curriculum. In the new curriculum at HTW Chur, in addition to courses for imparting survey knowledge into the research methods in the field, there are now a greater number of project courses, in which elements of the scientific research process or an entire student research method are planned, carried out and documented independently (ibid.). Additional publications have come into existence within the context of a research project at the University of Applied Sciences Potsdam (see Box 14.1).

Among the various concepts and models for inquiry-based learning which are in part described in this book, the Zurich framework (Tremp and Hildbrand 2012) is especially suited in our view for providing a framework for the requirements on information science in terms of a concept for inquiry-based learning as worked out in this article (for more, see Mieg, in this volume).

The starting point for the Zurich framework is the belief that the main objective of academic studies is a "university education" (ibid., p. 104). Providing students with the ability "to think and act in a scholarly manner" (ibid.) can be derived as a general study objective from the postulate of a university education. The framework makes the aforementioned problems in developing a scholarly identity in information science clear: "A university education thereby focuses on the development of an academic personality, which is characterized in equal degree by creativity and methodological skill, and which is committed to scholarly attitudes and values" (ibid., p. 104–105, translated).

In our view, one of the strengths of the Zurich framework is that, at the course level, there are no requirements for the compulsory use of certain teaching formats, which may not really be transferrable to the specific basic conditions of a university and its curricula under certain circumstances. Rather, it encourages retaining the diversity of forms of teaching and developing the strengths of each for integration into the framework at the level of curriculum development. The visualization of the frameworks can be found in this volume in the article by Mieg (Fig. 1.3).

Using the Zurich framework, a curriculum need not necessarily be completely redesigned and based entirely on extensive student research projects. Rather, it is much more important to provide students early with a general overview of the research process as reflected in the specific subject culture. It is possible to explain, practice and reflect on the different stages of the research process that build on one another in a modular way within the various courses. If the principle of "research as a central idea" is maintained

Box 14.1: *Developing Research Competencies in the Information Professions*

In 2012–2014, a BMBF research project at the University of Applied Sciences Potsdam investigated the interdisciplinary competencies in the professional practice of information specialists: "Akademische Kompetenzen in den Informationsberufen (AKIB)" ("Academic competencies in the information professions"). One of the results was the empirical identification of the core competencies of this professional field as a metacognitive reflective competence. On the one hand, this is expressed in the taking on of roles in conjunction with the intermediary position of information professionals; on the other, however, it also points to the important core task of information scientists in the generation of data via data ("metadata" such as catalogs or other "finding aids"). Against this background, an e-learning-based "self-study course on scientific work" was developed for students and continuing education participants in the Department of Informational Sciences, with the aim of familiarizing them with the concept of university study as research right from the first semester on. Unlike other introductions to scholarly work, the model – which has been designed to be appealing with interactive multimedia – focuses less on formalities and more on research attitude. It is available to students throughout their studies, beyond the workshop module in the first semester, in the mode of peer learning.

Accompanying this, an online training course was developed for lecturers teaching blended learning courses concerning implementing the format of inquiry-based learning, which likewise addresses the metacognitive approaches of the professional field and which is based on connectivist didactic approaches. Understanding the metacognitive situation of "learning how to learn" is especially important for instructors in this context (cf. AKIB n.d.; Hobohm et al. 2015; Pfeffing et al. 2018).

Another important component of the commitment of the University of Applied Sciences Potsdam on the topic of analyzing and conveying competency in information science within the meaning described here is the establishment of the internationally innovative field of "informational didactics" with a newly established professorship.

throughout the entire curriculum, then students should be socialized to such a degree that they are prepared to carry out their research project as a "final project."

The activities associated with implementing inquiry-based learning as a didactic guiding principle in the Department of Informational Sciences at FH Potsdam will be described in greater detail below. The process can be described in a manner analogous to the Zurich framework in terms of fundamental didactic ideas and the institutional levels.

FH Potsdam provides good basic conditions for developing inquiry-based learning formats and integrating these in the degree programs at the university: In addition to a large-scale third-party project for inquiry-based learning "FL^2" (inquiry-based learning – instructional research), a development program for interdisciplinary courses focused on inquiry-based learning has existed for years (cf. depiction of the Interflex program in the article by Prytula et al., in this volume). The aim of these tools is to link research activities within the university with teaching. The Department of Informational Sciences' requirements for systematically anchoring inquiry-based learning in the curricula of the degree programs are favorable:

1. The Department of Informational Sciences is research-oriented and has strong third-party funding.
2. It follows the link between research and teaching in the further development of the curricula for all degree programs. Thus didactic elements of inquiry-based learning, for example, are implemented in all three reaccredited bachelor's degree programs, which will start as of the 2016/17 winter semester.
3. Instructional student research projects have been successfully carried out for years.

Concrete planning for the bachelor's degree programs explicitly integrate inquiry-based learning. The implementation strategy was developed in the same way as the Zurich framework to the effect that inquiry-based learning is not focused on individual, large-scale project phases, but as a didactic principle throughout the entire curriculum.

In the new curricula of the three bachelor's degree programs that are occurring in a partially integrated manner, a teaching format was introduced right in the first semester with the workshop module (2 semester hours per week), which made the research process in information science tangible right at the start of the course of studies through independent student research projects. This workshop module enables the didactically accompanied implementation of the first student research projects. Thus the research-based project work is to be practiced in a didactic form and transferred to practical knowledge.

What is especially important about the concept is that all instructors in the degree programs are involved in teaching in the workshop module. For example, it should hereby make the methodological breadth of information science tangible to students. Moreover, the didactic fine-tuning among teachers requires a consistent understanding of the different methodological and epistemological approaches to their discipline. During the course of study, the "workshop" is included repeatedly as a didactic form, e.g. in relatively comprehensive "project and supplementary seminars" (in part as interdisciplinary InterFlex courses) or, insofar as is useful to the content or didactic intent, in partial aspects of other courses.

According to the Zurich framework, the use of the other forms of teaching should be done in a reflective manner in that the instructors situate the teaching method in the research process in order to also consistently anchor the focus on the research process where the acquisition of specialist knowledge is in the foreground in terms of content, and to allow reflection on the transfers of accumulated knowledge to the research process.

14.4   Outlook: On the Perspective of Inquiry-Based Learning in Information Science

The most important measure for promoting inquiry-based learning in information science is promoting the awareness that research-oriented behavior is an essential basic competence not only in information science, but also in practical occupations related to information science. An important tool here is in experimenting with the form of inquiry-based learning in information science, in the research accompanying these activities and in obtaining feedback regarding the relevance of the research-oriented behavior in the information professions postulated in this article, for example by means of ongoing follow-up studies of graduates from the degree programs for information science and establishing other forms of theory-practice transfer.

It is also necessary to strengthen and increase the visibility of information science research at the level of science politics, because inquiry-based learning requires lively research at the academic training institutions. To this end, German information science must first grow stronger as a discipline in quantitative, institutional but also discursive-methodological terms, as explained in detail above. The publication of basic textbooks and handouts in German must be intensified. The discipline's status as a "small subject area" must also be pursued more intensely in terms of science politics and be reflected in the funding lines of the science-promoting institutions. The relevance of information science research will play an important role in this. The research affinity of the discipline, which has already been fostered to some extent by the Bologna Process, must be further increased, for example through the continued development or redevelopment of master's (and bachelor's) degree programs in information science, as well as through increased funding by third parties and, in particular, through the shared acceptance of research as the core activity of the research and teaching of the subject, which are strongly anchored in practice.

In addition, the relevance of research-oriented behavior for the dynamic professional field of information professionals must be promoted at the level of the information professions. Within this context, information-science research facilities must also establish themselves as agents in the transfer from theory to practice, that is, as information facilities within the sense of practical action based on evidentially founded information.

A quantitative and qualitative intensification of both internal and external scientific communication is needed in order to realize this agenda. Since the previous activities, statements and position papers failed to demonstrate the desired success, new strategies and formats of knowledge transfer need to be developed. Complementary to this strategy, what we have stated thus far will result in a completely distinct research program for informational didactics and the transfer of knowledge, which consists of working out the specifics of various information assets against the background of the prerequisites and practices of the respective, relevant knowledge cultures, as well as of the development of suitable didactic formats for the transfer of information and knowledge (cf. also Ballod 2007). Information literacy is not equally universal, despite the apparent public perception to the contrary due to the ubiquitous availability of information and knowledge resources. Rather, the correct handling of information and knowledge requires the systematic and scientifically secure construction of specific information-related competencies based on the development of meta-reflective, research-oriented behavior.

References

Akademische Kompetenzen in den Informationsberufen (AKIB) (n.d.). *Projektwebsite.* Retrieved 11 April 2016 from http://AKIB.fh-potsdam.de

Ballod, M. (2007). *Informationsökonomie - Informationsdidaktik: Strategien zur gesellschaftlichen, organisationalen und individuellen Informationsbewältigung und Wissensvermittlung.* Bielefeld: Bertelsmann.

Bawden, D./Robinson, L. (2012). *Introduction to Information Science* (Foundations of the information sciences). London: Facet.

Booth, A./Brice, A. (Hrsg.). (2004). *Evidence-based practice for information professionals: A handbook.* London: Facet.

Greifeneder, E. (2014). Trends in information behaviour research. *Information Research, 19*(4), 159–170.

Hider, P./Pymm, B. (2008). Empirical research methods reported in high-profile LIS journal literature. *Library & Information Science Research, 30*(2), 108–114.

Hobohm, H.-C./Pfeffing, J./Imhof, A./Groeneveld, I. (2015). »Reflexion« als Metakompetenz: Ein Konzeptbegriff zur Veranschaulichung akademischer Kompetenzen beim Übergang von beruflicher zu hochschulischer Qualifikation in den Informationsberufen. In W. K. Freitag/R. Buhr/E.-M. Danzeglocke/S. Schröder/D. Völk (Hrsg.), *Übergänge gestalten: Durchlässigkeit zwischen beruflicher und hochschulischer Bildung erhöhen* (S. 173–191). Münster: Waxmann.

Kuhlen, R. (2013). Information – Informationswissenschaft. In R. Kuhlen/W. Semar/D. Strauch (Hrsg.), *Grundlagen der praktischen Information und Dokumentation* (6. Auflage) (S. 19–42). Berlin: De Gruyter Saur.

Pfeffing, J./Mauch, M./Hobohm, H.-C. (2018). Die Potenziale Forschenden Lernens heben – eine Online-Weiterbildung zur Moderation von Lernprozessen für Hochschullehrende. In J. Lehmann/H. A. Mieg (Hrsg.), *Forschendes Lernen. Ein Praxisbuch* (S.472-485). Potsdam: FHP.

Schuldt, K./Mumenthaler, R. (2015). Forschungsmethoden in die Praxisausbildung einbinden? Ansätze an der HTW Chur. *Libreas. Library Ideas, 11*(27). Retrieved 15 March 2016 from http://libreas.eu/ausgabe27/04schuldt/

Tremp, P./Hildbrand, T. (2012). Forschungsorientiertes Studium – universitäre Lehre: Das »Zürcher Framework« zur Verknüpfung von Lehre und Forschung. In P. Tremp/T. Brinker (Hrsg.), *Blickpunkt Hochschuldidaktik: Vol. 122. Einführung in die Studiengangentwicklung* (S. 101–116). Bielefeld: Bertelsmann.

Umlauf, K. (2011). Bibliotheks- und Informationswissenschaft. In K. Umlauf/S. Gradmann (Hrsg.), *Lexikon der Bibliotheks- und Informationswissenschaft* (S. 91–93). Stuttgart: Hiersemann.

Umlauf, K./Fühles-Ubach, S./Seadle, M. (Hrsg.). (2013). *Handbuch Methoden der Bibliotheks-und Informationswissenschaft: Bibliotheks-, Benutzerforschung, Informationsanalyse.* Berlin: De Gruyter Saur. Retrieved 15 March 2016 from http://www.degruyter.com/doi/book/10.1515/9783110255546

Weinberg, A. M./et al. (1963). *Science, Government, and Information: The Responsibilities of the Technical Community and the Government in the Transfer of Information.* Washington D.C. Retrieved 15 March 2016 from http://eric.ed.gov/?id=ED048894

Life Sciences

Inquiry-Based Learning in Medicine 15

Thorsten Schäfer

At each new encounter with a patient, medical students are challenged to engage in inquiry-based learning, at least implicitly. Currently, great efforts are being made to explicitly integrate inquiry-based learning and research into the curricula in the study of medicine. As such, however, special basic conditions apply to the medical studies.

15.1 Characteristic Features in the Field of Medicine – Basic Conditions for Inquiry-Based Learning

The goal in medical training is a physician who is trained scientifically and practically, who is capable of autonomous and independent medical practice, continuing education and constant continued development. Training is intended to provide basic knowledge, abilities and skills in all subjects that are required for comprehensive healthcare for the population. Training to become a physician is carried out on a scientific basis and in a manner that is practice and patient-related [...].

This is what is stated in paragraph 1, subparagraph 1 of the *Approbationsordnung für Ärzte* or German Medical Licensure Act for Physicians (abbreviated as: ÄApprO; source: Approbationsordnung für Ärzte, 2002, translated), which governs medical studies in Germany down to the smallest detail. It defines the subjects and interdisciplinary areas to be taught, prescribes seminars, courses and internships including total cumulative hours for the part of the studies dealing with fundamental science in Annex 1, specifies what are currently 22 clinical subjects, 14 interdisciplinary areas and 5 block placements as

T. Schäfer, Prof. Dr. med. (✉)
Universität Bochum, Medizinische Fakultät, Studiendekan der Medizinischen Fakultät,
Bochum, Germany
e-mail: Thorsten.Schaefer@rub.de

© The Author(s) 2019
H. A. Mieg (ed.), *Inquiry-Based Learning – Undergraduate Research*,
https://doi.org/10.1007/978-3-030-14223-0_15

compulsory study content in paragraph 27, and defines the type, content and scope of exams within the university and the nationally uniform written state examinations (*Staatsexamen*) applicable throughout Germany.

The so-called Model Clause (paragraph 41 ÄApprO) in the Medical Licensure Act opens up the possibility of replacing the first state examination, which is focused on the basics, with an equivalent examination, thus enabling greater integration of the curricula and one's areas of focus. Nevertheless, all medical students must pass a written state examination after the 10th semester, and an oral-practical state examination after the 12th semester.

The German institute for medical and pharmaceutical examinations (*Institut für medizinische und pharmazeutische Prüfungsfragen* or IMPP), which was commissioned to create the national written examinations, publishes what are known as topic catalogs, which list the examination contents as keywords for the basic subjects as well as the clinical and clinical-theoretical subjects. It is not just the relevant textbooks that are geared towards these extensive catalogs and serve to facilitate targeted exam preparation. The courses offered at the university have been subject to the student demand for exam relevance. Courses that are not directly relevant to the examination are, at best, perceived with special interest by few students due to the enormous volume of material and considerable exam pressure in medical studies.

Doubtless specifying the range of subjects, defining the common study content and nationwide examinations for aspiring physicians serves as quality assurance in medical studies; however, it also insulates those studies as compared to most other degree programs that have experienced significant advancements, individualization and reorientation due to the Bologna Process.

Practice orientation and scholarliness are the milestones on which medical studies should focus, according to paragraph 1 of the ÄApprO. As such, the "and" is sometimes also understood as "despite" or "instead of" in the political debate over the provision of care in a country-doctor setting. In the discourse about the orientation of medical studies, however, a shift towards academic qualification is currently being observed.

15.2   General Experiences with Inquiry-Based Learning in Medical Studies

Inquiry-based learning does not appear in the framework of medical studies outlined above. As a general rule, medical students are not required to prepare their own academic work. Nonetheless, there is a high percentage of students who often develop interest in medical research during their studies and who pursue a doctoral dissertation in addition to, rather than as part of, their medical studies. At the same time, a very broad range of topics as well as spectrum of quality can be observed. This aspect will be revisited below.

Due to the specifications of the ÄApprO and the IMPP, the curricular internships related to aspects of basic science in physics, chemistry, biology, anatomy, physiology and biochemistry are oriented towards promoting an understanding of fundamental relationships and promoting basic skills. Both the independent choice of methods and autonomous analysis and interpretation of the data are lacking, as are the time and remaining resources – and ostensibly the exam relevance – to allow experimental approaches with open questions that are to be developed.

At many locations, the proof of performance for the cross-section of "epidemiology, medical biometry and medical information technology" to be provided after the first state examination starting in the 5th semester includes a systematic introduction into scientific work and evidence-based medicine as a compulsory curricular program and allows students to experience the basics of research and the creation and application of new knowledge.

Based on the position paper from the Federal University Assistants' Conference (BAK) from 1970, Huber (2009, p. 9) cited the features of inquiry-based learning specified therein:

- independent selection of the topic,
- independent 'strategy,' in particular with reference to methods, experimental design, research,
- corresponding risk of errors and detours on the one hand, an opportunity for chance discoveries, 'fruitful moments'... on the other,
- working according to the demands of science (e.g. adequate examination of existing knowledge, endurance…),
- self-critical examination of the result with regard to its dependence on hypotheses and methods,
- endeavor to present the achieved result in such a way that its meaning becomes clear and the way in which it was reached is made verifiable.

The fact that "such strongly emphasized independence" represents a high goal, but must first develop over various stages, is relativizing.

Given this understanding, curricular medical studies certainly include a high proportion of inquiry-based learning, albeit learning has hitherto been more implicit: In addition to the theoretical attention, the patient-orientation required in the ÄApprO is provided in the curriculum, in particular through "bedside teaching," block placements, and three 16-week tertiary sessions of full-time clinical-practical work in academic teaching hospitals during the "practical year" at the end of the course of studies. Of a total of 476 hours of teaching at the bedside, half of this must be in the form of a patient demonstration in a group of no more than six, and one patient by a student in a group of no more than three students.

There are direct parallels to the characteristics of inquiry-based learning in the case of the situation at the bedside: Students choose the strategies and methods themselves, build on existing knowledge, and independently formulate hypotheses based on the results of the interview and examination, e.g. in terms of diagnosis and differential diagnoses, investigate and test these hypotheses in a critical and unbiased manner, experience errors and detours, as well as incidental findings and "fruitful moments." Their results must be presented in such a manner that the way in which the results were reached is comprehensible and verifiable. With an assumed workload of about 30 credits according to ECTS, this inquiry-based learning at the bedside represents a significant proportion of the curricular teaching in the twelve semesters of medical studies. Not all agents are aware of the significance of this type of instruction in sharpening scientific thinking.

At many locations, for example at the Ludwig-Maximilians-Universität Munich and at the University of Heidelberg, structured doctoral programs have been very consciously set up for medical students in order to provide an optional offering to support independent academic work on the one hand, and in order to improve the quality of medical doctorates in terms of the structural conditions and to sustainably improve the process and the results on the other. These offerings range from support in the application phase of a doctoral project, the mutual obligation between doctoral student and advisor, the guarantee of support and infrastructure, and support through theoretical and practical training to scholarships for doctoral students with particularly ambitious doctoral theses.

Since the ÄApprO was amended in 2002, attempts have been made in some model degree programs, for example the University of Hamburg and the Charité, Berlin, to anchor scientific thinking and activity, and inquiry-based learning, in the curriculum. This is exemplified by the study reforms in the Faculty of Medicine at Ruhr University Bochum, for example.

15.3 Inquiry-Based Learning Based on the Example of a Model Degree Program and an Integrated Reformed Degree Program

In 2003, parallel to a reformed standard curriculum, the Faculty of Medicine at Ruhr University Bochum launched a model degree program, which was characterized in particular by a targeted problem, practice and patient orientation. For nine years, 42 students per year were enrolled in this independent, problem-oriented learning degree program. After evaluating this model project, a new "integrated, reformed degree program in medicine" was created, which combined the advantages of the model degree program in medicine with those of a reformed standard curriculum for a large number of students; for all 300 students in the 2013/14 winter semester, and even 330 new students since 2014/15.

15.3.1 Problem-Based Learning in the Model Degree Program

The model degree program in medicine dispensed with the systematic transfer of knowledge in lectures. Instead, students were involved in a topic-centered curriculum with concrete patient cases, documented cases in the first four semesters, and then increasingly with real patients. These cases were selected in such a way that general knowledge, clinical theory and clinical knowledge were developed through this involvement. The development followed the classification system of problem-based learning (Schmidt et al. 2011).

The cases were analyzed and processed in seven steps by groups of seven students, each group being under the guidance of a trained tutor:

1. Clarification of comprehension questions for case presentation
2. Limitation of topics
3. Brainstorming with activation of existing knowledge
4. Forming hypotheses
5. Formulating concrete learning objectives for the group
6. Time for independent learning
7. Presentation and discussion of learning outcomes.

The time provided for independent learning was flanked by courses in the form of seminars and practical tutorial. Using this unbiased approach, students were trained

- to engage with new issues,
- to select the topics themselves,
- to accept the risk of errors and detours, but also to experience "fruitful moments,"
- to use their available knowledge and to research critically,
- to check the results in a self-critical manner and with other group members and to present these results comprehensively.

Problem-based learning was supplemented, inter alia, by a "vertical educational track" anchored in the study regulations on the topics of health economy, scholarliness, methodology and research, in which scientific thinking and work methods were to be presented and built up over the first six semesters, and implemented in students' own tasks and reports in a manner that was exam relevant.

In later semesters, scientific symposia were integrated into the program, in which researchers from the Faculty of Medicine presented their scholarly work and newest findings, and discussed these with students. The problem orientation of this model degree program appears to strengthen the interest in continued autonomous, scholarly work. An initial analysis of the rate at which students obtain doctoral degrees as compared with reformed conventional curriculum suggests this.

This model degree program for 42 new students was planned as a pilot project and was implemented in parallel with a reformed conventional curriculum of approximately 260 new students. On the one hand, this parallelism provided excellent opportunities for researching various educational strategies, especially as the students in the model degree program were chosen by lot from among the applicants; on the other hand, the school posed significant logistical challenges for the faculty. In a two-year planning process that involved multiple departments, a new degree program was therefore developed based on the evaluation results; it has been offered to all new students at the Faculty of Medicine at Ruhr University Bochum as an "integrated, reformed degree program in medicine" since the 2013/14 winter semester.

15.3.2 Inquiry-Based Learning and Learning to Research in the Reformed Degree Program

Inquiry-based learning is now anchored in the curriculum in three stages:

The basic, systematic scientific education in the first four semesters, or *the first stage*, is accompanied by problem-based learning, in which concrete, topic-oriented patient cases are processed based on the aforementioned seven steps: Hypothesis formation based on knowledge in a scientifically founded excursus with the other members of the team, research in the event that there are open questions as well as the presentation, critical questioning and fact-based defense of the learning outcomes are the main features of research-oriented, unbiased and self-determined learning. The tutors, all of the lecturers at the Faculty of Medicine, thereby have the task of "allowing" the group process "to play out," and they should introduce as little as possible in terms of content.

In *stage two*, which is obligatory for all students, the foundation of scientific thinking and working are systematically processed. This occurs in compulsory courses as lectures and practical tutorials during the fifth semester within the context of the proof of performance for "epidemiology, medical biometry and medical information technology." At the end of the semester there is a written exam on theoretical knowledge. Learning objectives during this stage include not just getting to know and assessing research findings, but also internalizing the research process itself, from the development of a precise research question about the suitable choice of method, the analysis, and the presentation and critical discussion of the results to classifying these in the current state of research.

In stage three, students must select a main area in which they wish to deepen their knowledge of previously learned theory in small groups and in scholarly discourse. There are three topics to choose from in sixth-semester seminars:

1. Basic biomedical research
2. Clinical research
3. Evidence-based medicine

Organized beneath these three main themes are various small group courses focused on ongoing research projects, which provide the participants with immediate, practice-oriented insight into the research process and room for their own research-based work.

15.4 Outlook for Inquiry-Based Learning in Medicine – What Needs to Be Done?

The call for stronger practice orientation in medical training has grown in recent years as part of the concerns surrounding providing medical care to the population. At the same time, however, there is a growing conviction that the doctors we are training today not only need to have internalized the present "state of the art" and must act with great knowledge, sophisticated practical skills and appropriately for the profession. As medical advances continue to increase, today's graduates must also be able to understand the advances of tomorrow (and beyond) that are relevant to them, to analyze the relevancy of those advances for their own patients and utilize them for those patients' benefit, and must be as prepared and able as possible to contribute to these advances themselves.

15.4.1 Recommendations of the German Science Council (Wissenschaftsrat) for the Further Development of Medical Studies

In 2012, the German Science Council started the work program "Stand und Perspektiven der humanmedizinischen Modellstudiengänge" ("Status of and perspectives on model degree programs in human medicine"). In this program, ongoing degree programs were examined with respect to the question of which reform elements have been successful, and what conclusions could be drawn for the advancement of medical studies in Germany.

Concerning this, in 2014 the German Science Council presented its "Empfehlungen zur Weiterentwicklung des Medizinstudiums in Deutschland auf Grundlage einer Bestandsaufnahme der humanmedizinischen Modellstudiengäng" ("Recommendations for the further development of medical studies in Germany on the basis of a survey of model degree programs in human medicine") (Wissenschaftsrat 2014). The recommendations are summarized in five principles. These deal with (1) competence orientation, (2) integrated patient-oriented curricula, (3) scientific competencies, (4) interprofessional education and (5) focusing the curricular content. With regard to item 3, which is relevant here, the German Science Council stated the following in its abstract (p. 7, translated):

> Scientific competencies: Physicians must be able to examine their own actions in more complex care situations with regard to basing them in evidence and against the background of new medical findings, in order to arrive at a decision that relates to the individual patient. Thus scientific thinking and activity forms the basis for the adequate, patient-oriented selection of diagnostic and therapeutic measures. The compulsory acquisition of scientific competencies in the course of studies is thus a necessary prerequisite for responsible medical practice.

In concrete terms, the German Science Council recommends the introduction of a longitudinal educational track, the courses or modules of which build on one another, extending over multiple semesters with the aim "that knowledge, skills and attitudes toward scientific thinking and activity when working through problems in practice, as well as the process of scientific knowledge generation and assurance can be practiced by students themselves." The format of problem-based teaching has proven itself in its practical application.

What is new for medical studies – but common for nearly all other degree programs – is that conducting one's own research is required, in the course of which scientific competency is to be proven, whereby this research is to become an elementary component of the curriculum. It is stated that the German Science Council is aware of the fact that this will necessitate a cultural change in medicine. The arguments are easy to understand, but at the same time, practical questions are raised regarding the current basic conditions outlined above, which likewise must be reformed in the sense of the advancement of medical studies in Germany. This also includes providing the necessary resources, because the above-mentioned requirements suggest a considerable additional support effort.

15.4.2 New: A National Competency-Based Catalog of Learning Objectives for Medicine (NKLM)

A very concrete, promising approach to the establishment of inquiry-based learning in medicine can be found in the development of the national competency-based catalog of learning objectives for medicine (NKLM) and for dentistry (NKLZ) (Hahn and Fischer 2009). The Gesellschaft für Medizinische Ausbildung (Society for Medical Education) and the Medizinische Fakultätentag (German Medical Faculty Association), in coordination with the member societies of the Arbeitsgemeinschaft der Wissenschaftlichen Medizinischen Fachgesellschaften (Working Group of Scientific Medical Societies), are currently working on a multidimensional catalog of competencies and operationalized learning objectives which should be acquired by the end of twelve semesters of medical studies. In the process, the physician should not be seen as just a "medical expert" with a wealth of medical knowledge, but rather it is stressed that additional roles are integrated into this expertise. Based on the CanMEDS framework of the Royal College in Canada (actually developed for medical continuing education), in the NKLM and NKLZ, physicians' roles as scholars, communicators, team members, health advisors and advocates, responsible parties, managers and professionals have been underpinned by corresponding competencies.

The subject of "inquiry-based learning in medicine" is expressed here in particular in the physician's role as scholar. Here, the NKLM defines four core competencies, the first of which is that graduates are lifelong learners, who improve and maintain their professional activities by means of constant continued education. Critical reflection on one's own level of knowledge, uncovering knowledge gaps, defining one's own learning needs, effective implementation of suitable learning strategies and adequate documentation and implementation of the learning outcomes for the benefit of the patients are specific goals in this category.

Secondly, as defined by the NKLM, physicians should be able to critically evaluate scientific information and the sources of that information, and should be able to apply it in a suitable manner to their own actions. Here, the NKLM integrates the principles of evidence-based medicine, which are both credo and challenge to science-based, individualized medicine.

Thirdly, scholarliness also includes teaching competencies for various target groups. Here, the education and instruction of patients and relatives, and the training of medical students and students in other health professions, is explicitly specified.

Fourthly, as innovators, aspiring physicians should contribute to the formation, dissemination, application, and translation of new insights and practices. In order to develop and practice these competencies, physicians are recommended to do their own practical work, going beyond the understanding of the philosophy of science and the knowledge of ethical and legal principles of research. This includes research work including the following stages: the derivation of a research question and testable hypothesis; systematically obtaining information on the current state of the research; and planning and carrying out a research project, including documentation and disseminating the research findings. Thus the research activities correspond to the recommendations of the German Science Council for strengthening scientific competencies within the context of the advancement of medical studies in Germany.

That such an integration of inquiry-based learning and scientific work in the medical studies curriculum is possible is shown by the advancement of medical studies abroad. Within the context of the Bologna reform, for example, medical degree programs in the Netherlands and Switzerland were converted into graduated, modularized degree programs, in which an independent scientific thesis within the context of the bachelor's and/or master's degree program is obligatory.

15.5 Conclusion

The variety of new projects on inquiry-based learning and on scholarly thinking and working at medical schools, the recommendations of the German Science Council for the advancement of medical studies in Germany and the agreement on scientific competencies in the national competency-based catalog of learning objectives for medicine and dentistry are conspicuous signs of a "change in culture" in medicine towards integrating independent, scholarly work in the medical curriculum (Fischer and Fabry 2014). It is to be hoped that this change in culture will be constructively and rapidly accompanied by a change in the basic conditions and will inspire scholarliness and a practice orientation in the course of studies.

References

Approbationsordnung für Ärzte vom 27. Juni 2002 (BGBl. I S. 2405), die zuletzt durch Artikel 2 der Verordnung vom 2. August 2013 (BGBl. I S. 3005) geändert worden ist Bundesgesetzblatt I 2405, Bundesministerium für Gesundheit 2002.
Fischer, M. R./Fabry, G. (2014). Thinking and acting scientifically: Indispensable basis of medical education. *GMS Zeitschrift für medizinische Ausbildung*, 31(2), Doc24. doi:https://doi.org/10.3205/zma000916.

Hahn, E. G./Fischer, M. R. (2009). Nationaler Kompetenzbasierter Lernzielkatalog Medizin (NKLM) für Deutschland: Zusammenarbeit der Gesellschaft für Medizinische Ausbildung (GMA) und des Medizinischen Fakultätentages (MFT). *GMS Zeitschrift für medizinische Ausbildung*, 26(3), Doc35. Retrieved 05 May 2015 from http://www.egms.de/en/journals/zma/2009-26/zma000627. shtml

Huber, L. (2009). Warum Forschendes Lernen nötig und möglich ist. In L. Huber/J. Hellmer/ F. Schneider (Hrsg.), *Forschendes Lernen im Studium. Aktuelle Konzepte und Erfahrungen*. (S. 9–35). Bielefeld: UniversitätsVerlagWebler.

Institut für medizinische und pharmazeutische Prüfungsfragen (2015). *Gegenstandskataloge für den schriftlichen Teil des Ersten Abschnitts der Ärztlichen Prüfung (IMPP-GK1) und Gegenstandskataloge für den schriftlichen Teil des Zweiten Abschnitts der Ärztlichen Prüfung (IMPP-GK2)*. Retrieved 05 May 2015 from https://www.impp.de/internet/de/medizin/articles/ gegenstandskataloge.html

Royal College of Physicians and Surgeons of Canada (o.J.). *The CanMEDS Framework*. Retrieved 05 May 2015 from http://www.royalcollege.ca/portal/page/portal/rc/canmeds/framework

Schmidt, H. G./Rotgans, J. I./Yew, E.H.J. (2011). The process of problem-based learning: what works and why. *Medical education*, 45(8), 792–806. doi:https://doi.org/10.1111/ j.1365-2923.2011.04035.x.

Wissenschaftsrat (2014). *Empfehlungen zur Weiterentwicklung des Medizinstudiums in Deutschland auf Grundlage einer Bestandsaufnahme der humanmedizinischen Modellstudiengänge*. Köln: Wissenschaftsrat.

Inquiry-Based Learning in the Life Sciences

16

Natascha Selje-Aßmann, Christian Poll, Matthias Konrad Tisler,
Julia Gerstenberg, Martin Blum, and Jörg Fleischer

16.1 Trends in the Life Sciences as Determining Factors for Teaching and Research

The life sciences comprise numerous disciplines; these study physiology, anatomy, behavior, development, evolution, ecology and disorders of living organisms as well as the use of organisms in natural or technical procedures. Life sciences include biology, biomedical research and pharmaceutics, biochemistry, biophysics, bioinformatics, agricultural and nutritional science as well as food technologies, bio-based economy and the use of biogenic resources. The life sciences contribute not only to our understanding of basic

---

The term research-based learning is used here throughout to describe what is subsumed under undergraduate research experience (URE) in English speaking countries. In the German academic culture, research-based learning aims at a high level of self-dependence on the part of the student.

The authors are coordinators of a research-based learning project for undergraduates, "Humboldt reloaded – Wissenschaftspraxis von Anfang an" ("Humboldt reloaded – scientific practice right from the start") at the University of Hohenheim in Stuttgart, Germany (www.uhoh.de/humboldt-reloaded). They actively participate in research and teaching at the Schools of Natural and Agricultural Sciences.

N. Selje-Aßmann, Dr. Ph.D. (✉)
Institute of Agricultural Sciences in the Tropics, Section Animal Nutrition
and Rangeland Management, University of Hohenheim, Hohenheim, Germany
e-mail: n.seljeassmann@uni-hohenheim.de

C. Poll, Dr. Ph.D.
Institute of Soil Science and Land Evaluation, Section Soil Biology, University of Hohenheim, Hohenheim, Germany
e-mail: christian.poll@uni-hohenheim.de

© The Author(s) 2019
H. A. Mieg (ed.), *Inquiry-Based Learning – Undergraduate Research*,
https://doi.org/10.1007/978-3-030-14223-0_16

171

mechanisms of living organisms and ecological systems; new research opens up novel possibilities to elucidate and treat human diseases as well as securing food for a growing world population.

A high degree of empiricism is intrinsic to the life sciences. The state of scientific knowledge in the life sciences is based on observations and experiments with which researchers describe, measure and analyze the conditions and behavior of nature. Methods are chosen to ensure the reproducibility of results. Many studies require sophisticated methodologies, e.g. advanced imaging, "omics" approaches and the like. Thus, the ability to acquire knowledge in these disciplines very much depends on development and availability of methods. Methodological advances and improvements may yield data of higher quality, allow novel conclusions and open up new areas of research (e.g. brain research, gene therapy, stem cell technologies, etc.). In recent years, rapid technological advances in many fields, including information technology, data processing, genetic engineering, or molecular biology, have led to a rapidly increasing complexity of methods. As a result, life sciences are characterized by an exponentially growing volume of knowledge and fragmentation into numerous sub-disciplines.

This development impacts on university teaching and higher education. New challenges arise with respect to the volume of knowledge that is taught, or the discrepancy between traditional text book knowledge and the results of modern research. Combining highly specialized subject areas with practical and methodical approaches in a meaningful way presents additional challenges for teaching in higher education. In addition to a sound knowledge base and understanding of biological relationships, which are increasingly explored more broadly, students ought to develop competencies in terms of research methodology such as purposeful planning, executing and evaluating experiments as well as analytical and critical thinking. With a possible career in research in mind, students have to learn how to work collaboratively in a group, on campus and in an international context.

M. K. Tisler, Dr. Ph.D. · M. Blum, Prof. Dr. Ph.D.
Institute of Zoology, University of Hohenheim, Hohenheim, Germany
e-mail: matthias.tisler@uni-hohenheim.de; martin.blum@uni-hohenheim.de

J. Gerstenberg
University of Hohenheim, Hohenheim, Germany
e-mail: j.gerstenberg@uni-hohenheim.de

J. Fleischer, apl. Prof. Dr. Ph.D.
Institute of Biology/Zoology, Martin Luther University Halle-Wittenberg, Halle (Saale), Germany
e-mail: joerg.fleischer@zoologie.uni-halle.de

In the light of limited human and spatial resources, imparting the described wealth of knowledge and developing the required competencies place high demands on lecturers that will be barely accomplished via the traditional curricula. Given the high numbers of students in present-day study programs, life sciences are often taught in large classes of 100 participants and more. Such courses make it difficult to establish a close link to state-of-the-art research, especially in terms of the necessary use of modern devices and techniques. This development is all the more problematic if one considers the close connection between the life sciences and the current state of research. This may not only lead to demotivated students, it also reduces personal contact between students and lecturers. Consequently, it is difficult for the latter to assess the level of knowledge of an increasingly heterogeneous student body and to adequately address knowledge gaps.

It is essential to strengthen the students abilities to accumulate knowledge and research competence in a self-dependent manner. This ability is of particular importance, given the rapid increase in knowledge that we face, as well as the associated shorter half-life of the current state of knowledge in life sciences. Life scientists working in academia and industry must continuously have a critical look at current research findings, technical developments and modern experimental approaches, as well as the resulting new insights and hypotheses. However, it is by no means sufficient to enable future life scientists to (self-dependently) acquire and reproduce already existing knowledge. They will be the ones in charge of ensuring future insights and innovations, and to deal with new technological opportunities in a responsible way, for the benefit of society in the midst of global competition and in the face of global challenges. For this reason, academic teaching should focus more on key competencies such as analytical, creative and reflective thinking, on acquiring specific scientific skills and on furthering the capacity for teamwork.

How can the acquisition of these competencies be fostered in the life sciences, given the high numbers of students and limited resources? How can the concept of "research-based learning", put forth in German-speaking countries under the formative influence of Ludwig Huber (2009), be integrated into curricula of the life sciences? In the tradition of the "Humboldtian model of higher education", teaching is essentially derived from the research process. Students develop competencies in a dynamic and unbiased process in order to self-dependently gather new insights. In the following, we will outline specific characteristics of the life sciences that have beneficial or inhibiting effects in terms of an increased use of research-based learning in academic teaching. Moreover, strategies to counteract inhibitory effects as well as advantages of research-based learning will be discussed.

16.2 Research-Based Learning: Advantages and Facilitating Conditions

The implementation of research-based learning in the life sciences is favored by the concept of research itself, as well as by the sequential structure of the research process. The experimental nature of research allows an easy understanding of the concept of research.

However, beginners often have a biased understanding of the research process in which data collection is overrated, while the proportion of literature review, statistical planning, data analysis and publication is underestimated. Research is often perceived as a linear process, while in practical terms it consists of small steps, setbacks, discarding and reformulating of hypotheses and the like.

Many research topics in the life sciences are extremely complex. However, in many cases, they can be separated into sets of specific research questions, which individually require less background knowledge. Such questions can be addressed in the setting of research-based learning, with limited efforts and a small subset of required methods. For example, most students will not be able to elucidate the complex processes of neural circuits in the central nervous system. Within the context of research-based learning, however, they could study neurotransmitters used by cells of the brain or spinal cord and how they communicate with other cells. Dividing complex research topics into small, easy-to-address research questions thus facilitates the participation of students in the research process. Students get introduced to the research process by carrying out experiments, collecting and evaluating their own data. This process is supported by the fact that the complexity of research-based learning can easily be adapted to the students' respective knowledge and skills. Students can perform simple experiments under the guidance of a supervisor, for example during a course, and they can perform independent (and less guided) research during an internship (i.e. research-based learning in the classical meaning). This transition from receptive to self-guided learning supports the students in their developing self-awareness as scientists.

The structure of the study program reflects the importance of experimental data collection and methodological development in the life sciences. The curricula contain a wide range of courses and tutorials, in which students apply modern research methods. It would be relatively easy to apply the concept of research-based learning within such courses. The format of research-based learning is variable; it may consist of courses held in regular intervals during the semester, of whole-day courses that last for a few weeks, of internships during summer break and seminars or student projects. Moreover, the scope of research-based learning can vary, i.e. it can cover the entire research process related to a research question (Fig. 16.1) or it focusses on specific aspects such as scientific writing, statistical data analysis or literature review. The latter may include the elaboration of the research topic as well as the identification of the current state of research, the drafting of hypotheses and the design of statistically sound experimental set-ups. Depending on the research question, appropriate methods must be acquired, developed or validated before collecting data in the experimental part of the work. The data are (statistically) evaluated and discussed in relation to the research question. An essential part is the documentation of the research process in a comprehensible and reproducible manner, and making the results available to the research community. Several authors published examples of how research-based learning could be implemented in the curricula of life-science curricula (e.g. Brewer and Smith 2011; Ott and Carson 2014; Resendes 2015; Ward et al. 2014).

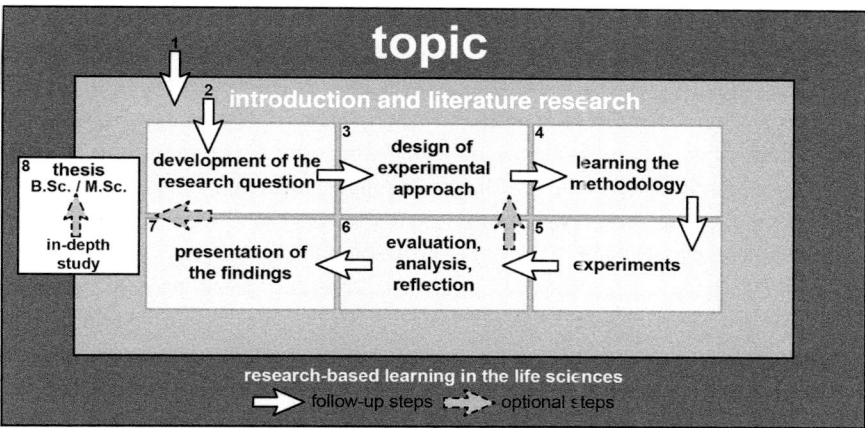

Fig. 16.1 Schematic diagram of the sequential structure of a research-based learning project in the life sciences

Research-based learning is probably firmly established in many curricula in the life sciences, for example in the form of internships or small research projects, which are often not referred to as research-based learning. Last but not least, as in other disciplines, students conclude their studies with a thesis during which they work, in large parts independently, on their research question. Thus, experiencing research-based learning in other formats before is the perfect preparation for a successful bachelor or master thesis.

After selecting a topic (1), students perform a literature review to understand the theoretical background needed for implementation of the research (2). Participants subsequently develop their research question(s) and hypotheses, and design a suitable experimental setup (3). Students practice the methodology (4) before they perform the experiments and collect data (5), which are subsequently evaluated and discussed (6). Finally, the results and conclusions are presented to the (academic) public (7). Optionally, insights obtained during this process may result in a new cycle of questions and experiments (3–6), or the project may connect to a more in-depth course or become integrated into a thesis (8).

The latter reasoning could help motivate supervisors to take part in research-based learning. Lecturers that engage in full-fledged research at the same time (which is the standard at German universities) are often faced with the problem of reconciling their teaching with their scientific projects. The concept of research-based learning provides a workable solution for this conflict of interests. Replacing conventional courses and tutorials, which constitute a significant part of the teaching activity and which do not provide new scientific knowledge, with research-based learning projects may produce novel and exciting results, not only for the students benefits but for the supervisors as well. In most cases these will be preliminary results on for example the variability of methods, the optimization of experimental designs or testing of new methods. Such preliminary experiments are often time- and labor-consuming. Including these experiments in research-based learning allows the supervisor to conduct preliminary research despite the scarcity of resources, and provides students with a sense of achievement. The overlap between a student's research project and the research interests of the supervisor results, therefore, in the increased motivation of both, students and supervisors. Our experience shows that spending time in a research-based context is more meaningful to students than teaching formats, which simulate the research process based on an arbitrarily selected research question.

The high relevance of research for future professional activities implies that students of the life sciences have a keen intrinsic interest in research questions and a pronounced motivation for true research activities (cf. Multrus 2012). Thus, enhanced student motivation constitutes another beneficial factor for the implementation of research-based learning in the life sciences. This is particularly true in cases of research-based learning projects addressing topical issues such as climate change, gene therapy or genome editing, healthy nutrition or conventional versus organic agriculture. Such topics relate directly to the everyday reality of students, which should elicit special interest. In addition, the personal contact to scientists and the favorable ratio of students to supervisors may contribute to a high intrinsic motivation of the students. Students' self-perception as "researchers" can contribute to their satisfaction with the study program in a major way.

16.3   Meeting the Challenges of Research-Based Learning

Favorable conditions that facilitate the implementation of research-based learning contrast with a number of unfavorable factors that restrict research-based learning in the life sciences. These include costs, organizational issues and time-related aspects of research topics and applied methodologies, as well as the rather hierarchical construction of knowledge in the so-called hard sciences (cf. Healey 2005). Significant expenditures of time and money required for research-based learning may be the most limiting factors.

In the life sciences, sizeable costs derive from the use of expensive consumables (e.g. fine chemicals), instruments and equipment. High acquisition costs can be avoided by linking a student's research question to ongoing research projects in the supervising institute or department. Alternatively, expenses can be reduced by restricting the research question to aspects that can be answered using a reduced set of consumables and equipment. If the concept of research-based learning is incorporated in the mission statement of the university, financial and personal resources that are still being used for conventional course work may be reallocated in part or full to research-based learning projects.

Furthermore, limited laboratory space and availability of instruments may constrain the realization of research-based learning projects. This issue again may be solved by integrating students' projects into current research questions of the involved institution. However, it is difficult to circumvent the restricted flexibility of experiments in terms of time management. This may be due to limited infrastructure (workstations and equipment), only temporary availability of biological sample materials (e.g. due to vegetation periods or generation cycles) and the at times considerable duration of experimental procedures (e.g. long-term observations or incubations, sequential extraction steps and the like). Time requirements and progress of an experiment strongly depend on the research question and the methodology applied and may require the students' presence in the laboratory or in the field during a given time window with little chance for rescheduling the tasks. It therefore can be difficult to coordinate research-based projects in the context of inflexible timetables of study programs. Thus, research-based projects may best be placed during semester breaks or other suitable time windows in which students are in charge of their time management.

In the German academia, concepts of research-based learning, that were developed in the soft sciences, often stress the importance of self-dependent development of research questions, decision making, and completion of research projects by the learners, in order to enhance motivation and learning outcome. Laborious analyses and complex experimental approaches in the life sciences, however, prevent pure student-led research-based learning or at least makes it quite difficult. Undergraduates in general lack technical and methodological skills and access to the required instruments in order to plan or carry out such projects completely self-dependently. This problem is further exacerbated by legal requirements and restrictions (e.g. animal welfare legislation, occupational safety regulations, environmental protection act, and genetic engineering law). These can significantly restrict the choice of research questions suitable for student projects and necessitate additional training in good laboratory practice and the specific methodology. Thus, projects need to be planned and carried out in collaboration with experienced supervisors. Supervision may be required as well for the application of statistical methods, as imparting statistical basic knowledge in lectures and tutorials often does not enable students to adequately evaluate individual experiments.

Research-based student projects that are incorporated into ongoing research of the supervising staff are unique with respect to content and preparation and can usually accommodate only a small number of participants, due to the aforementioned limitations. Thus, the time requirements for academic staff to supervise research-based projects are significantly higher compared to standard courses that are given repetitively each year. A reasonable compromise could lie in addressing the same research question in a recurring manner year after year, e.g. to analyze a soil sample or the composition of the vegetation at a given site in order to allow for long-term observations and to illustrate the dynamics by comparing the data to those of previous generations of students. At the same time, the effort for planning and organization can be minimized in such projects. These must relate to ongoing research topics at the supervising institutions, however, in order to qualify as research-based project, and such approaches may not be applicable in every field of research.

If research-based learning is implemented at an early phase of the study program, supervision of undergraduates can be particularly time-consuming, depending on the background of the students, e.g. in terms of general knowledge and skills in literature research, scientific writing, or application of statistics programs, which can be taught in formats with higher numbers of participants. Even if a synergy between teaching and research can be achieved, the increased time requirements compared to standard teaching may negatively impact on research efficiency. Research-related criteria dominate over didactics of teaching, when applying for positions or third-party funding, i.e. research output is considered more important than successful teaching. This reality results in the prioritization of research activities by academic staff and complicate engagement in time-consuming teaching formats such as research-based learning.

A major difference between standardized course work and research-based projects is the frequent failure of experiments in the life sciences, in which even well-established routine methods can fail at times. Failed experiments as well as the rejection of a hypothesis require patience, diligence, and a high degree of tolerance towards frustration. This can negatively impact on student motivation, especially in the context of short-term projects (Linn et al. 2015). However, this experience enables supervisors to familiarize students with the fact that experiments frequently do not precisely result in the expected outcomes. Students recognize right from the start that the research process is tedious and difficult, and progress can only be realized in small steps.

Last but not least, reflection on the concept of research-based learning is not as widespread in the life sciences as in disciplines with higher affinity to didactical issues, social-learning theory and pedagogics. The unfortunate tendencies towards lecturing very large classes and a constantly increasing amount of basic knowledge favor an instructive learning culture aiming at knowledge transfer. The deep expert knowledge of increasingly specialized researchers reinforces the impression that students are not able to conduct their own research. The discipline-specific learning culture and the discrepancy between highly specialized and basic knowledge thus may be another obstacle to the wide-spread implementation of research-based learning in the life sciences.

16.4 Conclusion

It is becoming increasingly difficult to teach an ever expanding and continuously developing knowledge, while the acquisition of competencies such as the ability to self-dependently acquire new knowledge, to critical, analytical and solution-oriented reasoning is becoming increasingly important for a successful professional career. Research-based learning can significantly contribute to the development of these competencies and therefore should be integrated into study programs at an early stage. In the life sciences, programs frequently have structural requirements due to a strong practice-orientation of these disciplines.

For learners and supervisors, research-based learning is an extremely time-intensive format, and requires thorough planning in terms of time management, feasibility and adaption to the individual abilities of students. The dependence on often costly resources together with complex methodologies, legal and ethical issues restrict the idealized concept of free research-based learning in the life sciences, i.e. the engagement in independently developed, intrinsically motivated research question by the learner themselves.

Instead of tying up resources in formats that merely simulate research, we highly recommend to integrate research-based learning into ongoing research projects of lecturers, in order to synergistically use personnel and financial resources for research, learning and teaching, and to achieve a high motivation of students and supervisors at the same time. The implementation of research-based learning undisputedly changes the study content. The intense engagement with a research question fosters the deep understanding of a specific topic but does not provide a broad knowledge base. Thus, research-based learning can be a significant pillar, but not the sole format in higher education. Against the backdrop of sizeable student cohorts, lectures represent important and efficient teaching formats for conveying the necessary basic knowledge. To extent the implementation of research-based learning in the life sciences, several aspects need to be considered: a reflection on study contents in terms of knowledge and skills; a true change in the culture of learning and teaching; the dissemination of the concept of research-based learning in combination with improved didactical training of researchers; and the support of academic staff when introducing research-based learning. In so doing, it is crucial to demonstrate how research-based learning can be used for the mutual benefit of learners and supervising staff and, ideally, for acquiring new scientific insights.

References

Brewer, C.A./Smith, D. (2011). *Vision and change in undergraduate biology education – A call to action*. American Association for the Advancement of Science. Retrieved 26 May 2015 from http://visionandchange.org/finalreport.

Healey, M. (2005). Linking research and teaching: exploring disciplinary spaces and the role of inquiry-based learning. In R. Barnett (Ed.), *Reshaping the university: new relationships between research, scholarship and teaching* (pp. 67–78). Maidenhead, McGraw-Hill, Open University Press.

Huber, L. (2009). Warum Forschendes Lernen nötig und möglich ist. In L. Huber/J. Hellmer/F. Schneider (Hrsg.), *Forschendes Lernen im Studium. Aktuelle Konzepte und Erfahrungen* (S. 9–35). Bielefeld: UniversitätsVerlagWebler.

Linn, M.C./Palmer, E./Baranger, A./Gerard, E./Stone, E. (2015). Undergraduate research experiences: Impacts and opportunities. *Science, 347*. DOI: https://doi.org/10.1126/science.1261757.

Multrus, F. (2012). *Forschung und Praxis im Studium. Befunde aus Studierendensurvey und Studienqualitätsmonitor* (S. 14–15). Konstanzer Online-Publikations-System (KOPS) URI: http://nbn-resolving.de/urn:nbn:de:bsz:352-222461.

Ott, L.E./Carson, S. (2014). Immunological tools: Engaging students in the use and analysis of flow cytometry and enzyme-linked immunosorbent assay (ELISA). *Biochemistry and Molecular Biology Education, 42*(5), 382–397.

Resendes, K.K. (2015). Using HeLa cell stress response to introduce first year students to the scientific method, laboratory techniques, primary literature, and scientific writing. *Biochemistry and Molecular Biology Education, 43*, 110–120.

Ward, J.R./Clarke, H.D./Horton, J.L. (2014). Effects of a research-infused botanical curriculum on undergraduates' content knowledge, STEM competencies, and attitudes toward plant science. *CBE- Life Science Education, 13*, 387–396.

Inquiry-Based Learning in Public Health/Health Sciences

Kati Mozygemba, Ulrike Lahn, Tobias Bernhardt, and Anne Dehlfing

Public health sciences is still a relatively recent field of study at German universities and universities of applied sciences; it encompasses efforts to prevent disease, extend life and promote health (DGPH 2015), thus clearly pursuing a political mandate. In the present text, we will first characterize public health/health sciences on the basis of four characteristic features. We will ask about their relevancy to teaching in the field and, in particular, for implementing inquiry-based learning; we present examples of the implementation of inquiry-based learning in the health sciences, and, finally, reflect on these in a critical light.

K. Mozygemba, Dr. (✉)
Universität Bremen, Fachbereich Human- und Gesundheitswissenschaften, Institut für Public Health und Pflegeforschung, Abteilung Versorgungsforschung. Bremen, Germany
e-mail: kati.mozygemba@uni-bremen.de

U. Lahn, Dipl. Soz.
Fachhochschule Dortmund, Fachbereich Angewandte Sozialwissenschaften,
Dortmund, Germany
e-mail: ulrike.lahn@fh-dortmund.de

T. Bernhardt, MA
Jade Hochschule, Fachbereich Bauwesen Geoinformation Gesundheitstechnologie,
Wilhelmshaven, Germany
e-mail: tobias.bernhardt@jade-hs.de

A. Dehlfing, MA PH
Universität Bremen, Fachbereich Human- und Gesundheitswissenschaften, Institut für Public Health und Pflegeforschung, Abteilung Versorgungsforschung, Bremen, Germany
e-mail: anne.dehlfing@uni-bremen.de

© The Author(s) 2019
H. A. Mieg (ed.), *Inquiry-Based Learning – Undergraduate Research*,
https://doi.org/10.1007/978-3-030-14223-0_17

17.1 Characteristic Features of Public Health as Basic Conditions for Inquiry-Based Learning

17.1.1 Public Health as a Scientific discipline

Public Health as "Holistic" Alternative to Medical Studies The field of public health has developed in Germany since the 1980s, with increased development in the 1990s, in conjunction with efforts to create an academic quality initiative in the healthcare system, which bundles a broad spectrum of healthcare occupations having differing qualification levels, educational institutions and professional settings. Public health prefers to consider health and healthcare holistically, critically reflect and limit the power of interpretation of medicine in the health sector, and develop other perspectives. Thus public health has offered, and continues to offer, a significant complement to traditional medical studies, a new perspective on continuing education and the career paths for physicians in Germany associated therewith (Polak 1999; von Troschke 2002). Initially designed as a course of study to be pursued part-time alongside employment, public health quickly developed into a degree program with various opportunities for specialization, which also signaled the academization and professionalization of healthcare occupations, for example physical therapy or speech therapy (Blättner 2012). Development away from a "vertical, hierarchical professional structure" is also being supported (Immenroth 2012, p. 57, translated).

Public Health as a Multidiscipline with a Transdisciplinary Orientation Public health involves a range of different core subjects, which represent different disciplines of science and their perspective on the common subject; the health of the population. These include: epidemiology, statistics/methods, medical basics, social and behavioral science basics, health promotion and prevention, health economics, healthcare policy, healthcare management, work, environment and health, law and ethics and research into the healthcare system (Dierks 2012). In addition, scientific aspects of nursing practice and theory were integrated such as nursing science, nursing education and nursing management (von Troschke 1999). Public health/health sciences are characterized by a transdisciplinary approach to health policy and practice or, respectively, to the transfer of knowledge to healthcare practice. Combining the various foci provides those who will be employed in the healthcare system in the future with a basis for the core competencies, for example competency in interprofessional cooperation. For example, these competencies have been documented in the Careum paper (Sottas et al. 2013), a position paper on reforming the training of health professionals in the twenty-first century, which emphasizes networking between those who will be working in the healthcare sector in the future.

Public Health as Applied Science Public health is an applied science. A mandate that emphasizes the connection between science and healthcare can be seen as early as Winslow's definition of public health (Winslow 2001), which was formulated in 1920 and adopted by the WHO in 1953 (Polak 1999). According to Noack (1999), the goals are to control and regulate health systems, to create basic social conditions for health, and to maintain and promote the social and organizational conditions for health. Dierks (2012) specifies that the goal of public health is in educating professionals in planning and decision-making in the healthcare system, and in developing, implementing and evaluating health-promoting and preventive programs, and likewise in founding health research and teaching. A clear definition of the field is lacking, however, which makes it difficult to distinguish between the different study orientations and the comparability of degrees (Dierks 2012). To date, problems associated with the application orientation such as the handling of different professional and disciplinary communication and process cultures have scarcely been systematically addressed (Schröder-Bäck 2014). Additional challenges include dealing with the pitfalls associated with labor law in transdisciplinary commissioned research and the need for a specific research ethics relating to public health, as well as the lack of epistemological considerations on the epistemology and methodology of the subject (ibid.).

The Heterogeneity of Students and Instructors The wide range of occupations and scientific disciplines that deal with health and the different paths to qualification substantiate the heterogeneity of both instructors and students in the public health. Thus, according to the Bremen student survey QUEST (2010/2012), a majority of new students have completed vocational training, work experience or experience through social engagement (Universität Bremen 2014). They are therefore older and more experienced than students in other disciplines. Moreover, the QUEST analysis further characterized this student group as pragmatic and dutiful – and less theoretical. Political involvement, artistic-cultural activities or experiences abroad are less common in the public health group as compared with students in other departments (ibid.). In addition, it is largely female students who are interested in the field. The percentage of women is over 80 percent (ibid.). To date, however, there is still a lack of reflection on gender and diversity within the subject culture and by the healthcare professions. The instructors are also characterized by heterogeneity. The majority of instructors recently came from independent scientific disciplines such as medicine, biology, economics or sociology and, as a rule, were qualified through a continuing education degree program or by working on health-related issues in their field of origin. The field has been changing since the first graduates of undergraduate degree programs in the field first took academic positions.

17.1.2 Didactics in Public Health

The plural disciplinary constitution, the adaptations due to the Bologna Process and the applied approach need not be an argument for strongly regulated B.A. and M.A. instruction. The exclusive concentration on a transfer of knowledge that focuses entirely on subject-specific knowledge also reaches its limits if students are to be enabled to establish interdisciplinary and transdisciplinary connections between theory and practice (Völker 2004).

The desire for greater interdisciplinary alignment, discussions about a common methodology and theory of cognition, a sense of history, and options in dealing with theory-practice problems in the case of commissioned research can foster the development of innovative didactic models for holistic teaching and learning. Projects such as that of the "Kooperationsverbund Hochschulen für Gesundheit" (Cooperation Network of Universities for Health) comment on the guiding didactic principles, which are supposed to ensure that students have essentially comparable qualifications (Hochschulen für Gesundheit e.V. 2001). The Deutsche Gesellschaft für Hochschuldidaktik (German Society for University Didactics) also has a health science working group focusing on the subject. A systematic didactical reflection with regard to the above-mentioned challenges is the exception, however. This is made apparent by the small number of publications on the topic (Reiber 2012a). According to Reiber, insofar as it occurs at all in health science instruction, this reflection is made in reference to literature and findings from general higher education didactics (ibid.).

The multi- and transdisciplinary references and the explicit call for the applicability of the contents, as well as the heterogeneity of the teachers and students, could make the inquiry-based learning approach (cf. Mieg in this volume) interesting in public health. Inquiry-based learning could provide instruments that move the discipline away from the multiplicity of perspectives represented by the individual disciplines towards theoretically and methodologically based inter- and transdisciplinarity, thereby connecting both students and instructors with one another. Van Wickevoort Crommelin (n.d.) summarizes the following points as shared characteristics of inquiry-based learning approaches as follows:

1. The problem and question, as well as the methods of answering, are self-chosen and possibly self-developed, and are reflected upon in an exchange with others (students, instructors, the public).
2. The procedures are based on scientific principles, and the research process and the results are critically reviewed.
3. Interdisciplinarity will be considered and the findings will be presented to a (professional) public, for example the student body or practice partners.

Whether and the degree to which inquiry-based learning offers solutions here will be examined below.

17.1.3 Inquiry-Based Learning in Public Health

Learning arrangements that are intended to promote interdisciplinary development in public health include "Regional Health Universities," for example (Sottas et al. 2013). This didactic approach was pursued in the 1970s and aimed to strengthen the integrated training of health professionals across professional boundaries and care sectors (ibid.). However, this will not build a bridge to inquiry-based learning. Reiber explicitly addresses the benefit to the public health sciences associated with inquiry-based learning (Reiber 2012a, 2012b). She sees potential for multidisciplinary reflexivity in education, for example: Research results from differently designed studies could be received in a multi-perspectivist and critical manner using inquiry-based learning, and different research paradigms could be discovered. This would thereby make it possible to grasp the applied approach of the field through research activity and thus foster students' understanding of public health and professional self-understanding. Likewise, it would be possible to develop the ethically based power of judgment needed in the profession (Schröder-Bäck 2014). Inquiry-based learning could thus help involved practice partners to understand which competencies students could bring to the professional practice.

To our knowledge, there has been no systematic review to date of inquiry-based learning in public health. The implementation of inquiry-based learning in public health and the design of public health studies seem to be situated in the curriculum at individual institutions of higher learning. One example of embedding inquiry-based learning in the public health can be found at the institute for educational and health-care research in the health sector (InBVG) at the Bielefeld University of Applied Sciences (Weyland and Nauerth 2013). Here, the entire course of studies in teacher education for the healthcare occupations includes inquiry-based learning. It is integrated in both the master's and bachelor's degree programs and includes both small-scale research as well as multi-semester projects (ibid.).

Another example is the "FLexeBel – Forschendes Lernen zur Vorbereitung auf komplexe und interdisziplinäre Berufsfelder" ("FLexeBel – inquiry-based learning in preparation for complex and interdisciplinary professional fields") project at the University of Bremen. It is aimed at the implementation of inquiry-based learning in all teaching modules of the master's degree program in "healthcare provision, health economics and healthcare management" (FLexeBel 2015) ["Gesundheitsversorgung, -ökonomie und -management"]. The bachelor's degree program at the University of Bremen also includes inquiry-based learning. The seminar on occupational health management in "daycare centers" settings, which was financially supported, designed and carried out within the context of the ForstA project (research-based study right from the start) was exemplary. The goal was to implement occupational health management in daycare centers using inquiry-based learning. Over the course of two semesters,

1. theoretical fundamentals regarding occupational health management were taught,
2. practiced using virtual examples and
3. applied to the actual situation in daycare centers.

The measures for introducing inquiry-based learning into public health sciences are part of the overall strategy for the implementation of inquiry-based learning at the University of Bremen (cf. Kaufmann & Schelhowe, in this volume).

17.2   Critical Discussion and Outlook for the Field of Public Health

As a didactic concept, how can inquiry-based learning help address the specific challenges faced by public health (e.g. the holistic theoretical/practical relevance and the difficult integration of multidisciplinary perspectives)? In the following, we highlight some points that go beyond purely programmatic requirements and should be discussed in public health in order to pave the way for innovative didactic concepts such as inquiry-based learning. This includes sufficient reception and elaboration of the concept of inquiry-based learning for public health didactics, for example. This will make more orientation options available to public health instructors for planning their teaching projects – in a very practical way on the one hand, and in epistemological engagement with their own subject on the other. Both aspects will be examined below, whereby they are, in part, relevant to the approach to inquiry-based learning beyond public health as well.

On the practical side, for example, inquiry-based learning emphasizes an equal learning alliance in which students are guided through the research process in the sheltered environment of a seminar. Associated changes in role expectations and demands on the organization of the lesson design in terms of time and content can create confusion and should not be left unexamined. In the example of implementing health management in daycare centers, the more flexible organization in the inquiry-based learning setting met students' needs. Small group work made it possible to organize working hours flexibly and individually outside of a fixed lecture schedule. Students with part-time jobs or responsibility for schooling or care particularly appreciated the benefits. *Here, the process-oriented setting of inquiry-based learning countered the heterogeneity of the students.*

The more flexible and group-specific learning settings also created difficulties, however, which indicate that innovative teaching formats such as inquiry-based learning in public health should already be taken into consideration when planning curriculum for B.A. and M.A. studies. Examples include *clashes with established, administrative structures and work regulations* – whether these be examination rules, role expectations in a hierarchical teaching/learning system that is focused on grading, time constraints, forms of collaboration, and so on. This may thus be associated with additional work for both instructors and learners that should not be underestimated in order to ensure that activities are timely and conform with administrative expectations (e.g. by means of exception rules).

In addition to questions concerning the concrete design of teaching and learning settings, it is generally necessary to consider how the concept of inquiry-based learning can be designed constructively under the conditions of multidisciplinary public health and possibly even lead to interdisciplinary teaching and learning. For us, the key to this lies in reflection during the research and learning process. According to Huber, these should include three levels of reflection according to the humanistic cognitive ideal: "the self-reflection of scholarship as a mode of rational cognition, the self-reflection of the subject through scholarship, and the reflection on the common good to be promoted thereby" (2009, p. 3 et seq.; for details, see also Huber, in this volume).

The first two levels of reflection are still in their infancy in the science culture of public health: The cognitive tools used by public health come from other disciplines. They are shaped by different scientific cultures and tend to stand side by side. As yet, there has been no systematic reflection on the understanding of science with regard to public health, the situatedness of the knowledge and the researchers, as well as the ethical responsibilities of the health professionals and those conducting research in the health sector. Inquiry-based learning could introduce well-founded reflection into the learning setting, thereby also supporting instructors who may also lack the theoretical and analytical foundations of the different core disciplines. Without reflection on the understanding of science and research as the basis for the research process, this could lead to more research-oriented learning, as in the daycare example. This leaves the applicability of the research and public health understanding of itself, as well as the homogeneity of the students as researchers and professionals in the field of health policy, unexamined.

Another item from discussions regarding inquiry-based learning in public health sciences concerns *the relevance of the findings for third parties, i.e. for scientific contexts as well as for practice partners* (cf. Huber 2009). The "third party" is first and foremost the scientific community: the seminar group, the department or a scientific forum. Here, Huber (2009) refers to requirements that can also be met by student work within the students' abilities, and not to trailblazing research innovations that alter a scientific community. This pertains to requirements that do not call into question the contents of the everyday scientific work of teachers and scientific staff (cf. ibid.). According to Tremp (2014), the students are the main addressees of the presentation of results. Critical aspects of the orientation towards third parties emerge, for example, when the relevance of the topic for practical partners fails to coincide with the scientific relevance of a topic, such as when the *goals of applicability and commissioned research and the goals of scientific insight* diverge. Both areas of relevance should be critically and explicitly reflected upon in relation to the research and learning process in the seminar, however. This constant work of reflection must not fall prey to the elaborate organization of time and activity in the process of inquiry-based learning in public health.

And what happens if the "third parties" are healthcare enterprises or charities that want to continue working with the seminar results and do not focus on the research and learning process? The third parties being addressed are thus primarily students' potential employers. Mutual expectations will be exaggerated, clients will expect economically beneficial results and students will be less concerned with the learning process of scientific reflection than with output, which is to say with the effort to deliver a "product." In addition, concentration on the "product" places the process-critical reflection of the students' approach and the assessment of their scientific work at risk.

A problem with which inquiry-based learning settings could be confronted is shown in the example of corporate inquiries that seek to implement inquiry-based learning in certain health-related corporate contexts. This is an aspect that is initially positive, as it speaks to the positive external perception of degree programs in the health sciences and provides students with an option to acquire practical occupational experience without interrupting their studies. What is vexing about these requests, however, is the content and scope of the services requested. Examples include coordinating and carrying out a national representative survey for quality assurance or the call for tenders for a complete evaluation of outpatient healthcare activities. From a student perspective, this creates a kind of internship construct which, in the best-case scenario, makes it possible for the student to join the company upon graduation and, in the worst-case scenario, must be presented as a "failed project" in the seminar. Here, companies bear neither (personnel or material) costs (e.g. for the data collection, transcriptions or travel) nor risks. From the beginning, it should therefore be very clearly agreed with the practice partner that in the case of inquiry-based learning, what is at stake is the research and learning process in the sheltered environment of the university, and not added economic value. If this discussion is not held, questions will remain as to the degree to which self-exploitation is being promoted as part of the university's organizational and value culture, especially in applied disciplines such as health sciences, by providing services without an economic quid pro quo. In developed professions, for example in the planning field (architecture, civil engineering), professional associations and organizations frequently prohibit institutions of higher learning from undertaking low-cost projects that could also be carried out by professional planning offices; see, for example, the fee structure imposed on architects and engineers acting as public contractors (HOAI). As a multidiscipline, public health still needs to find its own way in this regard.

In summary, it should be said that, as an innovative, didactic concept in public health, inquiry-based learning requires conducive disciplinary conditions pertaining to the structure of higher education if it is to develop good, reflective research and a self-reflective research attitude, as well as multi- and transdisciplinary collaboration. In public, if desired and implemented well, it can initiate sustainable sensitization and qualification processes for both young scientists and instructors as well, in order to meet the challenges of the young discipline.

References

Blättner, B. (2012). Public Health-Inhalte in anderen gesundheitswissenschaftlichen Studiengängen. In F. W. Schwartz/U. Walter/J. Siegrist/P. Kolip/R. Leidl/M. L. Dierks/R. Busse/N. Schneider (Hrsg.), *Public Health. Gesundheit und Gesundheitswesen* (S. 807–810). München: Urban & Fischer.

DGPH (2015). *Was ist Public Health?* Retrieved 29 October 2015 from http://www.deutsche-gesellschaft-public-health.de/informationen/public-health

Dierks, M.-L. (2012). Public-Health-Ausbildung in Deutschland und Berufsfelder der Absolventinnen und Absolventen. In F. W. Schwartz/U. Walter/J. Siegrist/P. Kolip/R. Leidl/ M. L. Dierks/R. Busse/N. Schneider (Hrsg.), *Public Health. Gesundheit und Gesundheitswesen (S. 799–804)*. München: Urban & Fischer.

FLexeBel (2015). *Forschendes Lernen zur Vorbereitung auf komplexe und interdisziplinäre Berufsfelder (FLexeBel)*. Retrieved 29 October 2015 from http://www.ipp.uni-bremen.de/ forschung/abteilung-1%2D%2Dversorgungsforschung/projekte/?proj=633

Hochschulen für Gesundheit e.V. (2001). *Leitbilder für das Projekt Multimedialer Kooperationsverbund: Hochschulen für Gesundheit*. Retrieved 29 October 2015 from http:// blog.hochges.de/wp-content/uploads/2013/04/leitbilder_hochschulen-fuer-gesundheit.pdf

Huber, L. (2009). Warum Forschendes Lernen nötig und möglich ist. In L. Huber/J. Hellmer/ F. Schneider (Hrsg.), *Forschendes Lernen im Studium* (S. 9–35). Bielefeld: UniversitätsVerlagWebler.

Immenroth, T. (2012). Employability als Ziel dualer Pflegestudiengänge. *In A. Nauerth/U. Walkenhorst/R. von der Heyden (Hrsg.), Hochschuldidaktik in pflegerischen und therapeutischen Studiengängen* (S. 57–74). Berlin: Lit Verlag Dr. W. Hopf.

Noack, H. R. (1999). Public Health an der Schwelle zum 21. Jahrhundert: Tradition, Modernisierung, Herausforderung und Vision. In G. Polak (Hrsg.), *Das Handbuch Public Health. Theorie und Praxis. Die wichtigsten Public-Health-Ausbildungsstätten (S. 8–36)*. Wien u. a.: Springer.

Polak, G. (1999). *Das Handbuch Public Health: Theorie und Praxis. Die wichtigsten Public-Health-Ausbildungsstätten*. Wien u. a.: Springer.

Reiber, K. (2012a). Hochschuldidaktik für gesundheitsbezogene Studiengänge. Eine theoretische Grundlegung. In R. Richter/C. Baatz (Hrsg.),*Tübinger Beiträge zur Hochschuldidaktik, 8(2012)*, Retrieved 29 Octiber 2015 from https://publikationen.uni-tuebingen.de/xmlui/ handle/10900/43953

Reiber, K. (2012b). Kompetenzentwicklung durch forschendes Lernen in pflege- und gesund-heitsbezogenen Studiengängen. In A. Nauerth/U. Walkenhorst/R. von der Heyden (Hrsg.), *Hochschuldidaktik in pflegerischen und therapeutischen Studiengängen* (S. 17–28). Berlin: Lit Verlag Dr. W. Hopf.

Schröder-Bäck, P. (2014). *Ethische Prinzipien für die Public-Health-Praxis: Grundlagen und Anwendungen*. Frankfurt/New York: Campus Verlag.

Sottas, B./Höppner, H./Kickbusch, I./Pelikan, J./Probst, J. (2013). *Educating Health Professionals: n Intersectoral Policy Approach* (careum working paper 7). Zürich: Careum Stiftung.

Tremp, P. (2014). *Forschendes Lernen als Profilmerkmal einer Universität: Kommentierung der Beispiele aus der Universität Bremen und Fragen an das Lehrprofil*. Retrieved 18 April 2015 from http://www.uni-bremen.de/fileadmin/user_upload/single_sites/qm/Hochschuldidaktik/ Bremen_Lehrprofil_Bericht_TREMP.pdf

Universität Bremen (2014). *Studierendenbefragung QUEST*. Retrieved 29 October 2015 from http:// www.uni-bremen.de/de/quest.html

Van Wickevoort Crommelin, A. (o.D). *Forschendes Lernen – Genese, Ansätze und geeignete Formate*. Retrieved 18 April 2015 from http://www.uni-greifswald.de/fileadmin/mp/1_studieren/ Qualitaetssicherung/interStudies/Forschendes-Lernen_Genese-Ansaetze-Formate.pdf

Völker, H. (2004). Von der Interdisziplinarität zur Transdisziplinarität? In F. Brand/F. Schaller/ H. Völker (Hrsg.), *Transdisziplinarität: Bestandsaufnahme und Perspektiven* (S. 9–28). Göttingen: Universitätsverlag Göttingen.

Von Troschke, J. (1999). Public Health in Deutschland. Aus- Fort- und Weiterbildung in den Gesundheitswissenschaften. In G. Polak (Hrsg.), *Das Handbuch Public Health. Theorie und Praxis. Die wichtigsten Public-Health-Ausbildungsstätten* (S. 205–216). Wien u. a.: Springer.

Von Troschke, J. (2002). Geschichte und Entwicklung von Gesundheitswissenschaften und Public Health in Deutschland. *Public Health Forum, 10*(3), 4–5.

Weyland, U./Nauerth, A. (2013). *Forschendes Lernen in der Lehrerbildung für Gesundheitsberufe* [Poster]. Fachhochschule Bielefeld.

Winslow CEA (2001). Winslow's definition of public health. In *Encyclopedia Britannica* (S. 740). Vol. 15. London, England: Encyclopedia Britannica Inc. [cf. Winslow CEA (1920). The unfilled field of public health. Modern Medicine 2, 183–191.]

Inquiry-Based Learning in the Natural Sciences

18

Andrea Ruf, Ingrid Ahrenholtz, and Sabine Matthé

18.1 Characteristic Features in the Natural Sciences in Terms of Inquiry-Based Learning

Instruction in the natural sciences of biology, chemistry, the marine sciences and physics is inconceivable without reference to research. Students are trained to take up the profession of "scientist" and faculty often recruit or recommend doctoral students from among former students in their own courses. This practice includes a high proportion of course elements in which students themselves become active such as internships, tutorials and excursions, which usually already correspond precisely with the method of working or at least the methods being used in current research (see Box 18.1 for an example in genomics research).

Interdisciplinary and project-like courses dealing with concrete, socially relevant topics were established due to reform initiatives at universities in the 1970s and the environmental protection and conservation movements in the 1980s (Fichten et al. 1978; Wildt 1981; Jung 1997). In the area of the natural sciences, for example, students have dealt with forest dieback, pollution from chemicals or the effect of radioactivity on the environment.

A. Ruf, PD Dr. (✉)
Fakultät für Natur- und Sozialwissenschaften, Universität Vechta, Vechta, Germany
e-mail: andrea.ruf@uni-vechta.de

I. Ahrenholtz, Dr. · S. Matthé
Carl von Ossietzky Universität Oldenburg, Fakultät für Mathematik und Naturwissenschaften, Oldenburg, Germany
e-mail: ingrid.ahrenholtz@uni-oldenburg.de; s.matthe@uni-oldenburg.de

© The Author(s) 2019
H. A. Mieg (ed.), *Inquiry-Based Learning – Undergraduate Research*,
https://doi.org/10.1007/978-3-030-14223-0_18

Box 18.1: *Tapping the Potential of Undergraduate Researchers – The Genomics Education Partnership (GEP).* **Reprinted from Genetics Society of America (2015) with permission**
Recent reports on undergraduate education have emphasized the crucial role of authentic research experiences. A genomics research article published in the May issue of G3: Genes|Genomes|Genetics allowed 940 undergraduate students not only to engage in original scholarship, but also to be authors on a peer-reviewed scientific paper. The research, on the evolution of an unusual chromosome in fruit flies, was powered by the contributions of students at 63 higher education institutions across the US, coordinated by the Genomics Education Partnership (GEP).

"By organizing the efforts of 'massively parallel' undergrads, we can solve problems that would defeat other methods," says GEP program director Sarah Elgin of Washington University in St. Louis. "At the same time, students learn how to handle the messiness of real data, to evaluate different kinds of evidence, and to justify their conclusions."

The GEP is a collaboration between faculty at a growing number of institutions and the Biology Department and The Genome Institute at Washington University in St. Louis. The GEP's goals are to introduce bioinformatics into the undergraduate curriculum and to integrate research experience into the academic year. With this classroom-based approach, many more students can access educational opportunities normally restricted to those who secure one of the small number of summer research spots available to undergraduates.

The GEP faculty and staff oversaw the project and drafted the paper, but each of the 940 students listed as a co-authors performed original research and read and approved the manuscript before submission. Many students also provided important comments that were incorporated into the final version.

The GEP students tackled the investigation of the "dot" chromosome of Drosophila fruit flies. The dot chromosome gets its name from its tiny size; next to the other fruit fly chromosomes, it looks like a compact dot.

Scientists are interested in the dot chromosome because its DNA is tightly packaged in a form called heterochromatin – a state normally linked with relatively inactive genome regions that contain only a few rarely expressed genes. But despite being packed into heterochromatin, a large region of the dot chromosome carries a similar density of actively expressed genes compared to other, non-heterochromatic parts of the fruit fly genome. Non-heterochromatic DNA is known as euchromatin.

How has this unusual state affected evolution of the dot chromosome genes? To investigate, the GEP team wanted to compare the dot chromosome to a euchromatic region from a different chromosome. But this exploration required a high quality genome sequence from several different Drosophila species, not just Drosophila melanogaster, the species in which the dot chromosome has been most intensively studied.

(continued)

Box 18.1: (continued)

Draft genome sequences for other Drosophila species were already publicly available, but because the dot chromosome carries many repetitive sequences, the genome data was sometimes unreliable. That's because repeat sequences cause trouble for the software that stitches together the fragments of raw sequence data – like a jigsaw puzzle with many pieces of the same color and shape, it's hard to figure out which fragments belong where.

In this case, humans do a better job than computers. The GEP was able to correct errors in the draft genome assembly by breaking the work up into chunks and distributing it among hundreds of students. The students carefully examined each region they were assigned and paid attention to small differences in repeated sequences that gave them clues on how to put the puzzle together. In areas where there were gaps in the sequence, the students submitted requests for laboratory scientists at the Genome Institute to perform additional sequencing to cover these regions. "The students do a significantly better job at improving the sequence than the software does," says Elgin.

The team improved sequences from the dot chromosome and a euchromatic comparison region from three species of Drosophila that, together with D. melanogaster, are separated by 40 million years of evolution. To help them compare genes across the different genome sequences, the students used multiple types of evidence to predict the start, stop, and splice sites for each gene. These "punctuation marks" are critical to understanding how DNA is transcribed into RNA and translated into proteins. Start and stop sites tell the cellular machinery where to begin and end the translation of a sequence, and splice sites define where to chop out intervening sequences – introns – from the regions that code for proteins – known as exons.

Each chunk of sequence was examined by at least two independent groups of students, so they could cross-check findings and fix errors. The end result was a high quality data set that allowed the team, led by GEP staff member Wilson Leung, to statistically compare the properties of the dot chromosome to the euchromatic region in all four species.

This comparison revealed that most of the distinctive properties of the D. melanogaster dot chromosome are conserved across species. Dot chromosome genes have longer introns and more exons than the comparison region, as well as a higher density of repeat sequences. The accumulated repeats – mostly remnants of now inactive transposable elements – can partly explain why dot chromosome genes have larger introns (the introns contain more repeats), though it doesn't explain why the genes tend to have more coding exons.

Dot chromosome genes also showed fewer traces of the effects of natural selection. This agrees with theoretical predictions that natural selection should be less effective on heterochromatic genome regions.

(continued)

Box 18.1: (continued)

The analysis also uncovered a tantalizing clue to one of the ways dot chromosome genes could remain active despite being stuck in a heterochromatic state. The researchers found that dot chromosome genes contain fewer of the "C" and "G" bases (of the famous A, T, C, G components of DNA) than do genes in the euchromatic region. Because Cs and Gs bind together more tightly than As and Ts, the DNA strands that make up dot chromosome genes are likely easier to unwind, which might allow better access to the DNA for the proteins that turn genes on and off. Further research will be needed to test this idea.

The GEP students not only advanced science with their work, but they also learned about genetics and genomics in a hands-on way. This translated to greater educational benefits for the students.

"We think a lot of the benefit comes from asking students to weigh the evidence; sometimes it's contradictory, sometimes one clue is more reliable than another, sometimes the students need to dig a bit deeper," says Elgin. "Basically we're teaching them to look carefully at data and be suspicious, be skeptical."

The GEP has previously measured the program's educational performance and found that students learn more about genes and genomes compared to students who did not participate in a research-based genomics course. The GEP students also self-report similar gains in their ability to analyze data and understand the research process as those who had spent a summer working in a research lab. Given enough time (on average, around 45 h of class time), GEP student gains even exceeded those of summer research students.

"Faculty are sometimes skeptical that this kind of project will work for their students. But the GEP includes a diverse range of schools serving different types of students and the learning gains were similar across every category we tested. I believe any student can benefit," says Elgin.

Read more at http://scienceblog.com/78332/tapping-the-potential-of-undergraduate-researchers/#uEKWMOtzd4iMIDjC.99

Following the study reform related to the Bologna Process (i.e. the introduction of graduated and modularized degree programs), universities have, for the most part, definitively renounced the continuation of the project formats (Kruse 2009), especially as the increase in the number of students and their growing heterogeneity in skills, knowledge and interests have made it necessary to further develop the teaching concept. Instead, elements of inquiry-based learning were integrated into the curricula in less extensive formats or exclusively for selected students. With the additional funding by for example the federal

Teaching Quality Pact, however, many institutions of higher education are rethinking this project tradition and are implementing similar or adapted formats in the natural sciences, for example

- project workshops and "tu projects," ZEWK Berlin (ZEWK 2015);
- Supervision of laboratory internships, TU Darmstadt (Homann 2011);
- Humboldt reloaded, University of Hohenheim (Universität Hohenheim 2015);
- interdisciplinary research competence, University of Bielefeld (Lenger et al. 2013).

18.1.1 Understanding of Inquiry-Based Learning and Teaching Within the Context of the Natural Sciences

In the natural sciences department at the Carl von Ossietzky University in Oldenburg, inquiry-based learning and teaching is understood to mean the interaction between students and researchers whereby scientific curiosity is increased, scientific work practiced and new knowledge generated. Students should thereby practice and intensify their competencies in areas that include a capacity for problem solving and analysis, reflection, collaboration in a team, internationality, project management, independence and responsible time-management.

In particular, the students should:

- develop, plan and implement their own research ideas,
- orient their research ideas towards the international standard for the field,
- establish personal and individual contacts with active researchers,
- be integrated into the research project of working groups and
- give their studies an international focus.

For this reason, instructors must

- include their own research into their teaching practice,
- acquire and apply (didactic) methods that promote students' independent scientific work,
- develop new forms of teaching and learning in communication with other instructors and
- get involved in student initiatives.

This catalog of requirements makes it clear that inquiry-based learning really cannot refer to an individual course or module, but must instead run like a common thread through the curriculum.

18.1.2 Properties of Academic Studies in the Natural Sciences in Relation to Inquiry-Based Learning Using the Example of the University of Oldenburg

Academic studies in the natural sciences and in mathematics have some favorable characteristics that facilitate integrating elements of inquiry-based learning. (1) The natural sciences are not subjects with mass appeal, especially at the level of master's degree programs. Professional master's degree programs are tailored to the research interests of the research groups, since this is where the natural sciences recruit young academics. More than ¾ of new students in the school of mathematics and the natural sciences at the University of Oldenburg find an introduction to research to be important or very important (Albrecht 2015), which is significantly more than the average for all students in their first semester of university. (2) Furthermore, internships and tutorials are traditionally important components of a course of studies which extend through all phases of those study programs. Research methods are usually practiced in internships and tutorials, and sometimes students work on predetermined or autonomous projects. (3) The staff-to-student ratio is frequently good since, in addition to the instructor, additional student or scientific personnel are involved in classes. (4) Project work and thesis projects are often completed within the research groups, e.g. in the research laboratories. This establishes close contact with researchers and makes the standards required of scientific work tangible for students. (5) In chemistry and physics, for example, experiments that are also conducted in lectures demonstrate current research topics and methods. In addition, many degree programs have already established project or block formats years ago that allow a comprehensive and often interdisciplinary treatment of a topic with a great deal of flexibility in terms of time. (6) The fact that there are many qualification positions for completing a doctorate or for postdoctoral qualification for teaching staff facilitates the research orientation in teaching. The young scientists bring a great deal of new impetus to teaching and enthusiasm for their field. (7) In addition, there is usually research-related and modern equipment available in the laboratories and workspaces since the research groups attract a great deal of third-party and special funding. (8) It is also important that scientific standards be applied in the international competition in the natural sciences; scientists compete for funding and publications within an international community. Both advanced study programs for postgraduates and research topics therefore have an international focus.

In addition to these aspects, which are favorable for inquiry-based learning, there are also unfavorable factors in the natural sciences. (1) Firstly, the study groups in many courses are very heterogeneous in terms of previous knowledge and motivation. (2) A secondary-school diploma (*Abitur*) or other university entrance qualification does not guarantee a minimum standard of knowledge in mathematics and the natural sciences. (3) In most disciplines, a great deal of prior knowledge is needed in order to develop a research question, the methods are often specialized, complex and expensive to implement. (4) Generally, interdisciplinary questions that are derived from everyday knowledge do not lead to testable hypotheses. (5) In many natural-science-related subjects, it is very important to systematically develop knowledge in a manner oriented toward the logic of the discipline (Fichten 2010). (6) In addition, the above-mentioned high turnover of non-professorial teaching staff in qualification positions has a negative impact, such that personnel are often inexperienced in instructing students and have little opportunity to systematically develop the teaching competence that is so critical for the format of inquiry-based learning.

18.2   Experiences with Inquiry-Based Learning in the Natural Sciences in a Project at the University of Oldenburg

18.2.1 Measures and Formats

With all of this said, inquiry-based learning is more than a didactic trick, and instructors must conduct research themselves and be integrated into an environment in which scientific activity is actively being pursued. Convinced that there are many different ways and formats through which research and teaching can be linked (Healey 2005), various measures were supported at the University of Oldenburg and subsequently documented and evaluated. In addition to enriching the curriculum with additional personnel, teaching and learning formats that allow inquiry-based learning have been newly established and expanded. This includes the student labs that already exist for elementary school classes for the topics of the Wadden Sea, the human senses, the Green School, energy, automation technology and chemistry and that were expanded as research facilities for prospective teachers. Student labs are course formats in which school classes conduct experiments in facilities and using the equipment belonging to the university, and who are led by university students. In so doing, students can work on their own research questions concerning teaching-learning settings. The implementation of these measures was accompanied by higher education didactic courses for the lecturers, which were tailored to the change of perspective in inquiry-based learning.

18.2.2 Modules/Courses Concerning Inquiry-Based Learning

In many research areas, distinct formats have been developed so that inquiry-based learning can be especially well implemented. Here, most projects emphasized the ability of students to develop their own questions or to identify problems. A few examples of this from among the various thematic contexts have been outlined in Table 18.1:

18.2.3 Summary Overview and Classification

In order to integrate more elements of inquiry-based learning in the degree programs, a total of 17 different formats were developed and introduced. Most of the new courses have been developed for the professional master's degree programs, and many are also directed

Table 18.1 Examples from the degree programs in the natural sciences at the University of Oldenburg in which the new inquiry-based learning formats have been integrated

Format	Brief description	Degree program	Credits
Theoretic (chemistry)	Students will formulate and work on their own questions, derive hypotheses and implement these autonomously on the computer with support from scientists. Participants will program their own quantum chemical program of any level of complexity and solve problems as a team with guidance.	Bachelor's program in chemistry	6
Student lab project module in automation technology (engineering)	School students learn automation technology based on the example of robots that are easy to build and program. The increase in knowledge among school students is recorded empirically by the university students. Students gain insight into didactic research and study the effectiveness of their own teaching.	Two-subject bachelor's degree in engineering	6
Proteomics (marine science)	Biological issues from current research topics are processed and solved. To go deeper into the topic, students give presentations on current publications. Students evaluate the published data statistically and categorize it. A tie-in to the thesis work is possible.	Master's degree program in microbiology	12
Meta-analyses of marine biodiversity (marine science)	Students develop their own initial hypotheses in small groups. Suitable data records will be handed out or students will search for data from the published literature independently, then evaluate the data and present the results. The hypotheses they formulate themselves will subsequently be investigated in laboratory experiments. A tie-in to the thesis work is possible.	Master's degree program in marine environmental sciences	12
Independent research project (biology)	Students suggest projects that they could also work on at a partner institution, for example abroad. Support personnel is available to all students for questions. The goal of the project is to make independent scientific work possible. A tie-in to the thesis work is possible.	Master's degree program in biology	15
Teaching-learning lab in laser optics (physics)	Students independently build the resonator on the basis of calculations made in the group so that the resonator can be used to operate the laser. Due to the modular design, further courses relating to such experiments can build on this in coming semesters.	Bachelor's program in physics	6

(continued)

Table 18.1   (continued)

Format	Brief description	Degree program	Credits
Correlation and causality networks in complex systems (marine science)	The topic is the empirical reconstruction of correlation and causality networks based on multivariate data. The basics of theory and application of mathematical methods are taught in lecture units. Acquired methods can be applied to data that is provided or students' own datasets. In so doing, students develop and process their own questions.	Master's degree program in marine environmental sciences	6
Student lab in the Wadden Sea/ teaching-learning lab (biology)	Students first develop learning arrangements on the topic of the Wadden Sea. These are then implemented together with the school students, who work as independently as possible. University students reflect upon and optimize the learning arrangements using didactic research methods.	Two-subject bachelor's degree in biology	6

Source: author's representation

towards students in the bachelor's program. Another important element of independent research in the natural sciences is the preparation of a thesis, which is not listed separately here. Many of the courses containing elements of inquiry-based learning can be used as preparation for a thesis, however. The various formats include different tasks in the curricular acquisition of the competency to conduct independent research (on the basis of Deicke 2013):

Stage 1 – Receptive: Students acquire knowledge and abilities related to scientific research.
Stage 2 – Applying or referring only to literature: Students make a narrowly defined contribution to a larger research project or review literature.
Stage 3 – Researching: Students work on their own research project.

In order to be able to systematically record the depth to which, and in what respects, the new formats included elements of inquiry-based learning in the degree programs, instructors were asked to classify their courses according to the categories of inquiry-based learning: in the receptive, applying and researching stages, and in the categories of research results, methods and processes, respectively (according to Deicke 2013). The explicit designation of methods and the application thereof make this model especially suited for the natural sciences. This often relates to research methods and to the implementation in practical action. The classification shows a focus in terms of the research methods, namely at all three levels of student activation (receptive, applying and researching); this is how nearly half of the projects carried out were classified. It is also striking that approximately 40 percent of the projects were assigned to the receptive stage, whereby a move towards more demanding levels of learning is desirable. At the same time, there are at least five formats that instructors described as allowing students to go through the entire research process autonomously, although the degree programs have not undergone any fundamental structural changes. This confirms that the curricula in mathematics and the natural sciences are well prepared for inquiry-based learning formats and that these formats have long been considered, for example when selecting the appropriate forms of examination.

18.3   Conclusion and Outlook: Outlook for Inquiry-Based Learning in the Natural Sciences: What Needs to Be Done?

Overall, both teaching staff and students benefited from the above-mentioned projects and formats, and the evaluations demonstrated that both sides were satisfied or even enthusiastic. Nevertheless, difficulties did arise. Students first had to understand and accept the new learning concept; many were unaccustomed to being able to pursue their own ideas. Once students had undergone this change in perspective, however, it was possible for them to continue to work very well. It was also difficult to deal with heterogeneous study groups with varying previous knowledge and different motivations for engaging in a change in perspective. This turned out to be particularly difficult in bachelor's courses. Some classes were perceived as being too specific. The size of the study group substantially impacts the success of the format: Neither those groups that were too small (fewer than 3 students), nor those that were too large (more than 20 students) were able to satisfactorily implement the planned concepts.

18.3.1 What Are the Next Steps?

With regard to the systematic and sustainable establishment of inquiry-based learning, the projects made it clear that the degree programs already have the necessary formal structures. Nevertheless, steps for further development are necessary:

Adjusting the Staff-to-Student Ratio   Courses containing elements of inquiry-based learning require very intensive supervision and therefore would reduce the teaching capacity in other formats if established on a permanent basis. This would lead to the deterioration in the staff-to-student ratio in other courses. Therefore, a significant increase in the Curricular Standards (CNW) – the planned teaching hours for a student's education – for degree programs with evident elements of inquiry-based learning is absolutely necessary.

Analysis and Further Development of the Research Orientation in the Degree Program Curricula   A research orientation is an essential element of academic studies at the university. It is therefore appropriate to use this aspect to assess and, if necessary, adapt the degree programs in terms of continuous quality development. In so doing, the model developed by Wolfgang Deicke (Deicke, 2013) could be used. Each module can be arranged in this grid. That means that, in planning a degree program, an important aspect is the research orientation by applying inquiry-based learning. Based on this, the curriculum can be structured in terms of its systematic capacity building for independent research.

Integration into the Quality Development of Degree Programs The goal of sustainably establishing elements of inquiry-based learning can be achieved by systematically anchoring these in the curricula and the monitoring of success. The subject of elements of inquiry-based learning can be included as an operational goal in a quality-development system. As a result, inquiry-based learning will be anchored in such a way that it is reported on and the further development thereof documented. An indicator system would need to be worked out for this.

Impact Research Elements of inquiry-based learning in degree programs should be visible, further established and expanded so that students are better equipped to develop into autonomous, independent and responsible members of the global scientific community and society. In doing so, they should have acquired all of the competencies over the course of their studies that enable them to perform the corresponding functions as academics. Presumably, students who have experienced many elements of inquiry-based learning are therefore better able than other students to meet the educational goals of degree programs. Corresponding impact research must first demonstrate this, however.

18.3.2 Outlook

In the degree programs in the natural sciences, many practical and research-related elements already exist that make it easy to selectively integrate inquiry-based learning and self-determined action on the part of students. What is missing are formats adapted to the specific phase of a course of study (e.g. for motivation in the introductory phase of the course of study), a curricular build-up in research competence including interdisciplinary competencies, and systematic integration into a system in order to develop the quality of the degree programs, as well as comprehensive and fair concepts for sustainable establishment beyond the Teaching Quality Pact. What continues to be needed are concomitant impact research, in order to identify efficient models, and a reinforcement of the higher education didactic competence of the instructors through measures that are tailored to the scientific culture of natural sciences.

References

Albrecht, N. (2015). Studieneingangsbefragung 2014/2015. Retrieved 14 June 2015 from http://www.uni-oldenburg.de/lehre/evaluation/interne-evaluation/studieneingangsbefragung/
Deicke, W. (2013). *Implementing Research-Based Education: Challenges and Opportunities* [Powerpoint-Folien]. Zugriff auf Vortrag an der Humboldt-Universität zu Berlin am 14.06.2015 von http://www.unica-network.eu/sites/default/files/20121205%20UNICA%20Bologna%20Lab%20Deicke.ppt

Fichten, W./Jaeckel, K./Stinshoff, R., (Hrsg.). (1978). *Projektstudium und Praxisbezug. Reformmodelle der Lehrer- und Juristenausbildung*. Frankfurt/Main, New York: Campus.

Fichten, W. (2010). Forschendes Lernen in der Lehrerbildung. In U. Eberhard (Hrsg.), *Neue Impulse in der Hochschuldidaktik. Sprach- und Literaturwissenschaften* (S. 127–182). Wiesbaden: VS Verlag für Sozialwissenschaften.

Genetics Society of America (2015). *Tapping the potential of undergraduate researchers. More than 900 students co-author genomics research paper*. Retrieved 03 March 2016 from http://www. genetics-gsa.org/media/releases/GSA_PR_201505_GEP.html

Healey, M. (2005). Linking research and teaching: exploring disciplinary spaces and the role of inquiry-based learning. In R. Barnett (Hrsg.), *Reshaping the University: New Relationships between Research, Scholarship and Teaching* (pp. 67–78). Maidenhead: McGraw Hill/Open University Press.

Homann, U. (2011). *Qualifizierungskonzept und innovative Prüfungsform für die Betreuung von Laborpraktika in Studiengängen der Fächer Biologie und Chemie*. Retrieved 14 June 2015 from http://www.stifterverband.info/ wissenschaft_und_hochschule/lehre/fellowships/fellows_2011/ homann/darmstadt_homann.pdf

Jung, E. (1997). *Projekt – Projektunterricht: mehr als eine Methode*. Schwalbach: Wochenschau-Verlag.

Kruse, E. (2009). Projektstudium und Praxisbezüge im Bologna-Prozess. *Sozial Extra, 33*, 1/2, 42–47.

Lenger, J./Weiss, P./Kohse-Höinghaus, K. (2013). Vermittlung interdisziplinärer Forschungskompetenz: Lehren und Lernen von- und miteinander. *Zeitschrift für Hochschulentwicklung, 8*, 60–68.

Universität Hohenheim (2015). *Humboldt reloaded*. Retrieved 14 June 2015 from https:// studium-3-0.uni-hohenheim.de/ueberblick

Wildt, J. (1981). *Hochschuldidaktik und staatliche Studienreform. Zur Transformation des Projektstudiums im Spannungsfeld einer Studienreform von »oben« und »unten«*. Materialien und Berichte, Bd. 13. Bielefeld: Interdisziplinäres Zentrum für Hochschuldidaktik der Universität Bielefeld.

Zentraleinrichtung Wissenschaftliche Weiterbildung und Kooperation (ZEWK) (2015). Projektwerkstätten und tu projects. Retrieved 14 June 2015 from http://www.projektwerks- taetten.tu-berlin.de/menue/ueber_projektwerkstaetten_und_tu_projects/

Inquiry-Based Learning in the Engineering Sciences

19

Thorsten Jungmann

Creativity and a capacity for innovation are among the intended learning outcomes in Engineering Education. Engineers are expected to develop technical solutions for current and future technical and social problems. Inquiry-based learning as a didactic principle can be used to design the teaching-learning environments in such a way that, in addition to professional competencies, students can learn critical interdisciplinary competencies as well. Based on the research of Johannes Wildt, Ralf Schneider and Thorsten Jungmann (cf. Schneider and Wildt 2009, Ossenberg and Jungmann 2013), a research workshop for engineering students was developed and set up at the Technical University of Dortmund. The newly designed format and, above all, the special set-up and equipment on site are intended to close the gap between theoretical knowledge acquisition and practical engineering work.

19.1 Creativity and Innovation Cannot Be Learned by Rote Memorization

Engineers are creative problem-solvers. Their developments have an impact on people, society and the environment. Large development projects are handled by interdisciplinary teams, the members of which must have more than professional methodological engineering skills alone. In addition to creative problem-solvers, engineers who work using

T. Jungmann, Prof. Dr.-Ing. (✉)
Jungmann Institut, Herne, und Fachhochschule Bielefeld, Fachbereich Ingenieurwissenschaften und Mathematik, Professur für Ingenieurwissenschaftliche Grundlagen und Technikdidaktik, Bielefeld, Germany
e-mail: tj@jungmann-institut.de

© The Author(s) 2019
H. A. Mieg (ed.), *Inquiry-Based Learning – Undergraduate Research*,
https://doi.org/10.1007/978-3-030-14223-0_19

analytical calculation are also needed. Consequently, engineers should be able to generate creative, innovative ideas as well as transform their ideas into technically feasible, safe and sustainable solutions using the analytical methods of engineering sciences. It is not just fully trained engineers who are subject to a variety of requirements. At the start of a degree program in engineering, students are often already faced with conflicting expectations: "short periods of study, study abroad, soft skills, economic skills and, on top of that, good grades in the core engineering subjects" (Becker 2007, p. 1, translated).

A survey of career beginners conducted by Karl-Heinz Minks (cf. 2004, p. 34) brought to light the fact that, at the start of a career in engineering, the following abilities are especially decisive: working independently, communicating with others, organizing oneself and others, and assuming responsibility for processes and products. Engineering education is usually characterized by lectures and tutorials in the first few semesters, the primary goal of which is to impart basic professional knowledge to the students. In later semesters, the lecture format is then supplemented by laboratory- and project work. Experiments frequently take place in labs with guidance, with the findings already known in advance. The effect here is frequently reproduction rather than creativity.

The conflict of objectives in Engineering Education is training engineers to be scientists on the one hand, but also preparing them for the creative and engineering-related solution of technical issues on the other. In view of this conflict, the development of a new teaching-learning format on the basis of inquiry-based learning is proving to be productive.

19.1.1 Inquiry-Based Learning Fosters Creativity and a Capacity for Innovation

In addition to the remarks by Ludwig Huber (2009) and the Federal University Assistants' Conference (BAK) (1970) on inquiry-based learning (cf. Mieg, Pasternack, Reiber, Huber, in this volume), the definition developed by Karin Reiber and Peter Tremp stresses the open, unfinished character of research:

> Inquiry-based learning means an introduction into science through the medium of scientific reflection and forms of working. The skills of research are learned, as well as disciplinary knowledge. An attitude is practiced that is characteristic of scientific activities: wanting to know something, questioning a factual situation and one's own views at a critical distance. Inquiry-based learning can be characterized by the fact that the academic field is not treated as a finished and fixed education building and is not presented as a static possession of certain knowledge, but instead is developed through questions for which research seeks answers. (Reiber and Tremp 2007, translated)

As such, inquiry-based learning does not supplant the lecture as a teaching method. In addition to active, independent learning, receptive learning through a systematic or problem-related transfer of knowledge also has its place in teaching: "If there is a canon of knowledge capable of producing a consensus, this should be imparted during the overview" (Reinmann 2009, p. 42, translated). Examples of this include the rules for the execution of technical drawings as well as the process model of "systems engineering," which embeds the evaluation of the solution in the entire, systematically designed product development process. It is the understanding of such fundamental methods and their practiced application that allows the professional handling of creative ideas in the innovation process. Thus, for example, effective and professional communication about various solutions for a given technical problem is made possible by sketches and drafts completed in compliance with the rules for the execution of technical drawings.

Similarly, genetic and critical learning have their place in inquiry-based learning: Genetic learning or, in other words, the reproduction of research processes from the initial question to the result by students supersedes inquiry-based learning when the latter is too difficult, time-consuming or resource-intensive. Critical learning serves to reflect basic scientific questions and cognitive processes, to develop critical distance and to learn independent scientific work (ibid.).Gabi Reinmann (2009) advocates not viewing the problem-oriented approach as a central characteristic of inquiry-based learning as do, in her view, "nearly all authors who are currently discussing inquiry-based learning." She advocates returning to the core characteristics of inquiry-based learning as conceived nearly 40 years ago in the Federal University Assistants' Conference (BAK), but in so doing, to not exclude the complimentary forms of learning (genetic, receptive and critical learning). According to Reinmann, inquiry-based learning is taking place when

> [s]tudents conduct their own research (e.g. as a final paper) when they participate in a research project by taking on a single task (e.g. in the case of larger projects), when they perform research 'on a small scale,' thus research that is guided and for practice (education research within the context of courses) or when they are at least able to understand the research process (genetic learning). (Reinmann 2009, p. 43, translated)

Inquiry-based learning once again gained increased significance in the course of the Bologna Process. Based on the recommendations of the German Science Council (Wissenschaftsrat) (cf. Wissenschaftsrat 2001, p. 41) the use of inquiry-based learning for Engineering Education clearly demonstrated the following

- The objective of a degree program in engineering to acquire (a) the competence needed to deal with typical problems and tasks in professional practice and (b) the disciplinary knowledge which leads to the ability to make judgments in a scholarly examination of the subject, and which incorporates reflective competence and professional know-how with reference to the professional field of engineers.
- Engineering Education should promote and foster an attitude of inquiry-based learning, in order to enable future engineers to utilize their theoretical knowledge to analyze and shape the professional field and, in this way, carry out their activities not in a manner that is remote from scholarly pursuits, but rather with a research-centric attitude.

19.1.2 Inquiry-Based Learning in Engineering Education

How can inquiry-based learning be implemented in the engineering sciences? What could learning in the format of research look like in the engineering sciences? Synchronizing learning and research processes, as illustrated in Figure 19.1, shows us some of the possibilities.

The figure is based on the learning cycle according to Kolb (1984), which is shown inside. The outside of the figure models the sequence of activities typical for research projects in engineering.

The synchronized cycles start with the perception of a problem or a question. Curiosity can be the driving force both in the case of learning and in the case of researching. After the students have specified the problem and defined the system boundaries, the problem can be abstractly conceptualized or modeled. Immersion in the theory contributes to a conceptual understanding and supports both the development of a research question and the selection and establishment of a research methodology. The planning and implementation of the research project leads to activities such as experimentally checking the abstract concept or model, for example. When analyzing and interpreting the resulting data, students find out whether later concrete experiences with the research subject can be predicted using the abstract concept. Errors become apparent when the results are implemented

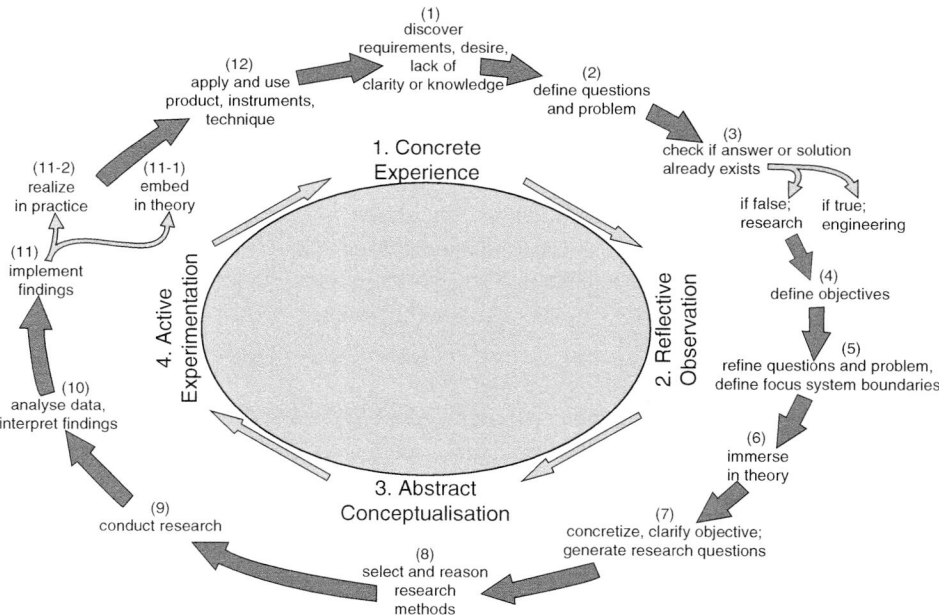

Fig. 19.1 The research cycle according to Jungmann (2011) synchronizes with the learning cycle according to Kolb (1984). (Source: author's representation)

in practice or are embedded in theory. The cycle starts again as soon as ambiguity or new issues arise after the implementation.

Based on the classification system proposed by Huber (2013), we distinguish between inquiry-based learning in the narrower sense and inquiry-based learning in the broader sense. In the narrower sense, inquiry-based learning is the format as described by the Federal University Assistants' Conference (BAK) 1970, in which students go through the entire research cycle largely autonomously in terms of methodology and content, based on a subject of their own choosing. Inquiry-based learning in the broader sense is the umbrella term for various formats, for example research-oriented learning or research-based learning. In this broad sense, inquiry-based learning can be implemented in Engineering Education, for example by having the students:

- delimit a problem,
- determine a state of the art,
- select methods,
- establish a model,
- perform experiments,
- interpret results in the context of methods and theory and/or
- publish results.

Students participate in individual phases of the research process or in the entire research process. This flexibility in the implementation of inquiry-based learning makes it possible to design teaching-learning processes, which result in the desired increase in competence in the field of professional, methodological and interdisciplinary competencies.

19.2   Where Does Inquiry-Based Learning Take Place in the Degree Program in Engineering?

Inquiry-based learning in Engineering Education can occur in various locations. Lecture halls and seminar rooms offer good opportunities for students to participate in lectures on research (results) and impart the canon of knowledge capable of producing a consensus based on the state of scholarship. In laboratories, students can perform experiments on equipment and machines on an industrial scale. Students can learn to do research away from machinery and equipment in the research workshop, a learning site specifically set up for this purpose, and which will be discussed in greater detail later in this article. Here, they learn to develop a critical attitude, and to question and discuss their own research findings and those of other. Each of the following sections examines one of the various locations for inquiry-based learning.

19.2.1 Inquiry-Based Learning in a Seminar Room: Tutorial, "Kreativität und Technik" ("Creativity and Technology"), TU Berlin

The technical realization of creative ideas in the course of construction is an essential element of research in mechanical engineering. In the tutorial, "Kreativität und Technik" ("Creativity and technology"), which is offered at TU Berlin within the context of their orientation studies, "MINTgruen" (MINTgreen)[1], the fundamentals of engineering design are conveyed before the students apply them in their own work. One individual application is the design of a mechanical timepiece. Students independently design the form, select the material and define the function of their timepieces. In so doing, they chose a strategy in terms of the methods being applied, experimental design and research. They are confronted with the corresponding risk of resting on errors and taking detours, of working in a scientific manner and portraying the results in such a way that, the significance is clear and the way in which those results were reached is verifiable. They work in teams, and are supported by tutors. Here, creativity is especially important because both tried and true solutions and innovative approaches to solving the problem come into question and are weighed against each other.

This teaching-learning scenario must be categorized as inquiry-based learning in the narrower sense. It exhibits essential features of inquiry-based learning and introduces students to situations within the context of projects that are competently dealt with in research-oriented behavior.

19.2.2 Inquiry-Based Learning in the Laboratory: Maastricht Science Programme, Maastricht University

In the "Maastricht Science Programme," students can help to shape their bachelor's degree program according to their own abilities and inclinations. In addition to core modules such as biology, chemistry and physics, the course of studies even includes elective modules such as "biomedical engineering." Here, the students work on currently relevant, still-unanswered research questions. They carry out their own small research projects, working closely with scientists from the university. They perform experiments in labs within the context of their research projects, for example in thermogravimetric analysis or gas chromatographic mass spectrometry. They document their findings and present them to the interested public at technical conferences and in journals.

This teaching-learning scenario corresponds to inquiry-based learning in the narrower sense, whereby the emphasis here is on learning the skills of research when dealing with highly modern lab equipment on the one hand, and the comprehensible planning and documentation of experiments on the other.

---

[1] Translator's note: MINT is the German equivalent of the English STEM.

19.2.3 The Dortmund Research Workshop for Engineering Students

In designing the research workshop described here, the focus was on motivation, effectively supporting the engineering students in their professional and personal development; special emphasis was placed on the development of creativity and a capacity for innovation that cannot be trained in a lecture hall or in specialist laboratory. Based on the didactic principle of inquiry-based learning, the research workshop for engineering students was designed as a teaching-learning environment in which students were trained to become innovative problem-solvers. The focus is on producing the aforementioned learning situations and occasions, thereby facilitating and promoting their own interest-based engagement with a topic from a research perspective. Subject areas include Industry 4.0, mobility concepts in megacities and resource efficiency in production technology.

In the standard spatial configuration (see Figure 19.2), the research workshop is divided into two areas that can be flexibly separated from one another. In the part of the research workshop shown on the left, students can work and discuss in groups, develop ideas for their own research projects or immerse themselves in literature. Moderation, research and visualization tools (1, 2) as well as literature (8) are thereby made available to them. The right part, which is delimited from the left by flexible partitions (2), is optimized for presentations and equipped with presentation media (6, 7). It is designed such that students can present the results of their research activity.

The Dortmund research workshop for engineering students is an activity that is part of the "Exzellentes Lehren und Lernen in den Ingenieurwissenschaften" (ELLI) ("Excellent teaching and learning in the engineering sciences") project funded by the Bundesministerium

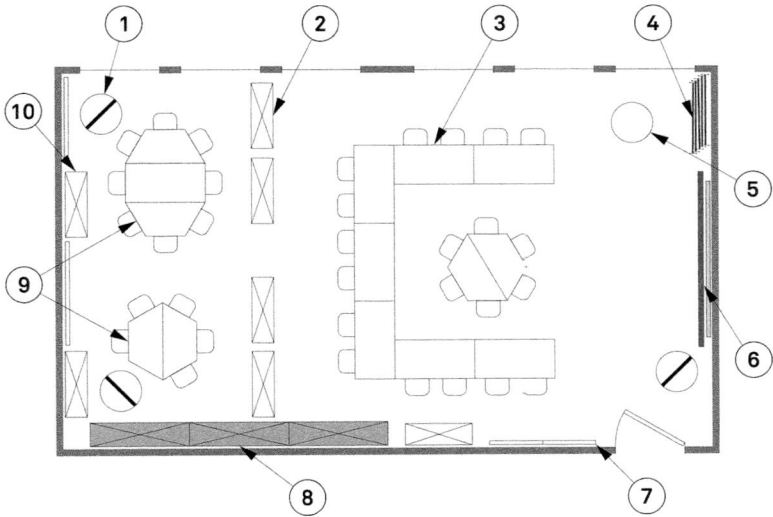

Fig. 19.2 Floorplan of the research workshop for engineering students at the TU Dortmund campus according to Jungmann und Ossenberg 2014. (Source: author's representation)

für Bildung und Forschung, within the context of which inquiry-based learning plays a prominent rule due to its special suitability for teaching in a manner that fosters innovation and creativity. With the ELLI project, the three project partners – RWTH Aachen, Ruhr University Bochum and Technical University of Dortmund – have taken on the task of effectively improving Engineering Education at their locations. The team at the research workshop is comprised of experienced scientists, academic staff and student assistants, who together design the various courses and make them accessible to students. At the Dortmund research workshop, there is a special task for student assistants who have a tutoring qualification, and who support students in their learning and working phases in inquiry-based learning.

19.2.4 Courses at the Research Workshop

The team at the research workshop and the materials provided support inquiry-based learning in the engineering sciences during free hours of operation, workshops, courses and experimental workshops.

During the *hours of operation*, students are free to use the research workshop. They have the opportunity to use the materials available in the research workshop – which include the experimentation sets or the moderation and presentation technology – for their own "research projects" (e.g. their bachelor's thesis) either individually or in small groups, or practice their next presentation. Furthermore, the students can seek advice from the tutors on scientific work during the hours of operation. The goal is for students to already start using the research workshop during the first semesters of their studies so that they can familiarize themselves with independent work on exciting topics early on while using a scientific methodology.

In addition to the hours of operation, the research workshop provides students with the opportunity to develop and refine key qualifications in *workshops*. Workshop topics include time and self-management, presentation techniques and scientific work. Depending on the topic, the workshops at the research workshop last between three hours and two full days. Students from the engineering sciences as well as other departments participate in the workshops. The resulting interdisciplinary perspectives on the workshop topics can be used beneficially, especially in inquiry-based learning processes. The workshops encourage students to engage in active and sustainable learning. Learned methods can be tried out immediately and then evaluated.

In addition to the workshops, which are self-contained, short thematic sections of the research cycle, the *course*, "Fit for Science – Wissenschaftliches Arbeiten in den Ingenieurwissenschaften mit Tablet-PCs organisieren und präsentieren" ("Fit for Science – organizing and presenting scientific work in the engineering sciences using tablet PCs" cf. May and Ossenberg 2015), has been established as part of the Dortmund research workshop. Students go through the entire research cycle in groups during the course. Collaborative scientific work is supported by mobile devices. Mobile devices particularly support the informal learning processes, for example using Evernote and other apps directed towards collaboration and productivity. They allow students to work on their topics across various platforms outside of their university courses and provide the opportunity to document not only the results of the informal learning processes but also the progression thereof in a comprehensible manner.

Experiments are frequently used in the engineering sciences. Research questions are answered empirically or data relevant to finding a solution is identified with the help of experiments. The significant step of experiment planning precedes the task of actually conducting the experiment. As a rule, the complexity of a problem or question is reduced by means of abstraction and idealization, as well as by appropriate assumptions, so that these can be examined in the experiment. The innovative teaching-learning format "FLExperiment" was developed in order to enable the students to acquire the skills needed to do so. Various experimentation sets, which are available in the research workshop, allow students to get their first experiences with technical experiments without having to rely on the availability of laboratory equipment. FLExperiments allow students to plan and conduct experiments without expensive lab equipment. By doing so, the students learn to hypothesize and confirm or disprove by conducting experiments. They practice writing a scientific report documenting their experiment, including the experimental setup, methods, materials used, research results and conclusions.

After conducting several FLExperiments in *experimentation workshops*, students will have acquired the basic skills necessary to plan, perform and evaluate experiments. In the further course of their learning, tutorial support for the researching learning processes replaces the methodical guidance. Peer-learning and peer-review are initiated and fostered. Students work on parts of the research cycle during the early stages of the FLExperiments. As learning progresses, there is a transition from partial processing to going through the entire research cycle.

19.3   Summary and Outlook

Inquiry-based learning as a didactic principle can be used to design the teaching-learning environments in such a way that, in addition to professional competencies, students can learn critical interdisciplinary competencies as well, especially in the engineering sciences. Its special suitability for competency-oriented, student-centered and, at the same time, science-related degree program design makes inquiry-based learning a preferred didactic principle in engineering programs, especially as there are numerous points of contact for inquiry-based learning, e.g. laboratory internships and experimental lectures.

There are challenges posed by the practical implementation of inquiry-based learning, especially in terms of curricular embedding or, respectively, in assigning credits for the student workload. In particular, it is necessary to consider the special organized and informal learning processes when calculating and awarding credit points.

References

Becker, F. S. (2007). Was heute von Ingenieuren verlangt wird. Markttrends, Erfahrungen von Berufsanfängern, Erwartungen von Personalverantwortlichen und Karrieremechanismen. In J. Grüneberg/I. G. Wenke (Hrsg.), *Arbeitsmarkt Elektrotechnik Informationstechnik 2007* (S. 13–32). Berlin: VDE-Verlag.

Bundesassistentenkonferenz (BAK) (1970). *Forschendes Lernen – Wissenschaftliches Prüfen.* Bd. 5. Bonn: Schriften der Bundesassistentenkonferenz.

Huber, L. (2009). Warum Forschendes Lernen nötig und möglich ist. In L. Huber, J. Hellmer/ F. Schneider (Hrsg.), *Forschendes Lernen im Studium* (S. 9–35). Bielefeld: UniversitätsVerlagWebler.

Huber, L. (2013, 02. September). *Forschendes Lernen: Forschungs- und Entwicklungsaufgaben* [Eigene Mitschrift]. Vortrag an der FH Potsdam, Potsdam.

Jungmann, T. (2011). *Forschendes Lernen im Logistikstudium: Systematische Entwicklung, Implementierung und empirische Evaluation eines hochschuldidaktischen Modells am Beispiel des Projektmanagements* [Dissertation]. TU Dortmund, Deutschland.

Jungmann, T./Ossenberg, P. (2014). Research Workshop in Engineering Education: Draft of new Learning. In *Proceedings of the 2015 IEEE Global Engineering Education Conference (EDUCON).* Konferenzbericht der Engineering Education towards Excellence and Innovation, Tallinn University of Technology, Tallinn, Estland (S. 83–87).

Kolb, D. A. (1984). *Experiential learning: experience as the source of learning and development.* Englewood Cliff NJ: Prentice Hall.

May, D./Ossenberg, P. (2015, März). Fit for Science: A course for teaching to organize, perform and present scientific work with mobile devices. In *Proceedings of the 2015 IEEE Global Engineering Education Conference (EDUCON).* Konferenzbericht der Engineering Education towards Excellence and Innovation, Tallinn University of Technology, Tallinn, Estland (S. 176–183).

Minks, K.-H. (2004). Kompetenzen für den Arbeitsmarkt: Was wird vermittelt, was vermisst? In Stifterverband für die Deutsche Wissenschaft e.V. (Hrsg.), *Bachelor- und Masteringenieure. Welche Kompetenzen verlangt der Arbeitsmarkt? Positionen* (S. 32–40). Essen: Stifterverband für die Deutsche Wissenschaft e.V.

Ossenberg, P./Jungmann, T. (2013). Experimentation in a Research Workshop: A Peer-learning Approach as a First Step to Scientific Competence. *International Journal of Engineering Pedagogy (iJEP), 3* (2013), 27–31.

Reiber, K./Tremp, P. (2007). Eulen nach Athen! Forschendes Lernen als Bildungsprinzip. In B. Berendt/H.-P. Voss/J. Wildt (Hrsg.), *Neues Handbuch Hochschullehre. Lehren und Lernen effizient gestalten. [Teil] A. Lehren und Lernen. Neue Lehr- und Lernkonzepte.* (Griffmarke A 3.6). *Berlin: Raabe.*

Reinmann, G. (2009). Wie praktisch ist die Universität? Vom situierten zum Forschenden Lernen mit digitalen Medien. In L. Huber/J. Hellmer/F. Schneider (Hrsg.), *Forschendes Lernen im Studium. Aktuelle Konzepte und Erfahrungen. Bd. 10. Motivierendes Lehren und Lernen in Hochschulen* (S. 36–52). Bielefeld: UniversitätsVerlagWebler.

Schneider, R./Wildt, J. (2009). Forschendes Lernen und Kompetenzentwicklung. In L. Huber /J. Hellmer/F. Schneider (Hrsg.), *Forschendes Lernen im Studium. Aktuelle Konzepte und Erfahrungen. Bd. 10. Motivierendes Lehren und Lernen in Hochschulen* (S. 53–69.) Bielefeld: Universitäts Verlag Webler.

Wissenschaftsrat (2001). *Empfehlungen zur künftigen Struktur der Lehrerbildung.* Berlin: Wissenschaftsrat.

Inquiry-Based Learning in Mathematics 20

Ingolf Schäfer

As Huber (2009) states, inquiry-based learning as a higher education didactic method is subject to strong criticism from many quarters. The issue of the unity of research and teaching, which serves as a central pillar for the educational-theoretical justification of inquiry-based learning, is called into question both in principle and pragmatically. This article will present inquiry-based learning in mathematics as an idealized process on the one hand, and in a real implementation on the other. This will be done against the backdrop of cultural-historical activity theory according to Roth and Radford (2011), which more precisely defines the theory for mathematics learning based on Leontiev (1978).

20.1 Introduction

Inquiry-based learning has become increasingly important as a method of higher education didactics in recent years. As such, inquiry-based learning is also regarded as a bridge between the traditional demand for unity of research and teaching, and newer demands in a pluralistic world that is characterized by the ability and willingness to learn throughout one's life.

Within mathematics, the primary trend in inquiry-based learning consists of very broad attempts to establish inquiry-based learning as part of mathematics instruction. Please refer to the PRIMAS project of the European Union (see Box 20.1) as exemplary for many other projects. Although PRIMAS and similar projects have created a large public for the topic of inquiry-based learning within mathematical didactics so that at conferences of the Gesellschaft für Didaktik der Mathematik (Society for the Didactics of Mathematics), for

I. Schäfer, Dr. (✉)
Universität Bremen, Fachbereich Mathematik/Informatik, Bremen, Germany
e-mail: ingolf.schaefer@uni-bremen.de

© The Author(s) 2019
H. A. Mieg (ed.), *Inquiry-Based Learning – Undergraduate Research*,
https://doi.org/10.1007/978-3-030-14223-0_20

> **Box 20.1:** *The PRIMAS Project of the European Union*
> At 14 institutions of higher learning in 12 European countries, instructional materials are being created, teacher training sessions held, and support provided in the implementation of instruction, all of which serve to introduce inquiry-based learning into instruction in mathematics and the natural sciences. The project describes the goals of PRIMAS as follows (Projekt PRIMAS n.d.):
>
> > PRIMAS has taken on the goal of getting more higher education students, school pupils and graduates interested in school subjects and fields of study from mathematics and the natural sciences. Partners of PRIMAS are convinced that more pupils would be enthusiastic about these subjects if their natural curiosity were stimulated and strengthened through inquiry-based and discovery learning. The pupils will learn to observe phenomena, to ask questions, to look for solutions independently, and to reason. The pupils should not and cannot discover everything themselves. However, they should be allowed to experience how a mathematician or natural scientist proceeds in order to get a fair picture of these subjects and the careers associated therewith

example, regular sections are held on inquiry-based learning in schools, this has found little resonance in higher education. The same is true internationally: although inquiry-based learning is currently widely considered within the school context, it does not play a recognizable role in higher education.

Within the context of the "matheFL: inquiry-based learning right from the start?" project at the University of Bremen, an attempt was made right from the first semester to utilize inquiry-based learning in project groups in order to strengthen and maintain student motivation (Bikner-Ahsbahs et al., 2013). The examples from the implementation used in the text are taken from this project. The matheFL project is sponsored by the University of Bremen within the context of the initiative for inquiry-based learning (cf. Kaufmann & Schelhowe, in this volume).

20.2 Definition of Terms and Theoretical Frameworks

Huber (2009, p. 10, translated) defines inquiry-based learning as follows:

> In contrast to other learning methods, inquiry-based learning is characterized by the fact that learners shape, experience and reflect on the process of a research project, which is aimed at obtaining insights that are of interest to third parties, doing so throughout all the essential phases of said project; from developing questions and hypotheses, selecting and implementing the methods, through testing and presenting the results, either by working independently or in active collaboration with an overarching project.

It already seems difficult to fulfill this definition for courses within a normal course of study. At the start of a course of study, however, it may even seem impossible: much like the current research situation in any scientific discipline, the requirements for independent research or active participation in a project generally demand a much more substantive and, above all, methodical knowledge than can be provided in a school education. Two specific problems become apparent for mathematics. On the one hand, the structure of mathematics is ordered in a strictly deductive manner. There may be no gaps in mathematical proofs. On the other hand, there is currently no research being conducted in the areas directly covered by lectures for beginners; instead, it is frequently conducted in sub-areas motivated by applications, which then require very extensive additional knowledge just in order to understand the research questions in these areas. Obtaining insights that are of interest to third parties within an introductory lecture seems nearly impossible.

Huber (2009) explains the use of inquiry-based learning in various ways: To begin with, he argues at the level of education. Here, the scientific method serves to gain insight by self-reflection, and the engagement with which science is pursued is what makes it possible to go beyond a school education and training (Huber 2009, p. 11 et seq.). At the level of general competencies, the project-like approach of inquiry-based learning most likely offers the opportunity to practice key qualifications such as cooperation, communication, and managing time and work in a natural way (Huber 2009 p. 13 et seq.). Finally, Huber emphasizes the importance of inquiry-based learning for "deeper learning" (for details, see also Wulf, in this volume). Here, deeper learning means that it is not a sluggish knowledge of facts that is being learned, but rather "a living ability that can be actively used in new situations and flexibly modified" (Huber, 2009, p. 15, translated). This does not require completed knowledge, but rather more generalizable and generative action strategies (ibid.). As Huber points out, the approach to authentic problems such as those that may arise within the context of inquiry-based learning provides the best prerequisites for this.

In activity theory according to Wolff-Michael Roth and Luis Radford (2011), activities are social processes that occur within the context of a culture. Each activity consists of individual actions, each of which relate to objects and goals or motives. Roth and Radford describe knowledge as the awareness of possible actions, crystallized as an abstract concept which must be recreated by the individual in concrete situations. Thus, learning can be understood as a process of objectification, meaning an increasing awareness of what one is doing at the moment, and what that means. In so doing, the abstract concept allows one to gain insights through the respective specific manifestation in which action is taken. This view is particularly suitable for the understanding of mathematics learning as this is about examining abstract concepts, such as those of a triangle or vectors, in specific manifestations.

It will be useful here to take a closer look at the processes involved in inquiry-based learning using this concept of learning from activity theory, which is based on the work of Leontiev (1978). In so doing, "researching," "inquiry-based learning" and "completing tutorials" are the activities that are relevant in this context.

To begin with, it is immediately apparent that Huber's above-mentioned definition of inquiry-based learning is formulated as an activity. The motive for the activity is to (help) design, experience and reflect on a research project, and the activity includes activities such as developing hypotheses, choosing the method, presenting the findings, etc., so that, in the end, insights are obtained that are of interest to third parties.

In order to understand research in mathematics as an activity, we must first establish that the motive for mathematical research is to identify generally valid correlations and to demonstrate their validity, thus to formulate and prove mathematical propositions. Although there are areas of mathematics that have other motives, for example applying or algorithmizing, these are not a part of the mainstream of mathematical research. Mathematics is therefore described as the "proving discipline." Boero (1999) examined the activity of producing proofs in greater detail and, by analyzing the working processes of mathematicians, developed a model comprised of six stages:

1. non-specific exploration of an area of interest;
2. formulating a generally valid claim pursuant to the conventions in mathematics;
3. specific exploration of the claim;
4. identification and ordering of the steps of the proof in a chain of deductions;
5. writing proofs in the context of mathematics (publication);
6. (optional stage) all parts of the proof formulated according to the rules of formal logic.

It is natural to understand these stages as actions associated with the activity of proving and mathematical research per se, whereby activity is understood within the meaning of Roth and Radford (2011). When considering specific proofs, it is possible to apprehend these broad activities much more precisely and identify the respective goal.

However, in the case of the form of learning that is common in STEM subjects, a lecture with a tutorial, other activities are realized in the tutorials. On the one hand, one is confronted with a concrete task, the solvability of which has already been established, and the essential process consists of repeating and applying processes and methods from the lecture. If one views "completing a tutorial" as an activity unto itself, the motive consists of acquiring routines for problem-solving and to reach a prescribed level of points in order to obtain a proof of performance (the proportion thereof varying, depending on the student). Even if exercises are proof tasks, at least the essential first two stages in the Boero model are omitted. Tasks that are more open-ended, which include processing these two stages, are virtually non-existent.

According to Schneider and Wildt (2009), the activities "inquiry-based learning" and "researching" can be described in a manner that is consistent with the categories of research activity, although the frames of reference are different. All activities of the Boero model – which of course represent the specifics of mathematical research – can be classified as activities in inquiry-based learning. If we take the intention that the course of study is intended to enable students to conduct independent research as the starting point, it becomes clear that the pure teaching-learning format of a lecture with a tutorial is not suitable for producing a broad repertoire of required sub-activities. Conversely, this does not mean that lectures with tutorials would be pointless; rather, they provide an important part of the set of tools needed in stages 4 and 5 of Boero's model.

20.3   Exemplary Analysis of Projects from "matheFL"

This section will present the implementation of inquiry-based learning in mathematics within the "matheFL" project (Bikner-Ahsbahs et al., 2013) and, at the same time, will analyze the work of one project group from an activity-theory perspective. The examples discussed here occurred in conjunction with the lecture "Linear Algebra 1," within the context of an intensified course on linear algebra for students of secondary-school teaching.

The groups were allowed to select their topics from a list of very general topics, for example perspective, population growth, ranking, mixture, ratios, and resources. Good topics should be able to arouse a certain degree of interest in students, and at the same time should provide the mechanism that makes it possible to connect the mathematical theory gained during the semester to an individual application. The group's first task was to come up with their own research questions on the topic. The instructor then commented on these questions where applicable and, if necessary, the group then narrowed these down, expanded them or discarded them and replaced them with other questions over the course of the project. The only requirement was that the research questions should relate to the lecture on linear algebra.

Every two weeks, the progress of the project was documented in a shared wiki document, both so that the groups could keep one another informed and so that support could be provided. Entries in what was known as the "research wiki" included a brief description, who in the group did what during the period of time in question, what progress was made, what problems occurred or what changes were made, and documentation of the sources read or consulted. The groups received feedback on their entries and, where applicable, help and advice on the documented problems.

Each group received individual feedback on the final presentation from the instructor. In addition, in the last session in the semester, the individual groups reflected on their experiences in the project. The course concluded with the submission of the written papers. As a special incentive, the three best papers were published in an anthology for the course and the three groups with the best presentations were asked to give a slightly more elaborate version of their presentation, again as part of a lecture series for interested pupils.

This raises the question as to whether the aforementioned implementation also satisfies Huber's criteria mentioned in Section 3. The project process is based on the external progress in the research process, i.e. research questions were asked, then investigated in a methodically controlled manner. In so doing, the research questions were potentially changed. At the end, the results of the research had to be presented and written down. Structurally, the procedure thus fulfills Huber's criteria.

The support intensity varied widely, however. To what extent can the groups really act independently, or to what extent is the procedure scientific if it is completely independent? Experience has shown that all groups sought assistance and advice, or received help through the feedback on entries over the course of the research. Nevertheless, significant differences in the need for support were discernable: Approximately half of the groups simply needed confirmation that they were on a reasonable path with their deliberations, and these groups tended to have questions concerning details. These groups independently sought out and analyzed literature, adjusted their research questions, generated examples, and were able to complete their presentation and written paper without much help. This constituted *working very independently*. A third of the groups required stronger incentives, i.e. reference to concrete literature, specific concepts that one could consider, or assistance with helping themselves set up an example. These groups were also limited in their ability to select their topic themselves. Here, we would say this was *working largely independently*. The remaining sixth required substantial assistance. These groups was limited in their ability to independently design and reflect on their topic, even with literature or concrete examples. We would classify these groups as *working largely with support*.

Huber also stipulates that the knowledge generated should be potentially interesting for third parties. The knowledge produced, however, depends on the respective progressions of the group work. In Bikner-Ahsbahs et al. (2013), it is therefore suggested that the approach used in the project be referred to as "research-like learning," when that approach is similar to a research process, based on research questions and knowledge interest. In any event, in the present round of projects, 8 out of 24 groups generated knowledge that could be of interest to third parties. Five groups modelled practical situations using the methods of linear algebra, and three groups attempted to identify mathematical structures in phenomena. Although, in principle, this knowledge is available in the literature, when linked to a concrete phenomenon, it is nevertheless an interdisciplinary example and in this sense of interest to third parties.

20.4 Exemplary Progression of the "Projection and Perspective" Group

The following presents the progress of a group by way of example. Starting just from the title, "Projection and Perspective," after some research, the group formulated three questions:

1. How are three-dimensional objects mapped onto a two-dimensional surface?
2. What are perspectives and what perspectives are there? What is the connection between these perspectives and linear algebra?
3. How are projections represented in mathematics?

After another session, an additional question arose: What is the projective space? The group then split up (relevant excerpt from the research wiki):

December 18, 2011

After a lengthy investigation of the research questions, we determined that the questions are too general or are difficult to process. For example, we realized that, given the subject of rotation, the question "3D in 2D" is too complex and would take too much time given the scope of the course.

Then we came up with the idea of putting projections into the context of linear algebra: What is the relationship between projections and maps?
Are there projections that are maps and vice versa?

December 20, 2011

Member 1: I researched projective space and was able to find out that this is an extension of affine space. Upon researching further, however, I discovered an interesting topic: photogrammetry [...]. This deals with the reconstruction of three-dimensional objects from two-dimensional images and thus falls within projective geometry.

Member 2: I researched how objects are projected onto a graph. In addition, I have dealt with subspaces for projections. Going through the calculations, I determined that I needed to do some catching up on the subject of vectors. So first I refreshed my knowledge of vectors, and at the moment I am still trying to better understand the different types of projections.

As can be gleaned from the above, some group members were working on projections and others were trying to figure out what a projective space was all about, which appears to have been a bridge back to linear algebra for the group. In doing further research, the group came upon the topic of "photogrammetry," which later became the main subject of interest. The entries in the research wiki also clearly show how they still were still working on understanding the terms, however. Finally, the group came up with three content areas: projections (central and parallel projections) as linear transformations, the geometric object of "projective space" and the reconstruction of three-dimensional objects from various two-dimensional projections.

In its presentation, the group limited itself to the first two areas due to time constraints. During the reflection session at the last meeting, the students stated that the questions from the audience made them notice that they were still not fully clear on the connection between the areas. The three areas were brought together in the final report, in which the explanation of the projective space was significantly richer than it had been in the presentation.

In the beginning, the research questions were of a type that tried to make something accessible: The first question was not yet necessarily mathematical, but instead posed the technical question, "how does it work?" With the second question, the students attempted to gain an overview of the topic (i.e. that of perspective) and its relationships to linear algebra, which would then be mathematized in the third question. The topic of photogrammetry gained importance as a result of studying the literature and discussions with the lecturers. The wiki even indicates that an object-related interest in photogrammetry developed: students' engagement with linear transformations, equivalence classes and vector subspaces became more intense and their engagement with the mathematical contents gained in depth.

Looking at the project group from the point of view of action theory, one sees that the group clearly shows some of the actions from Boero's model. Group members initially explored their area in a general and unstructured way; for example, they developed ideas about the connection between projections and linear transformations, which came together as concrete hypotheses, which can be found (mostly only implicitly) in the research wiki. They researched in a structured manner, for instance by concentrating on two and three-dimensional projections. Even when the group failed to fully understand the necessary terms in some areas, that understanding improved as a result of reflection. Thus, in this way, not only did learning incorporate methods, research processes and social interactions, but content-related learning was also promoted.

20.5   Outlook

As the example shows, the fundamental idea of inquiry-based learning in the sense of "research-like learning" (Bikner-Ahsbahs et al., 2013) can already be implemented with students within mathematics. In so doing, however, no "small" research results can be expected; instead, one may expect interesting examples, models and applications.

A later point in time for such a course would be appropriate in order to arrive at a "purer" implementation of inquiry-based learning. This is when the "Undergraduate Research Opportunities Program" at the Massachusetts Institute of Technology and similar programs begin and demonstrate the basic feasibility, for example. Nevertheless, to date there have been no large-scale implementations which appeal not only to individual students in a given year of study, but that are, instead, more broadly established. Furthermore, space must also be created in the course of study to accommodate this. This often does not exist in the narrowly controlled curriculum in mathematics, especially for students in teacher education. It is students in teacher education in particular, however, who need these kinds of experiences in their studies so that later, when they are teaching, inquiry-based learning can become a fruitful form of learning in STEM instruction in school as described in the PRIMAS project.

References

Boero, P. (1999). Argumentation and mathematical proof: A complex, productive, unavoidable relationship in mathematics and mathematics education. *International Newsletter on the Teaching and Learning of Mathematical Proof, 7*(8). Retrieved from http://www.lettredelapreuve.org/OldPreuve/Newsletter/990708Theme/990708ThemeUK.html on 2018-04-16

Bikner-Ahsbahs, A./Dreher, F./Schäfer, I. (2013). Forschendes Lernen von Anfang an? – Plenumsprojekte in Analysis und Linearer Algebra. In L. Huber/M. Kröger/H. Schelhowe (Hrsg.), *Forschendes Lernen als Profilmerkmal einer Universität* (S. 73–90). Bielefeld: UniversitätsVerlag Webler.

Huber, L. (2009). Warum Forschendes Lernen nötig und möglich ist. In L. Huber/J. Hellmer/ F. Schneider (Hrsg.), *Forschendes Lernen im Studium. Aktuelle Konzepte und Erfahrungen* (S. 9–35). Bielefeld: UniversitätsVerlagWebler.

Leontiev, A.N. 1978. *Activity, consciousness, and personality*, Engelwood Cliffs, NJ: Prentice-Hall.

Projekt PRIMAS. (n.d.). *Ziele von PRIMAS – PRIMAS – Deutschland*. Retrieved from http://primas. ph-freiburg.de/primas-overview/das-projekt-primas/ziele-von-primas 2015-03-01

Roth, W.-M./Radford, L. (2011). *A Cultural-Historical Perspective on Mathematics Teaching And Learning*. Rotterdam: Sense Publishers.

Schneider, R./Wildt, J. (2009). Forschendes Lernen und Kompetenzentwicklung. In L. Huber, J. Hellmer/F. Schneider (Hrsg.), *Forschendes Lernen im Studium. Aktuelle Konzepte und Erfahrungen* (S. 53–68). Bielefeld: UniversitätsVerlagWebler.

Art and Design

Inquiry-Based Learning in the Arts

Elke Bippus and Monica Gaspar

21.1 Points of Contact Between Inquiry-Based Learning and Art Practices

The foundational publications on inquiry-based learning (inter alia, Huber 2009) demonstrate that there is a clear overlap between the emancipatory objectives of the higher education didactic principle, which has been discussed since the 1970s, and educational concepts in the fine arts: Students' self-responsibility and autonomy regarding their methods and topics, practice and experience as a productive aspect or the necessity that the activity have social relevance are some of the aspects that both educational concepts have in common. The objective of engaging in a process of constantly questioning any existing statement with inquiry-based learning can also be associated with concepts that have been valid in the arts since the 1960s.

Apart from a few exceptions, however, the notion of inquiry-based learning is scarcely used, despite elements of other concepts circulating in art education. In an age in which education and research have gained media and political attention, even in the liberal arts, we are even being increasingly warned about the inflationary use of the words "research" and "new knowledge." According to the art historian, James Elkins, these terms should "be

This article is based on the results of the "Ästhetische Praktiken nach Bologna" project ("Aesthetic practices after Bologna") (2013–2016; Zurich University of the Arts, 2013), a collaboration between the Swiss Federal Institute of Technology in Zurich (ETH), the Berne University of Arts (HKB) and the Zurich University of the Arts (ZHdK). We would like to thank the SNF for its financial support and Monika Kurath, Priska Gisler, Anna Flach and Drilona Shehu for their critical comments.

E. Bippus, Prof. Dr. (✉) · M. Gaspar, Lic.Phil.
ZHdK Zürcher Hochschule der Künste, ith Institut für Theorie, Zürich, Switzerland
e-mail: elke.bippus@zhdk.ch; mgaspar@bluewin.ch

H. A. Mieg (ed.), *Inquiry-Based Learning – Undergraduate Research*,
https://doi.org/10.1007/978-3-030-14223-0_21

confined to administrative documents, and kept out of serious literature" (Elkins 2006, p. 129). Elkins advocates using established terms such as "inquiry," "investigation," "project" or simply "work" to refer to the practice of research in the arts. Given the manifold problems of the term "research" in the context of what is known as "artistic research" (Badura et al. 2015), which will not be presented here, we will address the central characteristics of inquiry-based learning below, and discuss these characteristics within the context of art education.

21.1.1 Emphasis on Autonomy

The basis for inquiry-based learning – like that of art education – is a personal project. From this perspective, education is not measured as a learned, retrievable pool of transmitted knowledge, but rather in the individual's own "seeking and finding, problematizing and understanding, 'astonishment' and invention, investigating and communicating" (Huber 2009, p. 13, translated). Inquiry-based learning educates because students *engage in* scholarship themselves, and not because they learn and acquire something that is complete. According to the relevant literature, inquiry-based learning does not necessarily impart career-relevant knowledge, but instead promotes the "core competencies for the ability to work in highly qualified occupations or professions," for example "dealing with uncertainty," which is used and practiced in research, and sustained "deep learning," in which "the learner organizes, elaborates on and critically reflects on his or her own knowledge" (Huber 2009, p. 17, translated). The ambivalence of these skills, which are known as core competencies for highly qualified occupations, have been discussed since no later than the end of the 1990s. This is because they also justify the new "capitalistic spirit" and are also an expression of profound changes in the now project-based organizational form of our society, in which the boundaries between employment and lifeworld are increasingly blurred and the professional world is determined by the dynamics of change and competition. The new capitalist spirit has integrated characteristics such as "autonomy, spontaneity, rhizomorphous capacity, multitasking [...], the search for interpersonal contacts" and highlights these as guarantees for success, which are "taken directly from the repertoire of May 1968" (Boltanski and Chiapello 2007, p. 97).

21.1.2 Scholarship as a Social Process

The goal of inquiry-based learning is making science tangible as a social process, and this puts it squarely in the tradition of those intellectual forefathers who saw the university as an educational institution. They assumed that students become self-reliant by treating them as though they already are. While inquiry-based learning sees this self-reliance as being guaranteed by systematically running through a research cycle which makes cognitive and emotional experiences possible, a pre-structured research cycle is problematic from the perspective of the arts. Such a cycle is necessarily finalistic in the sense that it implies an end that occurs as soon as one communicates the knowledge or problem-solving. In the arts, on the other hand, not only can problems remain unbiased as to the result, there is in fact an implicit demand that they remain open and negotiable. At issue are the complexity of problems and the proliferation of possible reflections thereof, and "an individual solution […] to a universal condition" (Geyer 2008, p. 62), as the artist and theoretician Andrea Geyer writes.

A second aspect of scholarship as a social practice is participation. Participation in a research cycle in the area of inquiry-based learning requires that all participants, i.e. instructors and students, be empowered: Each assumes responsibility vis-à-vis the group. In the literature, inclusion is doubly characterized as strengthening social competencies and at the same time having a disciplining effect in that a community is formed, in which there is mutual monitoring.

The focus of a collaborative research activity corresponds with developments in the arts since the 1980s that adhere to the concept of collective authorship, as in the media arts. This is distinct from the individualistic concepts of (art) learning; pointing the way are the concepts of the "dividuum" or atomized subjectivity, which question the assumption of an "undivided" and self-contained living entity, and which describe a non-individual singularity using the terms "dividuum" and "dividuality" (Raunig 2010). Artistic practice is linked to the ability to delegate artistic decisions and to recognize and contextualize the complex relationships of one's own work. In the arts, the production of knowledge is commonly understood to be a social process that can be communicated through collective discussion, exhibiting or presenting one's own work, and that is made tangible as a moment of insight.

21.1.3 Reflexivity and Criticality of Inquiry-Based Learning

Like art since the 1960s, the concept of inquiry-based learning is linked to the idea of institutional critique: for example, by questioning every established knowledge structure and every educational concept. Accordingly, the question of whether art is teachable is among the paradoxical and productive characteristics of teaching art. Moreover, since the 1970s, institutional criticism as an art movement – which attempts to use its critical reflections to maintain or open up new, autonomous scope for action – has led to the de-territorialization of the classroom or, concretely, to an "educational turn" in the form of open teaching concepts and experimental structures: The Bologna Process with all its discontents "is also seeing an unprecedented number of self-organized forums emerging outside institutions, as well as self-empowered departures inside institutions" (Rogoff 2008, p. 6).

As the educational theorist Münte-Goussar discusses, for example, despite critical approaches, inquiry-based learning can also be used as another optimization technique for neoliberal, market-oriented educational concepts. Inquiry-based learning promises a self-educating and self-organizing, resilient, flexible subject that can adapt to the diverse demands of today's lifeworld. This subject promises to correspond with the connection between knowledge and creativity as a new central productive force and appears to have been furnished with the ability to make child's play of dealing with non-hierarchical, non-bureaucratic forms of organization. Originally it was artistic forms of employment in particular that were characterized by a project and team orientation, flexibility, a short-term nature and uncertainty, which became exemplary given these new neoliberal requirements (Von Bismarck and Koch 2005).

Values such as self-determination and self-actualization that have traditionally been associated with art are now part of the requirement profile for managers in the neoliberal working world. The use or even the appropriation of ideas and ideals that are emancipatory and related to educational policy for a neo-liberal maximization of profits makes it necessary, in our opinion, to take a closer look at inquiry-based learning and emancipatory educational practice. In so doing, we should point out those aspects that oppose the capitalist apparatus of justification – the "attractive, exciting life prospect, while supplying guarantees of security and moral reasons for people to do what they do" (Boltanski and Chiapello 2007, p. 25) – in order to reveal differences and prevent, and to prevent short-circuiting self-education with the logic of self-optimization. This is because these days, demands of autonomy and attributions of responsibility are likewise the instrument of a new exercise of power that is conducive to the ideology of a neoliberal market.

21.2   Art Education in Its Sociopolitical Framing

Art education is always rooted in the context of historical, social, cultural and theoretical developments and debates. It is therefore not surprising that there are always revisions and new conceptualizations of teaching methods. These concepts appear to be committed to the fundamental objective of developing areas of freedom and opportunities with students, in which an attempt is made to develop an individual position within a state of constant self-questioning and the artistic experiment that can hold its ground in the face of current artistic and social events. Instructors in the "free arts" emphasize explicitly that their objective is to support the individual development of an artistic personality (Gisler and Shehu 2016). Since in many ways, art always reflects social developments and phenomena, it is necessary to relate to contemporary issues which are debated in discourse and practice in order to develop a critical and at least temporarily emancipatory individual attitude and practice, and to create the necessary areas of freedom. Reflection on art education is thus accompanied by different, ever new reference points. For several decades, these have been digitality, gender, ecology, economization, postcolonialism and knowledge.

Art education and its objectives of not just preserving, but rather expanding areas of freedom under the respective current conditions, of responding critically and resisting normative requirements and of claiming relevance in society are not exactly supported by the declaration, adopted in Bologna in 1999, of a shared European higher education area. A wave of critical reactions and engagement with the Bologna reform on the part of art institutions has generated extensive literature. It should be noted that the reform promotes the tendency to draw a distinction between research institutions and teaching institutions and thus supports the establishment of mass and elite universities. Many of the developments triggered by the Bologna Reform are critically reflected by representatives of inquiry-based learning, as well as by artists and scholars who teach. Numerous academies in Germany and Austria have availed themselves of the opportunity to continue the "fine arts" as a study program that awards a *Diplom*, instead of adapting the B.A./M.A. system, using critical and even resistant strategies towards the Bologna reform.

In Switzerland, on the other hand, the Bologna reform was implemented in all departments, and the former schools of arts and crafts were "upgraded" to universities of applied sciences. Art colleges in Switzerland follow in the tradition of vocational schools of arts and crafts, which brings with it certain difficulties when integrating methods of inquiry-based learning. With the exception of the Geneva School of Art and Design, according to their own self-conception, the schools of arts and crafts in no way aimed to educate fine or free artists, but instead trained them as typographers, photographers, lithographers and graphic designers. This tendency, which dates back to the 1870s, and which was significantly marked by the Arts & Crafts movement, reinforced that instruction was related to industrial needs and was not at all academic in nature. As a consequence, there were hardly any specialist-subject classes in Switzerland in which it would have been possible to study the fine arts until well into the second half of the twentieth century. The absence of an academic tradition was also noticeable when it came to research approaches. One exception to this was the "F+F School of Art and Media Design in Zurich": The Swiss artist Serge Stauffer developed a theory of art as research in the 1970s (Hiltbrunner and Helmhaus Zürich 2013). In contrast to the academies for the visual arts, this was characterized by the development of more comprehensive concepts of art and design and a reform-oriented pedagogy.

With the research project "Aesthetic practices after Bologna" ("Ästhetische Praktiken nach Bologna," Hochschule der Künste Bern 2019), we examined the effects of academization in the training courses for the graphic arts/fine arts, design and architecture at Swiss institutions of higher learning. Using a praxeological and cultural-critical approach, we addressed the question of how aesthetic practices are mediated, how these practices were impacted by the research imperative since Bologna, and whether it is possible to discern the formation of specific epistemic cultures for the respective departments. Various authors have stated that in Switzerland, the research assignment – which was swiftly institutionalized and bureaucratized as a "top-down" decision in the form of research institutes – was issued to the art colleges *before* a significant scene for artistic research existed. In the course of this development, what is considered *research* within the arts is that which is classified and recognized as financeable research by the funding agencies. The findings of our research project made it clear that it is not the discipline itself that determines the form and content of its research, but rather a group of mainly non-specialist actors (representatives of the established university disciplines, those in senior positions related to higher education policy, administrative personnel or interdisciplinary bodies comprised of heterogeneous institutions).

The results of our research show that the art departments assume that they are meeting students on an equal footing as artists. They wish to keep education as free as possible of structural requirements. In the field of design, the metaphor "shoulder to shoulder" is frequently used in order to describe a de-hierarchized, process-oriented understanding of teaching and learning. Unlike some recent studies of German art colleges, which suggest a potential to transfer artistic research to the concept of inquiry-based learning, the studies of the "Aesthetic practices after Bologna" make it clear that the open, experimental and sometimes fuzzy understanding of research in everyday teaching differs from that of artistic research. It therefore seems necessary to grasp research in a pluralistic way so that research approaches are not reserved for master's degree programs in the form of artistic research. In consequence, a methodically rigorous and systematic conception of research should not be pitted against experimental, tentatively seeking, unconventional research that is not goal-oriented. This would reduce the complexity and heterogeneity of research approaches and knowledge forms alike.

21.3 Research in the Arts – Alternative Educational Scenarios

Since art colleges received an official research assignment, the question of which specific forms of knowledge and cognition are generated and transmitted through the arts and in artistic and aesthetic processes is also currently being debated, in addition to the question of what is meant by research in the arts. Artistic research, which is increasingly institutionally anchored at art colleges, is currently often perceived as the academization and narrowing of the research-experimental scope of art. As a result, representatives of a research-experimental approach distance themselves from artistic research while campaigning for aesthetic thinking or research in the arts, which is claimed to be a counter-model to scientific research. Thus, for example, the journal "MaHKUscript. Journal of Fine Art Research" was recently established as the successor to what had been "MaHKUzine. Journal of Artistic Research" (2006–11), and is undertaking a reflexive critical shift in perspective by questioning the meaning of "research" and "knowledge production" in contemporary *artistic production* (and specifically not in artistic research).

Finally, based on three concepts that are currently exerting a determining influence on considerations of education in art, we would like to outline *alternative educational scenarios*: a) unlearning, b) maintaining the "safe space" and c) inquiry-based art in the broad field of social and political action.

21.3.1 Unlearning

In the day-to-day work with students, it is remarkable that their ideas about art and its characteristics, possibilities and functions frequently stem from superficial and reductionist polarizations between art and science or between theory and practice. These judgments (and prejudices) are conveyed through their artistic work, which they develop and implement independently since, as mentioned, there are no assignments in the fine arts. In individual mentoring, in plenary or in group critiques, students practice and reflect in critical engagement with their engagement with their concerns and the depiction thereof. In this regard, no generally binding knowledge nor generally binding practice is imparted. Rather, what is required is a constant self-criticism of one's own practice, aesthetics and thinking. To this end, however, it is indispensable to reflect on the subjective practice and subjective knowledge in relation to universal or general historical as well as contemporary phenomena and developments that are of an aesthetic, ethical or political nature. To this extent, art education is always a self-exploration. When working with students who are methodically pursuing research approaches and practices, it is striking that engagement with the concepts of knowledge and knowledge production have gained increased significance, and that an attempt is being made to achieve emancipation from the Eurocentric perspective. In this context, the concept of learning is less at issue than that of *unlearning*. This term, which originates with postcolonial theory, is linked to a critical engagement with "how knowing occurs" as opposed to "what one knows," to use the words of Gayatri Spivak, the central thinker of postcolonialism and aesthetic education (Spivak 1990). Unlearning means reflecting on one's own privilege as a loss or in other words, to recognize that one's own privileges and the ways of thinking and worldviews that are developed therewith (can) always have a disabling effect (ibid.).

In art, the need to unlearn is manifested in the reflective statements of artists who teach. As the Austrian artist Reiner Ghanal writes in an interview for the PARSE Journal of Artistic Research, for example:

> Investigating Euro-centrism and cultural arrogance, I could use myself as a good and readily available exemplar. I came to better understand myself and my biased cultural background, a process that is still ongoing, hence, I'm still unlearning. (Ganahl 2015, p. 67)

There appears to be little reflection on this aspect of unlearning in the discussion on inquiry-based learning. Thus, for example inquiry-based learning is often traced back to and founded on the Humboldtian educational ideal without taking a scientific-critical perspective (Huber 2009, p. 14). The nexus between "learning" and "unlearning" must be considered in the analysis of educational processes and of processes of autonomous knowledge production so that we can then ask why only a certain "knowledge" is requested and who is developing which educational motivations and when (Castro Varela 2008). Such reflections can be triggered in various ways, and what is urgently needed in the field of art is a practice that is in itself connected with an inherent reflection upon that practice.

21.3.2 Maintaining the "Safe Space"

Both inquiry-based learning and art studies cultivate protected spaces for the development of new ideas. The protected space of an academic institution can be understood as a metaphor for moments "of speculation, expansion and reflexivity" (Rogoff 2008, p. 2). The safe space is not a sound, autonomous world, however, but instead is comparable to a laboratory, a space in which to meet and experiment, and which is open to all sorts of uncertainties and conflicts, for a variety of positions. Given the pressure of the creative industry and the art market and their dictates of efficiency, innovation or productivity, such spaces are seriously at risk.

21.3.3 Inquiry-Based Art "in the Expanded Field"

In addition to safe spaces, art education also calls upon those that address the demarcations between public-social and institutional-private space. Here it is worth mentioning the use of non-commercial spaces operated by artists (alternative spaces beyond the "white cube," i.e. beyond the exhibition of art in the typical white gallery space) or project work in conflict zones. In this context, methods of transdisciplinary research between art, scholarship and society become relevant in order to tackle research itself and to answer questions such as: "How can we develop a new, democratic understanding of research? How can we initiate research processes that potentially involve all members of society, depending on the research question, the field of investigation and the nature of the problem?" (Peters 2013, p. 12, translated). In this case, this is a matter of additional participation, i.e. participation in constituting urgent questions and problems. It is therefore not about the accumulation of knowledge, but rather about questioning the logic of knowledge such as hegemonic forms of knowledge.

21.4 Summary

Education within the art world is described as the process-oriented work of open-ended experimentation and speculation, which is subject to unpredictability, and which requires a high degree of self-organization and self-criticism. Art is always called upon to tackle the boundaries of what has been established and to explore unexpected possibilities. From art it is expected to problematize normative social and political conditions and make alternative spaces possible – and not just for research.

References

Badura, J./Dubach, S./Haarmann, A./Mersch, D./Rey, A./Schenker, C./Toro Pérez, G. (Hrsg.). (2015). *Künstlerische Forschung. Ein Handbuch.* Zürich, Berlin: diaphanes.

Boltanski, L./Chiapello, E. (2007). *The New Spirit of Capitalism.* 1st ed. 2005. London, New York: Verso.

Castro Varela, M. d. M. (2008). Maria do Mar Castro Varela im Interview mit Vina Yun. Das Begehren neu ordnen: Autonome Wissensproduktion in postkolonialer Perspektive. *Frauensolidarität, 1,* 10–11.

Elkins, J. (2006). On Beyond Research and New Knowledge. In Elkins, J. (ed.), *Artists with PhDs. On the New Doctoral Degree in Studio Art* (pp. 111–133). Washington DC: New Academia Publishing.

Ganahl, R. (2015). Strange teaching. The Artist as Excellent and Miserable Teacher. *PARSE Journal, Göteborg: Platform for Artistic Research Sweden*, 1, 65–74. Retreived 25 April 2016 from http://www.parsejournal.com/article/strange_teaching/

Geyer, A. (2008). Notes on teaching art and feminism. In S. Schaschl-Cooper/B. Steinbrügge/R. Zechlin (Hrsg.), *Cooling Out. On the Paradox of Feminism* (pp. 58–66). Basel: Kunsthaus Baselland.

Gisler, P./Shehu, D. (2016). Performative Kapazität der künstlerischen Autonomie. Ethnographische Beobachtungen im Hochschulkontext. In U. Karstein/N. T. Zahner (Hrsg.), *Autonomie der Kunst? Zur Aktualität eines gesellschaftlichen Leitbildes* (Reihe: Kunst und Gesellschaft). Wiesbaden: Springer Verlag.

Hiltbrunner, M./Helmhaus Zürich (Hrsg.). (2013). *Serge Stauffer: Kunst als Forschung. Essays, Gespräche, Übersetzungen, Studien*. Zürich: Scheidegger & Spiess.

Hochschule der Künste Bern (2019). *Ästhetische Praktiken nach Bologna*. Retrieved 4 March 2019 from https://www.aesthetischepraktiken.com/

Huber, L. (2009). Warum Forschendes Lernen nötig und möglich ist. In L. Huber/J. Hellmer/F. Schneider (Hrsg.), *Forschendes Lernen im Studium* (pp. 9–35). Bielefeld: Universitätsverlag Webler.

Peters, Sybille (Hrsg.). (2013). Das Forschen aller – ein Vorwort. In Dies. (Hrsg.), *Das Forschen aller. Artistic Research als Wissensproduktion zwischen Kunst, Wissenschaft und Gesellschaft* (pp. 7–21). Bielefeld: transcript.

Raunig, G. (2010). *Etwas mehr als das Commune. Dividuum und Condividualität*. Grundrisse. Zeitschrift für linke Theorie und Debatte, 35. Retrieved 25 April 2016 from http://www.grundrisse.net/grundrisse35/Etwas_Mehr_als_das_Commune.htm

Rogoff, I. (2008). Turning. In e-flux journal #0 – november 2008, (p 1–10).

Spivak, G. C. (1990). Strategy, Identity, Writing. In S. Harasym (Hrsg.), *The Post-Colonial Critic*. New York/London: Routledge.

Von Bismarck, B./Koch, A. (Hrsg.). (2005). *Beyond education. Kunst, Ausbildung, Arbeit und Ökonomie*. Frankfurt am Main: Revolver.

Inquiry-Based Learning in Design

22

Matthias Beyrow, Marion Godau, Frank Heidmann,
Constanze Langer, Reto Wettach, and Harald A. Mieg

The University of Applied Sciences FH Potsdam is known for its wide-ranging design education: Product and communications designers have been trained here since 1992, interface designers since 2003. In order to highlight the potentials as well as the difficulties and limitations of inquiry-based learning in the discipline of design, several design professors from the department who had already implemented inquiry-based learning in their teaching practice were invited to a discussion in August of 2015:

Matthias Beyrow is a professor of corporate identity and corporate design in the degree program in communication design.

Marion Godau is a professor of the history of design, culture and art and researches the discursive construction of design history.

M. Beyrow, Prof. · M. Godau, Prof. · F. Heidmann, Prof. Dr. (✉) · C. Langer, Prof.
R. Wettach, Prof.
Fachhochschule Potsdam, Fachbereich Design, Potsdam, Germany
e-mail: beyrow@fh-potsdam.de; godau@fh-potsdam.de; heidmann@fh-potsdam.de;
langer@fh-potsdam.de; wettach@fh-potsdam.de

H. A. Mieg, Prof. Dr.
Humboldt-Universität zu Berlin, Georg-Simmel-Zentrum für Metropolenforschung,
Berlin, Germany
e-mail: harald.mieg@hu-berlin.de

© The Author(s) 2019
H. A. Mieg (ed.), *Inquiry-Based Learning – Undergraduate Research*,
https://doi.org/10.1007/978-3-030-14223-0_22

Frank Heidmann studied geography and is a professor of software interface design in the degree program in interface design.

Constanze Langer is a professor of visual interface design in the degree program in interface design.

Reto Wettach is a professor of physical interaction design in the degree program in interface design.

Moderation: Harald A. Mieg; textualization: Josefine Matthey.

22.1   Scientific Research in Design

Mieg: What role does scientific research play in design?

Heidmann: There is art and there is art studies; there is media and there is media studies; thus there is design and design studies, too. Design studies is basic research that deals with the history, theory and perception of design. The concept of *research about design* was established based on the work of Christopher Frayling (1994). This must be distinguished from *research for design*, the results of which include new design methods and processes, for example, as well as the knowledge transfer of other disciplines (e.g. cognitive sciences, information technology, material sciences) for design. The third and most difficult-to-grasp category, *research through design*, expresses that an artifact itself is the embodiment/materialization of research and generates new knowledge. In this way, the "state of the research" is not just conveyed verbally, but graphically as well. Design may thus become a third class of research. It is *a "science of applied, everyday problem-solving."* This opportunistically utilizes the method sets of other disciplines, for example of ethnology.

Godau: In the case of a new discipline, it is an inevitable development that, initially, methodological use be made of other disciplines. In design, we do not have a unified "textbook" that sets forth design methods that can be used in a precise manner. At best, the educational model at the Ulm School of Design (HfG Ulm), which conceives of design as a social and not as a formal task, could be considered to some extent as such. According to the philosophy of the HfG Ulm, products should be developed based on their purpose. HfG Ulm was founded back in 1953 and dissolved 15 years later; since that time, a lot has changed in the field of design.

Langer: Naturally many methods have been adapted and introduced from other disciplines, the reason for which is that designers are interested in bigger problems and *want to "save the world."* Nevertheless, design also has its own research methods – these are simply not summarized in a single compendium. Designers have always worked with variant formation after changing the practical variables, for example. This is a typical design method that has not been "stolen."

Beyrow: I believe that design studies will never be a science that produces definitive answers (*Bescheidwissenschaft*), but rather a *supporting science (Begleitwissenschaft)*. That means that design studies will never claim to fundamentally alter other reference disciplines, since it can only partially "find its way around" in those disciplines. It can provide suggestions for the restructuring of these disciplines and contextualize existing specialist knowledge, however. Nevertheless, design studies will never take on the role of appointed evaluating authority. But we can hope that we will eventually be able to develop an intellectually supportive instrument.

Wettach: I believe that design has contributed much to the social canon of knowledge. An example of this is how early graphic design in the 1990s changed people's viewing habits with the advent of the Mac. We are happy to be inspired by methods, but in the meantime, this evolution also has a repercussion on other disciplines that *we* inspire. For example, the designers Bill Gaver, Tony Dunne and Elena Pacenti developed the technique of "cultural probes," in which data about users' thoughts, feelings and values can be collected with the aid of small artifacts. This is a qualitative method that has since been adopted in sociology.

Godau: If design is an academic field of study, then it is a hybrid, because we have both a technological approach and an individual-intuitive art approach. And, in any case, we also have a humanities approach. Design studies is still growing, however. When sociology, along with other academic disciplines, first saw the light of day, it had the exact same problem. This also happened to psychology, which was decried as "dream interpretation." Historically, I see it as a structural process that is always the first step on the way to becoming a discipline.

Heidmann: I believe that design does not fit into the canon of the human, natural, technological and engineering sciences. These categories of science develop their state of the research through the verification and falsification of hypotheses. Transferring these to design would also mean having to evaluate the results of the design process. Designers would find this difficult.

Beyrow: I would describe this as a fear of allowing a different scale. We feel at home in the taste we have elaborated and in our assessment; that's worth a lot. After all, we would not be able to use scientific methods to relieve a user of making any design decisions. Therefore I would say that design is a kind of *navigator*: We must try to make very complex connections understandable and visible so that the client or other designers are able to follow and participate in the discussion. Accordingly, we are the ones who also develop solutions to these problems. The navigator may be a type that is not easily represented in other sciences. This also means that we need to create access to and an understanding of other industries if we are to develop appropriate solutions for them.

Heidmann: Bruno Latour (2009) stated that it is designers who can "save the world" – if anyone can. Design is very social because it seeks to solve worldly problems, and it rarely operates in a void. Latour described five quality criteria of design that bestow on it the privilege of assuming this role of problem-solver:

1. humility and modesty towards "fundamental" disciplines such as engineering, architecture;
2. attention to detail;
3. the possibility of opening up artifacts to interpretation and giving them meaning;
4. the property of design as a subsequent task that always builds on something that already exists;
5. the introduction of morality, which is the basis for evaluating how "good" a design is.

This makes it clear that designers can withdraw and be empathetic. And since they try harder to generate solutions, they have a more playful approach than other sciences. That is exactly what we need in the twenty-first century. It is a discipline that covers everything. That can also be a strength. In the approach to "design science" within the philosophy of science, the fact that design is *not subject to the traditional understanding of science* is regarded as a strength. Classical science is one path to knowledge; design is another. It is the opposite of an experiment; the results are not generalizable.

Beyrow: Design as a discipline is also about acting from another level – in contrast to occupations and job profiles that are more oriented towards the skilled crafts and trades (such as media design). The thing is: is it necessary? Is "good craftsmanship" not enough?

Heidmann: But what about scientific verifiability? When I use an "eye tracker" (a device that records a person's eye movements) to examine a newly designed logo, I can confirm or refute the design hypothesis of the designer. If we want to view design as more than a skilled craft and trade, we have to let that happen. Finally, whether a logo is well received by the recipient can be empirically operationalized.

Langer: Eye tracking and other methods of evaluation do not necessarily just scare designers because these methods can falsify something, but because they were not used to it in their design education. In design education, the state of the research has always been determined by the verbal discourse. Written discourse – in other words publishing, responding to one another in writing and therefore making the discourse a resource that can be consulted – is something that scarcely exists. That's why we still have small groups in design. It is now time for designers to pay attention to it.

Godau: I find it good to evaluate a new design using eye tracking or other methods. This is the case with marketing methods as well, however: you can only ever represent what is. There is also the principle of habituation, which cannot be foreseen. A new aesthetic when launching a product may initially be met with displeasure and it may take users a while to adopt that aesthetic.

22.2 Inquiry-Based Learning in Design

Mieg: And what does that mean as a consequence for inquiry-based learning?

Godau: I would like to make a distinction between research and inquiry-based learning. For me, in the case of inquiry-based learning, an orientation towards design pedagogy is the priority. And my thesis would be that the question of what inquiry-based learning is in design is premature, because we have no design pedagogy.

Heidmann: My concept of inquiry-based learning is very opportunistic. I simply draw on various methods. Integrating current research findings into one's teaching goes along with inquiry-based learning. Ludwig Huber (2009) calls for *going through the entire research process,* for example – in other words, defining questions and delimiting these again – and this has a lot to do with the normal design process. It's also about delimiting, gathering knowledge, designing something. But at the end of the design process, what you have is an artifact and not a scholarly paper. This is a different output, but the basic process is not dissimilar in research and design studies (Heidmann et al. 2011), especially in the later semesters.

Wettach: I would like to develop a slightly different position straightaway, one that I realize is also becoming more and more important in practice: For me, the *scholarly paper is in the foreground* in the course. I use it as a common thread that runs throughout the course. In this sense, the paper is not documentation that is written at the end of the course, but ideally, I use its structure to establish inquiry-based learning instead. It is therefore used to provide students with written reasoning.

Langer: In principle, inquiry-based learning is about first finding the right question. This is also integrated in the design discipline right from the start: Students must tolerate uncertainties in order to find a topic that is interesting and relevant to them. This is a very painful process, as it is often only then that they realize how interesting a subject is. In design education, some instructors keep students in limbo for a long time. In inquiry-based learning, the focus is also often heavily placed on this *"leaving in limbo."* For design, that is almost boring, since that is already the practice there. There, the question is more about how to narrow the matter down again. The literature on inquiry-based learning shifts the focus to project work, away from lectures. But design actually needs to move further away from project work and back to various distinguishable formats.

Beyrow: My reaction to inquiry-based learning was that I no longer defined tasks but instead defined problems, for example "Here is a baker who wants to sell more bread rolls." As a designer I have to think about which tools I can use and which are the correct tools for this specific baker. What is a challenge here is that we cannot initially work in a way that is solution-oriented, but have to open up the problem area first This will be very disorganized and confusing at first, and it will be necessary to condense it once again in the middle of the semester. In other words, inquiry-based learning also means putting the artist *in a state of surprise,* because they discover everything that a topic may entail. I try to establish simply finding a topic as training for students. As a faculty member, however, I must make a point of eventually requiring actual designs. For me, these are two separate processes.

Heidmann: Naturally, research thrives on the fact that one very often fails and experiences disappointments. This is hard for design students, because you want to have a great product in the end. Feedback can then have a very demotivating effect. Take the example from Matthias Beyrow: If it turns out that people no longer buy bread at the bakery because they've discovered that grain is unhealthy, then that's not a design issue. But as a teacher, you would not say that. And Reto Wettach requires immediate designs in his course, for example, which is something we also disagree on. Admitting that something does not work in research is also part of the early stages of a research process. *Dealing with failure* is unpleasant in other research disciplines as well, but it is especially true in the design disciplines. This also means admitting this to students and not requiring ten posters for an exhibition at the end, for example. We in design would have to deal with these demands somewhat differently in courses that focus on inquiry-based learning.

Wettach: Work done for the bachelor's degree should show that students can apply designs, while work done for the master's degree should also represent a contribution to other designers. In this context we do a lot for the development of methods and tools, for example both in the area of prototype tools and also in the development of new interaction paradigms.

Heidmann: What has proven itself: Doctoral students are especially capable of practicing inquiry-based teaching, since they can also do research in teaching. Unfortunately, at FH Potsdam, we can only hire doctoral students through third-party funded projects. However, inquiry-based learning should not only be made a topic in projects with a limited time-scope, but needs to be continuously and constantly anchored in teaching practice in higher education. Therefore, it is our job as professors to advance and implement inquiry-based learning.

22.3   Advantages of Inquiry-Based Learning for Students

Mieg: How do students benefit from participating in inquiry-based learning?

Godau: Inquiry-based learning is good for opening your own horizons and asking yourself what current topics are. Students are forced to look for questions themselves, which better prepares them for their future.

Beyrow: Students benefit from the fact that they have a different kind of insight when they ask these research questions. We have to make them understand that you cannot "just do it like that." We want to develop concepts and not just act by following formulas. And when you internalize that, you have to ask questions and be able to tolerate the fact that there are 24 equally exciting and good solutions in the class. We do not work towards a universal solution, but instead work using very different approaches, all of which could work, because all can present good arguments.

Langer: And students should understand what citation means, but also that there is a difference between tasks that are aimed at writing a 20-page paper or at developing a design project. And of course that looks different.

Heidmann: Of course, it is also about showing the students an alternative career path to the design firm/agency. The majority of them want to study design in order to create a portfolio or to develop an app, for example, than make a small contribution to developing methods for measuring attractiveness.

Langer: This is the strength of the university as an educational facility that it is able to show this variance in professional careers. That means that we have to educate people who can weigh these and make their decisions on that basis.

Beyrow: We are working on a new type of designer here, partly because we have learned it differently ourselves and want it to be different. In their professional futures, students will also always have to deal with the products of research. This requires intellectual analysis, a strategy that we teach with inquiry-based learning.

Langer: Writing a paper can also advance a design portfolio in a completely different way and set it apart from others. Ultimately, it is always about creating a transfer benefit to other disciplines.

Wettach: I notice this a lot in my practical work with designers who sometimes have great difficulty defending their designs argumentatively. In the case of a presentation, a layperson must be able to decide for themselves whether the design is good or not, or must be provided with a rationale for why it is a good solution.

Beyrow: Correct. Perhaps we can provide designers with the capability to communicate better with inquiry-based learning. In other words, not to say: "This is great because I made it," but instead to lay out reasons and approaches as is done in modern art as well.

22.4   Outlook for Inquiry-Based Learning in Design

Mieg: What is your outlook on, and what are your wishes for, inquiry-based learning in design?

Heidmann: Since the founding of our design program, it has been reflected time and time again in the evaluations that we have a theory and method deficit. There are many reasons for this: We do not coordinate enough, we interpret our modules very freely, there is not one documented state of the research. In their primary studies (*Hauptstudium*), students have comparatively little theoretical knowledge. Although their approaches are intuitively correct and they can design and program, there is nevertheless a lack of factual and methodological knowledge. We need to work on that.

Wettach: I'm surprised how quickly students forget. I also think that we are no longer up-to-date with our evaluation methods, especially when it comes to the qualitative area. I would like for us to do more in the area of cultural probes, for example. Out of the lab, into real life!

Godau: In the course, "Das große Wie. Forschungsmethoden im Design" ("The big How. Research methods in design"), which I designed with Harald A. Mieg, a student raised an interesting question: "Why do we still design for old needs instead of deliberately influencing them?" And I think that is something where inquiry-based learning can help us to think independently about how to influence; not in the sense of "saving the world," but exploring the possibilities and limitations of working as a designer.

Beyrow: I have had the experience of doing research with students on the topic of university logos – it was absolutely impossible. Students were unable to research, analyze and present ten university logos per person. Scholarly research is one of the basic competencies that we should teach as an institute of higher learning, however. This must be approached with new teaching formats. If 10–20% of the courses that we offer are not decidedly design-focused, but instead focus on research results, then inquiry-based learning will also be more wisely accepted.

Langer: The range of possibilities is what is so exciting: getting to the bottom of research questions, but also sometimes making arbitrary/intuitive suggestions. We should also show this range of possibilities to students as approaches (Box 22.1). For me, inquiry-based learning is not a means to confirm what we are already doing, but to try something new.

Box 22.1: Student Interaction Design Research Conference – A Conference for Students by Students (Jacob Buur)

The faculty at the University of Southern Denmark trains students in publishing papers on their own IT Product Design graduate program is positioned between a design school tradition of studio-based learning in active projects, and a university tradition of theoretical basis and scientific argumentation. From the inception of the program in 2001, professor Jacob Buur and colleagues were intent on teaching students to conduct their own research, as the field of interaction design is evolving so rapidly that methods learned 1 year may be obsolete a few years later. One means of achieving this was to challenge students to develop their skills in scientific work: Oral exams turned into research seminars; Projects were completed with a research report in conference paper format.

This led to the need for a venue where students could present their work in a broader community, not just to professors and clients. So in 2005, the University of Denmark established the Student Interaction Design Research Conference (SIDeR), which has been run every year since, in universities and design schools across Scandinavia and The Netherlands, with some 100+ participants. What makes the conference special is that it is organized by students for students. Students submit their papers to double-blind review by junior researchers and faculty; they present, discuss, and organize workshops as in a regular conference. Over time, the standard of student papers has improved as other programs started adapting similar teaching principles. Today, the students don't stop at SIDeR: they submit papers to a range of regular and high-level conferences in the design community – and are often accepted.

What do the students write about? The IT Product Design program is both international and cross-disciplinary, and accepts students with a background in design, engineering, business, anthropology, or communication. Therefore, they also address a wide range of themes and employ diverse research methods; these include: Design ethnographic research (to understand human practices and the role of technologies), research through design (to investigate concepts by building, to critique prevailing perceptions in society), action research (to develop new design methods and practices in organizations), and conversation analysis (to understand how people interact with each other and with designed objects).

Since the early years of SIDeR the focus on research in learning has trickled down to the undergraduate design classes, so that those students have also begun writing up their own research experiments, and several of them get papers accepted at the conference each year.

References

Frayling, C. (1994). Research in Art and Design. *Royal College of Art Research Papers, 1*(1), 1–5.

Heidmann, F./Klose, A./Vielhaber, J. (2011). Erlebbar machen von Forschung für Studierende an Fachhochschulen. In W. Benz/J. Kohler/K. Landfried (Hrsg.), *Handbuch Qualität in Studium und Lehre* (S. 1–20). Stuttgart: Raabe Fachverlag für Wirtschaftsinformation.

Huber, L. (2009). Warum Forschendes Lernen nötig und möglich ist. In L. Huber/J. Hellmer/ F. Schneider (Hrsg.), *Forschendes Lernen im Studium (S. 9–31).* Bielefeld: UniversitätsverlagWebler.

Latour, B. (2009). Ein Vorsichtiger Prometheus. Einige Schritte hin zu einer Philosophie des Designs, unter besonderer Berücksichtigung von Peter Sloterdijk. In M. Jongen, S. van Tuinen/K. Hemelsoe (Hrsg.), *Die Vermessung des Ungeheuren. Philosophie nach Peter Sloterdijk* (S.356–373). München: Wilhelm Fink Verlag.

Inquiry-Based Learning in Architecture

23

Reform is needed in architectural education: The complexity of building tasks (new materials, new standards, internationalization, etc.) needs to be practiced more during training. Taking the path of supplementing the course of studies with special subjects does not seem promising; architectural studies would become overloaded and inaccessible to study. Inquiry-based learning offers an alternative: Students implement their own research projects (often with practice partners) and, in this way, deal constructively with structures and buildings. This article will present, inter alia, a format for inquiry-based learning that could be groundbreaking for architectural education in Germany: the Undergraduate Research Opportunities Program (UROP).

23.1 Design and Project Orientation as Constraints on Inquiry-Based Learning, as a Special Feature of Architecture

The education in architectural programs that is offered in Germany at universities of applied sciences, universities, institutions of higher learning, schools of fine art and comprehensive universities is focused on occupational qualification as an "architect," a professional title that is protected by various chamber by-laws. Thus the requirements for vocational training are clearly linked to occupational tasks – primarily the planning of buildings. The Federal Chamber of Architects specifies four main areas of emphasis as occupational tasks in the "Guideline for career qualification - architects" (*Leitfaden zur Berufsqualifikation – Architekten*, Bundesarchitektenkammer 2007, p. 4, translated):

L. Albrecht, Dipl.-Ing., M.Sc. (✉)
Fakultät Architektur + Raumplanung, Technische Universität Wien, Vienna, Austria
e-mail: luise.albrecht@tuwien.ac.at

© The Author(s) 2019
H. A. Mieg (ed.), *Inquiry-Based Learning – Undergraduate Research*,
https://doi.org/10.1007/978-3-030-14223-0_23

- Design, technical, economic, social and ecological planning of buildings as well as urban planning therefor;
- coordination, steering, control of planning and execution of a project;
- consulting as well as support and representation of the client in all matters related to the planning and execution of a construction project;
- the creation of expert reports.

Learning how to design is usually done in the form of *project work* – in design projects. Naturally, the term *project* is used very differently within a subject culture. In keeping with the educational reform movements in the 1970s, architectural programs were designed so that they were project-oriented or converted into project-based studies. At the time, the following (groups of) features of a project were identified: Practical and vocational relevance, problem orientation, reference to social reality, interdisciplinarity, complexity of the task (Positionspapier zum Projektstudium im Rahmen der Studienreformdiskussion 1979, pp. 2–3). These features are sometimes included in the current project definitions at various institutions of higher learning; however, in my view, frequently, not all of these components are implemented within the projects. An example of such a reduction is the feature of interdisciplinarity mentioned above. Due to the complexity of building tasks, specialized sectoral planning (such as building services, structural design, etc.) is involved when designing and building. Thus it would be possible to identify a project with an interdisciplinary orientation based on the integration of a project intensification (one of the different directions of sectoral planning), for example, or based on the regular involvement of other disciplines, which is recognizable from the curriculum. A random sampling of study plans at the institutions of higher learning shown in Table 23.1 showed that only a few curricula in bachelor's degree programs in architecture are consistently interdisciplinary.

In the case of project work in a course of studies, different priorities are generally set both in terms of the scale – thus possibly from the smallest object to furnishings, rooms, homes, and even urban districts – and in terms of the orientation of the content, in other words a design with a focus on design detailing, for example. If one examines the curricula in architectural programs, the project (in particular of design projects in the broader sense mentioned above, thus including project intensification) takes up a considerable portion of the program. This article will examine a random sampling of current study plans based on the exam regulations for bachelor's degree programs in architecture at eight German institutions of higher learning in order to determine the percentage and scope of *design projects* (see Table 23.1). Accordingly, a trend that can be identified in the eight study plans examined is that obligatory design projects in the bachelor's degree account for approximately 30–45 percent. As such, ordinary design projects generally comprise 8–12 credit points; some institutions of higher learning have supplementary modules with 3–5 credit points in the discipline (for example, for the above-mentioned design detailing).

Table 23.1 Percentage of design projects in architectural studies

University	Total of semesters	Total of credits	Credits per design project (%)	Characteristic features: internship, etc.
TU Berlin	6 (180)	180	81 (45%)	Design projects and project-integrated intensification
UdK Berlin	8 (240)	215	93 (43%)	5-month office internship (25 LP)
HCU Hamburg	6 (180)	180	80 (44%)	Design projects and impromptu designs
HTW Konstanz	6 (180)	150	54 (36%)	1 semester practice phase
FH München	6 (180)	180	65 (36%)	Continued additional modules
TU München	8 (240)	180	58 (32%)	2 semesters abroad
FH Potsdam	8 (240)	240	90 (38%)	Includes office internship
University of Stuttgart	8 (240)	210	70 (33%)	1 semester option of: Study abroad, research

Source: Author's representation, last updated in the fall of 2015

Note: The percentage of the curriculum was determined based on the specified compulsory design projects (including project-integrated intensifications or impromptu designs) within the credit points specified at the home university. Thus phases of study abroad or office internships planned for in the curriculum were not included in the calculation

23.2   Research and the Understanding of Research in Architecture

The relationship to research differs so widely in architecture that a rudimentarily uniform understanding of research is not even approximately identifiable or definable. The range in terms of the view of research ranges from statements by architects with reference to their own (designing) actions such as "I design in a research-oriented manner" to the statement that their own actions have nothing in common with research. These statements likely already reflect the complexity of design activities, which has thus far only been understood to some extent in scientific studies (cf. Führ 1999; Ammon & Froschauer, 2013). According to Banse (1999), in addition to the "stereotypical or routine procedures," design activities have comprised an overlapping of methodical, heuristic and creative intellectual processes.

Since many architects do not consider their own activity to be research-oriented and do not perceive research to be a competence that pertains to their profession, they have a somewhat rejecting attitude towards research. Here, research and scholarship are presumably implicitly equated. Thus this attitude makes the implementation of inquiry-based learning for designing in architecture programs difficult.

In the discipline of architecture, there are numerous fields of research with a scholarly orientation. The group comprising humanities research includes historical, theoretical, cultural-political, artistically oriented disciplines, for example. Also included are design-related or project-related studies, which must be carried out as a basic examination for individual projects (especially in architectural competitions) or as typological research, for example. The "traditional" field of research in architecture, for example in the field of heritage conservation and architectural history, is the building archaeology (e.g. of a historical building or settlement/city). Research in the natural sciences mainly includes technology or material-related topics.

Such research is difficult to implement unless integrated within a design project because of the common curriculum organization in architectural programs outlined above. Research time is almost always included in design projects. A survey of design supervisors at the FH Potsdam showed that students would invest about 5–30 percent of the working time in research activities. Students' assessment of the percentage of time spent on research was identical in a seminar at TU Wien with approximately 20 participants. The subject areas include studies on the location and/or use in particular. Such preliminary and design-related activities vary widely, depending on the topic, the sources involved, and the basic design approach. Frequently historical issues and analyses (housing stock, functional relationships, infrastructure, green space) are also included in the subsequent planning. Ultimately, this time spent researching when designing is not referred to as "research," but rather "(preliminary) studies." These studies are also part of the professional practice: They are referenced as "basic evaluation" (*Grundlagenermittlung*) in the Fee Schedule for Architects and Engineers (HOAI) in Service Phase 1 (special services: "survey, site analysis") (HOAI 2013, Appendix 10). The difference between "research" and "(preliminary) studies" may appear to be marginal in some disciplines; however, architects who implicitly correlate research and science have usually not participated in scholarship within the meaning of a methodological process in their own education and are accordingly unable to pass this experience on.

23.3   Sample Formats

Even with the usual basic conditions, in particular a predetermined curriculum and prepared class schedules, inquiry-based learning can be further developed in architectural education. Research questions are frequently handled in many "small" (mandatory) electives, usually comprising 2–4 credit points. "Real research" is frequently divided into partial subjects that lend themselves to processing, which can be worked on by and with students, especially in the theoretical subjects (architectural history, architectural theory, heritage conservation). What is important here is not that students be able to understand their own actions as input to "real research," but rather as a valuable, small building block in the big picture. Frequently, portfolios are required as output from this research that consist of a mixture of graphic, photographic and written documentation. As a general rule (depending on the previous knowledge of the participants and previous courses at school and in the degree program), these research seminars must be accompanied by intensive and methodical support. In many cases, crash courses for research, citation or a writing workshop are worth recommending as additional offers. Two developments should be highlighted in conjunction with inquiry-based learning: education research in conjunction with targeted skills development on the one hand, and UROP on the other.

23.3.1 Peer-Feedback and Student Research Projects

A few institutions of higher learning have set up special modules in which students can pursue research in the area of architecture, usually instead of a design. At TU Berlin, the corresponding module is called the "student research project" (Lehrforschungsprojekt). As a general rule, all participants in a student research project work "on a shared, predetermined topic. Students work on subtopics within this framework and create a report" (Modulhandbuch 2015, module no.: 60363). This module is only offered within the master's degree, however.

It must be said that a particular weakness of many architecture students is written expressiveness, a competency that is given short shrift in the curricula in architectural programs (cf. Schmitt 2013). "Written expressiveness," as well as "structured thinking" and "analytic capability," can be classified together in the competency category known as *cognitive competencies* (cf. Hobohm et al. 2015, p. 176) and, without a doubt, form the basis of scholarly work and research. Unlike architectural studies, instructors in the humanities deal intensively with students' texts and deal out constructive criticism of the same. In most architecture curricula, very few texts are written within compulsory courses. Instructors who ask for written reports as proofs of performance often find students' texts "unacceptable" and are unable to remediate the deficit within a seminar. Here, it makes sense that constructive criticism in architectural programs not be limited to a few (and seldom selected) seminars, but to integrate them more frequently and compulsorily in the course of studies. One possibility for integration into the curricula is "peer feedback" (see Box 23.1), in which students provide written constructive criticism of their fellow students' texts.

> **Box 23.1: Peer Feedback**
> Similar to the "peer review" review process for scholarly articles, peer feedback is a review process by members of a specific peer group; in this case, students. In doing so, the students give each other qualitative feedback. In the formalized feedback procedure, students assess the submissions of fellow students based on a questionnaire and, at the end of the process, also receive qualitative feedback on their own submission. The process may be carried out anonymously or with names revealed.
>
> As a general rule, peer feedback is conducted in classes in such a way that students give and receive similar amounts of feedback. The number of feedback responses that they must create (and maintain) is set in advance. It is recommended

(continued)

Box 23.1: (continued)

that there be at least two feedback responses per work output so that students receive different perspectives. In addition to key questions for the assessments, it would be best for rules of constructive feedback to be worked out together with the students so that a positive attitude in the feedback is generally guaranteed.

The method consists of three elements essential to the learning process: (intensively) reading the texts of fellow students, writing feedback and receiving it for their own work. This teaching element can promote (self-)reflection by means of the differentiated assessment of unfamiliar work with an actual/target comparison, which is also carried out in comparison with the work the student has submitted themselves.

In architectural studies, the culture of constructive criticism is usually poorly established. For this reason, students should receive training in which they practice giving constructive criticism based on a similar example before actual feedback responses are given to fellow students. In teaching, the use of online media is an effective strategy for conducting peer feedback. The "Workshop" activity within the e-learning platform Moodle is used for this purpose at the University of Applied Sciences Potsdam (for more detail, see Mauch and Albrecht 2014).

23.3.2 The Undergraduate Research Opportunities Program (UROP)

To date, students in bachelor's degree programs in architecture have had barely any curricular opportunity to do their own research. In many cases, the only way for them to participate in scientific research is to work on externally funded projects on a project basis as student assistants. In the United States, the Undergraduate Research Opportunities Program (UROP) was developed to give bachelor's degree students the opportunity to participate in scientific research. A UROP was launched for the first time in 1969 at the prestigious Massachusetts Institute of Technology (MIT) in Boston. Since then, a UROP has been established at almost all US universities; similar programs can be found in Great Britain, Singapore and at RWTH Aachen since 2008.

The respective programs have certain similarities (Laursen et al. 2010, pp. 1–4):

- The research projects are "real science," and thus they are of interest to the scientific community.
- The research project designated for an individual student or a team of students is well-defined in advance and is connected in some way to an ongoing effort in the research group, or to an area of scholarly interest of the supervising researcher.

- This involves working intensively on the research topics either as a multi-week immersion, often full-time for 10 weeks during the summer, or over the duration of an entire academic year.
- Individualized guidance is provided by an experienced scientist.

As a rule, projects are publicly announced. Depending on the project and program, students can be credited with academic achievements. Often, the project is associated with financial support. As a rule, these basic conditions can spur the interest of both supervising researchers and bachelor's degree students in participating in the program. In the US, UROPs are an important component of higher education culture, especially when it comes to competing with one another and for the best students. In UROPs, research partnerships are typically concluded within the disciplines. The number of participants in each respective "partnership" varies from project to project, and from program to program, ranging from a partnership of just two to small groups that often have different levels of qualification in the United States: Bachelor's degree students, master's degree students and post-doctoral researchers work together here.

At the University of Applied Sciences Potsdam (FHP), the UROP was conceived and launched by the author as part of the project "FL^2 Forschendes Lernen – Lehrende Forschung" (FL^2 inquiry-based learning – instructional research). To date, there have been two nine-month cycles for bachelor's degree students of the three degree programs of the FHP Department of *Architecture and Urban Design*. Up to five undergraduate students of the department can participate in each cycle and receive professional and financial support. In preparation, and as an important basic condition for amended study and examination regulations, a new option was created: instead of an office internship, students could complete scholarly work in the form of a UROP and receive credit points for this work. It was unclear what interest the program would attract from the students, however. Potential supervising researchers were involved early in the concept. They created short, introductory project descriptions before the respective tenders.

The UROP supervising faculty was also involved in the issue of how and in what medium the research results should be presented. Many institutions of higher learning such as RWTH Aachen University, for example, organize UROP conferences to present the results of their research. Each year, a National Conference on Undergraduate Research (NCUR) is held in the United States at which undergraduate students present their research results (more than 3000 presentations). Supervisors and students at FH Potsdam prefer that students make their own first *publication* as a result presentation of their UROP research, which of course does not exclude extending this to include presentations and conferences. The scope of the publication approximately corresponds to a typical journal article. Deadlines were set to allow the UROP research to be published in a joint publication. Students can freely select the phase during which this research is done; depending on the degree program and the semester, this research falls into different time periods.

Since, as a rule, this is the first time that architecture students will have the opportunity to go through an entire research process, supervisors should not expect any previous research knowledge. The author of this article set up a *supervisory colloquium* in Potsdam in order to support those who are new to research. This offers both general methodological assistance in research beyond subject-specific and topic-specific questions, and opportunities for exchanges among UROP participants. Depending on the focus of the ongoing UROP projects being worked on, research competencies – starting with the limitation of the topic, and ranging from researching strategies and writing a synopsis to support in obtaining the image rights for the publication – are discussed and strengthened at the colloquia, which are held on a monthly basis. If content-related decisions are also made within the supervisory colloquium (for example, a specifically developed research question), the specific research supervisors are informed, and the students are asked to discuss content-related decisions with these experts. In the long term, as soon as a UROP culture is established in a university, a program similar to MIT's "Research Mentor Program" could be set up, in which experienced UROP students support those who are new to UROP.

23.4   Outlook

At the moment, institutions of higher learning are placing increased pressure on architecture departments or faculties to do more research, and in particular to attract more external funding. In response to this, research conferences have been and are being initiated at some institutions of higher learning (for example TU Berlin, BTU Cottbus, TU Darmstadt, TU Vienna). In Switzerland, all ten architecture colleges met in 2015 for a joint research conference (Solt 2015, p. 12). Such events are primarily aimed at increasing the visibility of architectural research and partly at representing what architectural research is understood to be. Networking is usually a goal as well. Research conferences form an important component in the establishment of research in architecture. Without "real" research interests, without research practice in the sense of a methodical process, inquiry-based learning is difficult to establish and pass on.

A changed attitude towards research in architecture could and should begin much earlier, preferably as soon as the study begins. In the first week of a pilot project implemented at FH Potsdam by the author, new students were encouraged to develop open research questions associated with a building survey and drafting exercise at Potsdam's Belvedere on the Pfingstberg. This assignment provides instructors with a great deal of insight. They are able to get to know a variety of unexpected questions that new student have with regard to architecture, many of which could unexpectedly be approached in an interdisciplinary way (although answering most questions would exceed the scope of a dissertation). For the new students, this exercise provides an insight into the variety of possible topics in the selected subject area. At the same time, this exercise aims to detect an individual's own areas of interest and support curiosity – an important moment in the research process. Research-based learning and teaching could be further developed by means of a variety of even smaller teaching elements across all phases of architectural studies.

In order to bring about long-term changes, UROPs need to be further developed and strengthened. The aim of this expansion would be to ensure that the up-and-coming next generation is more likely to have come to know research in the sense of a methodological process even during their studies. Establishing research in architecture would have numerous benefits: a financial benefit for the institutions of higher learning in terms of attracting external funding, an individual benefit for each graduate in personally developing a critical (research) attitude, and the professional benefit of a methodical process for the basic evaluation and "preliminary investigations" in architecture.

References

Banse, G. (1999). Entwerfen im Spannungsfeld von Methodik, Heuristik und Kreativität. *Wolkenkuckucksheim: internationale Zeitschrift für Theorie und Wissenschaft der Architektur,* 4(1), Retrieved 10 July 2015 from http://www.cloud-cuckoo.net/openarchive/wolke/deu/ Themen/991/Banse/banse.html

Bundesarchitektenkammer (2007). *Leitfaden Berufsqualifikation der Architekten/innen.* Retrieved 10 July 2015 from http://www.bak.de/architekten/ausbildung/leitfaeden-zur-berufsqualifikation/ leitfaden-zur-berufsqualifikation-architekten-1.pdf

Führ, E. (Hrsg.). (1999). Entwerfen – Kreativität und Materialisation. *Wolkenkuckucksheim: internationale Zeitschrift für Theorie und Wissenschaft der Architektur,* 4(1).

HOAI (2013). *Verordnung über die Honorare für Architekten- und Ingenieurleistungen (Honorarordnung für Architekten und Ingenieure - HOAI) Anlage 10 (zu § 34 Absatz 4, § 35 Absatz 7) Grundleistungen im Leistungsbild Gebäude und Innenräume, Besondere Leistungen, Objektlisten.* Retrieved 10 July 2015 from http://www.gesetze-im-internet.de/hoai_2013/ anlage_10.html

Hobohm, H.-C./Pfeffing, J./Imhof, A./Groeneveld, I. (2015). Reflexion als Metakompetenz. Ein Konzeptbegriff zur Veranschaulichung akademischer Kompetenzen beim Übergang von beruflicher zu hochschulischer Qualifikation in den Informationsberufen. In W. Freitag/R. Buhr/ E.-M. Danzeglocke/S. Schröder/D. Völk (Hrsg.), *Übergänge gestalten: Durchlässigkeit zwischen beruflicher und hochschulischer Bildung erhöhen* (S. 173–191). Münster: Waxmann.

Laursen, S./Hunter, A.-B./Seymour, E./Thiry, H./Melton, G. (Hrsg.). (2010). *Undergraduate Research in the Sciences: Engaging Students in Real Science.* New York, NY: John Wiley & Sons.

Mauch, M./Albrecht, L. (2014). Online-gestütztes Peer-Feedback als Baustein Forschenden Lernens. In N. Apostolopoulo/H. Hoffmann/U. Mußmann/W. Coy/A. Schwill (Hrsg.), *Grundfragen Multimedialen Lehrens und Lernens. Der Qualitätspakt E-Learning im Hochschulpakt 2020. Tagungsband GML^2 2014* (S. 265–280). Münster: Waxmann.

Modulhandbuch WiSe 2015/16 für Studiengang Architektur Master StuPO2011 (2015). Retrieved 10 July 2015 from http://www.planen-bauen-umwelt.tu-berlin.de/fileadmin/f6/Studieng_nge/01_ Modulkataloge/Arch_M_StuPO2011_WiSe15-16.pdf

Positionspapier zum Projektstudium im Rahmen der Studienreformdiskussion (1979). Tagung: Projektstudium für Bauingenieurwesen, Architektur und Raumplanung, Dortmund.

Schmitt, G. (2013). Mehr Schreibkompetenz für Planer und Architekten. *Arbeitsmarkt Umweltschutz und Naturwissenschaften, 21*(43), 6–8.

Solt, J. (2015). Was ist Architekturforschung? *Tec21: Fachzeitschrift für Architektur, Ingenieurwesen und Umwelt, 15*, 12.

Individual Disciplines

Inquiry-Based Learning in Business Administration

24

Georg Müller-Christ

In many cases, it is assumed that research-oriented teaching means imparting existing research designs to students or allowing them to participate therein. This article puts forth the idea that new research designs can be developed through the involvement of students in the research process.

24.1 Teaching-Learning Situation in Business Administration

What has changed in the academic process of transferring knowledge that has led to students suddenly being transformed into "young researchers"? They should participate in and promote the process of creating knowledge. But what existed prior to this? And what didactic conditions (still) exist in business administration?

Prior to this change of paradigm, a course of study all the way up to the higher semesters consisted of individual processes of adopting existing bodies of knowledge. The advantage of this kind of academization, and thus of imparting education as a higher problem-solving ability, is its verifiability: Students who have acquired the given body of knowledge at a level that instructors consider high receive good grades. Those who only partially master the wealth of knowledge receive bad grades. Business administration has always been a discipline where the body of knowledge consists of *explicative and technological statements*. These quasi-normative statements dictate which actions are beneficial to corporate success. For business research, this functional perspective ("what works is true") means looking for generalizable cause-and-effect relationships in practice

G. Müller-Christ, Prof. Dr. (✉)
Universität Bremen, Fachbereich Wirtschaftswissenschaft,
Fachgebiet Nachhaltiges Management, Bremen, Germany
e-mail: gmc@uni-bremen.de

© The Author(s) 2019

H. A. Mieg (ed.), *Inquiry-Based Learning – Undergraduate Research*,
https://doi.org/10.1007/978-3-030-14223-0_24

(empirical research) or deducing cause-and-effect relationships from concepts (theoretical research).

The challenge for business administration now lies in the fact that it is permanently increasing the body of knowledge in all its functional areas (procurement, production, marketing, human resource management, etc.) in terms of explicative and technological statements, thus making the "mountain of knowledge" that the students are supposed to climb ever steeper. Acquiring that knowledge then demands the memorization of large bodies of knowledge, which leads students to have an attitude of passive consumption, then apply the *ethos of their own discipline* during learning as well: Achieving the prescribed or self-imposed goal efficiently, which is to say with the least possible effort, seems to be the prevailing maxim of action.

Research-oriented teaching requires a higher emotional, mental and temporal effort on the part of both parties. While the students are at least formally protected from excessive strain due to the workload concept, instructors face the risk of an unmanageable support effort, especially when it comes to modules with larger numbers of attendees. In seminars with a manageable number of participants, the well-known didactic forms of research-oriented learning such as roleplays, simulation games, case studies and project-based studies have long been used in business administration. Nonetheless, according to empiricism, these forms are primarily used with the objective of *discovery learning*. Research in the sense of discovery means that students themselves discover existing bodies of knowledge in alternative, didactic ways. This applies in particular to roleplaying and business games as well as case studies, criticism of which Henry Mintzberg (2004) dealt with intensively. Students are encouraged to use inductive processes, where logical thinking leads them to conclusions that instructors have long known and that relate to context-free cases from the past (Mintzberg 2004). Project-based studies initially have an open design and can be considered a basic condition for different motives between a targeted transfer of knowledge and freely chosen research into a new topic.

24.2 How Does Something New Become a Part of Business Administration? Different Research Designs

Theories are considered statement systems, which can contain numerous propositions and hypotheses about correlations. Finding new hypotheses can also be the goal of research-oriented learning. It makes a difference whether research is conducted *within the context of justification or of discovery*, especially when it comes to teaching. In the context of justification, hypotheses are usually subjected to an empirical examination, while in the context of discovery, new hypotheses are obtained. The search for how something new comes into the world implies research within the context of discovery, and that this takes place with new forms of knowledge. In business administration, known paths of knowledge are likewise deduction and induction. Less well-known is abduction; intuition is employed even less frequently. These four forms of knowledge acquisition are briefly explained in terms of their ability to bring something new into the world (cf. Fig. 24.1).

24.2.1 Distinction Between Fundamental Paths of Knowledge

The discussion concerning the fundamental paths of knowledge is being pursued with continuing intensity in cognitive science and the philosophy of science. These can be distilled into the following distinction.

Deduction: Deduction is the *form of knowledge in the context of justification*. It consists of drawing specific propositions from general propositions. If, for example, the premise applies that when there is an increase in the production volume, the costs also increase (general proposition), then observing an increase in the production quantity leads to the conclusion that costs are also rising. Rising costs can then be determined empirically. Deduction cannot really generate new insights, only propagate existing ones (Brühl 2015).

Induction: This method is frequently used in business administration. Practical corporate behavior should be explained by showing the correlation between a case and, ultimately, corporate success (in the form of profit). Best practice concepts have been and still are very popular in management research since the release of the bestseller *In Search of*

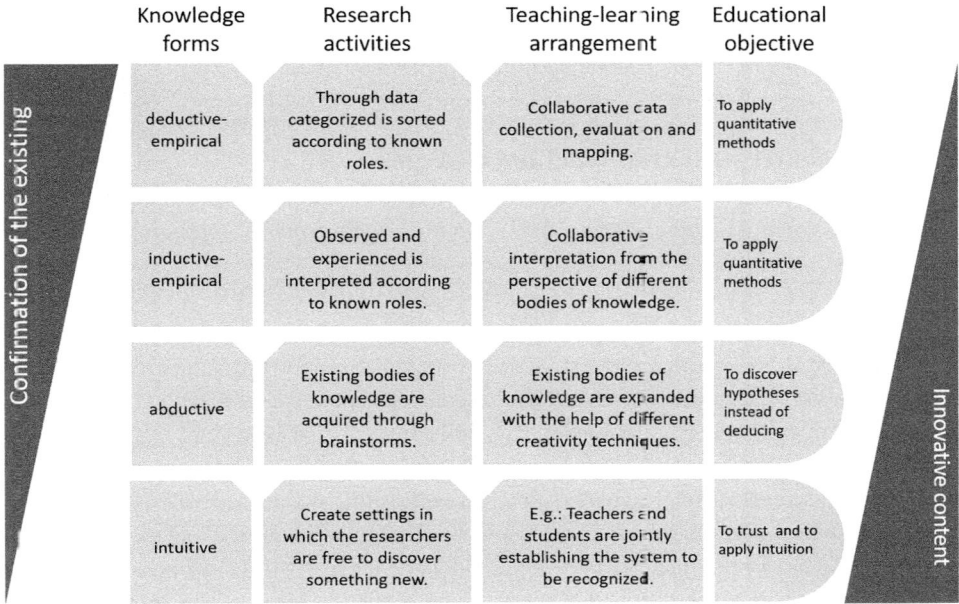

Fig. 24.1 Matrix of the cognitive processes in research-oriented learning. (Source: Author's representation)

Excellence (Peters and Waterman 1984). New insights usually only lead to imitation and thus the *duplication of existing patterns of action*.

Abduction: In terms of formal logic, the problem that triggers abduction is the following: There is only one event known, and no law and no constraint from which anything can be logically concluded. Creativity is therefore required in order to deduce a generalizable hypothesis from an event. For Charles Sanders Peirce, who introduced and described abduction, it is a lightning-fast insight that only occurs upon conclusion of a process when faced with a problem and based on knowledge of the facts, and that tends to be hampered by logical rules of reasoning (Reichertz 2013).

Intuition: Intuition in its narrower sense is inspiration, and thus the development and experience of knowledge that was not previously present in the person seeking or researching. These intuitive flashes of inspiration, gut decisions or ideas can barely be rationally explained, and their formation and origin can hardly be substantiated. Intuition does not simply encounter people unprepared in everyday life. Intuition is present in the moment in which seekers or researchers concentrate fully on a topic or a task and get into a "flow." In other words: *Intuition is most likely to come to the prepared mind*.

The distinctions made in Fig. 24.1 are of a categorizing nature. In the practical research process, different types of cognition alternate. Even with purely deductive-empirical research, new insights can arise through abduction or intuition: the view of the data suddenly gives rise to an insight that was not there before. Some explanations as to the teaching-learning arrangements for research-oriented learning in this research design will be provided below, based on the simplification that work tends to be deductive in quantitative empirical research, inductive in qualitative social research, and abductive and intuitive in systemic research (cf. for more detail Müller-Christ 2015).

24.2.2 Research-Oriented Teaching Design

Research-oriented teaching design I: Technological statements through quantitative research

This research-oriented teaching design best fits the notion that research-oriented learning *entails the entire research process*. Students should have the opportunity to get to know a research process from the definition of the research question, the derivation of hypotheses, the translation into an empirical design, data collection, data analysis and interpretation to publication (Huber et al. 2013). It is possible to become familiar with the process in a lecture, but true rapprochement only occurs when performing the process oneself. Such processes are shaped in teaching within the framework of project modules and theses.

The challenge for instructors lies in communicating the methods in this field of research. This can be prepared by lectures, but a "dry run" of this sort does not mean that students can recognize the methodological challenges in their research process and cope well. Supporting students is therefore very costly in terms of time and personnel. It is only possible to get through such a process over the course of a semester if the questions are very limited. Until now, it has been difficult for students to obtain empirical survey data; however, online surveys facilitate and reduce the costs associated with access to representative data volumes considerably.

Certainly there are areas of business administration that cling to the old belief that only quantitative research is scientific, because it has standardized, validated procedures that allow for generalizable statements. This attitude is particularly obvious when international publications are sought as a result of research. The results of quantitative research, especially within the context of justifying hypotheses, are easier to publish than the results of qualitative research in the context of discovery because of their international comprehensibility.

Research-oriented teaching design II: Hermeneutic statements through qualitative research

Hermeneutics is the method of understanding recognition of life situations. Anyone who proceeds in a hermeneutic way would like to understand and explain interdependencies and perhaps even contexts of meaning such that they can understand and relate to them. This reconstruction of social occurrences utilizes methods of social research by means of observation, interviews or case analyses. If students participate in this *process of social reconstruction* in a research-oriented teaching-learning arrangement, they usually learn how to conduct and evaluate qualitative surveys with interviews or observations within the context of project papers and final papers. Since the time and money for extensive surveys are usually too limited, a few interviews are subjected to an evaluation using content analysis and new hypotheses are then derived inductively. Often, there is no capacity left to clarify whether the found hypotheses are really new or have been dealt with in literature for some time, or perhaps even already discarded. Perhaps this is not so relevant, however, since research-oriented learning is more likely to enable students to shape the process of discovery and reasoning according to scientific criteria.

The crucial bottleneck for students in this research-oriented teaching design is access to suitable interlocutors within the specified period of project work. In my experience, research topics related to leadership issues are very popular with students. The big challenge for the instructors is the distinction between the positive effect of discovery learning and the actual finding of a new hypothesis. *Interpretation as the assignment of meaning* is easier for the instructors, who have more substantial background experience than the students. Students are presumably more likely to discover something new for themselves.

Research-oriented teaching design III: Generating hypotheses using system constellations

The system constellation method is a method of acquiring knowledge in which people are placed spatially as elements of a system. They visualize the system by showing the relationships of the elements to one another through their distance and their line of gaze. System constellations work using *transverbal spatial language*: People are able to understand the system embodied by proxies in spatial relationship in a relatively similar way without the need for verbal communication. Representatives for the elements arrive at a representative perception of the state of the elements that they represent, and can often clearly verbally communicate how changes in the system affect their perceptions. In constellations, it is very important that the representatives only pay attention to their physical condition and track the changes, but do not reflect thereon. Thinking processes can prevent the detection and perception of differences. They can be avoided by placing the representatives such that they are concealed so they do not know which element they represent. The silent assignment of the representative, for example, by the constellation facilitator appears to position the representative perception as well. For the sake of brevity, the method cannot be discussed in detail. However, there is already a considerable body of introductions to and reflections on the method in the organizational literature associated with consultation (e.g. Rosselet 2012).

The teaching concept using the system constellation method is still new compared to the first two teaching designs and is used by only a few teachers (Müller-Christ 2015). It is important to mention right from the start that the use of system constellations requires the *guidance of an organizational constellation facilitator*. The representative perception of the representatives must be enticed and supported sensitively, and students' options must be taken into account. The use of system constellations should be systematically taught and practiced; however, it can be learned quickly. The system associated with this research-oriented teaching design is presented by Müller-Christ (in press) based on a sample constellation. The question of how constellations can be evaluated as *innovative methods of qualitative social research* is also addressed therein.

24.3   The New Role of Instructions in a Systematic, Research-Oriented Teaching-Learning Process

The research-oriented teaching design III changes the entire teaching-learning process with its systemic perspective. In the first two designs, instructors act by dint of their substantive superiority in terms of content: They have more experience and more knowledge in applying quantitative and qualitative empirical methods, and presumably they learn very little as a result of student findings. In the systemic perspective of the research-oriented teaching design III, instructors become a *learning guide*, because something new is sought, in collaboration, which the instructor did not know before either. Therefore what is at issue is the creation of a teaching-learning setting in which a space of exploration, discovery and wonder (Scharmer and Käufer 2014) is created with the students, a space where they can seek something new together. In order to do so, instructors must step down from their infallible position and learn to view that which is familiar to them in a new way with the students. This repositioning of instructors and learners is a challenge, especially in business administration, because those who are actually teaching become learners again, and those who hitherto have been mere consumers of bodies of knowledge actively appropriate their own learning process. If both parties agree on the format, a creative space of joint research can emerge, which is a lot of fun for all those involved, and which allows astonishment and new questions to arise. Perhaps business administration and management theory is just waiting for incentives of this kind? (Box 24.1)

Box 24.1: Collaborative Research in Business School: Benefits from the Research Group Model. (Extracted from Bartkus et al. 2010)

Although business students account for approximately 22% of undergraduate degrees in the U.S., business is one discipline that has been largely absent from the discussion about undergraduate research. One of us (Bartkus 2007) has noted, for example, that business projects accounted for fewer than 3% of the presentations at the National Conference on Undergraduate Research in 2007 and that business faculty make up less than 1% of the members of the Council on Undergraduate Research.

Given the importance of undergraduate research and the under-representation from colleges and schools of business, Bartkus (2007) introduced the Research Group model to encourage greater involvement by faculty and students. Since it began to evolve in 2004, the Research Group in the Jon M. Huntsman School of Business at Utah State University has continued to evolve and provide benefits to both students and faculty members. Here we describe the structure, benefits, assessments, and implications for future development of the model.

Research Group Model: An Overview

The model, developed at the Huntsman School, summarizes its mission this way:
The Research GroupTM is a not-for-profit consortium of business and university scholars, corporate leaders, and qualified undergraduate students dedicated to the advancement of high quality research experiences. Its mission is to provide students the opportunity to develop core competencies in the use of the scientific method as it relates to business and public policy issues. In doing so, students become better prepared for success in graduate school and their chosen careers. The guiding motto of The Research Group is "Research that Matters." (Bartkus 2007, p. 8)

As a consortium, the administrative structure of the model is relatively straightforward. Students enter the program as "associates" (as opposed to students) and work under the guidance of "partners" (as opposed to faculty). These titles are intended to reflect the notion that students are gaining relevant work experience, which has been cited as an important consideration for employment and admission to graduate business programs.

To further ensure that the experience is relevant, the model encourages students to publish in peer-reviewed publications and/or present at scholarly research forums such as at the National Conference on Undergraduate Research. Students who

(continued)

Box 24.1: (continued)

succeed in those areas become eligible for promotion to the "senior associate" level where they continue their research and also mentor incoming associates.

Students and faculty members are also required to obtain training and certification in human-subjects research through the university's institutional review board. This certification is the national standard and provides students with a bona fide credential. Additionally, students can receive awards from the Huntsman School in recognition of their research scholarship (e.g. annual Awards for Scholarly Merit). The school also designates one deserving student each year as the outstanding undergraduate researcher. In these ways, students gain both relevant experience and documented recognition of research productivity.

In sum, the model takes the traditional educational concept of undergraduate research and administers it under the auspices of a professional research organization. The result? Both students and faculty develop a greater sense of ownership and pride in the program.

Benefits for Students

The research group has developed five new initiatives specifically designed to provide benefits for our students:

1. The Consumer Outlook is an online survey-research program, from which participating students gain experience in questionnaire design, sampling, data collection, analysis, and reporting. The resultant research is intended to be published in a peer reviewed outlet and/or presented at a research forum.
2. Deli-Nation.Com is an online publication that reports on events in the restaurant industry. Students work as editors, staff reporters, writers, Web masters, and video producers to develop and operate this social-media site within the business school.
3. The Research Group Quarterly is an online, open-access journal dedicated to publishing collaborative business research, interviews with business leaders and scholars, and book reviews. Students serve on the editorial board, review articles, and manage other administrative issues related to the operation of a publication.
4. Opportunities for engagement with other business-school programs provide students with mutual support and create additional research synergy.
5. Opportunities to engage with corporate entities and issues expand students' experiences. Corporate engagement occurs when an external organization collaborates with the business school.

    Each of these initiatives is intended to further enhance a student's critical thinking and communications skills through real-world applications and involvement with a faculty mentor.

References

Bartkus, K. R. (2007). Fostering Student/Faculty Collaborations Through the Research Group Model: An Application to Business Schools. *CUR Quarterly, 28*(2), 6–10.

Bartkus, K. R./Olsen, D./Mills, R. J./Hills, S. B. (2010). Collaborative Research in Business School: Benefits from the Research Group Modell. *CUR Focus on the web, 31*(1), 5–8.

Brühl, R. (2015). *Wie Wissenschaft Wissen schafft*. Konstanz: UTB-Verlag.

Huber, L., Kröger, M./Schelhowe, H. (Hrsg.). (2013). *Forschendes Lernen als Profilmerkmal einer Universität. Beispiele aus der Universität Bremen*. Bielefeld: UniversitätsVerlagWebler.

Mintzberg, H. (2004). *Manager statt MBAs. Eine kritische Analyse*. Frankfurt, New York: Campus Verlag.

Müller-Christ, G. (2015). Nachhaltiges Management: Systemisch(er) Forschen und Lehren für eine gelebte Transdisziplinarität. In W. Leal Filho (Hrsg.), *Forschung für Nachhaltigkeit an deutschen Hochschulen* (S. 97–115). Wiesbaden: Springer Spektrum.

Müller-Christ, G. (im Druck). Forschungsorientierte Lehre in der Betriebswirtschaftslehre mit Systemaufstellungen. In J. Lehmann/H.A. Mieg (Hrsg.). *Forschendes Lernen: Ein Praxisbuch*. Potsdam: Verlag der Fachhochschule Potsdam.

Peters, T. J./Waterman, R.H. (1984). *Auf der Suche nach Spitzenleistungen*. Landsberg: Verlag Moderne Industrie.

Reichertz, J. (2013). *Die Abduktion in der qualitativen Sozialforschung. Über die Entdeckung des Neuen* (2. Aufl.). Wiesbaden: Springer Verlag.

Rosselet, C. (2012). *Andersherum zur Lösung. Die Organisationsaufstellung als Verfahren der intuitiven Entscheidungsfindung*. Zürich: Versus Verlag.

Scharmer, C.O./Käufer, K. (2014). *Von der Zukunft her führen. Theorie U in der Praxis*. Heidelberg: Carl-Auer Verlag.

Inquiry-Based Learning in Cultural Studies

Margrit E. Kaufmann

In accordance with the subject of culture, the presentation of inquiry-based learning in cultural studies (Kulturwissenschaft)[1] has multiple perspectives: The decentralized view of instructors and researchers is supplemented by the central perspective, in which the author (as an academic expert in diversity at the University of Bremen) participates in efforts to improve teaching and learning (Kaufmann 2013; Kaufmann & Schelhowe in this volume; Satilmis in that volume).

25.1 Characteristic Features in the Field of Cultural Studies as Basic Conditions for Inquiry-Based Learning

In the last 20 years, cultural studies has been constituted and established as a transdisciplinary professional profile centered on cultural theories and concepts. This is reflected, among other things, in the fact that in 2014, upon the establishment of a "Cultural Studies Society" as a scientific association, an institutional framework was created for the subject. Degree programs in cultural studies are available, for example, in Bayreuth, Berlin, Bremen, Frankfurt/Oder, Lüneburg, Koblenz and Constance. This young subject is defined by its lack of clear disciplinary borders, because it crosses traditional subject-specific demarcations and approaches questions in a multi-perspective manner. This transdisciplinary, polyphonic interaction is largely based on cultural theories; the British concept of

---

[1] The German discipine "Kulturwissenschaft" is not congruent with the British concept of "Cultural Studies."

M. E. Kaufmann, Dr. (✉)
Universität Bremen, Wissenschaftliche Expertin für Diversity der Universitätsleitung und Fachbereich Kulturwissenschaften, Bremen, Germany
e-mail: mkaufm@uni-bremen.de

© The Author(s) 2019
H. A. Mieg (ed.), *Inquiry-Based Learning – Undergraduate Research*,
https://doi.org/10.1007/978-3-030-14223-0_25

cultural studies; interpretive, postcolonial cultural anthropology; a proximity to literary studies; cultural history and cultures of remembrance, ethnopsychoanalysis; cultural mediation; intercultural and transcultural communication; postcolonial, gender and diversity studies; and media studies. In this sense, one often speaks of a plurality of cultural stud*ies* (Kulturwissenschaf*ten*). The subject matter of cultural studies research includes:

- the emphasis on processuality and the complexity of the cultural,
- everyday cultural phenomena and experiences,
- the interactions and relationships between cultural groups,
- the positioning of subjects within collectives with corresponding identity constructions and
- meaning and significance in the context of the change in macrostructural basic conditions.

That which is local is perceived within the context of globalization and transnationalization processes (Marcus 1998). Diversity and inequality research is one of the central areas of study and research in Bremen.

The behavior of "discovery," which is decisive for ethnography (Breidenstein et al. 2013, p. 13), is characteristic of the style of learning by doing research in cultural studies. This approach of discovery allows "lived experience" (according to Claude Lévi-Strauss) to be implemented by means of field research practices and methods. This has to do with the discipline-of-origin, ethnology, and its colonial history. Accordingly, the discipline endeavors to decolonize itself with questions about the power of definition and authorship, about the "crisis of representation" and questions about "Writing Culture" (Kaufmann 2013, p. 126 et seq.). Cultural studies as it exists today therefore calls into question research conducted about the other, which is to say the scientific objectification of the subject being studied. As a field, it counters this scientific "othering" (Fabian 1993, p. 337), as a production of otherness, and posits a postcolonial position in the search for new possibilities of collaborative, ethically acceptable knowledge production.

Inquiry-based learning in cultural studies thus consists of a critical-reflective process of a discovering acquisition of knowledge and production of knowledge within the context of teaching theoretical foundations, empirical tools and practical implementation. The cyclical course of an ethnographic research process is similar to the phase of inquiry-based learning, in which both theory and empiricism are linked and the process is not linear, but is to be understood as recursive, evolutive design (ibid., p. 45 et seq.), which repeatedly applies different steps to itself. By way of illustration (Table 25.1), the phase model of inquiry-based learning developed by Huber (2013, p. 248) is compared to the ethnographic research process (Kaufmann 2013, p. 131 et seq.).

Table 25.1 Comparison of the phases of inquiry-based learning with the phases of ethnographic research

Phases of inquiry-based learning (according to Huber 2013):	Phases of cultural-scientific, ethnographic inquiry-based learning (according to Kaufmann 2013):
1. Introduction	1. Providing research access
2. Identifying a question	2. Developing a question
3. Processing information	3. Defining the research design (Exposé relating to the state of the research and the theory contexts)
4. Acquiring methodological knowledge	4. Data collection
5. Developing a research design	5. Rendering the progression of the research as text (journal, logs, transcriptions, documents)
6. Conducting a research activity	6. Data analysis and interpretation (mediation between theoretical and field contexts with the aim of modifying and expanding theories)
7. Preparation and presentation of the results	7. Presentation of the research and its results (research reports, publications, presentations, including reflection on the procedure, the course of the relationship and one's own role)
8. Reflection	

Source: Author's representation

25.2 General Experiences with Inquiry-Based Learning in Cultural Studies

The usual distinction between research and practice projects does not really apply to cultural studies (Kaufmann, 2015). This is because projects that relate to the transfer of scholarship to practice in cultural studies include parallel research projects and practice-oriented, application-oriented research projects. Students are involved in the research projects of the instructors through "cognitive apprenticeship" (Tremp 2005, p. 345). This means that they are involved in all scientific thinking and action processes. Cognitive apprenticeship, as a kind of "cognitive master teaching" (ibid.), introduces students and doctoral students to the scientific community, specialist discourses and research areas (Kaufmann 2013, 2015). Inquiry-based learning does not present the subject-specific characteristics as a conglomeration of knowledge to be passively received, nor does it teach students using a top-down approach; instead, students actively participate in the production of knowledge. Cognitive apprenticeship promotes "team-play" (Ghaffarizad et al. 2015) between instructors and students and particularly supports collaborative learning, since the teaching-learning processes become a common concern of instructors and students alike. They get to know each other better through joint research questions and goals, becoming mutually supportive, collaborative "accomplices" (Kaufmann and Koch 2015a).

By integrating students into their research and what are termed transfer projects (*Vermittlungsprojekte*), it is possible to promote up-and-coming scholars, taking into account inequality factors. This is because instructors sensitize themselves to the different learning and research conditions of the students through student-oriented collaboration in inquiry-based learning. Thus, inquiry-based learning promotes dealing more consciously with diversity among students and instructors, and with discrimination and its factors during a course of study. Huber (2015) describes diversity among students and instructors on four levels, which I extend to six by adding the latter two:

- requirements, conditions and activities associated with teaching and learning,
- teaching-learning research forms (methods),
- interests of students and instructors,
- subject matter of teaching, learning and research,
- forms of communication and relationship,
- objectives of learning and research.

In inquiry-based learning in cultural studies, diversity is the subject of research, the topic of teaching, the methodological-didactic element and the basis for a mutual perception of instructors and students that is sensitive to difference and inequality. This involves the conscious handling of personal, professional and status-related differences between the students as well as among the instructors.

25.3   Inquiry-Based Learning throughout the Learning Cycle

The objective of cultural studies (shown here at the University of Bremen, for example) is directed both towards the acquisition of technical, theoretical, analytical, methodical and practical competencies, as well as what are known as "key competencies" in the fields of social affairs, ethics, diversity awareness and mediation. The acquisition of competency in the learning cycle within the "student lifecycle" corresponds to the processual ethnological research practice. The term "learning cycle" refers to processual, experience-based student learning, including the respective learning style. It travels in parallel to the student lifecycle. All activities related to studies are summarized under the concept of "student lifecycle," beginning with the application and admission of students for entry into a course of study, to their transition to working life and alumni work (Schulmeister 2007, p. 230). The curriculum is also designed in such a way that its building blocks can be related to the establishment of a research cycle:

In keeping with the entry into the student lifecycle, the learning cycle in the first academic year is dedicated to arriving within the course of study, the field and its community. After orientation week, students learn the central goals, questions and tasks of the discipline in introductory compulsory modules, and acquire technical basic skills for reading and writing texts, sharpen their senses for a research orientation, and practice the presentation of results. Introductions to basic questions are combined with exercises and small group work by the teaching organization in order to establish a relationship with the students right from the start, and to provide subject-oriented assistance.

Students subsequently attend courses on the subject classification system and in regional specializations as compulsory elective options in the second year of study, the core phase of the student lifecycle. In the third semester during this phase, they already acquire central research competencies through the intensive two-semester method training, which is implemented as a process of learning by doing research according to the learning cycle (Kaufmann 2013). Workshops support the writing of scientific texts and thereby attempt to take into consideration diversity among the students.

The final phase, which is the end phase of the student lifecycle in the third year of study, primarily supports independent work during and after graduation. This phase includes a practice module, major and minor modules in the compulsory elective area, a self-study module and, lastly, the final module. In the practical module, students complete at least 6 weeks of work placement in some field of cultural practice. In the self-study module, they deepen their selected focus and prepare themselves for the final thesis. The practice and self-study phase also leaves room for study or an internship abroad. The entire curricular course of the learning cycle along the student lifecycle, from introductions to the discipline and the independent testing of methods with the assistance of research workshops to independent inquiry-based learning, prepares students for an empirically or theoretically designed bachelor's thesis, the writing of which is supported by means of supervisory seminars and working groups. At the University of Bremen, the introduction of the regularly offered student conference "ResearchInsights" will not only present research results to a public audience, but will also put up issues and research settings for discussion, and train students in different forms of imparting knowledge.

25.4   A Method Module as an Example

Inquiry-based learning is already being implemented successfully in ethnologically based cultural studies, which considers the *students' own research experience* as a central element of academic studies when starting the bachelor's degree program with a large number of students (Kaufmann, 2013, 2015; Kaufmann and Koch 2015a, b). This will be explained briefly using the example of method training from the perspective of the individual responsible for the module. As stated by the German Rectors' Conference, "[…] the objectives and characteristics of inquiry-based learning can be realized especially well within the context of methodological training, since all of the central work steps of a research process as well as selected subject-related content and interdisciplinary competencies are essentially imparted by university instructors or acquired by students" HRK-Fachgutachten 2013, p. 75, translated).

25.4.1 What Are the Basic Conditions of the Module Subject?

In the methodology foundation module of the bachelor's degree program in cultural studies at the University of Bremen, which students complete in the third semester, students acquire cultural research methods by means of ethnographic field research experience. Here, they go through a whole research process according to the phase models of inquiry-based learning that have been presented, which extends from searching for a suitable field of research, developing a research question, and collecting and evaluating the data to writing the research report and, if possible, publication thereof. The module (described in detail in Kaufmann 2013) is offered in the winter semester with over 100 students who have cultural studies as a major or complementary subject. The person responsible for the module prepares the conceptual basics, undertakes the organization and coordinates the teaching team. The team consists of five instructors and five students from the previous year as tutors.

The aim of the module is "to provide students with basic methodological training that enables them to carry out, evaluate and describe their own ethnological and cultural (field) research" (Modulhandbuch 2012). It makes it possible to become familiar with and test cultural science tools, stimulate research and questioning, and make the experience of an entire research process tangible. Ethical questions about researching with and about people are fundamental. Social learning and research, both in the team and individually, promote methodical, theoretical, (professionally) practical, academic, social and ethical competencies.

By researching current socio-politically relevant issues, students also move locally in different social fields off campus (Kaufmann 2015). They experience complex, diverse learning research situations and inductively investigate explorative case studies through encounters with people and subject areas. The research experiences are reflected in the journals and in the accompanying research workshops. By defining the research design and the exposé, the methodological steps of the data collection such as participant observation and interviews are defined and recorded in notes, logs and transcripts. The evaluation is carried through the analysis, triangulation and interpretation of the collected data. A research report is prepared and a transfer of the results sought where possible, for example through publications, in order to promote self-reflection, as well as reflection on the group work and methods reflection in the research process.

25.4.2 How Is the Module Implemented?

The lecture, which is as interactive as possible, with two semester hours per week, binds the module together. It introduces basic methods of cultural research and leads students to form research teams and to perform their own fieldwork. It establishes basic methods and techniques which are discussed, mediates between the reading of basic texts and students' own handling of the methods, and guides the individual research steps. In doing so, it supports the research process and helps to document, analyze, interpret and reflect on the central results thereof. The faculty and doctoral candidates also provide stimuli for the individual steps, ideally as directly as possible from the immediate research.

The lecture is supplemented by four research labs, which are conducted jointly by instructors and tutors for two semester hours per week. They accompany and support the research process. Students from the previous year serve as tutors, building on their own experiences. They support inquiry-based learning by means of their concrete experiences, redesign the module on an ongoing basis from the perspective of the student, and contribute significantly to quality assurance.

In the labs, the students work in teams on the research documents that they themselves have created. They go through the work steps together and discuss any problems that arise. Through the process-related work, the research reports are written on an ongoing basis throughout the semester. This does not proceed for all groups and fields of research in a manner that is equally effective. An openness to the various research conditions is therefore important here.

Working both individually and in teams, students implement the research steps in teams that are assembled such that they are as diverse as possible, ideally in groups of three and based on previous experience. In so doing, care should be taken to form teams based on research interests as much as possible so that everyone feels comfortable with their team. The teams then focus on a research topic, working together on access to the field and on a central question. This collaboration supports diversity awareness and mutual assistance. It is supplemented by the students' own work, both in the data collection as well as in the reading and writing of texts. In addition, the internet platform "Stud.IP" is used as a teaching and learning tool. It also serves for framing and bundling as well as communication between the various levels and persons involved. On the e-learning platform "Stud.IP," students can work together on their data and texts.

25.4.3 What Is the Purpose of Conducting Research?

As a rule, students choose their research topics and fields themselves. However, instructors offer them opportunities to establish connections to their own research topics and fields in the sense of cognitive apprenticeship and collaborative, intricate forms of knowledge production. For example, a study on the diversity of students was conducted on the campus of the University of Bremen (Kaufmann 2013). Here, based on a joint decision, the student research dovetailed with the researchers' research on "Diversity in Organisationen – Unternehmen und Hochschulen" ("Diversity in Organizational Businesses and Institutions of Higher Learning"). They contrasted "Quest," the student survey on diversity at the Charitable Center for Higher Education Development (Centrum für Hochschulentwicklung, CHE), with diversity categories and references inductively developed from the student perspective. Through this research with students from other disciplines, study-relevant factors and diversity categories were surveyed which go far beyond the current categories of inequality. Inquiry-based learning on diversity was used to sensitize researchers, assistants and representatives of the institution to the different lifestyles as well as study and learning conditions among the students. The results were incorporated into the diversity processes of the University of Bremen.

Appropriate power-critical approaches to dealing with research ethics, based on academic tradition, raise fundamental questions about the forms of social and cultural coexistence and the norms, values and traditions of our rapidly changing, complex societies. Students' research revolves around fields of research on migration, refugees and asylum, artists and cultural professionals, subcultures and interest groups, social institutions and projects, cuts in social services and forms of protest, as well as social norms, stigmas and discrimination. The focalized areas, groups and institutions where societal problems arise correspond to a part of the spectrum in which cultural scholars later work. Instructors and students enter the social fields with this research orientation and the collaborative forms of knowledge generation. Inquiry-based learning can therefore be made a "link between a research and a vocational orientation" (Kaufmann 2015). It promotes the transfer between scholarship and society as a reciprocal process. After all, cultural studies needs these fields of practice as fields of research and work, and society, in turn, needs the concepts, methods and research that arises from scholarship.

25.5 Outlook for Inquiry-Based Learning in Cultural Studies: What Needs to Be Done?

Inquiry-based learning in cultural studies requires communicative and developmental spaces for good collaboration within the teaching team and with students, as well as space for negotiating transdisciplinary and transcultural processes (Kaufmann and Satilmis 2015). In principle, there is an equal need for reaching an understanding on the notions of subject-cultural specific forms of inquiry-based learning and for didactic training. According to the reformed degree program structure and modularization, inquiry-based learning processes with a corresponding scope for the heterogeneous student body are possible, although the module structure makes longer research phases more difficult. We therefore need to explore how longer phases can be made possible. It may be necessary to redesign module plans.

When individual modules attempt to keep the emphasis on processuality throughout the research, this makes them demanding and they tend to become overloaded. Working on curricular interlocking, this works against the "Zurich framework" model (Hildbrand and Tremp 2012, see also Mieg, in this volume). The theoretical and empirically oriented modules are easier to link, for example. Evaluation and accompanying research is needed in order to support the curricular integration of the modules and the way the student lifecycle fits together with the learning cycle. In cultural studies at the University of Bremen, for example, an accompanying research project is based on the question of how the student lifecycle can fit together with the learning cycle. The micro-, meso- and macro-levels of the design of the teaching-learning processes are systematically linked when implementing inquiry-based learning in cultural studies:

At the *micro-level*, at issue is the implementation of individual steps and elements of inquiry-based learning so that they are made tangible in their context as a research and learning cycle. In so doing, it is always about setting the framework and balancing guidelines with decision-making and experience opportunities of the students. With appropriate guidance and support, it increases students' motivation to study by fostering self-reliance. Subject-oriented work performed in small groups supports the sensitization of personal teaching and learning conditions and thus promotes educational justice.

At the *meso-level*, it is about explicating, documenting and communicating the concept of the degree program. In addition, individual modules can be relieved by harmonizing them better within the meaning of the Zurich framework. They can then cover partial aspects of the research and do not need to map the whole research questionnaire. Tutorials and research workshops can be expanded into free research laboratories. Relations with research partners, fields and topics can be sustained for long-term research as permanent field sites in institutions and neighborhoods. The aim is to academically accompany urban transformation processes and to contribute to the design of processes through collaborative research. These measures must be embedded in the quality cycles and degree program developments.

At the *macro-level*, there are links with university management and its planning. A greater number of instructors, sufficient existing rooms and connections between university planning, subject didactics and the everyday activities of teaching and learning are needed. As it is work-intensive for instructors to develop different courses and to respond to needs individually, inquiry-based learning requires more intensive supervision. Thus, structurally, priority is given to having sufficient resources and the smallest possible support ratio for inquiry-based learning.

References

Breidenstein, G./Hirschauer, S./Kalthoff, H./Nieswand, B. (2013). *Ethnografie. Die Praxis der Feldforschung*. Konstanz/München: UVK Verlagsgesellschaft.

Fabian, J. (1993). Präzenz und Repräsentation. Die Anderen und das anthropologische Schreiben. In E. Berg/M. Fuchs (Hrsg.), *Kultur, soziale Praxis, Text. Die Krise der ethnographischen Repräsentation* (S. 335–364). Frankfurt a.M.: Suhrkamp.

Ghaffarizad, K./Kaufmann, M. E./Koch, H./Kurzawski, B./Reuter, A./Seufert, P. (2015). Forschendes Lernen als Team-Play. Gemeinsamer Bericht von Studierenden und Lehrenden über den Tag der Lehre 2014 am Institut für Ethnologie und Kulturwissenschaft. Resonanz. *Magazin für Studium und Lehre an der Universität Bremen, 3*, 9–14.

Hildbrand, T./Tremp, P. (2012). Forschungsorientiertes Studium – universitäre Lehre: Das »Zürcher Framework« zur Verknüpfung von Lehre und Forschung. In T. Brinker/P. Tremp (Hrsg.), *Einführung in die Studiengangsentwicklung* (S. 101–116). Bielefeld: Bertelsmann.

HRK-Fachgutachten (2013). *Employability und Praxisbezüge im wissenschaftlichen Studium*. Retrieved am 14 June 2015 from http://www.hrk-nexus.de/fileadmin/redaktion/hrk-nexus/07-Downloads/07-02-Publikationen/Fachgutachten_Employability.pdf

Huber, L. (2013). Methodische Anregungen für den Umgang mit pragmatischen Schwierigkeiten im Forschenden Lernen. In L. Huber/M. Kröger/H. Schelhowe, *Forschendes Lernen als*

Profilmerkmal einer Universität. Beispiele aus der Universität Bremen (S. 247–255). Bielefeld: UniversitätsverlagWebler.

Huber, L. (2015). Vielfalt in der Lehre – Heterogenität als Chance. Forschendes Lernen als ein Weg. In M. E. Kaufmann/K. Ghaffarizad/F. Hoffmann/F. Suckut (Hrsg.), *Diversity @ Uni Bremen: exzellent und chancengerecht?! Dokumentation* (S. 27–29). Bremen: bik.

Kaufmann, M. E. (2013). »Wir haben selbst neue Wissenszusammenhänge geschaffen!« Forschendes Lernen zu "Diversity" in der Kulturwissenschaft. In L. Huber/M. Kröger/H. Schelhowe (Hrsg.), *Forschendes Lernen als Profilmerkmal einer Universität. Beispiele aus der Universität Bremen* (S. 123–142). Bielefeld: Universitätsverlag Webler.

Kaufmann, M. E. (2015). Forschendes Lernen als Bindeglied zwischen Forschungs- und Berufsorientierung in geisteswissenschaftlichen Studiengängen. In P. Tremp (Hrsg.), *Forschungsorientierung und Berufsbezug im Studium. Blickpunkt Hochschuldidaktik, Buchreihe der dghd* (S. 151–170). Bielefeld: Bertelsmann.

Kaufmann, M. E./Koch, H. (2015a). Die Lehrenden als Kompliz_innen im forschenden Lernprozess. In K. Rheinländer (Hrsg.), *Ungleichheitssensible Hochschullehre* (S. 219–236). Wiesbaden: Springer VS.

Kaufmann, M. E./Koch, H. (2015b). Forschendes Lernen zum Umgang mit Heterogenität als Instrument in der qualitativen Evaluationsforschung. In S. Harris-Hümmert/L. Mitterauer/P. Pohlenz (Hrsg.), *Heterogenität der Studierendenschaften: Herausforderung für die Qualitätsentwicklung in Lehre und Studium, neuer Fokus für die Evaluation?* (S. 113–128). Bielefeld: UniversitätsverlagWebler.

Kaufmann, M. E./Satilmis, A. (2015). In-Between Disciplines. Forschendes Lernen als Frame für die Gestaltung transkultureller und -disziplinärer Lernräume. In H. Schelhowe/M. Schaumburg/J. Jasper (Hrsg.), *Teaching is Touching the Future. Academic Teaching within and across disciplines* (S. 349–352). Bielefeld: UniversitätsverlagWebler.

Marcus, G. E. (1998). *Ethnography trough Thick and Thin*. Princeton: Princeton University Press.

Modulhandbuch (2012). *Bachelorstudiengang Kulturwissenschaft*. Bremen: Universität Bremen.

Schulmeister, R. (2007). Der Student Lifecycle als Organisationsprinzip für E-Learning. In R. Keil, M. Kerres/R. Schulmeister (Hrsg.), *eUniversity – Update Bologna* (S. 45–77). Münster: Waxmann.

Tremp, P. (2005). Verknüpfung von Lehre und Forschung. Eine universitäre Tradition als didaktische Herausforderung. *Beiträge zur Lehrerbildung, 23/3*, 339–348.

Inquiry-Based Learning in Geography

26

Jacqueline Passon and Johannes Schlesinger

26.1 Geography – More Than the Sum of Its Parts

Global challenges such as climate change, scarcity of resources, food security or the energy transition, to name just a few, are not only central themes of the twenty-first century, but also the field of geography. In order to be able to cope with these phenomena, scientists and enlightened citizens are needed who are familiar with both natural science-related phenomena and procedures from the social sciences, and who can use resources responsibly. As a discipline, geography is situated both in the natural sciences and in the liberal arts and social sciences. Thus geography is predestined to account for the challenges in the sociopolitical dialogue, to address these, and to make an important contribution to overcoming these problems. In addition, like other subject areas, geography has not escaped efforts to define individual subfields, which have ultimately led to the German-speaking geographic system of scholarly segregation along a dividing line between the natural sciences and the social sciences (Gebhardt et al. 2011, pp. 71–83; Elverfeldt and Egner 2015, p. 319 et seq.).

Due to the complexity of the topics outlined above, as well as the variety of methods and procedures that characterize the subject, it is already clear that the approach of *inquiry-based learning* has tremendous potential, especially in geography. Moreover, this methodology could also overcome barriers within the field.

J. Passon, Dr. (✉) · J. Schlesinger, Dr.
Albert-Ludwigs-Universität Freiburg, Fakultät für Umwelt und Natürliche Ressourcen,
Physische Geographie, Freiburg im Breisgau, Germany
e-mail: jacqueline.passon@geographie.uni-freiburg.de; j.schlesinger@svgeosolutions.de

© The Author(s) 2019
H. A. Mieg (ed.), *Inquiry-Based Learning – Undergraduate Research*,
https://doi.org/10.1007/978-3-030-14223-0_26

26.2 Predestined for Each Other: On the Nature of Inquiry-Based Learning and Points of Reference in Geography

26.2.1 Points of Reference in the Field of Geography

According to the definition by the German Geography Society, the field of geography deals with the earth's surface, with landscapes, with the people and with locations, as well as with people's material and cognitive environments. Thus geography examines the physical and social world in which we live. It is also about the mutual relationships between the physical and social environment and the associated spatial impact. As we have already made clear, geographical problems arise in both the natural sciences and in the liberal arts, social sciences and economics. Looking at the degree programs offered by the geography departments in the German-speaking countries and their range of studies makes it clear that current questions in geography include the intertwined processes of "global change" and globalization, as well as global relationships between the environment, culture and economy, resource management and sustainability (especially in terms of water and soil), urban development and business development, or political ecology and vulnerability.

With this in mind, the aim of the study of geography is for students to acquire skills and methods that enable them to gain insights into physical and social processes within the concrete context of places and regions, and to contribute to solving problems. In doing so, geographic insights are generated using methods from both the natural sciences (e.g. field and laboratory analyses), and from the social sciences, as well as history (e.g. survey and interview techniques, observation or source analysis). This results in a variety of techniques used in the discipline. These include dealing with geographical information systems (GIS), remote sensing (satellite and aerial image analysis), laboratory methods, map interpretation, interview techniques and statistical analyses, as well as archival research or text and media analyses. The special characteristics of the field of geography can be summarized as follows:

- variety of topics and methods;
- interdisciplinary approach;
- multi-perspective view;
- multi-paradigmatic structure of the subject.

Based on the above, it is clear that, due to its conception, the field of geography makes the following demands on learners:

- Learning in multiple contexts: Not only must subject matter content be transferred to other contexts, but different problem statements must be developed on different scale levels.
- Learning from multiple perspectives: Subject contents must be examined from different perspectives. Because it is situated at the intersection of the natural sciences, social sciences and liberal arts, geography is particularly geared towards interdisciplinary work.

- Learning in multiple contexts: In the course of field research and project studies, learners are encouraged to develop subject content and solution strategies in multicultural teams.

Thus, essential prerequisites for *inquiry-based learning* already exist, as a result of which there are already numerous starting points for the use of this method in this subject. The following forms based on Huber (2009) are particularly suitable for geography:

- complex laboratory tasks in the field of physical geography where the paths of knowledge and results are open;
- investigation of specific individual case studies;
- excursions and field internships ("field studies") with open topics and methods;
- testing methods on problems not yet investigated within the context of courses or projects;
- planning or other simulation games, in particular for the subfields of economic and social geography;
- project studies of various sizes.

26.2.2 Experiences with Inquiry-Based Learning in the Field of Geography

As already indicated, the concept of inquiry-based learning is already practiced at various universities in different fields. The reasons for the (still) restrained application of this concept are mostly to be found in structural and practical difficulties. A survey of scientists in the field revealed that geography is facing the challenge of satisfying the autonomy requirements of inquiry-based learning in the limited time frames within the structures of modularized bachelor's degree programs, master's degree programs and teacher training contrary to instructive teaching and reproducing forms of learning. This means that time and lessons planning are very tightly organized, especially in the bachelor's degree, which does not allow a greater time expenditure for inquiry-based learning. In addition, the allotted material to be covered is strictly defined, which makes a freer topic selection for inquiry-based learning more difficult. Moreover, for some of the respondents, there is an additional difficulty in the fact that inquiry-based learning is not compatible with the forms of examination available, and thus no evaluation can take place. In addition, the lack of resources, especially in the form of staff, determines the situation in teaching at German institutions of higher learning. According to the respondents, the poor staffing of the institutions of higher learning in terms of instruction, the low value assigned teaching within the professional community, the lack of subject-didactic training among staff and uncertain prospects, especially for up-and-coming scientists, make it difficult to engage in consultation-intensive forms of teaching and learning.

Thus it is in no way surprising to find that personal involvement is often the engine that drives inquiry-based learning in higher education instruction at the cost of significant extra work for the individual(s) involved. Overall, it should be noted that the range of courses devoted to this teaching method tends to be isolated, i.e. the courses do not dovetail with other courses. Usually, they are offered as a block course or in semester-oriented seminars. In these seminars, students have the opportunity to develop their own questions and to implement them within the context of smaller studies and to search for solution strategies. In addition, the methodology was also tested during excursions and field exercises. In terms of the openness and design of the courses, the spectrum ranges from the specification of the problems up to completely open offers, in which the students must define a problem independently (variants of the inquiry-based learning in courses were tested at the geographical institutes of the universities of Frankfurt, Freiburg, Halle, Hamburg, Hanover, Jena and Potsdam, among others). Instructors provide support and advice in particular within the courses. It should also be noted that the courses are very often directed at students of teaching. It is argued that these students need to be prepared for the demands of the teaching profession and day-to-day school life. Practical experiences in the field of cooperative learning and work contexts are more important for these students than they are, for example, for master's students.

The results of the evaluation of the research-oriented courses at the geographical institutes at the universities mentioned above show that the students are very satisfied with this form of learning. It turned out that managing a thematic and/or methodological complex independently not only can lead to a deepening of technical and methodological competence, but can also train competencies such as teamwork and cooperation skills in particular. In this context, instructors have repeatedly pointed out that well-functioning and harmonizing groups have developed in courses of this sort that have developed a special group knowledge and strongly subsisted from one another's perspectives, a circumstance that is rather rare in "traditional" courses.

26.3 From Theory to Practices: Experiences with the "Freiburg Research-Oriented Teaching/Learning Approach"

How can students be specifically involved in research processes as suggested by Jenkins and Healey (2010)? And what would participation in research even look like? These and similar questions keep coming up regularly when preparing courses. At least according to the theory, the inquiry-based learning approach systematically introduces the way in which scientists think and work, and can enable students to understand and evaluate research processes and to apply the knowledge gained thereby. What this might look like in geographic teaching practice has since been tested over a ten-year period and manifested as a research-oriented approach to teaching/learning (see Fig. 26.1).

The Department of Physical Geography in Freiburg has maintained research partnerships in North, West and East Africa for many years. For this reason, it made sense to

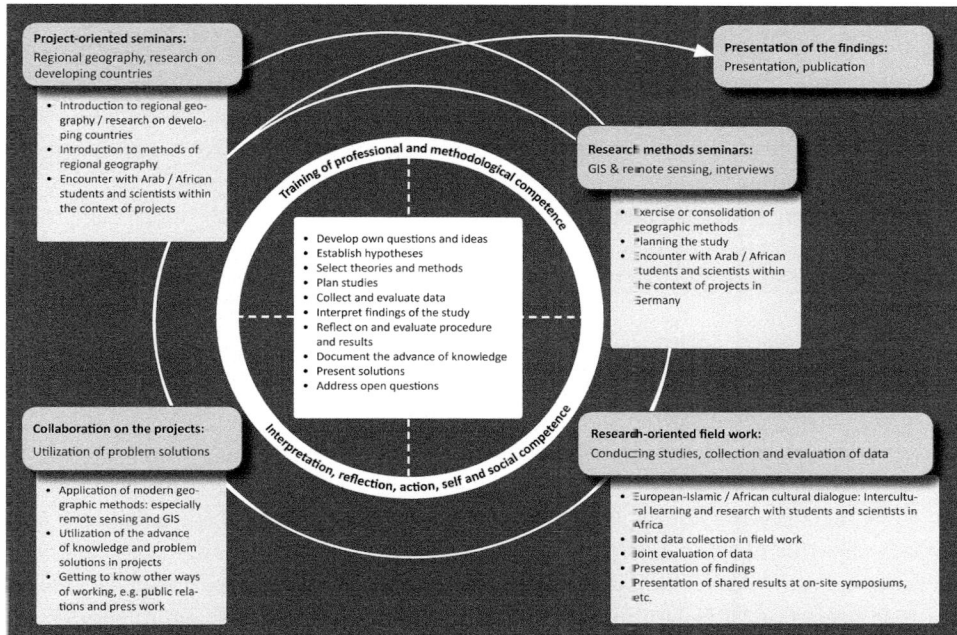

Fig. 26.1 The "Freiburger forschungsorientierte Lehr-/Lern-Ansatz" ("Freiburg research-oriented teaching/learning approach"). (Modified in accordance with Passon and Braun 2013, p. 42)

integrate the research projects in this field into teaching and to combine them with the inquiry-based learning method. The foundation for the approach to teaching/learning described here was laid with the project "Learning Through Dialogue" ("Lernen durch Dialog"), a research partnership funded by the DAAD and the Center for National Archives and Historical Studies in Tripoli (Libya) (Passon and Braun 2013). After successful testing, several modules were integrated into further exchange projects with West and East Africa with the intention of involving master's degree programs and teaching degree programs in research processes.

26.3.1 Preliminary Considerations

Since there is no unified theory or didactics of inquiry-based learning related thereto (Koch-Priewe and Thiele 2009, p. 271), it is necessary to draw on other learning theories as a background. Here, the approach of *discovery learning* is appropriate, which Bruner (1981), for example, defines as the self-learning interpretation of a knowledge area, whereby the instructor has only an observational and helping function. Learners should be trained to acquire knowledge independently and to solve problems that arise themselves. As a rule, discovery learning tends to handle problems rather "artificially" and allows learners to review and reflect on their solutions using model solutions (Bruner 1981). Ideally, inquiry-based learning goes one step further by focusing on unresolved research problems. Inquiry-based learning is also in no way merely a didactic trick to motivate students. Rather, the goal is to achieve "education through scholarship" (*Bildung durch Wissenschaft*, Huber 2004, p. 34) and to impart frequently required key competencies to the students (ibid.).

In considering which competencies should be taught in the research-oriented approach to teaching/learning, the following categories of competencies were formulated (for the structuring of the content, see Fig. 26.1):

- professional competence,
- methodological competence,
- analytic, reflective and occupational competencies, as well as
- self-competence and social competence.

A central concern of the approach to teaching/learning presented here is that it be possible to make the individual projects which are subsumed under this approach tangible to students in terms of the cultural and social dimensions, as is required for inquiry-based learning according to Huber, for example. In addition, these projects are to address the cognitive, emotional and social dimensions of learning (Huber 1998, 2003; Euler 2005). It is also important to create free space for students in terms of content. Individual teaching/learning projects should be designed so that students are actively challenged (Knowles 1975). They should be supported in thinking, planning, researching, learning, investigating and communicating with the lecturers or visiting scientists from countries such as Libya, Namibia, Cameroon or Ghana and other experts from different countries, as well as in connecting with other students.

26.3.2 Implementation

In concrete terms, research-oriented teaching/learning projects at the University of Freiburg extend over several semesters. As shown in Fig. 26.1, the projects are comprised of various modules, some of which are compulsory and some of which are elective. In addition, care is always taken to integrate the individual elements into the course of study in such a way that it is possible to accredit the seminar and project reports submitted by the participants as study-related achievements.

Project-oriented seminars with a regional focus or those that can be assigned to the subject area "Geographical Development Research" initially comprise the basis of the research-oriented teaching/learning projects. In addition, methodological seminars (e.g. introduction to or deeper look at geographic information systems, preparation of remote sensing recordings, preparation of interview guides or questionnaire) can be selected, in which the methodological knowledge required for the field visits is imparted or enriched.

The tasks set in these seminars are already directly related to the subsequent fieldwork. These courses also help students acquire the necessary theoretical, methodological and regional knowledge. Even in inquiry-based learning, the learner needs a solid foundation of knowledge in order to be able to think and act in a differentiated and creative way (Nuissl 2006, p. 222). Often, these seminars are already facilitating initial encounters with students and researchers in the country involved in the project cooperation. This is followed by the option of participating in the data collection for the respective research project at the institute during research stays in the various African countries, as well as of working on their own research question. To this end, attendance at block seminars that include project-specific preparation and intercultural training is required.

All research begins with a question, an idea or a problem. For this reason, practical questions form the starting point of the teaching and learning projects. The objective is to involve students in the implementation of research projects and to work with them to develop solutions that can also be applied in practice. A first task is to formulate research questions with the instructors and to define a study design, which requires intensive consultation and support from instructors. In so doing, hypotheses must be formulated, the research subject described and the research process defined. A research design is needed in order to move from a question to knowledge. Students must first acquire knowledge about the sequence of individual research steps as well as about research-related decisions that arise within the process. They must also be made aware that these research processes are variable and in reality rarely follow a fixed pattern:

1. impetus to conduct research
2. research subject and question
3. levels of analysis
4. project design
5. project implementation
6. reflection

In order to be able to work on the research questions, students must assess, select and apply models of research and research methods based on their suitability for the chosen problems. In addition, concrete research tools need to be developed (including interview guides, questionnaires, remote sensing data such as panchromatic and multi-spectral satellite scenes or aerial photographs), and preparations made for conducting the research. In concrete terms, this means that the research question has been found and the research design created in advance of the field work. Afterwards the data will be collected during the field work, and plans, sketches and/or maps will be developed. Collected data is evaluated by students using statistical software (R, SPSS), remote sensing programs or geographic information systems (GIS).

With regard to strengthening personal competencies, it should be noted that students work closely together with the partners, authorities or non-governmental organizations on-site at the respective projects. Autonomously planned and team-oriented or multicultural projects and case studies are created in this way. Some of the examples below are intended to clarify these explanations:

- GIS-based mapping of a section of the medina of Tripoli, Libya ("Learning through dialogue"): Mapping central commercial districts in Tripoli's Medina. The results of the mapping were made available to local urban planners.
- Film project on intercultural encounters in Libya ("Learning through dialogue"): Short film project on intercultural collaboration with scientists and students in Libya. The submission by three students won the DAAD Youth Award.
- Crowd sourcing of spatial data in practice in Cameroon ("LUNA project"): the OpenStreetMap (OSM) platform has made data accessible to the public with the assistance of interested citizens.
- Inventory and preparation of traditional recipes in Cameroon ("LUNA project"): Book project on the importance of indigenous vegetables for food security in an urban context. A book of recipes was developed in collaboration with peasant farmers and cooks; it deals explicitly with indigenous vegetables, their significance and use. The book was published by the World Vegetable Center, a project partner.
- Participation in a continuing education program for Ghanaian partners ("Urban Food[Plus]"): Students took on the role of instructor and passed on their acquired knowledge within the context of continuing education programs. The "Urban Food[Plus]" project also offers students the opportunity to carry out geodata acquisition using state-of-the-art technology.

In addition, engagement with students and partners from other cultures offers the opportunity to become familiar with and understand one's own culture or oneself better. In addition, the students participate in international symposia and meetings with representatives of German authorities abroad (e.g. embassies) or carry out press activities. In addition, they have the opportunity to work on the project as student assistants and to continue to apply or deepen what they have learned, especially in the field of remote sensing, GIS and cartography.

As shown in Fig. 26.1, at the heart of the teaching and learning projects is the development of interpretive and reflective competencies, as well as the training of specialist and methodological skills. Critical reflection on the research process in particular plays an important role. Students should learn to draw conclusions as to whether and how future work can be done more effectively in similar research and problem-solving situations. The emergence of reflective competence is certainly the biggest challenge and should be targeted, systematically guided and instrumented accordingly (Korthagen et al. 2002; Kroath 2004). Reflective moments should be like a "common thread" that runs through the entire process, and space and time must be provided for reflection. This can be done by creating an e-portfolio in which learners can visualize the development of their learning progress (Fichten 2010).

26.4   Summary and Outlook

The structure and implementation of the various courses (see Fig. 26.1) shows that the acquisition and deepening of specialist knowledge associated with student activity and the learning of methods through their application are central aspects of the teaching/learning projects. Controlled and autonomous learning phases alternate repeatedly, with the role of instructors constantly changing between acting as knowledge facilitators and as consultants. The systematic appropriation of the ways in which scientists and experts in professional practice think and work requires a high degree of independence and self-guidance.

The results of the course evaluation show that the students have chosen this form of learning for self-determined motives in particular (for example to achieve professional goals). In addition, it became clear that longer-term and more in-depth study of a complex of topics not only leads to more profoundly developed technical and methodological skills, but also makes it possible to acquire a kind of expert knowledge that is often neglected in university life due to the focus on output. However, the students emphasized two soft skills, "a capacity for teamwork" and "intercultural competence," that they have acquired in particular, which are more important than ever in a globalized work environment. By contrast, however, there is the enormous time expenditure that needs to be spent on such a course.

For geography, this very specifically raises the question as to how inquiry-based learning can be structured in a curricular and didactic-methodical way under the conditions of the current study structures, so that there can be a meaningful reciprocal relationship between research and teaching while simultaneously counteracting the current tendency to reduce university instruction to the level of school instruction. Consequently, further didactic-methodical considerations are required in order to permanently establish the developed procedure under the conditions of the current study structures. For technical and didactic reasons, it is worth strengthening the initiative of students by creating appropriate teaching/learning arrangements and disclosing their expectations. With the help of well-thought-out coaching, students' "own" research ideas and questions arise automatically.

Only if these conditions are fulfilled can students contribute to the development of geography by participating in real research questions. Last but not least, this methodology could also overcome barriers within the field. Kindling this fire is worth the effort.

References

Bruner, J. S. (1981). Der Akt der Entdeckung. In H. Neber (Hrsg.), *Entdeckendes Lernen* (S. 15–29). Weinheim: Beltz.

Elverfeldt, K. v./Egner, H. (2015). Systemtheorien und Mensch-Umwelt-Forschung. Eine geographische Perspektive. In P. Goeke/R. Lippuner/J. Wirths (Hrsg.), *Konstruktion und Kontrolle. Zur Raumordnung sozialer Systeme* (S. 319–342). Wiesbaden: Springer.

Euler, D. (2005). Forschendes Lernen. In W. Wunderlich/S. Spoun (Hrsg.), *Universität und Persönlichkeitsentwicklung* (S. 253–272). Frankfurt: Campus.

Fichten, W. (2010). Forschendes Lernen in der Lehrerbildung. In U. Eberhardt (Hrsg.), *Neue Impulse der Hochschuldidaktik: Sprach- und Literaturwissenschaften* (S. 127–182). Wiesbaden: Springer.

Gebhardt, H./Glaser, R./Radtke, U./Reuber, P. (2011). Das Drei-Säulen-Modell der Geographie. In H. Gebhardt/R. Glaser/U. Radtke/P. Reuber (Hrsg.), *Geographie. Physische Geographie und Humangeographie* (S. 71–83). Heidelberg: Spektrum.

Huber, L. (1998). Forschendes Lehren und Lernen – eine aktuelle Notwendigkeit. *Das Hochschulwesen, 46*, 1–10.

Huber, L. (2003). Forschendes Lernen in Deutschen Hochschulen. Zum Stand der Diskussion. In A. Obolenski/H. Meyer (Hrsg.), *Forschendes Lernen. Theorie und Praxis einer professionellen LehrerInnenausbildung* (S. 15–36). Bad Heilbrunn: Klinkhardt.

Huber, L. (2004). Forschendes Lernen. 10 Thesen zum Verhältnis von Forschung und Lehre aus Perspektive des Studiums. *Die Hochschule, 13*, 29–49.

Huber, L. (2009). Warum Forschendes Lernen nötig und möglich ist. In L. Huber/J. Hellmer/F. Schneider (Hrsg.), *Forschendes Lernen im Studium*. (S. 9–35). Bielefeld: UniversitätsVerlagWebler.

Jenkins, A./Healey, M. (2010). Undergraduate Research and International Initiatives to Link Teaching and Research. *CUR Quarterly, 30*, 36–42.

Knowles, M. (1975). *Self-Directed learning: A guide for learners and teachers*. New York: Association Press.

Koch-Priewe, B./Thiele, J. (2009). Versuch einer Systematisierung der hochschuldidaktischen Konzepte zum Forschenden Lernen. In B. Roters/R. Schneider/B. Koch-Priewe/J. Thiele/J. Wildt (Hrsg), *Forschendes Lernen im Lehramtsstudium* (S. 271–292). Bad Heilbrunn: Klinkhardt.

Korthagen, F./Kessels, J./Koster, B./Lagerwerf, B./Wubbels, T. (2002). *Schulwirklichkeit und Lehrerbildung. Reflexion in der Lehrtätigkeit*. Hamburg: EB-Verlag.

Kroath, F. (2004). Zur Entwicklung von Reflexionskompetenz in der LehrerInnenausbildung. Bausteine für die Praxisarbeit. In S. Rahm/M. Schratz (Hrsg.), *LehrerInnenforschung. Theorie braucht Praxis. Braucht Praxis Theorie?* (S. 179–193). Innsbruck: Studien-Verlag.

Nuissl, E. (2006). Vom Lernen Erwachsener. In E. Nuissl (Hrsg.), *Vom Lernen zum Lehren. Lern- und Lehrforschung für die Weiterbildung* (S. 217–232). Bielefeld: Bertelsmann.

Passon, J./Braun, K. (2013). »Lernen durch Dialog« – Denkanstöße zum Forschenden Lernen im Fach Geographie. *entgrenzt, 5*, 39–43.

Inquiry-Based Learning in History

27

Andreas Bihrer, Stephan Bruhn, and Fiona Fritz

The goal of the following article is to develop the prospects for the concept of inquiry-based learning in the subject of history. At the start of the article, the current state of the research will be outlined and a separate understanding of the underlying term will be discussed. Selected projects and fields for inquiry-based learning are presented before the article concludes with the development of new perspectives

27.1 Introduction and State of the Research

Forms and elements of inquiry-based learning are indeed used in the field of history at German institutions of higher learning, but so far only a few didactic reflections or programmatic contributions have been formulated: For example, bibliographic databases such as FIS Bildung and ERIC cite neither cross-sectional studies in current anthologies (e.g. Reiber 2007; Huber et al. 2009) nor individual publications; only a few project ideas are shown (e.g. Bihrer 2009; Battaglia and Bihrer 2010; Bihrer et al. 2010; Brauch and Bihrer 2011). This may be due to the state of the research on inquiry-based learning in

A. Bihrer, Prof. Dr. (✉) · S. Bruhn, Dr.
Christian-Albrechts-Universität zu Kiel, Historisches Seminar, Professur für Geschichte des frühen und hohen Mittelalters sowie für Historische Grundwissenschaften,
Kiel, Germany
e-mail: abihrer@email.uni-kiel.de; bruhn@histosem.uni-kiel.de

F. Fritz
Körber-Stiftung, Arbeitsbereich "Geschichte und Politik", Programm-Managerin EUSTORY;
History Campus, Hamburg, Germany
e-mail: fritz@koerber-stiftung.de

© The Author(s) 2019
H. A. Mieg (ed.), *Inquiry-Based Learning – Undergraduate Research*,
https://doi.org/10.1007/978-3-030-14223-0_27

general, since its conceptualization is still in its infancy (Huber 2014a), and the international technical debate has not led to any clearly defined concepts, even in the Anglosphere (Kossek 2009). Although descriptions of best practice examples, generalized pedagogical concepts, and ideas for university-based guiding principles have been published, it is often difficult to recognize or process other research in higher education didactics.

Against this background, and taking into consideration the different forms of empowering teaching and learning – which university administrators, in particular, want to label as inquiry-based learning or "research-led learning" due to the current attractiveness of the concept of research – it is also necessary to develop clearer definitions for the science of history and put up more clearly formulated concepts for discussion. Unlike the previous discussion (e.g. Huber 2004, 2014a; Reiber and Tremp 2007), inquiry-based learning should be clearly distinguishable from learning that is oriented towards problems, action or projects; of a genetic or discovering nature; and research-oriented or research-based. In the following, a definition is proposed, according to which the focus is not just on the change in perspective and role of students from learner to researcher – and evaluating this change – and the completion of all steps of a research cycle, as in the previous debate. Rather, two elements of this process should be given special significance There are two decisive factors – firstly the innovative research question developed by the students themselves (Brauch and Bihrer 2015), and secondly not only the generation of new knowledge that is of interest to third parties according to the standards of the subject, but also the presentation of the research results in a forum recognized by the scientific community. From this perspective, the mere creation of a wall news-sheet or a homepage is not enough; rather, the new findings must be addressed to the specialist community and issued in established forms of publication (Bihrer 2009).

27.2   Basic Conditions

In Germany, basic university conditions for the subject of history do not differ significantly from the circumstances of other major subjects in the humanities: Immense student demands are faced with low teaching capacities, which results in a poor level of support. As a result, larger projects in accordance with inquiry-based learning are limited. Employment opportunities for instructors in the subject of history are often limited to a few semesters, and (as in other subjects in the humanities) the course of studies is not designed as a narrow-based vocational education, due to the diversity of professional fields already outlined for students. The heterogeneity of students in terms of study progress, abilities or motivation is typical for courses in the field of history, which nevertheless need not be an obstacle to inquiry-based learning, since research assignments can be distributed at different levels within a project group. The greatest percentage of students have chosen the teaching profile for their history studies; the concept of inquiry-based learning is interesting for this circle, not least because this and similar didactic approaches are also being tested and implemented at the school level. Thus, not only a practical course of a research cycle, but also engagement with pedagogic and methodological issues is necessary for teaching students. For this purpose, the extension of the previous collaboration with subject didactics and teacher training is of particular importance. In addition, inquiry-based learning projects should be pursued in history as an academic discipline, but also in collaboration with non-university institutions such as archives, libraries or research centers.

Over the course of the Bologna Process, the basic conditions in Germany for the study of history have been reformed, as well as for other degree programs. Nevertheless, the central objectives of competence orientation and employability in the revised study regulations have generally been formulated as abstract competencies or judged solely on their usability for work and career. This revision of the examination regulations and study plans, as well as the formulation of module descriptions, has in many cases led to the development of a propaedeutic introductory phase of the course of study that is separated from research. The initial aim in this phase is to impart so-called basic knowledge, which complicates projects according to the stipulations of inquiry-based learning. In addition, modules have often been very narrowly defined, module descriptions established as binding content and didactic guidelines, and the connection of courses over several semesters hindered, which in turn hinders the implementation of projects based on inquiry-based learning. For this reason, at least the combination of previously separate teaching formats would have to be facilitated. In addition, the recognition of suitable forms of examination for inquiry-based learning should be realized (Huber 2009). Finally, in times of an actual or perceived overload on teachers and learners, it is essential that meaningful lesson planning in formats of inquiry-based learning be made possible by clearing out the curricula or reducing exam pressure, and that greater temporal leeway or at least planning certainty be allowed by clearly designating particularly labor-intensive phases.

In order to create better conditions for inquiry-based learning in the study of history, or even to establish the concept as a "curricular principle" (Reiber and Tremp 2007, p. 4), many of these changes can only be achieved through further development of the degree programs – which may, however, be problematic in the post-Bologna era, in which there is growing reform skepticism, in addition to disappointment with and fatigue of reforms. In the case of curricular readjustments, it is always necessary to consider that inquiry-based learning projects should not only be integrated at the end of the study course in the form of internships or practical semesters, but should also be implemented in the introductory phase of the course of study (general information about this, Huber 2004; for a course of study in history, Brauch and Bihrer 2015). A thematic approach should apply to all formats; however, that approach should retain a degree of technical specificity in its basic features: It must be possible to connect not only to other seminars, but above all to other institutions of higher learning so that degrees and requirements always remain comparable and, in the event of a change of university, acquired academic achievements can be recognized. The challenges for instructors associated therewith should be addressed through to reflection, evaluation, continuing education, greater networking among lecturers, and higher education didactic professionalization ("*Scholarship of Teaching and Learning*")

(Huber 2014b). Before inquiry-based learning can be established as a guiding principle for universities and used meaningfully by universities for profile development, these problems must first be tackled at the subject level.

27.3   Projects – Mapping and Perspectives

Although individual approaches to inquiry-based learning have been implemented into teaching and learning research pertaining to history as an academic discipline, this is in no way a systematic implementation or even penetration of the subject culture. In the following, we shall therefore undertake an initial mapping of those concepts of inquiry-based learning that are currently being pursued, planned or discussed in the field of history within higher education instruction in Germany. This overview, which in no way claims to be complete nor sets out to proceed in an exemplary manner, but rather seeks to etch out previously pursued guidelines, also serves as a starting point for a number of considerations of a conceptual nature that make it possible to demonstrate further prospects for history as an academic discipline.

27.3.1 Practiced Teaching Methods

In recent years, the demand that the study of history be oriented towards practice and competence has produced a variety of forms and formats, by means of which this reorientation is to be implemented in teaching. In so doing, inquiry-based learning approaches are not infrequently taken into consideration, whether consciously or unconsciously. In addition to the established fields and forums for student research – the qualification theses and colloquia – other concepts, which are also aimed at a non-university public, are being tested, with publication of the results as their goal (at least for some of the concepts): award-winning essay competitions; research studios which bring students into contact with doctoral candidates and post-doctoral researchers within the context of small conferences and workshops; and independently developed study trips that go through all the organizational phases, from ideas concerning fundraising to travel planning and implementation. Furthermore, participation in scholarly book projects (anthologies with student contributions, regional history encyclopedias, editions, etc.), readings before a lay audience (Schöck-Quinteros and Steffen 2013), the conception and implementation of historical tours or exhibitions, memorial work and formats of "re-enactment" or experimental archeology primarily rooted in popular culture should also be mentioned. This cursory listing may already be sufficient to show the wealth of variants that can be found.

27.3.2 History and Public Relations – Impetus from Applied History or Public History as well as National and Regional History

An important impetus for implementing practice-oriented approaches also comes from the field of applied history or public history, a still relatively recent trend in history in Germany, which deals with the public connection to history in all its facets. The growing importance of this sub-area is evident above all in university institutionalization, despite all the conceptual and methodological blurring that still characterizes the field in the German-speaking area (Nießer and Tomann 2014; Zündorf 2014). In addition to independent degree programs at the Freie Universität Berlin and the Universities of Mannheim and Bremen, we should mention the "Professur für Angewandte Geschichtswissenschaft – Public History" in Heidelberg, and the field of "Public History" in Hamburg. The latter has even replaced the "Allgemeine Berufsqualifizierende Kompetenzen" (general vocationally qualifying competencies) in the Department of History, thereby making the connection to the ideal of employability particularly evident. In terms of implementing inquiry-based learning approaches, the field of applied history/public history is of particular importance, as it places university research and education in direct relationship with public engagement with history, enters into and maintains collaborations with non-university institutions, reveals employment opportunities, and is dedicated to project acquisition. Thus institutional and – above all – subject-specific basic conditions are made available, by means of which the realization of research projects can find a direct and continuous input into teaching in order to support students in their involvement in the professional discourse on history in the long term, beyond the promotion of individual projects or the engagement of individual teachers. In this way, public interest in history is actively used to familiarize students early on with non-university representations and forms of mediation of the historical, and to introduce them to broader contexts, which may include not only the technical activity but also aspects of marketing or presentation skills.

Similar approaches are also being pursued in the departments of regional history, which are already in close contact with non-university institutions due to the orientation of their research field. Projects relating to regional history offer the advantage that they can usually be carried out in direct geographical proximity to the university location, and thus archives, history societies or other cooperation partners can be accessed without much financial or logistical effort. In addition, approaches of inquiry-based learning seem to be more trans-epochal at the level of regional history than in the area of applied history/public history that has a clear orientation towards contemporary history. However, inquiry-based learning should not be confined to what is assumed to be more familiar and accessible, but rather should encompass all epochs and topics of history. In this way, the heterogeneous interests of the students can be taken into account, even if different implementation options are available or changing methodological concepts may be useful, depending on the epoch.

27.3.3 From Theory to Practice: The Auxiliary Sciences of History

The question of epoch-specific methodology leads to another field which is currently in a position to make an important contribution to the implementation of inquiry-based learning approaches. We are talking about the auxiliary sciences of history, which are traditionally oriented towards the pre-modern age – a curriculum which is not uniformly defined, and which serves to open up the traditional source material in its original form. The auxiliary sciences have been under fire for some years because of their supposedly outmoded nature and their rigid classification system. This is a circumstance that is mainly reflected in the higher education landscape itself, where professorships with a corresponding denomination are often not filled again after being vacated or study programs in this area are being systematically reduced (Kümper 2014, pp. 10–13). On the other hand, it should be noted that working with sources in their original form as well as the analysis of manuscripts, documents, seals or inscriptions is a motivating factor for students that should not be underestimated. Here, history literally becomes "tangible" to them, and this is where the feeling of being able to interact directly with a bygone era and enter uncharted territory arises (Battaglia and Bihrer 2010). It is therefore not necessary to abolish the auxiliary historical sciences, which are still indispensable for sound engagement with all kinds of historical records. Instead, a methodological reorientation is needed, which takes into account changes in the basic conditions of the study of history and at the same time recalls its practical roots. Instead of instruction that is centered on lecturers, which merely aims to familiarize students with the classification system of the auxiliary sciences curriculum based on examples, an application-related, student-centered learning situation must be created which starts with a concrete application, offers selective assistance in the independent development of the material and ideally leads to the development of any transferable and applicable competence. It is only in this way that students become aware of the relevance of their own contribution to historical research to the historical record, thus retaining the motivation inspired by the "aura of the original" (Bihrer 2009, p. 78). Because of this reorientation of instruction, which partially breaks through the existing classification system, the proposal has recently been made to speak of practice-oriented „Materialwissenschaften "("material sciences," Kümper 2014) rather than theoretical and abstract auxiliary sciences – an approach that could prove promising in relation to teaching history.

27.4   Conclusion

What further perspectives can be formulated at a higher level following this overview? First of all, it should be noted that in all of the approaches and tendencies that have been presented, practice-oriented teaching does not necessarily imply inquiry-based learning. In forms of teaching and projects related to the field of applied history or public history, or as a result of research in regional history, it remains to be seen to what extent research processes are not only imitated by students, but also independently realized. So do these courses actually produce student publications that have developed from joint work in the seminar and that are clearly identifiable as individual achievements, finding their way into specialist discourse? It is only when these basic conditions have been met – which is to say the independent formulation of an innovative research question on the one hand, and product orientation on the other – that the buzzword "inquiry-based learning" becomes a viable concept, and imitation becomes serious participation.

In addition, taking into account the growing number of digital publication formats, it is critical to question the extent to which they can actually provide an alternative to "traditional" publication in print. This is because there are still serious reservations in the subject area with regard to online publications, not least because of the lack of quality controls, the abundance of information on the Internet, and the discontinuous management of many websites. Therefore, student contributions to the historical discourse should not be published online in the form of individual attempts, but instead should be linked to institutionalized platforms that are recognized within the subject area and (hence) continuous, that ensure the quality of the contributions, link the different projects with one another and conduct site maintenance in accordance with the requirements of a digital environment. Workspaces for public history (applied history) that already exist or that are in the start-up phase, as well as the relevant specialist portals, lend themselves to this task, since these could meaningfully integrate a component that has been defined in this manner into their public relations work. Ultimately, greater consideration of subject-specific standards can only be achieved through greater financial expenditures and the expansion of the existing personnel structure, so that in the long run, the question will be raised as to whether sustainable digital publishing is less intensive than the "traditional" printed publication formats.

In view of the university-specific basic conditions, it would also be desirable to expand funding opportunities and personnel capacities in order to improve the educator-student ratios in the subject in the long term and ideally to adjust them accordingly in response to the increasing number of students. Although interdisciplinary problems such as insufficient funding and overburdening of higher education structures place enormous limits on inquiry-based learning, in principle they cannot be considered to be arguments against an at least gradual implementation of this learning approach. A complete orientation of historical studies to research-related forms of teaching and learning is neither feasible nor meaningful. Rather, it seems worthwhile to integrate aspects of research activities into traditional teaching formats, for example in the form of smaller research processes that are independently organized by the participants. Furthermore, courses such as those presented could be created at the level of the curricula or through cooperation with external partners as a relief measure in order to create more freedom for students and lecturers alike.

A final point emphasizes the urgent need for further orientation courses in history, which relate individual projects to one another and evaluate them with regard to a subject-specific methodology – an approach that has yet to be developed. In addition, there is often no clear positioning relative to other forms of empowering learning, not least because of the lack of specialized subject matter and methodology. In particular, however, meaningful methods and study grids must be developed, which can then be used to determine the acquisition of competencies by students and the gradual promotion of autonomy within or by courses. The successful publication of research findings is by no means sufficient when speaking of successfully implementing the committed learning objectives of modern universities. Rather, it is necessary to specifically determine the learning successes and learning progress achieve by each individual participant – and at which point in time, and in which way – in the course of the research process, in order to be able to effectively manage the acquisition of skills and to continue to develop existing approaches in a systematic and purposeful manner. This is indispensable, not least in the sense of "broad support," because inquiry-based learning should not be an approach for shaping elitist educational structures. Here, an important impetus could be provided by history didactics, which is often still strongly oriented towards the teaching of history in school and the education of history teachers, in keeping with the requirements primarily directed at it in everyday university life. It is only in this environment that one can find those specialists, who are familiar both with the principles of empirical educational research and with the epistemological maxims of the subject area, and thus have the necessary competence to develop practical inquiry-based learning approaches with reference to history. This is because a sustainable implementation of inquiry-based learning can only come about if there is a change in the teaching culture in the subject, which requires higher education didactic guidance.

References

Battaglia, S./Bihrer, A. (2010). C 2.16: Vom Frontalunterricht zum forschenden Lernen: Kompetenzorientierung, Individualisierung und Praxisrelevanz in der universitären Lehre. In B. Berendt/H.-P. Voss/J. Wildt (Hrsg.), *Neues Handbuch Hochschullehre* (Ergänzungslieferung, 41. Band) (S. 1–22). Berlin: Raabe.

Bihrer, A. (2009). Natürlich, eine alte Handschrift… Forschendes Lernen in der Geschichtswissenschaft. In L. Huber/J. Hellmer/F. Schneider (Hrsg.), *Forschendes Lernen im Studium: Aktuelle Konzepte und Erfahrungen* (S. 70–78). Bielefeld: UniversitätsVerlagWebler.

Bihrer, A./Schiefner, M./Tremp, P. (2010). Forschendes Lernen und Medien: Ein Bespiel aus den Geschichtswissenschaften. In S. Mandel/M. Rutishauser/E. Seiler Schiedt (Hrsg.), *Digitale Medien für Lehre und Forschung* (Medien in der Wissenschaft, 55. Band) (S. 95–105). Münster u. a.: Waxmann.

Brauch, N./Bihrer, A. (2011). Die »Wikinger« als Lernanlass in der Geschichtslehrerbildung: Theoretische Überlegungen und erste empirische Befunde einer Studie zur Graduierung von Kompetenzen geschichtsdidaktischen Denkens. *Zeitschrift für Geschichtsdidaktik, 10*, 117–130.

Brauch, N./Bihrer, A. (2015). *FOGEL: Forschende Geschichtslehrer/innen*. Retrieved 1 April 2015 from https://www.histsem.uni-kiel.de/de/abteilungen/mittelalterliche-geschichte-und-historische-hilfswissenschaften/mitarbeiter/prof.%2D%2Ddr.-phil.-andreas-bihrer/forschungsprojekte

Huber, L. (2014a). Forschungsbasiertes, Forschungsorientiertes, Forschendes Lernen: Alles dasselbe? Ein Plädoyer für eine Verständigung über Begriffe und Unterscheidungen im Feld forschungsnahen Lehrens und Lernens. *Das Hochschulwesen, 1+2*, 22–29.

Huber, L. (2014b). Scholarship of Teaching and Learning: Konzept, Geschichte, Formen, Entwicklungsaufgaben. In L. Huber/A. Pilniok/R. Sethe/F. Szcyzyrba/M. Vogel (Hrsg.), *Forschendes Lehren im eigenen Fach: Scholarship of Teaching and Learning in Beispielen* (S. 19–36). Bielefeld: Bertelsmann.

Huber, L. (2004). Forschendes Lernen: 10 Thesen zum Verhältnis von Forschung und Lehre aus der Perspektive des Studiums. *Die Hochschule, 13* (2), 29–49.

Huber, L. (2009). Warum Forschendes Lernen nötig und möglich ist. In L. Huber/J. Hellmer/ F. Schneider (Hrsg.), *Forschendes Lernen im Studium: Aktuelle Konzepte und Erfahrungen* (S. 9–36). Bielefeld: UniversitätsVerlagWebler.

Kossek, B. (2009). *Survey: Die forschungsgeleitete Lehre in der internationalen Diskussion.* Retrieved 31 March 2015 from https://ctl.univie.ac.at/fileadmin/user_upload/elearning/ Forschungsgeleitete_Lehre_International_090414.pdf

Kümper, H. (2014). *Materialwissenschaft Mediävistik: Eine Einführung in die Historischen Hilfswissenschaften.* Paderborn: Schöningh.

Nießer, J./Tomann, J. (2014). Einleitung. In J. Nießer/J. Tomann (Hrsg.), *Angewandte Geschichte: Neue Perspektiven auf Geschichte in der Öffentlichkeit* (S. 7–14). Paderborn: Schöningh.

Reiber, K. (Hrsg.). (2007). *Forschendes Lernen als hochschuldidaktisches Prinzip: Grundlegungen und Beispiele* (Tübinger Beiträge zur Hochschuldidaktik 3 (1)). Tübingen: Universität. Retrieved 31 March 2015 from https://publikationen.uni-tuebingen.de/xmlui/bitstream/han- dle/10900/43870/pdf/TBHD%203-1-2007Reiber.pdf?sequence=1&isAllowed=y

Reiber, K./Tremp, P. (2007). A 3.6: Eulen nach Athen! Forschendes Lernen als Bildungsprinzip. In B. Berendt/H.-P. Voss/J. Wildt (Hrsg.), *Neues Handbuch Hochschullehre* (Ergänzungslieferung, 30. Band) (S. 1–14). Berlin: Raabe.

Schöck-Quinteros, E./Steffen, N. (2013). »Aus den Akten auf die Bühne« – Studierende erforschen »Eine Stadt im Krieg«: Ein geschichtswissenschaftliches Crossover-Projekt zwischen Forschung, Lehre und Theater. In L. Huber/M. Kröger/H. Schelhowe (Hrsg.), *Forschendes Lernen als Profilmerkmal einer Universität* (S. 195–209). Bielefeld: UniversitätsVerlagWebler.

Zündorf, I. (2014). Public History und Angewandte Geschichte – Konkurrenten oder Komplizen? In J. Nießer/J. Tomann (Hrsg.), *Angewandte Geschichte: Neue Perspektiven auf Geschichte in der Öffentlichkeit* (S. 63–76). Paderborn: Ferdinand Schöning.

Inquiry-Based Learning in Legal Studies

28

Roland Broemel and Olaf Muthorst

In addition to its content, a university education in law is characterized by the formats and subjects of its examinations, in particular the career-relevant first state examination in law. The high career relevance of the first state examination in law as well as its specific requirements mean that preparation for the state exam takes center stage for students even in the early stages of their studies. These specific exam requirements, as well as a high degree of uncertainty among students, uphold the traditionally widespread existence of commercial refresher courses, and at the same time limit the leeway for the individual faculties and instructors.

At first glance, this does not seem to result in a favorable environment for elements of inquiry-based learning. Irrespective of the regular calls for a reduction in the list of examination subjects or the further expansion of the examination formats (Wissenschaftsrat 2012, p. 62), exploratory learning offers students the opportunity to develop a basic understanding of the legal working method. On the one hand, such an understanding facilitates the ability to systematically handle large quantities of material. On the other hand, it also improves the capacity for differentiated reasoning and thus considerably increases the quality of the examination results. Inquiry-based learning can therefore also offer significant added value within the supposedly "tightly laced corset" set by state examinations.

R. Broemel, Prof. Dr. (✉)
Goethe-Universität Frankfurt, Fachbereich Rechtswissenschaft, Professor für
Öffentliches Recht, Wirtschafts- und Währungsrecht, Finanzmarktregulierung und
Rechtstheorie, Frankfurt, Germany
e-mail: broemel@jur.uni-frankfurt.de

O. Muthorst, Prof. Dr. iur.
Freie Universität Berlin, Fachbereich Rechtswissenschaft, Professur für Bürgerliches Recht,
Verfahrens- und Insolvenzrecht, Berlin, Germany
e-mail: olaf.muthorst@fu-berlin.de

© The Author(s) 2019
H. A. Mieg (ed.), *Inquiry-Based Learning – Undergraduate Research*,
https://doi.org/10.1007/978-3-030-14223-0_28

Starting points for inquiry-based learning can be found in the focus areas that emphasize in-depth study; above all, they are provided in the teaching format of the seminar. These have become less significant due to changes in the study regulations at many faculties within this course of studies. In terms of inquiry-based learning, seminars offer the opportunity to place greater emphasis on students' own initiative, for example in the development of the respective research questions.

28.1   Basic Conditions for Inquiry-Based Learning in Legal Studies

Pursuant to Section 5 (1) of the German Judiciary Act (*Deutsches Richtergesetz,* translated), qualification for the judicial office can be obtained by someone who "acquires a law degree at a university with the first state examination and subsequent legal traineeship with the second state examination; the first state examination consists of a university specialization examination and a state compulsory examination." Qualification for the judicial office is simultaneously the admission requirement for the other "traditional" legal professions: notary, counsellor in public administration, companies and associations. Although the international comparison shows – and it is repeatedly demanded within the profession (from among the chorus of critical voices, only Wissenschaftsrat 2012, p. 59 et seq., in particular 61 et seq.) – that law as a university subject is also conceivable with completely different curriculum designs and examination formats, the present state of legal studies at German universities is characterized by the orientation towards what the German Judiciary Act calls the "first examination."

This examination consists of a university section and a compulsory subject examination, the latter is the responsibility of state examination offices. Although the university portion in all departments is designed such that it is largely identical, with differences only in details, the state part of the first examination is considered the "actual" examination because of its supposedly greater comparability, in particular in terms of grading. The exam is predetermined by educational laws and regulations, both in terms of the examination formats and the subject matter of the examination. It is taken in a procedure that is considered strict and anonymous. The technical examination requirements, both in terms of scope of the material and the performance profile, are regarded as extremely high and difficult to predict. A great deal of career relevance is attributed to the final grade in the first exam and, in particular, the partial grade obtained in the state exam portion, since the examination format is considered by many – especially practitioners – to be particularly objective, reliable and valid due to its being externally assessed. In practice, this confidence in the efficacy of exams appears to be relatively stable as compared to the equally present awareness of margins of discretion, randomness in the testing process, and specific, non-specialist examination requirements.

On the other hand, the constant external assessment of university education, which must assert its relevance against private-sector revision books, can prompt positive standardization and quality-assurance effects. The level of education of German lawyers and the efficiency of German law are considered to be high, especially when compared internationally (Wissenschaftsrat 2012, p. 13 et seq.).

As stated above, the exams make up the dominant perspective of students of any teaching unit and its subject matter from the beginning of the course of study. As early as during the introductory phase of the course of study, students typically orient their learning behavior and the decision for or against their participation in courses, working groups or other courses towards preparation for the exams and their individual assessments of the examination requirements. There is considerable uncertainty about these requirements and the quality criteria for assessing examinations, especially during the introductory phase of the course of study (Broemel and Stadler 2014, p. 1212; Eork 2011, p. 61 et seq.). As a result of their previous learning experiences at school, students in the introductory phase of the course of study are typically accustomed to being able to pass examinations by reproducing and selectively transferring material from the classroom sessions. The specific requirements of exams in the form of case-solving require a contextualization of the learned material that goes well beyond the usual abstraction level of transference, however, and requires a case-solving technique that is independent of the content. Even though, in essence, this case-solving task requires competence in methodically meticulous interpretation and differentiated reasoning, students often neglect training this competence during exam preparation. The varying quality of the corrections, which are typically undertaken by grading assistants in the case of course-related examinations and assignments, and which often contain only abbreviated indications of the quality of the examinations and, above all, of concrete approaches to the improvement, also contribute to students' uncertainty regarding examination requirements. Not infrequently, students assume, up until the phase of exam preparation, that a good grade is attached to presenting the examiner with supposedly fitting keywords instead of convincing them through compelling rigor and quality of reasoning.

Apart from that, as their course of study progresses and especially during the run-up to the exam, students' need to choose courses that are relevant to exam preparation increases. Even with courses that are oriented directly towards the preparation of exam-relevant content, students expect each individual unit to be explicitly focused on their preparation in terms of the specific requirements of the written exams. In the final phase of the legal study, which would provide particularly good conditions for interdisciplinary inquiry-based learning due to the advanced status of the students, the students lack the time and the motivation for labor-intensive courses that are not directly related to exams (Broemel and Muthorst 2012).

28.2 Needs and Benefits of Inquiry-Based Learning in Legal Studies

The subject matter of legal studies attaches special importance to the integration of the individual sections and the lecture contents. This integration is a prerequisite for understanding the function of individual subareas. The structuring associated therewith makes it easier to manage large amounts of material and ultimately forms the basis for the ability to engage in the level of differentiated reasoning required in the examinations. This structuring, and not the available detailed knowledge, ultimately decides students' exam success, despite traditional student assumptions. Although exploratory learning trains a reflective approach to the methods of legal work, and thus focuses on establishing correlations, many students, confronted with the burden associated with the quantity of material and exam pressure, tends to result in a focus on traditional educational courses that are immediately relevant to exams.

A systematic view of the correlations between individual subareas is anything but a trivial learning objective in legal studies: It is of considerable importance both for understanding the function of individual regulations and for coping with the large amounts of material. During the introductory phase of the course of study, students are typically unfamiliar with legal methods. Although the contents of the courses are easily understandable, students in the first semesters and sometimes even beyond often find it difficult to recognize overarching and underlying structures, and to develop the system awareness that is essential for legal argumentation (Stadler and Broemel 2014; Bork 2011, p. 63). This difficulty is contingent, to some extent, on the subject matter of the field. The function and scope of individual concepts and institutions can only be fully grasped if one knows the implications for the areas being linked. This would require an understanding of at least the essential structures of the overall system (cf. Broemel and Stadler 2014, p. 1210 et seq.).

Students are thus faced with the difficulty that, regularly, the respective material for an area can only be understood in conjunction with the contents of the other areas and meaningfully applied to typically interdisciplinary issues. The high significance placed on integrating the individual subareas as well as on understanding interdisciplinary correlations makes studying more difficult at first. At the beginning of their studies, many students lack the overview of the structures in the curriculum that are scheduled for the later semesters. At the same time, the abundance of material that has already built up within a lecture, but even more so due to the large number of compulsory lectures each semester, often results in gaps in preparation and follow-up during the semesters (Broemel and Stadler 2014, p. 1209). Not infrequently, these gaps run through the entire course of studies and are only closed during the exam preparation or even make their way into the legal clerkship (*Referendariat*). Such gaps affect the ability to recognize the interconnections between regulations in individual subareas and to holistically understand the regulatory structure. Conversely, creating an understanding of the relationships and structures by orienting the content of legal studies towards integration would be particularly suitable for facilitating the learning and retention even of large amounts of material. A structural understanding makes it possible to classify new contents from lectures or textbooks, to understand its function and the implications thereof for other regulations, and to permanently recall the contents (Stadler& Broemel, 2014, p. 1215), since these contents often run parallel to other institutions, regulations or problem areas, which provides significant synergistic effects during the learning process. In summary, it can be said that the breadth of the material and the complexity of the possibilities for interlinking make it difficult to understand relationships and structures, and sometimes lead to a feeling of being over burdened among students.

In so doing, inquiry-based learning can make a significant contribution to understanding the legal working method and the added value of correlations as well as to a reflected methodical approach. Inquiry-based learning can significantly increase the quality and effectiveness of the learning process during the following period of study. An independent search for a research topic already sensitizes students to the fact that regulatory problems from everyday reality regularly concern different legal regulatory areas, the problem-related regulatory structure of which only arises as a result of their interaction. On the other hand, the search for a topic often forces students to first confront the question as to what constitutes a worthwhile analysis from a legal point of view. Inquiry-based learning thus provides a meaningful supplement to traditional tasks in the form of case-solving, which can lead to a certain narrowing of perspective and learning behavior, depending on the students' understanding (Wissenschaftsrat 2012, p. 56; and the contributions in Hof and Götz von Olenhusen 2012). Even if engagement with the content of lectures or practicing case-solving requires a high degree of methodological competence, the courses designed for inquiry-based learning more strongly favor a reflected approach to methods of legal argumentation by addressing method questions more or less directly. In addition to imparting interpretative techniques, this also applies to the open question as to the scope of legal methodology, which remains unresolved in jurisprudence, from the mode of interpreting standards or declarations of intent regarding an extended analysis of the functioning of regulatory structures to the processing of interdisciplinary references (for a broader understanding of the education, cf. the contributions in Hof and Götz von Olenhusen 2012).

Due to their subject matter and their resource-intensive support ratio, courses with elements of inquiry-based learning are especially suitable for teaching competencies that are often merely assumed in everyday teaching and testing of legal education, but not systematically taught. They directly address the criteria and added value of differentiated, balanced and problem-based reasoning. This deepening of methodological competence substantially promotes not only the students' learning success in the other, traditional courses but also the quality of the examinations (Stadler and Broemel 2014; Broemel and Stadler 2014). In addition to the rigor of the line of thought and emphasis, especially the persuasive power of reasoning (for more detail, see Broemel and Stadler 2014, p. 1209, 1211 et seq.), the essential quality criteria of examinations correspond to the skills and competencies that are taught and deepened in courses for inquiry-based learning.

Ultimately, the needs and benefits of inquiry-based learning depend upon the understanding of the research methods in one's own subject. The discussion on research methods and the methodical approach (Engel and Schön 2007; Stürner 2014; Röhl 2011, p. 70 et seq.) as well as on the subject matter of legal scholarship (Muthorst 2011, p. 9 et seq.) does not fail to have an effect on the concept of inquiry-based learning. For a methodical understanding which sees the goal of legal scholarship first and foremost in the reflected processing and systematization of practical legal questions, the application-oriented case solutions and the seminars based on dogmatic work do cover some part of inquiry-based learning that is not inconsequential. From this perspective, the need for additional steps towards implementing inquiry-based learning may be limited to the selective adaptation of existing course formats. Even a didactically focused understanding of research, that is, research as a systematic preparation of the legal material with the aim of receptivity, tends to result in a greater appreciation of the possibilities of using inquiry-based learning within existing structures. From the perspective of an understanding of legal methods that is less oriented towards application or reception, inquiry-based learning is also a starting point for sensitizing students to the breadth of the methodological spectrum of legal scholarship.

28.3   Starting Point for Inquiry-Based Learning in Legal Studies

The starting points for inquiry-based learning in legal education lie first and foremost in the traditional seminars and in the structuring of the focus areas. In addition, curricular support of the internships could enhance the incentives that are created by the experience of applying one's expertise.

Due to their comparatively small group size and above-average support intensity, seminars are traditionally among the courses with comparatively favorable external basic conditions in legal education (Bork 2011, p. 62 et seq.). In seminars with a traditional setup, students work on one of the pre-defined, content-related topics over a period of several weeks, write a seminar paper of 20–30 pages and present their work results in an oral presentation, which is followed by a discussion by the group. A seminar paper written with a high degree of reflection can meet the requirements for inquiry-based learning both in its development process and in its outcome. When working on the topic, students identify legal issues, work on the relevant state of legal research and, on this basis, formulate their own position, which is thoroughly founded on legal scholarship. Such an approach corresponds to the way in which many lawyers work. If the quality of the thought process and reasoning is appropriate, the term paper is easily suitable for publication in a scholarly journal. What is decisive for the scope of the research experience is the openness of the given topic and the autonomy with which students are able to set their own priorities within this topic and develop theses and arguments.

The frequently observed difficulties that students have in setting up and justifying the focus of the work on a topic make it clear how unfamiliar working independently on issues within a given topic is for students. Thus this task of identifying the research question represents a considerable part of the research process in that, on the one hand, the assessment of the suitability of a specific question requires an overview of the current state of the art of the respective research fields. At the same time, the conscious decision for or against a certain question increases the individual identification with the research subject. The more open-ended the assigned topics are, however, the less controllable the overall course is for the seminar organizers. The development of the individual seminar topics by the students makes the coordination of the content of the topics more difficult. In addition, identifying and laying out a suitable topic poses a difficult task that is prone to causing frustration (Bork and Muthorst 2013, p. 72 et seq.). Similar to the choice of a dissertation topic, after spending some time familiarizing oneself with an idea, it may prove to be either too complex or to have already been comprehensively worked through in legal scholarship. In general, law students are not used to dealing with difficulties that are typical of the research process such as intermediate results that are not foreseeable at the beginning or the ongoing adaptation of a line of thought, either from their courses, the working groups or the written exam preparation (Broemel and Muthorst 2012, p. 89, 94). The accentuation of inquiry-based learning thus requires that students receive ongoing support during the individual phases of the research process, and in particular when dealing with foreseeable obstacles and difficulties. Compared to traditional seminars, this research orientation does not necessarily increase the effort required for the ongoing support, but it does increase the visibility of the support need and thus the likelihood that students will avail themselves of the support effort. The additional expenditure of time is generally rewarded by the quality of the result and the learning success.

The individual focus areas to be selected, which the university portion of the first state examination in law will cover, thus provide special space for elements of inquiry-based learning insofar as they are already designed for deepening knowledge, and because the departments enjoy a certain leeway both in the design of the compulsory courses for the focus areas and in the examination formats (see Broemel and Muthorst 2012, p. 96). A seminar-like course could be combined with elements of inquiry-based learning in the focus area. This course could be combined with examination formats that assess the way in which typical difficulties and obstacles in the research process are handled. In addition to the manuscript that is prepared, justification for the selection of the respective research question as well as the ongoing reflection in a research journal could be the subject of an overall assessment, which would be included in the final grade of the university part of the first state examination in law. The latent tension between the risks inherent in each research process and the legal requirements for the conception and assessment of examinations, and in particular their comparability (Broemel and Muthorst 2012, p. 97 et seq.), can at least be reduced to a certain degree. Depending on the content orientation of the respective focus area, seminars that focus on inquiry-based learning could include connections to relevant neighboring disciplines. With the consideration of knowledge from administrative sciences or competition theory or other disciplines like sociology or psychology, for example, the methodological competence can be extended beyond interpretation questions and case solutions by a reflected approach to the processing of interdisciplinarity (regarding the desideratum, Wissenschaftsrat 2012, p. 56 et seq.; differentiating, on the other hand, the articles in Engel and Schön 2007). A systematic immersion in research elements in legal education would not least facilitate students' transition to the possibility of subsequent doctoral studies. In practice, research competence also provides the ability to adapt to the ongoing changes in the legal and actual basic conditions of a particular area of life, to align the premises of previously established regulatory structures with those changes and, if necessary, to draw appropriate conclusions. In legal practice, lawyers rely on the ability to update acquired bodies of knowledge in changed contexts, and to classify individual, newly emerging issues into broader bodies of knowledge with a moderate degree of abstraction. Inquiry-based learning then imparts a competence that is significant for practical work, that of transferring and further developing acquired knowledge in the face of dynamic changes.

This relevance of research competence for the lasting quality of practical activity, which is also known from other disciplines, likewise suggests that elements of inquiry-based learning be situated in the practice-oriented portions of legal studies. At present, students typically complete their intended internships independently of their legal education in their departments. A supplementary, systematic processing of the internships, which would transform the questions raised in the context of the practice into research questions, could make students much more aware of the connection between theoretical and practical issues. It could also increase students' ability to make differentiated observations and promote a reflective approach to understanding and coherence among students.

28.4 Conclusion: Perspectives and Desiderata for Inquiry-Based Learning in the Field of Legal Studies

In legal studies, inquiry-based learning promotes methodological competence and an understanding of overarching structures and their added value in legal scholarship, as well as a capacity for reasoning. Inquiry-based learning thus improves the quality of learning and exam success. Nevertheless, as they progress, students are increasingly reluctant to respond to course listings for courses that utilize inquiry-based learning, courses that are not directly geared towards teaching compulsory material or courses that focus on preparing for examinations. In view of this predicament, the prospects for inquiry-based learning lie in revealing the added value of an understanding-oriented approach for both the learning process and the quality of examinations, and to rigorously align courses towards inquiry-based learning in terms of their objective, support and evaluation.

Beyond this basic condition set by the first state examination in law and the corresponding list of examination subjects, the design of the focus areas offers departments considerable leeway to accentuate elements of inquiry-based learning in the content of the courses as well as in the examination formats. Inquiry-based learning could thus compensate for a deficiency in university education in the field of law (in detail, Röhl 2011, p. 67, 70 et seq.), which is sometimes criticized within the discipline.

References

Bork, R. (2011). Rahmenbedingungen der Juristenausbildung für eine rechtswissenschaftliche Fachdidaktik. In J. Brockmann/J.-H. Dietrich/A. Pilniok (Hrsg.), *Exzellente Lehre im juristischen Studium* (S. 59–65). Baden-Baden: Nomos.

Bork, R./Muthorst, O. (2013). Forschendes Lernen im Seminar im Bürgerlichen Recht für Anfänger. *Zeitschrift für Didaktik der Rechtswissenschaft, 01/2013,* 71–79.

Broemel, R./Muthorst, O. (2012). Forschendes Lernen in der Endphase des Studiums. In J. Brockmann/J.-H. Dietrich/A. Pilniok (Hrsg.), *Methoden des Lernens in der Rechtswissenschaft* (S. 89-103). Baden-Baden: Nomos.

Broemel, R./Stadler, L. (2014). Lernstrategien im Jurastudium. *JURA – Juristische Ausbildung, 36,* 12 (2014), 1209–1220.

Engel, C./Schön, W. (Hrsg.). (2007). *Das Proprium der Rechtswissenschaft.* Tübingen: Mohr Siebeck.

Hof, H./Götz von Olenhusen, A. (Hrsg.). (2012). *Rechtsgestaltung – Rechtskritik – Konkurrenz von Rechtsordnungen...: neue Akzente für die Juristenausbildung.* Baden-Baden: Nomos.

Muthorst, O. (2011). *Grundlagen der Rechtswissenschaft.* München: Verlag C. H. Beck.

Röhl, K. F. (2011). Die Wissenschaftlichkeit des juristischen Studiums. In J. Brockmann/J.-H. Dietrich/A. Pilniok (Hrsg.), *Exzellente Lehre im juristischen Studium* (S. 67–78). Baden-Baden: Nomos.

Stadler, L./Broemel, R. (2014). Schwierigkeiten, Lerntechniken und Lernstrategien im Jurastudium. In J. Brockmann/A. Pilniok (Hrsg.), *Studieneingangsphase in der Rechtswissenschaft* (S. 27–71). Baden-Baden: Nomos.

Stürner, R. (2014). Die Zivilrechtswissenschaft und ihre Methodik – zu rechtsanwendungsbezogen und zu wenig grundlagenorientiert? *Archiv für die civilistische Praxis, 214,* 7–54.

Wissenschaftsrat (2012). *Perspektiven der Rechtswissenschaft in Deutschland. Situation, Analysen, Empfehlungen.* Drs. 2558-12. Hamburg: Wissenschaftsrat.

Inquiry-Based Learning in Philosophy

Oliver Schliemann

The question that this article poses is: what role does inquiry-based learning play in philosophy? Remarkably, a short answer was already given 250 years before this question was ever asked. As Immanuel Kant wrote in his "Announcement of the Program of his Lectures for the Winter Semester 1765–1766":

> The method of instruction, peculiar to philosophy, is zetetic as some of the philosophers of antiquity expressed it (from ζητεῖν), In other words, the method of philosophy is the method of enquiry. It is only when reason has already grown more practised and only in certain areas, that this method becomes dogmatic, that is to say, decisive. (Kant 1765/1992, p. 293)

According to Kant, what is idiosyncratic about teaching philosophy is its "enquiring" nature. For Kant, this is in the nature of things, i.e. in the nature of philosophy (cf. ibid., p. 292). In contrast to many other sciences, there is no "common standard" of knowledge in philosophy (ibid., p. 294). It cannot be based on "experience or foreign evidence," in which, for example, history finds a common measure, nor can it "demonstrate" its theorems, such as in mathematics (ibid., p. 292 et seq.). The consequence is that there is no fixed stock of learnable knowledge in philosophy (ibid.) in which the "pieces" of assured knowledge to be imparted have already been "decided." For this reason, a student of philosophy cannot be *taught* through appropriate instruction. There is no universally binding philosophical knowledge that the student would only have to absorb and learn as such. Rather, they must seek this knowledge themselves: "In short, it is not *thoughts* but *thinking*," which he ought to learn (ibid. 292).

Because philosophy lacks knowledge, i.e. it lacks generally accepted answers to their questions, according to Kant, philosophical instruction must necessarily be exploratory.

O. Schliemann, Dr. (✉)
Universität Bielefeld, Abteilung Philosophie, Bielefeld, Germany
e-mail: oliver.schliemann@uni-bielefeld.de

© The Author(s) 2019
H. A. Mieg (ed.), *Inquiry-Based Learning – Undergraduate Research*,
https://doi.org/10.1007/978-3-030-14223-0_29

But what does that mean, exactly? What is the connection between the lack of knowledge and a scholarly, exploratory attitude? Where does inquiry-based learning take place in philosophy, and how can it be promoted?

29.1   On the Use of the Term "Inquiry-Based Learning" in Philosophy

The 1970 issue of the Federal University Assistants' Conference (BAK), "Forschendes Lernen – Wissenschaftliches Prüfen" (BAK 1970) ("Inquiry-based learning – Scientific testing"), also contains an initial statement on inquiry-based learning in philosophy. I am not aware of any philosophical institute, however, in which philosophy is taught with an explicit reference to these methodological considerations. Overall, there are scarcely any German publications on higher education didactics in philosophy. On the dust jacket of his 2007 anthology "Hochschuldidaktik Philosophie" ("Philosophy of higher education didactics"), Johannes Rohbeck still claims to have opened a new field of research with this volume (cf. Rohbeck and Philipsen 2007). Yet, to my knowledge, there are no empirical studies as to how philosophy is taught at German institutions of higher learning.

Even if no explicit link is evident between higher education instruction and the higher education didactic debate regarding inquiry-based learning, there is an explicit connection to inquiry-based learning at least in the field of teacher education. The Teacher Training Act of May 12, 2009 provides for what is termed a "practical semester" as part of teacher training in North Rhine-Westphalia. The "framework for the structural and content design of the practical semester in a master's degree program relating to teaching certification" ("Rahmenkonzeption zur strukturellen und inhaltlichen Ausgestaltung des Praxissemesters im lehramtsbezogenen Masterstudiengang") stipulates that "occupation-relevant scholarly theory and reflection [… should be linked with] a scientifically sound education in a *scholarly attitude"* (Landesrektorenkonferenz 2010, p. 4, emphasis added). At the University of Bielefeld, for example, this assignment has led to the explicit explanation of the role of inquiry-based learning in the practical semester in ("Guidelines for the Subject-Specific Implementation of the Bielefeld Practical Semester" / "Handreichung zur fächerspezifischen Umsetzung des Bielefelder Praxissemesters," cf. section B.2 of Fachgruppe Philosophie 2014, pp. 4–10). The research, which is linked here to the study of teaching students, is essentially not philosophical, but instead, and entirely in line with the country's conceptual framework, "school research" (cf. Landesrektorenkonferenz 2010, p. 6).

However, the lack of integration of German higher education philosophy into the higher education didactic debate regarding inquiry-based learning does not mean that inquiry-based learning is, by definition, not quite part of the study of philosophy at German universities. It is more difficult to track down such references that are merely "implicit," however.

29.2 What Does Inquiry-Based Learning Mean?

Huber conceives of inquiry-based learning as one of three types of "research-related learning" (and teaching). In addition to inquiry-based learning, this also includes research-based and research-oriented learning (cf. Huber 2014, p. 22). All three types refer to the process of research, which corresponds to the attitude described by Kant as enquiring ("zetetic"), in contrast to the "dogmatic" style of teaching. The three types of research-related learning differ, inter alia, in the degree of student independence, how open the subject of research is, and the relevance thereof to the scientific community, and are described in this volume by Mieg and Pasternack, for example.

According to Huber, in order to be able to speak of inquiry-based learning, it is of crucial importance that the students work independently: They should define problems, ask questions, conduct studies and evaluate and present their results *themselves*; in short, they should do their own research. This process is characterized by its being *zetetic*: The knowledge being pursued is not yet fixed, but rather sought. That which is sought in the research process is thus new, and not only for the researcher, as Huber emphasizes. According to him, "research processes are always also learning processes […], which are only distinguished therefrom by the fact that they are based on objective knowledge that is new or relevant not only to the subject, but for others as well" (Huber 2014, p. 23). The insights sought are not only subjectively new, which is to say new for the learner, but also objectively new. Inquiry-based learning is therefore independent and practical, zetetic and original.

29.3 John Rudisill's "Junior Research Seminar" at the College of Wooster

In his article "The Transition from Studying Philosophy to Doing Philosophy" (Rudisill 2011), John Rudisill contrasts the learning of philosophical content in the form of historically available positions and arguments (= "studying philosophy") with learning how philosophy is practiced, philosophizing or "doing philosophy" (ibid., p. 241). Rudisill describes philosophy with the aid of a series of learning objectives ("philosopher's skills"):

- the ability to interpret and analyze philosophical texts.
- the formulation and critical examination of the arguments of others and oneself,
- the application of terms and methods handed down through the history of philosophy to solve philosophical problems and
- the development and defense of one's own answers to philosophical questions (cf. ibid., pp. 243–244).

To promote these skills, the College of Wooster envisages a "junior-year seminar in philosophical research" (ibid., p. 241). It is an integral component of the curriculum for students majoring in philosophy (ibid.). The entire curriculum is designed to enable students to independently write a major thesis in the last (i.e., fourth) year of their studies (known as the "capstone project," ibid.). In this thesis, the students' task is to integrate the philosophical skills learned during the course of study into a broader research project, in which they draw conclusions about their own philosophical question(s) (ibid., p. 247 et seq.).

The junior research seminar is a one-semester course in the penultimate (i.e. third) year, which is intended to prepare the students specifically for this task. The seminar leads the students through a series of smaller tasks towards the goal of writing a term paper – with the length of a research article – at the end of the semester (ibid., p. 254). The tasks of the participants include, inter alia, (cf. ibid., p. 249):

- the preparation of an exposé for the final term paper including a bibliography containing at least ten titles,
- the presentation of an article relevant to their term paper in the seminar,
- the presentation of their own term paper project in the seminar,
- commentary on the term paper project of another student in the seminar.

A design principle of the course which clearly emerges from these tasks is the *principle of communication*, as I refer to it here. The last three tasks "force" students to initiate communication with their fellow students during various phases of the homework project. Students seem to underestimate the fact that research work usually arises through an intensive exchange with others.

Moreover, in these forms of communication, an additional principle emerges that I would like to call the *principle of imitation*. The presentation of one's own project corresponds to the professional research and colloquium lecture; commentary on such a lecture is a common procedure at scientific conferences. Just because performing these tasks imitates actual research communication, the previously described principle of communication is more than a merely formal or purely didactic principle; instead, it is a principle, the application of which, enables an activity to be learned, which itself is a part of actual research.

Rudisill's seminar can easily be described as a case of inquiry-based learning in Huber's sense: The condition of independent practice is largely fulfilled (I discuss the way in which to assess the restriction of independence by guidance below). Whether this practice is zetetic depends more on the content of the tasks. Based on general considerations regarding the handling of philosophical content, which I will explain in more detail below, however, I assume that Rudisill's seminar also fulfills this condition. The third condition, the desired originality of the results, is certainly only limited, at least according to claim. For this reason, students do not learn in an actual research context because one cannot expect them to produce results that are of interest to the research community before they finish their studies.

29.4 Inquiry-Based Learning in German Higher Education Philosophy

I have identified the autonomy with which the students perform their respective activities as part of a research project as a special feature of inquiry-based learning above. Insofar as possible, they should define problems *themselves*, ask questions, conduct studies and evaluate and present their results. In my experience, this is exactly what happens in theses – although theses are usually supervised by instructors, which may include agreeing on the topic or even interim discussions about the state of affairs, for example. In this respect, it is questionable whether one can speak of complete autonomy here. When one takes into account that research, as highlighted above, is a communicative process, however, it is clear that autonomy cannot mean the exclusion of any other person's participation. In my experience, the act of supporting thesis work is so general that it does not affect students' autonomy. Although the students are indeed in dialogue about their work, in the end, they must define the problems, ask questions, conduct studies and evaluate and present their results themselves. In terms of autonomy, therefore, the philosophical thesis definitely seems to be a case of inquiry-based learning.

A critical condition is the condition of originality brought into play by Huber, however. If the standard applied to this condition is that the results obtained also be of interest to third parties, and therefore worthy of publication, then I would say that at philosophical institutes in Germany, this claim is usually not made for theses, whether master's or bachelor's theses. Of course, ambitious work in this sense is certainly desirable, but neither the rule nor required. Rather, a claim to originality is usually associated with the dissertation. In the master's or bachelor's thesis, students tend not to research in the sense that they produce or strive for publication-worthy results. The traditional thesis is not research, but merely an imitation of research, asking a philosophical question and trying to answer it. This applies not only to the final thesis, but even more so to the entire course of study.

Furthermore, there is another obvious objection. Since this is an exam, what is achieved with the test should not be *learned here*, but must be proven to have *already* been *learned*. This does not preclude students from learning anything by means of their thesis and, insofar as they do research in the sense of the above criteria, the exam is certainly an example of inquiry-based learning in the literal sense. The concept of inquiry-based learning seems to be linked to the intention of using research for learning *during* a course of study, however. From this perspective, it would be misleading to call the thesis a case of inquiry-based learning.

Now, however, it is justifiable that the traditional term paper in philosophy be regarded as a "stripped-down" thesis to be written *during* a course of study. Thus it is not subject to the objection that has just been made of being "too late" to serve as a higher education didactic tool. It is questionable here whether one can speak to a sufficient extent of an independent performance by the students, however. Depending on the support concept, it is conceivable that the topic, the literature to be used, a concrete question or the structure of the term paper be prescribed or at least agreed upon, for example. Thus one may not have the same level of autonomy when writing a term paper as one would when writing a thesis.

This lack of autonomy can be explained by means of a didactic principle, which I would like to call the *training-wheel principle*, as based on Rudisill's formulation (cf. ibid., pp. 247–249). This principle is probably more familiar under the heading of "scaffolding," to which Rudisill also refers (cf. ibid., p. 248 et seq.). The training-wheel principle requires a gradual shift of responsibility for complex learning tasks from the instructor to the student. At the beginning of a course of study, instructors assume students' responsibility for certain aspects of the activity they are learning, like training wheels, allowing students to focus on other aspects. As a result of the continuing reduction of support on the part of the instructors as the course of studies progresses (see ibid., p. 249), students gradually assume responsibility for more and more tasks. Students must assume responsibility themselves for everything that the instructors do not (anymore). The fact that instructors sometimes provide topics, questions, literature or structure for philosophical homework can be understood very well in terms of such support wheels, which are removed over the course of study. Largely autonomous work tends to be the goal more at the end of the course of study. The way to get to this point is ideally to go through a series of tasks of reduced but steadily increasing student accountability.

When considering the thesis, the characteristic of independence emerges as a rather vague criterion. Is the autonomy of a natural science-related research project impaired if the experimental series are not carried out by the responsible researcher, but instead by assistants? Or how independent is a text that has been edited and corrected several times as a result of discussions with colleagues? It is unclear how much autonomy is required in order to deem it "inquiry-based learning." In any case, the control of certain conditions such as the specification of literature does not seem to exclude the possibility of students independently engaging in the literature, or in earnestly seeking an answer to a philosophical question. In this case, I think one could certainly speak of an exploratory (inquiry-based) term paper. The same applies to the other limitations on independence that have been mentioned. The extent to which a term paper is explorative therefore seems to require an assessment on a case-by-case basis.

In Rudisill's research seminar, I emphasized that students are asked several times to share their writing project, and interpreted this exchange as an imitation of the research process. In Bielefeld, there are two types of seminars, which likewise allow term papers to be dovetailed with seminars to some degree: "Philosophical Writing 2" in the bachelor's degree, and the "workshop seminar" in the master's. In the former, students write a short term paper of 2,000 words in intensively supervised sub-steps during the semester, while in the workshop seminar, students are asked to discuss the current state of a term paper, which they write in connection with a "regular" seminar. In the workshop, the students embark on a research-like exchange about their writing project, while "Philosophical Writing 2" focuses more on an explicit sequencing and reflection of the writing process while producing a term paper. These differences notwithstanding, the focus in both courses is centered on the (research) activity of the students. Even if these courses did not originate within the perspective of this keyword, they can be understood as examples of inquiry-based learning. The workshop seminar essentially corresponds to the popular idea of the colloquium; introductory events for writing term papers are currently being created at many German institutes of philosophy. Everywhere such courses are integrated into the course of study, even beyond Bielefeld, one therefore also finds inquiry-based learning in philosophy.

As is likely also true of Rudisill's Junior Research Seminar, however, the "workshop seminar" and "Philosophical Writing 2" are rather exceptional features in the philosophical curriculum. Ordinary philosophy seminars usually offer no such integration of a student writing project into the seminar. Although term papers are certainly often linked to seminar questions, the ordinary seminar neither systematically prepares for the writing of a paper, nor does it usually provide space for discussing student writing projects. The ordinary seminar usually deals with a certain subject matter in the form of one or more texts, which will be discussed during the semester with regard to the difficulties of comprehension and objective implications associated with it. Certainly there are student contributions, but these are usually not part of a larger writing or research project, but instead isolated performances aimed at obtaining a certain number of credit points.

Although the ordinary seminar therefore does not play a systematic role in students' individual research projects, they do, nevertheless, generally philosophize in these courses. Texts and arguments are analyzed together, theses are developed and reasons and counter-arguments weighed. All these are aspects of philosophical research, and to this extent the seminar is a place of inquiry-based learning. Learning in the seminar is also inquiry-based insofar as answers to questions are sought that are unknown at least to the participants. The fact that these are not necessarily answers worthy of publication should not be given too much weight. Publication-quality work can only be the perspective and not the concrete goal of philosophizing in a course of study. The more important aspect of inquiry-based learning may be found in the fact that the students learn to ask factually legitimate questions and to develop the corresponding answers with the help of philosophical tools. Rather, if these questions or answers have already been asked and provided in existing research, this even confirms that the students have researched and achieved the learning objective.

29.5   Conclusion

The opposite of inquiry-based learning and teaching is the dogmatic lecture. As such, at issue is the imparting of predetermined "pieces of knowledge." Kant's diagnosis of the state of philosophy can essentially still be agreed upon: there are still no, or hardly any, universally accepted questions. As such, there is still a need to focus on dealing critically with existing answers to philosophical questions. Philosophizing is therefore dependent on a historical knowledge of philosophy. Those who wish to philosophize successfully should show how far their own solution to a problem exceeds those of others; of course, in order to do so, one must be familiar with the solutions that have already been proposed.

Thus, the history of philosophy proves to be a kind of "quasi-dogmatic" area: This area is dogmatic insofar as there is, at least in broad terms, sufficient agreement as to which of the "pieces of knowledge" in the form of traditional positions and arguments ought to be learned. This area is not truly dogmatic, or even just "quasi-dogmatic," however, insofar as the positions and arguments to be learned here are not regarded as definitive solutions to philosophical problems, but as food for thought. To quote Kant once again, a philosophical classic must be regarded "not as the paradigm of judgment" in a specific philosophical matter, but rather "as the occasion for forming one's own judgment about him, and even, indeed, for passing judgement against him" (Kant 1765/1992, p. 293).

Inquiry-based learning therefore plays an essential role in philosophy, because the attitude that learners must have towards philosophical content in the form of given answers to philosophical questions need not be uncritical and receptive, but rather unbiased, scrutinizing, attentive, and therefore exploratory. Students must demonstrate this attitude in all sites where they exercise their philosophical activity: in seminars, in term papers and, of course, in their final thesis. These are all sites of inquiry-based learning in philosophy.

Of course, this attitude must first be learned. In philosophy, it makes sense to promote such research-oriented behavior by explicitly drawing attention to its own openness. New students in particular sometimes arrive with the expectation of seeking answers as to what is good, true and beautiful. It may be helpful to disappoint this expectation as expressly as possible and to make it clear that philosophy cannot be expected to provide simple answers to these questions. It is likewise helpful to illustrate the disunity of philosophy by presenting different views on one and the same problem. Feinberg and Shafer-Landau (2013) do so with their introductory text collection "Reason and Responsibility." The integration of student research projects into ordinary philosophy seminars also seems a promising way to promote a scholarly attitude. And finally, seminars that, like Rudisill's research seminar, explicitly focus on a students' research project are naturally particularly suited not only to promote a scholarly attitude, but also to provide students with a space in which to learn to combine various philosophical activities into a more complex research project.

References

Bundesassistentenkonferenz BAK (1970). *Schriften der Bundesassistentenkonferenz: Vol. 5. Forschendes Lernen - wissenschaftliches Prüfen*. Bonn: Bundesassistentenkonferenz.
Fachgruppe Philosophie (2014). *Handreichung zur fächerspezifischen Umsetzung des Bielefelder Praxixssemesters: Fachspezifische Teile - Philosophie*. Retrieved 02 March 2016 from http://www.uni-bielefeld.de/philosophie/lehramt/material/Handreichung-Philosophie-Entwurf.pdf
Feinberg, J./Shafer-Landau, R. (2013). *Reason and responsibility: Readings in some basic problems of philosophy* (Fifteenth edition). Boston: Wadsworth Cengage.

Huber, L. (2014). Forschungsbasiertes, Forschungsorientiertes, Forschendes Lernen: Alles dasselbe?: Ein Plädoyer für eine Verständigung über Begriffe und Unterscheidungen im Feld forschungsnahen Lehrens und Lernens. *Das Hochschulwesen, 62,* 22–29.

Kant, I. M. (1765/1992). Immanuel Kant's Announcement of the Programme of his Lectures for the Winter Semester 1765-1766. In Guyer, P & A. W. Wood (Eds), *The Cambridge Edition of the works of Immanuel Kant: Theoretical Philosophy 1755-1770, transl. and ed. by David Walford & Ralf Meerbote.* Cambridge & al: Cambridge University Press. 287-300.

Landesrektorenkonferenz der nordrhein-westfälischen Universitäten & Ministerium für Schule und Weiterbildung des Landes Nordrhein-Westfalen (2010). *Rahmenkonzeption zur strukturellen und inhaltlichen Ausgestaltung des Praxissemesters im lehramtsbezogenen Masterstudiengang.* Retrieved 2 April 2016 from http://www.schulministerium.nrw.de/docs/LehrkraftNRW/Lehramtsstudium/Reform-der-Lehrerausbildung/Wege-der-Reform/Endfassung_Rahmenkonzept_Praxissemester_14042010.pdf

Rohbeck, J./Philipsen, P.-U. (Hrsg.). (2007). *Jahrbuch für Didaktik der Philosophie und Ethik: Vol. 8. Hochschuldidaktik Philosophie.* Dresden: Thelem.

Rudisill, J. (2011). The Transition from Studying Philosophy to Doing Philosophy. *Teaching Philosophy, 34*(3), 241–271. doi:https://doi.org/10.5840/teachphil201134332

Inquiry-Based Learning in Sports/the Movement Sciences

30

Felix Riehl, Anna Dannemann, Robert Zetzsche, and Christian Maiwald

30.1 Characteristic Features in the Movement Sciences

The characteristic features of the discipline are placed prominently within the context of implementing inquiry-based learning in the modules for the sports and movement sciences degree program at the Chemnitz University of Technology.

30.1.1 Subject and Fields of Application

The movement sciences are characterized as a cross-sectional science, the content of which is the study of sports and movement from the perspective of various departments. With reference to the parent disciplines, the movement sciences and sports science are subdivided into areas belonging to the medical natural sciences, the liberal arts/pedagogy, and the social sciences (cf. Krüger & Emrich 2013, p. 18) The varied perspectives go hand in hand with a strong differentiation of the sports science degree programs. In addition to

F. Riehl, M.Sc. (✉) · A. Dannemann, M.Sc. · R. Zetzsche, Dipl.-Soziologe
Technische Universität Chemnitz, Fakultät für Human- und Sozialwissenschaften,
Institut für Angewandte Bewegungswissenschaften, Chemnitz Germany
e-mail: felix.riehl@hsw.tu-chemnitz.de; anna.dannemann@hsw.tu-chemnitz.de;
robert.zetzsche@hsw.tu-chemnitz.de

C. Maiwald, Prof. Dr. rer. nat.
Professur für Forschungsmethoden und Analyseverfahren in der Biomechanik,
Technische Universität Chemnitz, Fakultät für Human- und Sozialwissenschaften,
Institut für Angewandte Bewegungswissenschaften, Juniorprofessur Forschungsmethoden
und Analyseverfahren, Chemnitz, Germany
e-mail: christian.maiwald@hsw.tu-chemnitz.de

© The Author(s) 2019
H. A. Mieg (ed.), *Inquiry-Based Learning – Undergraduate Research*,
https://doi.org/10.1007/978-3-030-14223-0_30

an engagement with various sub-disciplines, the active and reflective engagement with different sports is part of the degree program (cf. Burk and Fahrner 2013, pp. 11–13). Due to this diversification, the labor market for students in sports science and the movement sciences is very heterogeneous. In addition to the school-related area, there are a variety of areas of activity in the extra-curricular labor market, such as the prevention and rehabilitation sector, recreational and competitive sports, sports economics, journalism and science (cf. Krüger and Emrich 2013, pp. 48–51).

A course of study in the movement sciences at Chemnitz University of Technology provides a broad range of topics in the field of sports and physical activity within its fundamentals. The focus is in the area of prevention and therapy, in which the majority of graduates later find their careers. The diverse contents in the relatively short training period are increasingly practice-oriented and have become more strongly focused on employability within the context of Bologna (cf. Spoun 2007, p. 47). In addition to specialist knowledge, the social and personal competencies which are needed in dealing with students, athletes, and patients play an important role (cf. Reiber 2010, pp. 18–20).

30.1.2 Problem and Selecting a Teaching Concept

An interest in deeper engagement with research and scholarship is not a priority for most students of movement sciences, as only a small proportion of graduates will work in the professional field within higher education and research and development. However, engagement with these subject areas is essential for critically addressing the knowledge acquired in cooperating departments before that knowledge is implemented into the practice of training and rehabilitation. In addition to the promotion of skills and the acquisition of expertise, the goal is to achieve transparency in the generation of knowledge in the sense of scientific work. In so doing, science should be made tangible as a process and be classified within a disciplinary context (cf. Huber 2009, pp. 13–14).

Students have their first contact with content relating to research methodology in the bachelor's degree program at Chemnitz University of Technology through their autonomous participation in a research project, as well as their first project within the context of their bachelor thesis. Methodological and statistical training and the imparting of epistemological knowledge is deepened over the course of the consecutive master's degree program.

Generating methodological knowledge within the context of sports science and the movement sciences represents a challenge when selecting a suitable teaching concept, which should take into account the range of subjects and their various perspectives and approaches, as well as enable students to set their own individual priorities. A traditional teaching concept appears to be less suitable for this. A comprehensive educational ideal such as that of inquiry-based learning, which goes beyond the teaching of subject-related competencies, is increasingly invoked as a maxim for the study. Here, learning is understood as a way of life and students are sensitized to question knowledge, beliefs and presuppositions (cf. Spoun 2007, p. 47).

30.2 Inquiry-Based Learning in the Movement Sciences

The motivations and the understanding of inquiry-based learning as a basis for teaching-learning concepts in the movement sciences are based on developments in research, teaching and higher education didactics. This serves as a starting point for considering existing modules and forms the basis for planning and implementing the "Wissenschaftstheorie und Forschungsmethodik" ("Philosophy of science and research methodology") course. This enables students to acquire some initial experience with implementing scientific thinking and research methodologies, and to identify specific challenges for future projects.

30.2.1 Research, Teaching, and Developments in Higher Education Didactics

The challenges of teaching methodological knowledge in sports science and the movement sciences are shaped by the Bologna Process, developments in teaching and learning research, and the discourse between teaching and research.

Fundamental changes of perspective in higher education didactics and teaching-learning research has resulted in a variety of models and concepts so that appealing teaching can be implemented at universities. As such, the focus has been increasingly shifted from input to the outcome of teaching, and oriented towards learning and learners. Ultimately, our understanding of the task of a higher education didactic expert has also changed from imparting knowledge to advising and supporting (cf. Schaeper 2008, pp. 197–199; Reiber 2006, pp. 6–9). These changes are based on a constructivist understanding of general didactics, in which learning is seen as an individual act of creating knowledge, skills, and competencies. This takes place in concrete situations and therefore, in addition to the learning topic, requires communicative interaction, a corresponding social form, and the embedding of media and methods (cf. Jank and Meyer 2014, pp. 286–303).

30.2.2 Fundamentals and Application of Inquiry-Based Learning

Within the context of higher education and taking into account changes within teaching/learning research, inquiry-based learning provides a versatile opportunity for teaching methodological knowledge in the field of movement sciences. According to the following features and integration possibilities described by Huber (2009), inquiry-based learning is oriented towards the phases of independently conducting a research project and the resulting cognitive, emotional, and social experiences. Essential features that distinguish inquiry-based learning from similar teaching concepts such as a student-centered structure, independent study, discovery and problem-based learning, or project-based studies, are the central facet of gaining new insights, as well as the social aspect of a "scientific community." The resulting teaching-learning concept can be integrated into the format of higher education instruction by having students take part in concrete situations and case studies, work on new problems, work-shadowing and participation in research laboratories and business simulations, and through their own studies.

At the Chemnitz University of Technology, opportunities for autonomous participation in research projects, in the form of research laboratories and processing simulated planning games, already exist within the context of the degree program in the movement sciences. Here, students from various departments gain insights into the concrete planning, conducting, and implementation of research projects. In the bachelor's degree program, it is possible to select from a variety of existing projects in different departments. Selecting from among the available projects is obligatory and an integral part of a module in the study regulations. The chosen project is then actively supported by the participants and terminates with a final report, which is a conducive contribution for the project leader in the evaluation and further processing of the research project. Thus, students have the opportunity to be introduced to specific elements of research at an early stage in a subject area of their choice. Examples include a sports medicine project for recording children's motor performance, or a sports education project for the temporal development of children's motor skills.

In sports science and the movement sciences, the "Wissenschaftstheorie und Forschungsmethodik" ("Philosophy of science and research methodology") course in the master's degree program is a focal point in implementing inquiry-based learning. Methodical and epistemological material is specifically addressed and transmitted over two semesters as part of an independently conducted research project. This represents the most extensive wealth of experience in the movement sciences within the context of inquiry-based learning and will therefore be described and explained in detail below.

30.2.3 Implementing and Evaluating the "Wissenschaftstheorie und Forschungsmethodik" ("Philosophy of Science and Research Methodology") Module

The various integration possibilities of inquiry-based learning are based on the general cycles of research activity and learning. The starting point comprises the basic phases of identifying a topic, formulating questions and hypotheses, creating a research design; and implementing and evaluating, as well as imparting, applying, and putting into practice. The research cycles overlap with the basic learning processes of experience, reflection, conception and experimentation (cf. Wildt 2009, pp. 5–6).

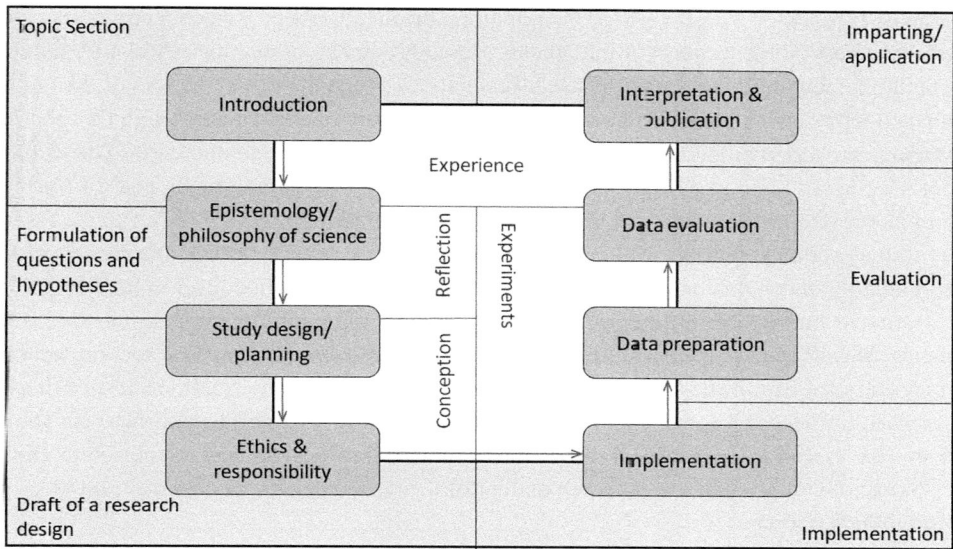

Fig. 30.1 Progression of the philosophy of science and research methodology module at TU Chemnitz in relation to the cycles of inquiry-based learning. (Source: Author's representation, modified in accordance with Wildt 2009)

After an introductory and informational event, the module which is implemented in the master's degree program at the Chemnitz University of Technology (see Fig. 30.1) begins with the topic and group identification phase. During this first section of the module, students are given a general orientation about the progression of the course and the opportunity to increasingly deal with their own research interests. After these initial experiences, the students find themselves in small research groups that persist throughout the module.

The subsequent phase involves deeper engagement with theory and the development of hypotheses. Here, groups of 4-5 students work independently and autonomously to engage with the theoretical status of their chosen research concerns. During this time, the lecturers and tutors are available to advise and assist in formulating a concrete question. At the same time, the students gain a theoretical insight into cognitive science and the philosophy of science.

The preparation and presentation of concrete research ideas and hypotheses is followed by a phase during which students elaborate on a suitable study design. In this section, the small groups receive a theoretical refresher on the planning and design of studies while they develop appropriate sequences of actions, tools and procedures for their own research project. The results of this and the previous phases are put forth in a presentation and a summary project proposal.

Ethical aspects are examined and an internal ethics committee is convened before data collection can occur. Here, the students are sensitized at a theoretical level to issues of responsible science and implement the knowledge they acquire in formulating an ethics proposal. Together with the lecturers and tutors, the small groups subsequently assess the ethical safety of the projects of the other research groups in an internal ethics committee. The implementation and survey phase takes place between the two semesters of the module and represents a transition between research planning and data analysis. In this phase, students are largely independent in terms of organization and implementation. The lecturers once again assume a supporting and accompanying role to ensure the goal of having completed data entry at the beginning of the new semester.

In the second semester, students run through various options for statistical evaluation and drawing a conclusion in alternation at a theoretical and applied level in the form of a lecture and tutorial. Within this context, students deal with descriptive and inductive statistics, as well as the transfer of findings to their own research project. This section, which represents the end of the entire research cycle, concludes with the small groups writing a scholarly article. Here, the preparatory work from the first semester and the evaluation from the second semester in the "Wissenschaftstheorie und Forschungsmethodik" ("Philosophy of science und research methodology") modules merge together and ideally lead to new findings.

According to David Kolb, another framework for planning and implementing inquiry-based learning is based on the four elementary learning processes of experience, reflection, conception and experimentation (cf. Staemmler 2006, pp. 46–50). In the progression of the module depicted here, it is initially assumed that students in the master's degree program have substantial theoretical and methodological experience. Students' engagement with various subject-related perspectives and topic areas, as well as the comprehensive, research-methodological consideration of the findings, forms the basis for topic identification in their own research projects. Reflection on one's own experience is necessary to identify existing inconsistencies or unresolved issues, which should enable a unique research question to be formulated. The following elements of research planning and research design can be summarized under the process of learning how to engage in conceptive processes. In doing so, the students are expected to engage in active and creative activities. By contrast, the data collection phases have an experimental character. Finally, the experiences and insights gained from the entire process form the basis for new research projects and are formally presented in the scientific article. The contents and methods of the individual phases of the module fulfill the competence requirements of sports and movement scientists on the job market to a large extent.

30.2.4 Support, Test Performances, and Formats

As students go through each section of the module, they receive support from the respective lecturers, tutors, and specific feedback from students in other research groups. This ensures that their own research process is reflected from different perspectives within the context of situational learning, and that it recreates the atmosphere of a scientific community. Here, participants receive the theoretical background for, and feedback on, the preliminary examinations from the lecturers. This enables the students to provide their content with an orientation and, ultimately, to assess what is and is not possible within their own research project.

It is a clear advantage that the tutors providing support have already completed this or a similar teaching-learning arrangements. Each tutor is responsible for two to three groups, supports the preparation of content-related aspects and is available for questions regarding the working method and group conflicts that arise. A special feature of this form of support lies in the relationship between the tutors and students, which is on an equal-terms basis, and in the function of imparting knowledge between participants and lecturers.

Another level of support is mutual feedback from the individual research groups. The results of the various sections and sub-points of the research cycle are loaded into a digital portal and can be viewed there by the other students. Using a fixed matrix, two to three research groups generate feedback in the form of peer reviews for the respective group. Thus participants receive feedback, again on equal terms, and in the form of a scientific community. The advantage of this is that the small groups deal with both the content and methodological aspects of others and that constructive criticism is likely to be more readily accepted and implemented.

As already indicated, students in the individual research groups have a variety of preparatory work and examinations. Fourteen smaller preliminary examinations (e.g. a short essay on the topic of "What is science?", presentation of the research question, written submission of a project proposal, or presentation of the descriptive evaluation) are integrated into the cycle for the entire module. The elements of the three central exams are the reproduction of knowledge via cognitive science and philosophy of science, an application-oriented exam on research methodology and statistics, and the final textualization of the research process and outcome in the form of an article. The aim of including such diverse forms of examination and focus is to meet the needs of different types of learning and different career models. Here, there is a relationship to a large percentage of the work areas of sports and exercise therapists; these also pose a variety of challenges in everyday work, for example in working with patients and with children and youth. An additional focus in designing the teaching-learning concept for inquiry-based learning in the movement sciences degree program is on the number and manifestation of the exam prerequisites. This again aligns with the practical conditions in the work performed as a therapist and trainer, who rarely have exceptional one-time achievements, but who instead tend to guide a process with multiple intermediate outcomes. Even if individual advance performances are still occurring at the beginning of the research cycle, they will only be completed in the following phases exclusively in the research groups. At the content level, forms of scientific communication are required, such as presentations, essays, contributions to discussions and applications.

The topic of research methodology and philosophy of science, which was originally an abstract concept, is not only considered and questioned in a variety of forms, it also receives a concretely applied and technical perspective by means of the individual issues of the research groups. Thus, a variety of topics, ranging from university sports at universities in Saxony to the consideration of myofascial taping to the effect of cloth baby slings on the musculoskeletal system, thus meets the general and theoretical perspective of the philosophy of science and research methodology. This effects that subject-specific topics are considered critically, and that topics which are increasingly perceived as isolated are revived. In this way, an effort is made to establish the aforementioned bridge between practical and subject-specific requirements and methodological reflection.

In summary, higher education instruction and the "Wissenschaftstheorie und Forschungsmethodik" ("Philosophy of science and research methodology") module have incorporated a variety of content and methodological aspects into teaching and learning planning. The planning and implementation of the individual elements took place with the inclusion of new perspectives in higher education didactics and within the concept of inquiry-based learning. As such, the two basic research and learning cycles constitute guidelines for designing the module.

30.3   Challenges and Outlook

In recent years, students have conducted 23 research projects within the context of the course (last updated: December 2015). In so doing, both instructors and supervising faculty were able to gather many impressions and obtain much feedback, and students were given the opportunity to present their perceptions and perspectives within the framework of assuring the quality of the teaching, and by means of formal evaluation.

30.3.1 Evaluation of the "Philosophy of Science and Research Methodology" Module ("Wissenschaftstheorie und Forschungsmethodik")

The informal impressions of the instructors and supervising faculty point to a positive overall picture of the teaching-learning arrangement used for inquiry-based learning in the movement sciences. Numerous students have given positive feedback regarding the long-term collection and retention of acquired knowledge, and noted a perceived increase in methodological, social and personal competencies. The high-performance groups in particular found the constant challenge of meeting fixed deadlines and constantly being challenged a profitable experience for their future professional lives. The group work was primarily described as pleasant and supportive, and many students found the support and encouragement they received from various people and contact persons to be helpful.

These experiences and impressions were also reflected in formal evaluation by the students, which were conducted at the end of each semester as part of the quality assurance for the course. The majority of the participants were able to develop *an understanding of science and empirical research*. In addition, a large proportion of students reported having developed a *fundamental interest in research* within the context of increasingly non-scientific professional fields in the labor market for sports and exercise scientists.

While working on a project with a variety of intermediate performances, it became apparent that motivation dropped significantly at the end of each semester and less work was done on preliminary examinations. Another challenge was the familiarization with various topics, due to the heterogeneity of the degree program. Formulating constructive and responsive feedback requires attempting to understand new fields and applying knowledge that has already been acquired. The requirement to critically reflect on research projects and on questions of logic, statistics and the philosophy of science on abstract levels was a challenge, but was successfully mastered in the overall picture of the module. Participants in the module as well as the lecturers and tutors faced a variety of challenges in implementing the teaching-learning module of inquiry-based learning. Most experiences coincide with the problem areas and critical points of inquiry-based learning according to Huber (2009, pp. 22–28).

30.4   Conclusion for TU Chemnitz and Sports Science in General

In the future, the module needs to be designed and implemented more efficiently and in a way that conserves resources. This could be achieved, for example, by incorporating the online learning platform to a greater to degree, increasing automation of open processes (e.g. through templates and automatic evaluation processes) or restricting the selection of research projects.

This educational ideal can be used in sport science and the movement sciences to implement a promising instrument so that it is possible to take abstract topics like method teaching and the variety of subject areas in the study program into account. The active and creative participation of the students makes it possible to generate positive effects on attitude and interest towards abstract and complex topics such as research methodology and philosophy of science. Moreover, this can be used to ensure the transfer of competencies required by companies and within the framework of the Bologna Process. Addressing these issues by linking subject-oriented and non-subject-oriented competencies in a complex learning environment is one of the key benefits of inquiry-based learning. Moreover, the conception and implementation of this educational ideal within the framework of movement sciences must always take into account both conditions and resources. Furthermore, an active evaluation of the processes is considered necessary. Just as movement sciences are in the process of development, a great deal of movement is also expected in the implementation and design of inquiry-based learning.

References

Burk, V./Fahrner, M. (2013). *Einführung in die Sportwissenschaft*. Konstanz: UVK Verlagsgesellschaft mbh.

Huber, L. (2009). Warum Forschendes Lernen nötig und möglich ist. In L. Huber/J. Hellmer/F. Schneider (Hrsg.), *Forschendes Lernen im Studium. Aktuelle Konzepte und Erfahrungen* (S. 9–35). Bielefeld: UniversitätsVerlagWebler.

Jank, W./Meyer, H. (2014). *Didaktische Modelle*. Berlin: Cornelsen.

Krüger, M./Emrich, E. (2013). Die Wissenschaft vom Sport. In A. Güllich/M. Krüger (Hrsg.), *Sport. Das Lehrbuch für das Sportstudium (S.* 10–23). Berlin: Springer Spektrum.

Reiber, K. (2006). Wissen – Können – Handeln: Ein Kompetenzmodell für lernorientiertes Lernen. In C. Baatz/R. Richter (Hrsg.), *Tübinger Beiträge zur Hochschuldidaktik.* (2. Auflage) (S. 6–9). Tübingen: Arbeitsstelle Hochschuldidaktik.

Reiber, K. (2010). Kompetenzentwicklung durch forschendes Lernen in pflege- und gesundheits-bezogenen Studiengängen. In A. Nauerth (Hrsg.), *Hochschuldidaktik in pflegerischen und therapeutischen Studiengängen* (S. 17–27). Münster: LIT.

Schaeper, H. (2008). Lehr-/Lernkulturen und Kompetenzentwicklung: Was Studierende lernen, wie Lehrende lernen und wie beides miteinander zusammenhängt. In K. Zimmermann/M. Kamphans/S. Metz-Göckel (Hrsg.), *Perspektiven der Hochschulforschung* (S. 197–199). Wiesbaden: Verlag für Sozialwissenschaften.

Spoun, S. (2007). Ein Studium für's Leben. *Das Hochschulwesen, 55* (2), 46–53.

Staemmler, D. (2006). *Lernstile und interaktive Lernprogramme. Kognitive Komponenten des Lernerfolgs in virtuellen Lernumgebungen*. Wiesbaden: Deutscher Universitäts-Verlag.

Wildt, J. (2009). Forschendes Lernen: Lernen im »Format« der Forschung. *Journal Hochschuldidaktik, 20*, 4–5.

Inquiry-Based Learning in Sustainability Science

31

Ulli Vilsmaier and Esther Meyer

Inquiry-based learning is a key component of degree programs in sustainability science. Since the research field focuses on sustainability challenges, which often require an interdisciplinary or transdisciplinary approach, students are not only introduced to the basics of sustainability science, but also trained in cooperative forms of research. Thus a variety of study objectives are combined, which can be very well implemented in the mode of inquiry-based learning.

31.1 Characteristic Features in Sustainability Science as a Context for Inquiry-Based Learning

Sustainability science is a recently created field of research, which has developed in response to the discourse on sustainable development to address sustainability-related societal challenges. The concept of "sustainable development" was introduced by the United Nations' Brundtland Commission in 1987. It has become significantly more differentiated since the United Nations Conference on Environment and Development in Rio de Janeiro in 1992, and has entered into the international public discourse. It is informed

U. Vilsmaier, Prof. Dr. (✉)
Leuphana Universität Lüneburg, Methodenzentrum und Institut für Ethik und Transdisziplinäre
Nachhaltigkeitsforschung, Apl. Prof. für Transdisziplinäre Methoden,
Lüneburg, Germany
e-mail: vilsmaier@leuphana.de

E. Meyer, M.Sc.
Leuphana Universität Lüneburg, Institut für Ethik und Transdisziplinäre
Nachhaltigkeitsforschung, Lüneburg, Germany
e-mail: esther.meyer@leuphana.de

© The Author(s) 2019
H. A. Mieg (ed.), *Inquiry-Based Learning – Undergraduate Research*,
https://doi.org/10.1007/978-3-030-14223-0_31

by research on questions about the future, environmental problems, justice and other topics; however, it is not a result of scientific research, but rather an ethical concept (Michelsen
and Adomßent 2014). The ethically motivated core demands formulated in the final report
of the Brundtland Commission, "Our Common Future," include preserving the environment, achieving social justice and ensuring political participation (ibid.). To achieve this,
the Action Plan approved at the Rio de Janeiro UN Conference in 1992 highlighted the
role of science and the importance of cross-boundary research and a strong societal contextualization of science for sustainable development. In Agenda 21, Section 31.1, it states:

> The cooperative relationship existing between the scientific and technological community
> and the general public should be extended and deepened into a full partnership. […] Existing
> multidisciplinary approaches will have to be strengthened and more interdisciplinary studies
> developed between the scientific and technological community and policy makers and with
> the general public to provide leadership and practical know-how to the concept of sustainable
> development. The public should be assisted in communicating their sentiments to the scien-
> tific and technological community concerning how science and technology might be better
> managed to affect their lives in a beneficial way. (Agenda 21, Section 31.1)

The field of sustainability science emerged out of different disciplines and interdisciplinary fields of research at the turn of the millennium. The environmental sciences, global
change research, social-ecological research and human ecology played an essential role.
The cohesive factor in this heterogeneous research field lies in its normative orientation
towards sustainable development and thus in dealing with problems (Klein 2014, p. 74,
Ziegler and Ott 2015) "that jeopardize the long-term ability to safeguard conditions for
societal development" (Michelsen and Adomßent 2014, p. 43, translated) as well as solutions that enable sustainable development. In 2003, Clark and Dickson characterize sustainability science as a vibrant field that brings together different perspectives from the
natural, social and engineering sciences and medicine, as well as from fields of practice,
incorporating perspectives from the global north and south, but that is not yet an independent discipline itself (Clark and Dickson 2003, p. 8060).

Since then, numerous steps towards institutionalization have been taken. The number
of journals that include the term sustainability in their title has increased significantly.
Numerous academic institutes, chairs and degree programs on sustainability, sustainable
development and sustainability science(s) have been established. In 2010, the first Faculty
of Sustainability in Germany was founded by Leuphana University in Lüneburg. In the
field of sustainability science, internal structures are increasingly becoming apparent.
Nölting, Voß and Hayn suggest drawing a distinction between three levels of sustainability
research: the analytical level, which aims to create systems knowledge; the normative
level, at which target and orientation knowledge is developed; and the operational level, at
which conceptual or transformation knowledge is generated (Nölting et al. 2004, p. 254,
cited in Michelsen and Adomßent 2014, p. 43). This division emphasizes that, according
to its normative foundations, sustainability science not only aims to understand and

explain, but equally aims at transformation. Therefore, different forms of research are required to produce different types of knowledge.

In addition to established empirical and interpretative forms of research, transdisciplinary sustainability research has developed as a core pillar of sustainability science. It is an integrative form of research that transcends disciplinary and interdisciplinary research by addressing societal issues "in vivo," i.e. in their living context, together with societal actors who are related to the respective problem (Vilsmaier and Lang 2014). In this sense, transdisciplinary research is a cooperative form of research, which comprises not only scientists from different disciplines, but also actors from different social fields as researchers. It not only develops knowledge about a problem, but also induces a negotiation and design process to bring about solutions to a given problem.

Learning and experiencing transdisciplinary research practice has a prominent position in the education of sustainability scientists. Transdisciplinary sustainability research neither follows a consistent framework nor builds on an established body of knowledge, but rather requires the establishment and implementation of research processes for specific cases and contexts. Therefore, learning through experimentation and reflective learning have a prominent position (Michelsen and Adomßent 2014). Transdisciplinary sustainability research is therefore conducted in an *inquiry-based learning* mode.

31.2 Characteristics of Inquiry-Based Learning in Sustainability Science

For students of sustainability science, the heterogeneity of the subject requires not only a wide range of sustainability knowledge and research forms, but also a high degree of individual responsibility in developing their professional profile. Therefore, inquiry-based learning in cooperative, transdisciplinary projects provides a suitable framework. It provides students with the opportunity to complete an entire research process in a very independent and autonomous manner (Huber 2009). On the other hand, they acquire new content, methods and abilities independent of an instructor's program or a static curriculum. Furthermore, the learning process is strongly guided by students' particular interests and requirements related to the given research situation. Specifics of inquiry-based learning in sustainability science include:

Problem Orientation Research questions are derived from concrete societal issues and require a case-based development of research designs as well as integrating heterogeneous bodies of knowledge that draw on different subjects and disciplines. Inquiry-based learning in sustainability science therefore makes working in a problem-oriented, interdisciplinary manner a necessity. This includes the constitution of fields of research that often exist between established subjects and disciplines, and which are yet to establish a firm place in the landscape of knowledge. A challenge faced by students of sustainability science is in acquiring familiarity with the sustainability-relevant body of knowledge in order to be able to address the issues of concern.

Solution Orientation In sustainability science, the normativity of a science for sustainable development is accompanied by a solution orientation in research, which requires the production of different types of knowledge (systems knowledge, target knowledge, transformation knowledge) and the negotiation and processing of societal transformations. Inquiry-based learning in sustainability science is therefore characterized by mutual learning in cooperative, transdisciplinary settings (Vilsmaier et al. 2015). Students are particularly challenged by gaining an appropriate understanding of the role(s) as sustainability scientists, and by being confronted with different interests and multiple objectives in the research process.

Relatedness to a Case The orientation towards a concrete societal sustainability challenge requires case-based, transdisciplinary research, which encompasses a variety of analytical dimensions (Scholz and Tietje 2002). It claims to produce generalizable knowledge in addition to results for the specific case. Inquiry-based learning in sustainability science therefore requires a combination of idiosyncratic and nomothetic research (Krohn 2008), and often of qualitative and quantitative research (Scholz and Tietje 2002). Above all, these are associated with challenges in the formation of theoretical foundations and methodical designs. Sustainability science students therefore need a solid epistemological and methodological understanding.

Difference-Based Transdisciplinary sustainability research is an integrative form of research that aims to integrate different bodies of knowledge, models of research and cultures of cognition, perspectives and interests, as well as values and objectives. In order to achieve this, it is necessary to identify differences and make them accessible. Inquiry-based learning in sustainability science therefore requires the ability to identify and to deal with differences. Students are required to learn to read both their own position in the research process, their perspective and socialization within a particular research culture, their interests and objectives, as well as the positions and perspectives of others in order to facilitate integrative research (cf. Vilsmaier and Lang 2015).

Plurality of Methods Sustainability research requires a broad spectrum of methods that are applied in an integrative way. In addition to methods of empirical and interpretative research, different methods of cooperation, evaluation, research management and boundary work are used to elaborate on differences between perspectives, bodies of knowledge and roles in the research process. In this sense, inquiry-based learning in sustainability science requires not only the knowledge or appropriation of different methods, but also the ability to link and embed different types of methods. Thus, students of sustainability sciences require extensive methodological knowledge in combination with basic theoretical and methodological understandings that make possible integrative forms of research.

31.2.1 Inquiry-Based Learning in the Master's Degree Program in Sustainability Science at Leuphana University of Lüneburg

An example of inquiry-based learning in sustainability is the module "Transdisciplinary Projects" in the master's degree "Nachhaltigkeitswissenschaft – Sustainability Science" at Leuphana University of Lüneburg. The module covers two semesters and comprises 20 ECTS credits. It forms the core of the master's program and enables students to spend more than a year researching concrete sustainability challenges within the university's regional environment. Generally, there are three groups each year, with approximately 15 students working together with two lecturers and one tutor, as well as non-university actors, forming three team levels.

Level 1: *The student team.* It consists of students with usually very heterogeneous professional backgrounds. The bachelor's degrees of students in the master's program include studies from the natural sciences, social sciences, and the humanities. Student teams are therefore always multidisciplinary. They work together continuously over a 12-month period.

Level 2: *The academic team.* In addition to the students, this team includes the lecturers and the tutor. In team teaching, attention is paid to a multidisciplinary composition in which one person contributes theoretical-methodological expertise in the field of transdisciplinary research. Lecturers meet with the student group on a selective basis, usually once a week during the lecture period and on request.

Level 3: *The transdisciplinary team.* In addition to the students, teachers and tutors, this team includes actors from the field that is being studied in the transdisciplinary research project. The number and heterogeneity of the actors is variable depending on the case. Since the establishment of the transdisciplinary team itself is already a core learning step, it is usually only in the second half of the project that regular collaboration takes place, which can range from joint workshops to regular meetings in a steering committee.

According to the principles of inquiry-based learning (Huber 2009), students are given a great deal of autonomy at all levels. The specifications that students receive are first and foremost of a theoretical and methodological nature. They are taught in an accompanying lecture during the first semester. The lecture covers fundamentals of transdisciplinary research and process design. Furthermore, the students are supported by the instructors through specific lectures on request, and are guided to find important literature. In order to promote the principle of independent research, optional accompanying workshops are offered in which students can deepen their specific expertise and exchange perspectives and experiences on specific topics or aspects of the research process with fellow students from other project groups.

The transdisciplinary projects are based on the principles of transdisciplinary sustainability research developed by Lang and colleagues (Lang et al. 2012). The students' research process is divided into three phases (cf. Lang et al. 2012; Vilsmaier and Lang 2014). Phase 1 covers a variety of subject- and team-related tasks that serve to constitute the field of research. In phase 2, the research question is processed according to a research plan and solution-oriented knowledge is produced at the different team levels. Finally, Phase 3 serves to link the knowledge gained to scientific discourses on the one hand, and to societal contexts on the other. This should ensure that the results of the transdisciplinary research process are brought to fruition.

Phase 1: *The constitution of the field of research*. Students identify sustainability challenges in a given subject area (e.g. phosphorus management, community development, energy supply) supported by the instructors. In an iterative procedure, a research question is developed that is of interest from a scientific perspective and at the same time socially relevant. Students analyze the relevant state of the art and the societal preconditions for achieving sustainable development. Already in the course of developing the research question, students begin to collaborate with actors from the field, thereby taking into account heterogeneous perspectives on the issues of concern. This is the first step toward to building a transdisciplinary team. These initial tasks assist the students in forming a team and developing working structures. The potential of the multidisciplinary group as well as individual interests and learning objectives are made visible, roles and responsibilities are distributed among the students, and a project management is established. Phase 1 is completed upon the submission of a research plan after 6 months. At this point, students have elaborated the state of the research, built up and expanded the necessary knowledge and expertise in the group, and established collaboration routines as student and academic teams. The transdisciplinary team should be organized at this point (e.g. by establishing a steering committee).

Phase 2: *Processing the research question*. Based on the research plan and the established team and work structure, in-depth knowledge about the problem (system knowledge), objectives to be achieved (target knowledge) and knowledge about how desired goals can be achieved (transformation knowledge) is acquired in phase 2. Academics and actors from the field have different roles and tasks in the research process. In order to gain a better understanding of the problem, the plurality of perspectives and the corresponding knowledge and experience are developed and integrated. For example, students and teachers introduce scientific knowledge of the subject, while actors from the field bring knowledge acquired through professional practice or everyday routines. The integration of different bodies of knowledge aims at a deeper or even new understanding of a problem and is a key element of transdisciplinary research, which is methodically implemented by the students. In developing target knowledge, the heterogeneity of interests and goals of different actors comes into its own. Students play a central role in shaping a societal learning process. Phase 2 ends with the completion of the survey and integration of knowledge in the different dimensions. At the end of Phase 2, transformation is likely to have already begun, due to the fact that, by working in transdisciplinary teams, societal learning processes are induced. New constellations of actor in the field are formed, creating communicative spaces and cooperation opportunities, and may contribute to sustainability transformations.

Phase 3: *Re-integration of results into scientific communities and societal fields*. The results of a transdisciplinary project are prepared in various ways. Contributions are made to the scientific discourse and the specific case. Students write a scientific paper, which they prepare for potential publication in the journal "GAiA – Ökologische Perspektiven für Wissenschaft und Gesellschaft" ("GAiA - Ecological Perspectives for Science and Society"). In addition, the outcomes are prepared for relevant actors or societal fields. The form, language and type of content are adapted to the target group. Recommendations for action are also provided, and results are presented to relevant actors, e.g. to the Environment Committee of the City of Lüneburg. Phase 3 ends with a public presentation of the projects and research results, which brings together all actors involved, as well as the interested public. The informal part of the event serves to strengthen relationships between actors from different sectors of society, students and scientists, and offers the opportunity to explore further topics and forms of cooperation. For students, the research and cooperation ends upon submission of the paper and the handouts for practice. Nevertheless, for many of them, the continuity or implementation of results is important. Thus, it is not unusual for individual students to maintain contact or co-design follow-up activities beyond the duration of the course.

31.3   Conclusion: Potentials and Challenges of Inquiry-Based Learning in Sustainability Science

Sustainability science provides a basis for dealing with phenomena or problems not through objectivation and linear cause-and-effect relationships, but rather in a vivid way that takes into consideration the complexity of real-life situations and challenges. The shift in the research process is far-reaching. With Nicolescu, we can speak of a shift from "in vitro" to "in vivo" research (Nicolescu 2008) and, as a corollary, of overcoming the dichotomy of active research subjects on the one hand, and of passive research objects on the other (Vilsmaier and Lang 2014). Here a research topography crystallizes, which forms a new topos in the landscape of research. It spans the gap between the spheres of science that focus on generalizability, traceability and stability, and those concerned with the elusiveness of an ever-changing world. Transdisciplinary sustainability research can combine these two spheres by addressing case-based sustainability challenges. It uses existing knowledge and creates new knowledges and experiences when working on the case, and situated within the case, and thereby promotes the transformation of the concrete lifeworld situation.

By practicing transdisciplinary sustainability research in the mode of inquiry-based learning, the learning process combines the acquisition of theoretical knowledge, the rehearsal of research practices to generate new knowledge, and the shaping of societal transformation processes. Inquiry-based learning in sustainability science, based on concrete lifeworld situations is thus always learning *for* sustainable development. These constellations challenge students to actively position themselves in relation to the research field, which loses its object status. However, this normative moment of inquiry-based learning in sustainability science needs to be handled with caution so that students are not driven *either* into mere activism *or* traditional research based on separation (Latour 2002). The establishment of a new, cooperative research culture requires comprehensive reflection. It must make the issue of objectivation and its causes itself the object of reflection in order to challenge students' dedication in the struggle for a new form of research and the consolidation of positions and roles of (prospective) sustainability scientists. Like transdisciplinary research itself, this reflection is not a fixed program, but instead arises from the experience of a vivid research situation, which is experienced by learning.

References

Agenda 21: Retrieved 05 March 2019 from http://www.un-documents.net/a21-31.htm

Clark, W.C./Dickson, N.M. (2003). Sustainablity science. The emerging research program. *Proceedings of the National Academy of Science*, 100, 8059–8061.

Huber, L. (2009). Warum Forschendes Lernen nötig und möglich ist. In L. Huber/J. Hellmer/F. Schneider (Hrsg.), *Forschendes Lernen im Studium. Aktuelle Konzepte und Erfahrungen* (S. 9–36). Bielefeld: UniversitätsverlagWebler.

Klein, JT. (2014). Discourses of transdisciplinarity: Looking back to the future. *Futures, 63*, 68–74.

Krohn, W. (2008). Learning from Case Studies. In G. Hirsch Hadorn/H. Hoffmann-Riem/S. Biber-Klemm/W. Grossenbacher-Mansuy/D. Joye/C. Pohl/U. Wiesmann/E. Zemp (Hrsg.), *Handbook of transdisciplinary research* (S. 369–384). Berlin: Springer.

Latour, B. (2002). *Die Hoffnung der Pandora*. Frankfurt a.M.: Suhrkamp.

Lang, D.J./Wiek, A./Bergmann, M./Stauffacher, M./Martens, P./Moll, P./Swilling, M./Thomas, C. (2012). Transdisciplinary Resarch in Sustainability Science – Practice, Principles, and Challenges. *Sustainablility Science, 7/1*, 25–43.

Michelsen, G./Adomßent, M. (2014). Nachhaltige Entwicklung: Hintergründe und Zusammenhänge. In H. Heinrichs/G. Michelsen (Hrsg.), *Nachhaltigkeitswissenschaften* (S. 3–60). Berlin, Heidelberg: Springer Spektrum.

Nicolescu, B. (2008). In Vitro and In Vivo Knowledge – Methodology of Transdisciplinarity. In B. Nicolescu (Hrsg.), *Transdisciplinarity. Theory and Practice* (S. 1–22). Cresskill: Hampton Press.

Nölting, B./Voß, J.-P./Hayn, D. (2004). Nachhaltigkeitsforschung – jenseits von Disziplinierung und »anything goes«. *GAIA 13, 4/2004*, 272–279.

Scholz, R.W./Tietje, O. (2002). *Embedded case study methods. Integrating quantitative and qualitative knowledge*. Thousand Oaks: Sage Publications.

Vilsmaier, U./Lang D. J. (2015). Making a difference by marking the difference: constituting in-between spaces for sustainability learning. *Current Opinion in Environmental Sustainability, 16*, 51–55.

Vilsmaier, U./Engbers, M./Luthardt, P./Maas-Deipenbrock, R.-M./Wunderlich, S./Scholz, R.W. (2015). *Case-based* Mutual Learning Sessions. Knowledge integration and transfer in transdisciplinary processes. *Sustainability Science, 10*, 563–580.

Vilsmaier, U./Lang, D. J. (2014). Transdisziplinäre Forschung. In H. Heinrichs/G. Michelsen (Hrsg.), *Nachhaltigkeitswissenschaften* (S. 87–114). Berlin, Heidelberg: Springer Spektrum.

Ziegler, R./Ott, K. (2015). The quality of sustainability science: A philosophical perspective. In: J. Enders/M. Remig, *Theories of Sustainable Development* (43–64). London, New York: Routledge. Taylor & Francis Group (Routledge Studies in Sustainable Development).

Inquiry-Based Learning in Theology

32

Oliver Reis

32.1 Characteristic Features in the Field of Theology as a Constraint on Inquiry-Based Learning

Theology as a scholarly discipline exists only in a plurality of denominations, which is because theology in Germany is taught from a denominational perspective due to the teachings of the church. For this reason, churches grant individual instructors permission to teach, and also separately approve of the degree programs through accreditation procedures. In Germany, theology is distinguished by its position, situated between teaching in academic freedom while at the same time doing so on behalf of the church. Theology is not a study of religion, but rather the reflective and methodological engagement with the beliefs of a religious community from within the same religious community. Theological research therefore does not investigate God, which would overwhelm theology. Instead, it deals with the human testimonies of faith for the believers. Theology has developed significantly during the course of its more than 2000-year history. An early form of theology is apologetics, which shows that the Christian faith is compatible with ancient philosophies during the period in which Christians were persecuted. Another is dogmatism, which seeks to rationalize questions of faith according to internal standards in times of differences of faith.

Today, four theological subject groups have become established, ensuring an extremely high level of internal cultural diversity. This also has an impact in terms of research methodology: Thus

O. Reis, Dr. Dr. (✉)
Universität Paderborn, Institut für Katholische Theologie, Professur für Religionspädagogik mit dem Schwerpunkt der Inklusion, Paderborn, Germany
e-mail: oliver.reis@uni-paderborn.de

© The Author(s) 2019
H. A. Mieg (ed.), *Inquiry-Based Learning – Undergraduate Research*,
https://doi.org/10.1007/978-3-030-14223-0_32

- *biblical theology* is methodologically oriented towards literary studies and cultural studies,
- *historical theology* is oriented towards the work of reconstructing historical source materials,
- *systematic theology* is oriented towards classic hermeneutics within the humanities
- and *practical theology* is oriented towards empirical educational sciences.

This results in completely different teaching and research traditions, which tolerate one another, but which also observe each other critically.

In the theological teaching practiced in Germany, a great deal of skepticism can be observed towards the Bologna study reform and adapting material for didactics in general. Without idealizing pre-Bologna conditions, engineered ideas about the feasibility of learning tend to be rejected in theology. Each new higher education didactic concept is tested for its impact on freedom of thought and the free educational development of the individual. This emphasis on freedom is connected with the above-mentioned position of the church, but also with the fact that the faith of the individual as well as God himself cannot and must not be controlled for us. The theological subjects must deal with this unavailability methodically. A subject area such as dogmatic theology within systematic theology is going to have a much harder time understanding its own teaching as a didactic locus than, for example, religious education, which can more easily relate its subject—the people learning before God—to its own teachings.

Despite the confessional and professional diversity, theology has individual actors with a clear interest in didactic innovation of higher education, which can emphasize the main points in individual teaching projects and modules, depending on the situation on site at the specific institutions of higher learning. Theologians are involved in their own projects and use institutional support at the German institutions of higher learning that offer theological instruction, and that are committed to inquiry-based learning in a programmatic way. In some cases this has also led to the curricular anchoring of inquiry-based learning, for example in the master's degree program "Christentum in Kultur und Gesellschaft" ("Christianity in Culture and Society") at the University of Münster or in the master's module "Theologische Forschung" ("Theological Research") at the Technical University of Dortmund.

Due to the mentioned basic conditions, there is no systematic reception of inquiry-based learning in theology. The principle is received differently in the various denominations and in the subject areas, and is filled with different research ideas. Unlike principles such as competence orientation, the ideological resistance to inquiry-based learning has diminished because in theology inquiry-based learning is understood as a counter-impulse to school-like and mechanized learning. This facilitates the actor's reception in two contexts: (a) the training of religious instructors with a focus on the theory-practice problem that imparting subject-specific content leaves hardly any traces in the educational reality of religious instruction (cf. Zimmermann and Lenhard 2015, pp. 15–18), or (b) master's modules in the former theological degree programs awarding a *Diplom*, which are consciously conceived as free learning places in contrast to the perceived reduction of education by the Bologna process to the level of school instruction.

32.2   Experiences with Inquiry-Based Learning in Theology

32.2.1 Inquiry-Based Learning—An Attempt to Structure the Formats

What exactly is it that should be investigated under the heading "inquiry-based learning" in the discipline of theology? In order to be able to sort the individual phenomena, I would first like to merge the structuring of Huber (2014) and Reinmann (in this volume).

Huber makes a distinction between research-based learning (*forschungsbasiertes Lernen*), research-oriented learning (*forschungsorientiertes Lernen*) and inquiry-based learning (*Forschendes Lernen*). In his structuring, increasing participation in the complete research process is the guiding interest of those involved in the process. *Research-based learning* (or, better yet, research-based teaching [Ludwig 2011]?) orients teaching, and thus learning as well, towards students' existing research interests. This is reflected in the way in which the discipline teaches its research-related aspect. *Research-oriented learning* goes beyond an orientation towards research-relevant issues and includes a methodological processing of the question based on professional standards. Beyond the question and its method-guided processing, *inquiry-based learning* also emphasizes evaluation and presentation to third parties. Here it becomes clear that research always happens within a specific context. For Huber, even inquiry-based learning need not be objectively innovative; it is a learning process within the context of scholarship that is innovative for the individual. On the other hand, when Reinmann distinguishes between "understanding research," "practicing research" and "performing researching oneself," she discovers an order of competency development between the poles of receptivity and productivity. It is productive, in my opinion, not to parallelize the two orders, as proposed by Reinmann (cf. Reinmann 2015, p. 5), but to intersect them (see Fig. 32.1).

Huber distinguishes among phases of the research process, thus the subject matter, and Reinmann distinguishes among phases of the development process, thus the activity with the subject matter. In between, there are some relevant intermediate moments that are significant for theology. Thus, for example, it is possible to focus on the development of one's own technically workable question, i.e. to strive for research-based learning within the meaning of Huber, and to put this into a supported pre- and post-process, thereby emphasizing the receptivity and productivity equally, which corresponds to Reinmann's approach to practice research (cf. X1 in Fig. 32.1). At the end of the bachelor's degree, it would also be possible to make inquiry-based learning in the sense of Huber's knowledge-based object (as "understanding research" in the sense of Reinmann) a course that should help in the choice between an application- or research-oriented master's degree (cf. X2 in Fig. 32.1). Of course, the ideal goal would be for both orders to come together as students conduct their own research throughout the process. To capture the reality of theology, however, the focus is on the intermediate stages.

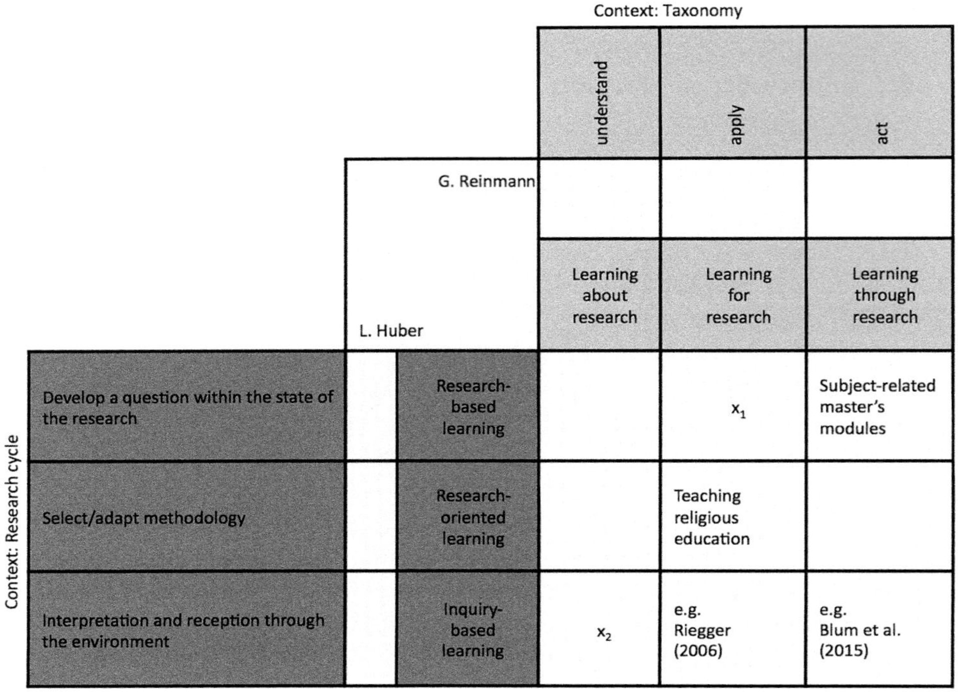

		Context: Taxonomy		
	G. Reinmann	understand	apply	act
	L. Huber	Learning about research	Learning for research	Learning through research
Context: Research cycle Develop a question within the state of the research	Research-based learning		x_1	Subject-related master's modules
Select/adapt methodology	Research-oriented learning		Teaching religious education	
Interpretation and reception through the environment	Inquiry-based learning	x_2	e.g. Riegger (2006)	e.g. Blum et al. (2015)

Fig. 32.1 Matrix of inquiry-based learning. (Source: author's representation) according to Huber (2014) and Reinmann (in this volume)

32.2.2 Formats in Theology

32.2.2.1 Link Between Theory and Practice in the Education of Religious Education Teachers

The training of religious education teachers includes various teaching projects that use inquiry-based learning in religious education courses to support internships or a whole practical semester.

The following projects exist in Protestant theology: In the case of Petra Freudenberger-Lötz at the University of Kassel, students conduct religious education and evaluate it according to the grounded theory research concept (cf. Freudenberger-Lötz 2007; Schmidl 2012). Heinz Streibl, at the University of Bielefeld, attaches great importance to class observation that is oriented towards the research cycle. At the University of Osnabrück, Caroline Teschner develops independent research questions with the students within the framework of action research; these questions influence the teaching design as guiding theses.

In terms of Catholic theology, the following examples can be mentioned: Guido Hunze works with video-based reflection talks and peer learning at the University of Münster (cf. Hunze 2010, pp. 257–259). At the University of Würzburg, Boris Kalbheim develops criteria for material analysis with students, conducts these analyses and has developed material for religious education (cf. Kalbheim 2013, pp. 203–206). Regine Oberle allows students at the Heidelberg University of Education to present their pupils' ideas on specific topics along the research cycle in order to improve subject orientation in religious education. In the case of Manfred Riegger from the University of Augsburg, students generate hypotheses through participatory observations that become relevant to classroom practice (cf. Riegger 2006).

Inquiry-based learning is used as a large-scale method to observe this in practice using research-oriented behavior, and to refer it back both to the theory of didactics and to religious didactic theory formation. Generally, the research cycle is not taught; instead, students in the practical phase are expected to apply the research cycle and generate results. Research reports often document and reflect on this research experience. This format can easily be construed as research-oriented learning in that research is pursued for the professionalization in the field of action. For inquiry-based learning, the contextual feedback of the results is usually missing. The results are not systematically evaluated and communicated in the teaching contexts or used for further development of the individual study biography, for example. The issue is about passing through the cycle itself and the associated research-oriented behavior, which raises awareness about which processes take place in religious education, how they are to be understood theologically and didactically, and which options for action arise therefrom. Furthermore, the self-determined framework for independent research is lacking. The didactic guidelines are tightly set in these teaching projects. The "Specialization Module Specialist Didactics: Religion, Bildung, Schule, Professionskunde" ("In-depth module for teaching methodology: religion, education, school, study of professions") of the Master of Education at the University of Münster is an example of how research-oriented learning can now be institutionally anchored in the training of religious instructors as a "practical obstacle course" (cf. "Religious Teachers – inside education" in Fig. 32.1).

Individual examples go a step further and ensure that the research results are made available to the specialist discourses. Particularly productive is the Kasseler research workshop, with its own publication series, "Beiträge zur Kinder- und Jugendtheologie" ("Contributions to child and youth theology"). Others take up the research results in order to directly influence the practice of action (for example in the case of Manfred Riegger in Augsburg, cf. Riegger 2006). In these examples, the entire process (of inquiry-based learning) is practiced.

32.2.2.2 Professional Courses with a Research Assignment

If inquiry-based learning is used in the subject modules, students should be given the opportunity to carry out independent learning processes. Usually, such research projects are assigned to the individual theological subjects. What is noticeable is that many projects can be identified in church history, e.g. at Ruhr University Bochum, the University of Oldenburg or the University of Tübingen. At the same time, there are projects in practical theology, for example at the University of Leipzig or the University of Frankfurt. The degree of support may fluctuate, but neither topics nor methodologies are specified; developing them is part of the project. The focus is on the discovery of a research-related question and its experimental work in a self-guided learning process in the sense of "self-research." When such modules are evaluated, the methodology is evaluated, but not as clearly as in the bachelor's and master's thesis. This is possible because it can be assumed that the students possess the essential knowledge and methodological skills. But that does not mean that the students are comprehensively informed about the concept of inquiry-based learning or that process itself was practiced. Inquiry-based learning remains rather implicit, while for students, the freedom needed for independent engagement with a personally relevant question is at the fore (cf. "Subject-related master modules" in Fig. 32.1).

This leads to the results being structurally continued (e.g. within the curriculum) in theses in only a few examples. This happens at the University of Münster and the University of Dortmund, for example. In some cases, the result is so innovative from the outset that it is brought to the public, as provided in the subject of church history at the University of Bochum and the University of Tübingen. The professional handling of the question then becomes important, in order for the result to be able to withstand public pressure.

32.3 Sample Implementation of Inquiry-Based Learning

In the following, I would like to present an example of a consistent orientation towards inquiry-based learning (see Fig. 32.1). In this presentation, I focus on the sequence of learning steps, which clearly shows how the research work is introduced in the teaching project, supported and used for further steps. The classification in the matrix (Fig. 32.1) takes place within the representation (see Table 32.1).

32.4 Outlook for Inquiry-Based Learning in Theology: What Needs to Be Done?

An essential task will be to network the previous approaches to inquiry-based learning in theology. Due to the confessional boundaries and the diversity of the subject cultures, the actors barely acknowledge one another and do not relate to one another. Usually, didactic approaches from general higher education are adopted and applied; however, a separate didactic discourse is still needed. Yet inquiry-based learning in particular has the potential to make theology more widely available to university didactics, since it does not involve a reputation for further reducing higher education to the level of school instruction or for stripping away the emphasis on expertise in the subject.

Looking at the Table 32.1, it is clear that only a percentage of the formats has found a place in theology and that, above all, "understanding research" is still not as well integrated into the projects. If inquiry-based learning continues to be implemented within the

Table 32.1 Project: Sifting through original sources, sorting and writing the history of German post-war Catholicism; research on church history projects (cf. also Blum et al. 2015). Guidance: Daniela Blum (University of Tübingen), Florian Bock (University of Tübingen) and Andreas Henkelmann (Ruhr University Bochum)

Step 1	Initially, several introductory sessions on post-war Catholic history and recurring tutorials on source study/analysis are offered. On the thematic level, the historical context in southwestern Germany is introduced.
Students develop a thematic body of knowledge. They practice in historical source analysis.	
Step 2	The joint training phase does not end with the material, but instead leads to codified archival practices, and thus to methodological competence, which students try out on practical examples (finding aids, etc.). The question for lecturers is what must be learned thematically and methodically in order to start the first archive phase. Lecturers take the liberty of deviating from some aspects of the seminar plan and dealing with other aspects in detail, if the research processes make this necessary.
Students become familiar with the method of working with the archive.	
Step 3	During the preparation phase, students form small groups to analyze source materials (files, minutes, etc.) for a self-developed historical question. There is a strong emphasis on the autonomous allocation of time and work by students. The development phase begins with a visit to the Diocesan Archives in Rottenburg. This is followed by a critical evaluation of the materials, whereby special emphasis is placed on freedom and independence in the finding of knowledge: Students find new source material, read it, develop a research question in view of the current state of the research, read the sources again in view of the research question, investigate other, possibly edited sources or secondary literature in the event that contexts are unclear, and create their own image in answering the question using the various building blocks of secondary literature and sources.
Students develop their own research questions through independent archival work and literature research.	
Step 4	In the midst of this preparation phase, a group session is held. The aim of this session is to "stop" the initiated learning process in order to reflect on it in terms of learning barriers. At the same time, it is about intensively discussing the key questions, as these are the starting point for further development. Without a key question, the search horizon cannot be reduced to a level that can be implemented with the seminar. The groups talk intensively about their experiences and results. Fellow students, not the lecturers, point out possible solutions for practical and content-related problems and act as experts on the level of question, subject and methodological competence.
Students articulate and reflect on the ambiguities or problems resulting from step 3.	
Step 5	This is followed by the second phase of on-site preparation. This phase is similar in a central point of the first phase, namely the source reading material. However, this reading should now refer specifically to the key question, however. This is done in the form of a literature search to contextualize the sources. The actual source analyses are subsequently conducted. Literature research and source analysis are therefore mutually dependent. As such, it is a circular process, not a linear one.
Students coordinate the key question, source analysis and literature research and construct a narrative about the self-developed question.	

(continued)

Table 32.1 (continued)

Step 6	At the end of the semester, the individual teams present their answers to
Students prepare their results for their target group and feed their narrative into a cultural context.	the seminar in a final session. For the additional proof of performance in the sense of a summative competence measurement, the individual presentations are prepared in the form of a newspaper article for the diocese newspaper ("Zeitschnitte" ["Cross-sections of time"] series in the Rottenburg *Sonntagsblatt*) or a scientific paper. In addition to sharpening the historical view of one's own local environment, the issue of perspective analysis, contextualization and addressee-related writing associated with the source work is sensitized.

study regulations, care must be taken to build up knowledge of what scholarship and research are all about as specific cognitive processes. For theology, this task increases the challenge of further developing one's own methodology and making it transparent and learnable for the students. In teaching practice, however, research-oriented learning is hardly realized; at best, in this case, "practicing research" consists of imitation. It is no coincidence that the few approaches to real "self-research" focus on research-based questions. However, those who hold true to the educational ideals of institutions of higher learning as claimed by theology should accept this challenge, however.

The crucial test only occurs when the teaching projects and modules accept the issue of testing, search for forms of testing "in research" and develop criteria that meet the specific learning results of the combination of activity and subject matter (see Table 32.1). So far, the tests of the object of measurement are more closely related to reflection on the research process (also: "On Research"; cf. Reinmann in this volume). Without further development of the examinations, inquiry-based learning in theology remains a rather unstructured form, which sustains itself through the high commitment of individual teachers and students (cf. Hunze 2010, p. 258).

References

Blum, D./Bock, F./Henkelmann, A. (2015). Der hochschuldidaktische Königsweg? Forschendes Lernen in kirchenhistorischen Seminaren. In F. Bock/C. Handschuh/A. Henkelmann (Hrsg.), *Kompetenzorientierte Kirchengeschichte. Hochschuldidaktische Perspektiven »nach Bologna«, Theologie und Hochschuldidaktik; Bd. 6* (S. 91–114). Münster: Lit Verlag.

Freudenberger-Lötz, P. (2007). *Theologische Gespräche mit Kindern. Untersuchungen zur Professionalisierung Studierender und Anstöße zu forschendem Lernen im Religionsunterricht.* Stuttgart: Calwer.

Huber, L. (2014). Forschungsbasiertes, Forschungsorientiertes, Forschendes Lernen: Alles dasselbe? *Das Hochschulwesen, 62* (1 + 2), 32–39.

Hunze, G. (2010). Die Gretchenfrage der Lehramtsausbildung: Wie hältst Du's mit der Praxis? – oder: Wie verzahnen, was sich nicht trennen lassen dürfte? *Engagement, 28* (4), 251–260.

Kalbheim, B. (2013). Zwischen akademischer Höhe und beruflicher Tiefe. Das didaktische Konzept »Forschendes Lernen« im theologischen Studium. *Pastoraltheologische Informationen, 33*, 193–206.

Ludwig, J. (2011). *Forschungsbasierte Lehre als Lehre im Format der Forschung.* Potsdam: Universitätsverlag Potsdam. Retrieved 06 April 2016 from http://pub.ub.uni-potsdam.de/volltexte/2011/4985/

Riegger, M. (2006). Wahrnehmen von Gottesbildern als forschend-evaluierendes Lernen. Reflexive Religionslehrerbildung an der Hochschule auf der Grundlage des symbolisch-kritischen Ansatzes. *International Journal of Practical Theology, 10,* 91–112.

Schmidl, S. M. (2012). *Die Professionalisierung Studierender durch Reflexionsgespräche, Aufgezeigt am Beispiel der Forschungswerkstatt »Theologische Gespräche mit Jugendlichen«.* Kassel: Univ. Press.

Zimmermann, M./Lenhard, H. (2015). *Praxissemester Religion. Handwerkszeug für Berufsanfängerinnen und Berufsanfänger.* Göttingen: Vandenhoeck & Ruprecht.

Overview: Perspectives

The final chapters deal with the prospects of inquiry-based learning for institutions of higher learning as well as for the economy and society. These chapters cover:

- Higher education development: the model for this is the University of Bremen, which has implemented the Zurich framework;
- Universities of applied sciences: attention is focused on projects funded by third-parties that also offer students the opportunity to conduct their own research;
- Digital media in teaching (technology-enhanced learning): the question is whether and how inquiry-based learning generally connects with the use of new media;
- Heterogeneity: it is argued that inquiry-based learning is an appropriate tool for dealing with increasing diversity among students in terms of prior knowledge, age or social and ethnic origin;
- Economy and society: the focus is on employability, i.e. the employability to which higher education studies is intended to contribute today.

One perspective on inquiry-based learning – for which, regrettably, we were unable to create a separate chapter – is that of continuing education. The box below gives an example of how inquiry-based learning has been used in continuing education for older students. Inquiry-based learning could also find its place in professional continuing education, from architecture to social work.

Box 1: Inquiry-Based Learning with Older Students

Markus Marquard, Managing Director of the Center for General Scientific Continuing Education (ZAWiW) at Ulm University

"Learning: for oneself, with others, for society": General scientific-oriented continuing education for interested older individuals is a central task of ZAWiW (cf. Marquard 2014). As a section in the department for Humanities at Ulm University, the ZAWiW is bridging the gap between academia and the citizens of Ulm with academic weeks, inquiry-based learning and extracurricular studies. The ZAWiW was founded in 1994 in response to the growing demand for general, multidisciplinary continuing education for the third age (U3A). The main task of the ZAWiW is to develop innovative educational programs that address the interests and continuing education needs of the participants, and that strengthen their own activities in the sense of inquiry-based learning.

Inquiry-based learning: Inquiry-based learning at ZAWiW is largely based on self-guided forms of learning; learners independently determine the topic of research and learning, as well as the research strategies and methods for handling the topic. Inquiry-based learning can be done both in individual work and in group work. It can be very theory-oriented and also practice-oriented; however, it should also always be supported scientifically and in accordance with the subject.

"Inquiry-based learning" working groups allow older people to self-determinedly research interesting issues based on their life and work experiences. Senior citizens independently develop the question in inquiry-based learning and identify appropriate methods with the encouragement and support of experts and older students (Stadelhofer 2006). They are supported by project leaders and older students when questions and problems arise or when there is a need for qualification, yet still conduct their own research.

The main topics of the working groups were regional history or contemporary witness work, cultural history and urban sociology, as well as topics from the fields of the natural sciences, economics, medicine and psychology. Over the years, however, working groups have also been formed on the topic of "Europe" or the topic of "old – young." Oblique research topics, or research topics that would otherwise often remain unaddressed and forgotten, are often taken up.

An important aspect of inquiry-based learning is the orientation of the research process towards the product and result, i.e. in the end, there are publications, exhibitions or other products that are made available to the public. Examples include exhibitions about Willy-Brandt-Platz in Ulm and the artist Richard Liebermann, brochures on the occupation period, the post-war period, about Wilhelmsburg as part of the Federal Fortress of Ulm, etc.

(continued)

Box 1: (continued)
Further developments and challenges

Inquiry-based learning was established at the ZAWiW early on, in the mid-1990s. Today, it is possible to identify developments which show that a review of the concept would be meaningful. Thus some of the working groups are struggling with the increasingly advanced age of their participants, which is reflected in the difficulty of integrating new learners into work on the one hand and, on the other, in the ever increasing age of the participants, who are sometimes at the limits of longevity, and who are no longer in a position (or have no desire) to participate to the same extent as before and contribute with a corresponding effort and a high degree of commitment to the work.

Stadelhofer, C. (Hrsg.). (2006). *Forschendes Lernen als Beitrag zu einer neuen Lernkultur im Seniorenstudium*. Neu-Ulm: AG-SPAK-Bücher.
Marquard, M. (2014). Lernen im Alter – Aktives Altern selbst gestalten! In K. W. Schönherr & V. Tiberius (Hrsg.), *Lebenslanges Lernen. Wissen und Können als Wohlstandsfaktoren* (S. 113–126). Wiesbaden: Springer VS.

Inquiry-Based Learning as a Teaching Profile at Institutions of Higher Learning – The Example of the University of Bremen

Margrit E. Kaufmann and Heidi Schelhowe

"Inquiry-based learning" is set to be promoted as a trendy concept. Numerous institutions of higher learning are involved in projects relating to inquiry-based learning and declare it a distinguishing feature of their teaching. This applies in particular to research-intensive universities. What does inquiry-based learning mean for higher education development? Is inquiry-based learning suited to serve as the strategic orientation of the entire institution? And how can this be implemented beyond a guiding principle and mere announcements at an institute of higher learning? How can the greatest possible number of actors be involved in these processes? And what should be taken into consideration in so doing? The following article addresses these questions and refers by way of example to activities and experiences in the profile development for inquiry-based learning at the University of Bremen.

33.1 Inquiry-Based Learning and Higher Education Culture(s): Reference to Teaching-Learning Research Traditions

Inquiry-based learning can neither be prescribed nor directly controlled by the university administration. In essence, it is essentially based on the Humboldtian educational ideal of the unity of research and teaching, relative to which institutions of higher learning position

M. E. Kaufmann, Dr. (✉)
Universität Bremen, Wissenschaftliche Expertin für Diversity der Universitätsleitung und Fachbereich Kulturwissenschaften, Bremen, Germany
e-mail: mkaufm@uni-bremen.de

H. Schelhowe, Prof. Dr.
Universität Bremen, Technologie-Zentrum Informatik und Informationstechnik, Bremen, Germany
e-mail: schelhow@tzi.de

© The Author(s) 2019
H. A. Mieg (ed.), *Inquiry-Based Learning – Undergraduate Research*,
https://doi.org/10.1007/978-3-030-14223-0_33

themselves differently. The University of Bremen, which was founded as a reform university in 1971 and selected as a "University of Excellence" (*Exzellenzuniversität*) in 2012, emphasizes this unity (Huber et al. 2013). The teaching profile of inquiry-based learning has a significant history in the project-based study here, what is known as the "Bremen model," as a teaching profile of the founding period (Schelhowe 2013). The course of study was initially organized for all subjects in the form of projects with interdisciplinary and socially relevant topics. Lectures and seminars were designed to support these projects. The aim was to promote a research-oriented, independent attitude in students. To date, this tradition of project-based studies has continued in various subjects and has been kept alive by individual instructors despite large-scale ("mass") studies (Robben 2013).

> Distinct experiences in interdisciplinary collaboration reinforce the research-oriented focus of instruction at the University of Bremen, and the internal culture of consensus enhances its implementation. What is characteristic of the teaching profile at the University of Bremen is thus the focus on research-based study from the beginning, the curricular anchoring of a comprehensive General Studies portion, as well as the supportive integration of e-learning portions in the teaching programs (Universität Bremen 2015b, translated).

These objectives are taken up, discussed and formulated in the process that has been initiated to develop and hone a guiding principle for teaching at the university. The guiding principle was developed by the Academic Senate's Teaching Commission, which was established for this purpose, reviewed and amended by all departments and deanships, and finally adopted by the Academic Senate, the supreme governing body of the university's self-government. This process, in which the involvement of students is of central importance, is based on numerous measures for the development and promotion of teaching.

If inquiry-based learning is anchored in the guiding principle, this raises questions not only about the characteristic features in the subject culture that must be taken into consideration, but about a common concept of inquiry-based learning as well. In the cross-university exchange, for example at the 2015 "Projekt nexus" meeting of the German Rectors' Conference, "Inquiry-based learning: subject-specific discrepancies and examination formats" ("Forschendes Lernen: fachspezifische Differenzen und Prüfungsformate"), the disunity in terms of concepts and applications of inquiry-based learning became clear. In his keynote address at this conference, for example, Ludwig Huber recommended drawing a distinction between inquiry-based learning in the narrowest sense, research-oriented and research-based teaching and learning.

The University of Bremen cooperates with Ludwig Huber and other experts in didactics with respect to inquiry-based learning, in particular with Peter Tremp and Tobina Brinkmann, who advised us on the understanding of the concept and its implementation. According to Ludwig Huber (2013, p. 248), the phases of inquiry-based learning are to be thought of as recursive loops. They consist of the introduction and identifying a question, developing information, acquiring methodological knowledge, developing a research design, conducting research, developing and presenting the results, and reflection. Going through a holistic research process structured in this way from start to finish is not possible in every module and not possible to the same degree in every course. There are ways to show how inquiry-based learning can be implemented, not only as a methodical, didactic principle in individual courses, but as an overall strategy of a scholarly attitude of instructors and students in the breadth of course offerings, however.

The "Zurich framework" concept (Hildbrand and Tremp 2012) lends itself to this, as it is oriented towards study activities in the curriculum and systematically links teaching and research. It takes the objectives of a course of academic studies as its starting point and focuses on the study activities. This model lends itself to structuring and simplifying the complex challenges that are implicated with inquiry-based learning (for more about the Zurich framework, see Mieg, in this volume).

33.2   Inquiry-Based Learning and Higher Education Development: Promote the Vanguard and Expand Inquiry-Based Learning

The measures of the administration of the University of Bremen with which inquiry-based learning is initiated, promoted and disseminated will be sketched out and discussed below. The "Semester Summit," a biannual discussion meeting between university board and students where the topics are current issues impacting studies and teaching, was turned into a work group dealing with inquiry-based learning at the University of Bremen, in order to come up with "recommendations" for the departments.

An important element for the overall university estimation of teaching and for the improvement of its quality is "Teaching Day" ("Dies Academicus"), which is held annually. On this day, students and instructors work together in the morning on improvements in teaching and studies (see Ghaffarizad et al. 2015), and participate in an interdisciplinary program in the afternoon. In the evening, a prize for excellence in teaching ("Preis für gute Lehre") is awarded. This prize acknowledges instructors whose examples from their day-to-day teaching practice are worth imitating as best practice.

In preparing the application for the second round of the federal and state governments' 2012 "Excellence Initiative" for the promotion of science and research at German institutions of higher learning, which refers to outstanding research, it was clear to the university administration that teaching and research belong together at the University of Bremen and that this must also be explicitly stated in the application (Schelhowe 2013, p. 11). When Heidi Schelhowe made inquiry-based learning her main focus in this phase during her candidacy for the position of Vice President Academic, it received a surprisingly warm reception from many areas of the university. It was possible to initiate a call for tenders for the promotion of inquiry-based learning projects using an internal university fund, which the state government provided the university so that it could prepare the Excellence application. Ten outstanding projects were selected with the objective of setting a standard for inquiry-based learning; the projects were assessed by experts, and participants trained, advised and evaluated in workshops.

New offerings for inquiry-based learning were increasingly integrated into the higher education didactic training courses in accordance with the profile development. Here, specific, subject-didactic courses are needed. The quality assurance and improvement measures that are implemented by the instructors also require additional resources. In order for inquiry-based learning to be carried out in a manner that reflects an awareness of and sensitivity to heterogeneity, and in order for student-centered teaching-learning research to be made possible, new connections were established between different areas of the institution. Inquiry-based learning was linked with the university's intersectional diversity processes (Kaufmann et al. 2015). At issue is the conscious handling of the diversity of the members and organizational units as a cross-sectional task with the objective of increasing opportunities, social inclusion and educational justice.

With funds from the "Teaching Quality Pact I," the joint federal-state program for improved study conditions and increased teaching quality in the Federal Ministry of Education and Research, it was possible to fund projects concerning inquiry-based learning and dealing with heterogeneity on a large scale from 2012 to 2016 under the title "ForstA – inquiry-based learning right from the start" ("ForstA – Forschend studieren von Anfang an – Heterogenität als Potential"), the intention being to permanently implement these projects. The Study Deans of the faculties and the faculty members were asked to develop related teaching concepts. As with the funding of the projects in the framework of the Excellence application, the objective was not just to promote the vanguard and to set standards. Rather, the program explicitly encroached on the subjects and departments so that *individual measures and steps* (e.g. in the methodology and didactics of so-called mass lectures as well) *were also promoted* and made visible, which has an impact on the overall inquiry-based learning profile. In the application and in its implementation, we therefore worked with a more strictly defined concept of "inquiry-based learning."

In terms of sensitization to the heterogeneity among students as a decisive aspect in improving studies and teaching, the university was involved with the "Quest" survey conducted among students in the major project "Diversity as opportunity" ("Vielfalt als Chance") at the Center for Higher Education Development (Centrum für Hochschulentwicklung, CHE), in parallel to promoting the quality agreement. The project is an anonymized survey on the diversity of students and their self-assessment of their success in their studies at institutions of higher learning (Kaufmann 2013, 2015). At the same time, the university participated in the "Different better!" ("Ungleich besser!") project of the Donors' Association for the Promotion of Humanities and Sciences in Germany (Stifterverband für die Deutsche Wissenschaft) and were subsequently audited for "Diversity University" (ibid.). Through engagement with nationwide diversity projects in conjunction with diversity research, didactic and structural approaches have been developed to raise awareness of inequality and how to deal with heterogeneity and diversity in inquiry-based learning (Kaufmann and Satilmis 2015; Satilmis, in this volume).

The starting point for the ForstA project was a SWOT analysis. The process identified critical phases in the course of studies upon which special emphasis is placed in the ForstA concept. This was oriented towards the "student lifecycle," from orientation week to the graduation phase, and focused on four pillars:

1. "September Academy" as a bridge from school to university, by means of which students come into contact with material and methods that are relevant to their subject;
2. the reform of the introductory phase of the course of study, whereby subject-related research is accentuated and components and methods of inquiry-based learning are incorporated into major courses;
3. the profiling of general studies in the sense of heterogeneous, autonomous research-related study in order to acquire key competencies and
4. support during the graduation phase and transition into professional fields by promoting learning communities and writing workshops.

The acting Vice President Academic, Thomas Hoffmeister, also fosters the focus on inquiry-based learning. As part of the Bündnis für Hochschullehre (Alliance for Higher Education Instruction), "Lehre Hoch N" ("Teaching to the nth degree"), to which the Stifterverband für die Deutsche Wissenschaft (Donors' Association for the Promotion of Humanities and Sciences in Germany) and other high-ranking foundations belong, he will be setting up a "Standing Conference for Excellence in Teaching" starting in 2016 (Götz 2015). The conference consists of 30 university members of all status groups – students, scholarly and non-scholarly contributors, and university instructors. The goal is to exchange information about quality criteria and opportunities for the further development of teaching within the university and in an interdisciplinary manner, to strengthen the unity of outstanding research and teaching, and to promote the widespread impact of innovative teaching projects.

33.3 Inquiry-Based Learning as a Degree Program Profile: Faculty-Cultural Concretization

The University of Bremen was again successful in the second competition, "Teaching Quality Pact" in 2015. "ForstA *integrated*" ("ForstA*integriert*") started in 2017 and built on the activities of "ForstA." It was intended to expand teaching excellence and to create an even stronger connection with research excellence. Going beyond projects to individual study phases, the focus is subsequently on the issue of coherent curricular processes in research-based study.

Vice President Thomas Hoffmeister explained the developmental perspective for teaching at the University of Bremen and the goal of "ForstA *integrated*" as follows: "We are building on experiences with inquiry-based learning in individual modules and projects; however, in the coming years, we would like to orient teaching in entire degree programs towards the concept at the University of Bremen" (Scholz 2015, translated). At the same time, the tried-and-tested program items from "ForstA" are being further developed. In contrast to the past, the program, "Uni-Start," is intended to offer students support not just before or directly at the beginning of their studies, but also throughout the first semester, for example through tutors and mentors. "Uni-Start" is intended to facilitate the transition to university and prepare new students for demanding inquiry-based learning.

The project, "Inquiry-based learning as a degree program profile" "Forschendes Lernen als Studiengangsprofil," FLASP), which was financed by the Higher Education Pact, was the pilot project for this concept, which, in contrast to the individual project promotion, oriented entire degree programs towards inquiry-based learning. To this end, from 2015 to 2017, three entire degree programs were examined and redesigned in terms of their curricular and modular design, and the didactic implementation. As in the case of promoting individual courses within the framework of the Excellence Initiative, this was intended to set standards and create excellent role models. The concepts for the bachelor's degree programs in biology and cultural studies and for the master's degree program in public health were selected (Universität Bremen 2015a). The goal of the FLASP project was to support the pilot disciplines with additional resources to develop their subject-specific access to inquiry-based learning and handling of heterogeneity with a high standard and high degree of visibility. The degree programs should be reviewed, planned and implemented with an eye towards promoting students' research-oriented behavior in order to show other degree programs possible paths to profile development as best practices. Decisive for the development of the degree programs is the collaboration of instructors, students, and those instructors responsible for the module who, after modularization, have the task of bundling individual courses into meaningful units according to their description in the module plans.

Inspired by the "Zurich framework" (see above, Hildbrand and Tremp 2012), the modules of the degree programs should be coordinated with one another in terms of curriculum and didactics in such a way that the students run through the various phases of research during the course of studies: "Planning and implementation should be such that, as students progress, they increasingly develop competence in assuming research-oriented behavior that may take effect when they take up a professional activity, or that prepares them to embark on a master's degree, doctorate or activity in research and teaching. A particular concern is reaching students across the breadth of their heterogeneous premises and interests" (Universität Bremen 2014, translated).

33.4   Unresolved Questions and Outlook: What Can Be Transferred from the Example?

The article makes it clear that every university must develop a teaching profile that accommodates its own teaching tradition and communication cultures. The University of Bremen can build on its tradition of project-based learning and is characterized by decentralized, low-hierarchical structures. What is true not only here, but presumably for all institutions of higher learning, however, is that inquiry-based learning can neither be set up from the outside nor easily implemented from above. It must evolve from teaching practice, which is to say, starting from the individual instructors and growing from their commitment. The University of Bremen is characterized by participatory approaches to teaching and academic studies. There are numerous opportunities for exchange in institutionally secured meetings on committees and through activities in working groups, workshops, further education, semester summit meetings or on the occasion of Teaching Day. The students' perspectives, their experiences as inquiry-based learners, are central to these processes. An important element in communicating about teaching, learning and researching is creating an "organ"—in our case, the "RESONANZ. Zeitschrift für Studium und Lehre" (Magazine concerning academic study and teaching), which, like the prize for excellence in teaching, contributes to establish a teaching and learning profile.

The "bottom-up" processes must be supported by binding statements by those bodies responsible for making decisions about the teaching profile at the faculty level, as well as at the university's administrative level. Instructors' commitment needs to be appreciated "from above," embedded in an overall strategy and structural anchoring. What a university administration can do with a specific strategy (and the resources promised and made available!) is to pool its forces and provide incentives to those who would face the challenges and provide assistance. It is important to set standards by means of what are termed "lighthouse projects" and to show what excellent teaching and inquiry-based learning could look like according to its narrow definition. At the same time, it also requires a low floor – easy access which allows all or at least many instructors to take steps in the direction of inquiry-based learning without a great deal of effort and without special conditions.

The University of Bremen is an example of the conscious, fruitful and absolutely necessary combination of inquiry-based learning and an orientation towards heterogeneity. Inquiry-based learning requires that diversity be consciously addressed. There are different prerequisites for institutions of higher learning that must be considered and included in the process of profile development. Some faculty or higher education cultures may not be consistent with inquiry-based learning. In that case, it would be wrong to jump on the bandwagon and follow the trend. There are many other valuable opportunities for profile development and quality improvement in teaching that address specific concerns and cultures, and that positively appeal to specific groups of instructors and students.

References

Ghaffarizad, K./Kaufmann, M. E./Koch, H./Kurzawski, B./Reuter, A./Seufert, P. (2015). Forschendes Lernen als Team-Play. Gemeinsamer Bericht von Studierenden und Lehrenden über den Tag der Lehre 2014 am Institut für Ethnologie und Kulturwissenschaft. *Resonanz. Magazin für Studium und Lehre an der Universität Bremen*, 3.

Götz, K. (2015). *Universität Bremen will »Ständige Konferenz für Exzellenz in der Lehre« einrichten* [Pressemitteilung vom 08.09.2015]. Retrieved 05 December 2015 from http://www.uni-bremen. de/universitaet/presseservice/pressemitteilungen/einzelanzeige/news/detail/News/universitaet-bremen-will-staendige-konferenz-fuer-exzellenz-in-der-lehre-einrichten.html

Hildbrand, T./Tremp, P. (2012). Forschungsorientiertes Studium – universitäre Lehre: Das »Zürcher Framework« zur Verknüpfung von Lehre und Forschung. In T. Brinker/P. Tremp (Hrsg.), *Einführung in die Studiengangsentwicklung* (S. 101–116). Bielefeld: Bertelsmann.

Huber, L. (2013). Methodische Anregungen für den Umgang mit pragmatischen Schwierigkeiten im Forschenden Lernen. In L. Huber/M. Kröger/H. Schelhowe (Hrsg.), *Forschendes Lernen als Profilmerkmal einer Universität. Beispiele aus der Universität Bremen* (S. 247–255). Bielefeld: UniversitätsverlagWebler.

Huber, L./Kröger, M./Schelhowe, H. (2013). *Forschendes Lernen als Profilmerkmal einer Universität. Beispiele aus der Universität Bremen.* Bielefeld: UniversitätsverlagWebler.

Kaufmann, M. E. (2013). »Wir haben selbst neue Wissenszusammenhänge geschaffen!« Forschendes Lernen zu ›Diversity‹ in der Kulturwissenschaft. In L. Huber/M. Kröger/H. Schelhowe, *Forschendes Lernen als Profilmerkmal einer Universität. Beispiele aus der Universität Bremen* (S. 123–142). Bielefeld: UniversitätsverlagWebler.

Kaufmann, M. E. (2015). Forschendes Lernen als Bindeglied zwischen Forschungs- und Berufsorientierung in geisteswissenschaftlichen Studiengängen. In P. Tremp (Hrsg.), *Forschungsorientierung und Berufsbezug im Studium. Blickpunkt Hochschuldidaktik, Buchreihe der dghd* (S. 151–170). Bielefeld: Bertelsmann.

Kaufmann, M. E./Satilmis, A. (2015). In-Between Disciplines. Forschendes Lernen als Frame für die Gestaltung transkultureller und -disziplinärer Lernräume. In H. Schelhowe/M. Schaumburg /J. Jasper (Hrsg.), *Teaching is Touching the Future. Academic Teaching within and across disciplines* (S. 349–352). Bielefeld: UniversitätsverlagWebler.

Kaufmann, M.E./Ghaffarizad, K. /Hoffmann, F. /Suckut, F. (Hrsg.), *Diversity @ Uni Bremen: exzellent und chancengerecht?! Dokumentation*. Bremen: Universität Bremen.

Robben, B. (2013). Projektstudium in Bremen. (K)Eine Entwicklungsgeschichte. In L. Huber/M. K röger/H. Schelhowe, *Forschendes Lernen als Profilmerkmal einer Universität. Beispiele aus der Universität Bremen* (S. 37–55). Bielefeld: UniversitätsverlagWebler.

Schelhowe, H. (2013). Zur Einführung: Forschendes Lernen als Profilelement einer Universität. In L. Huber/M. Kröger/H. Schelhowe, *Forschendes Lernen als Profilmerkmal einer Universität. Beispiele aus der Universität Bremen* (S. 11–20). Bielefeld: UniversitätsverlagWebler.

Scholz, E. (2015). *Qualitätspakt Lehre: Geldsegen für die universitäre Lehre* [Pressemitteilung vom 06.11.2015]. Retrieved 05 December 2015 from http://www.uni-bremen.de/universitaet/ presseservice/pressemitteilungen/archiv-2015/views/einzelanzeige-2015/news/detail/News/ qualitaetspakt-lehre-geldsegen-fuer-die-universitaere-lehre.html

Universität Bremen (2014). *Ausschreibung Forschendes Lernen als Studiengangsprofil.* Retrieved 05 December 2015 from http://www.uni-bremen.de/fileadmin/user_upload/single_sites/qm/ Ausschreibung_Forschendes_Lernen_2014.pdf

Universität Bremen (2015a). *Forschendes Lernen an der Universität Bremen – Förderung der Profilbildung.* Retrieved 05 December 2015 from http://www.uni-bremen.de/de/lehre-studium/ projektfoerderung/forschendes-lernen-profilbildung.html

Universität Bremen (2015b). *Lehre und Studium. Planung von Lehr- und Studienqualität.* Retrieved 05 December 2015 from http://www.uni-bremen.de/lehre-studium

Margrit E. Kaufmann is an ethnologist, senior researcher in cultural studies and Scientific Expert on Diversity for the University Board, as well as a member of the body of experts for ForstA ("Forschendes Lernen von Anfang an"/"Inquiry-based Learning Right From the Start").

Heidi Schelhowe is a professor for digital media in education in computer science and former Vice President Academic at the University of Bremen.

Inquiry-Based Learning from the Perspective of Universities of Applied Sciences

34

Margit Scholl

Universities of applied sciences in Germany (*Fachhochschulen*) have a track record of success and are increasingly regarded as universities of applied research. However, they lack the right to award doctorates, have no non-professorial academic teaching staff, and, historically, their faculty members have had a very high teaching load.

These days, research is necessary not only so that future challenges can be tackled but also so that study content is kept up-to-date, the teaching and learning environment is modern and equipped with multimedia capability, and scientifically sound, (socially) critical thinking is preserved. The qualification of students as future employees in companies, public administration, and institutions must be ensured by the institutions of higher learning and adapted to the current state of scholarship. Students should have practical opportunities to implement the postulate asserting the unity of research and teaching by becoming actively involved in scholarship. Inquiry-based learning, in particular, makes this possible. Third-party funded projects, especially at universities of applied sciences, can be used as a starting point for independent initiatives to help strengthen students' practical involvement in research processes, sciences, and knowledge management. The integration of research and learning into universities of applied sciences requires further structural support on the part of both the university administration and policymakers.

M. Scholl, Prof. Dr. rer. nat. (✉)
Technische Hochschule Wildau, Fachbereich Wirtschaft, Informatik, Recht, Professur für Wirtschafts- und Verwaltungsinformatik, Wildau, Germany
e-mail: margit.scholl@th-wildau.de

© The Author(s) 2019
H. A. Mieg (ed.), *Inquiry-Based Learning – Undergraduate Research*,
https://doi.org/10.1007/978-3-030-14223-0_34

## 34.1	Historical Understanding of Research and Teaching, and Current Issues

The German university reforms initiated by Wilhelm von Humboldt led to the type of research universities that are common today and were likewise adopted by the newly founded American universities. One hundred and sixty years later, the student revolts of the late 1960s led to a series of changes at German universities. Around 1970, university reform gave rise, among other things, to concepts aimed at linking research and teaching more effectively. This included project seminars, action research, and, most importantly, inquiry-based learning. Almost 50 years ago, the Federal University Assistants' Conference (BAK) published a programmatic paper on *inquiry-based learning*. Its tenets state that the following principles apply to university learning (BAK 1970, pp. 11–12, translated):

- *A scientific education and participation in science:* "First of all, 'scientific' means training by scientists, in a science, and for a science-dependent profession, which demands systematic, independent, and critical work in a certain area."
- *Process character:* "Science is a dynamic implementation or process of research and reflection, not the static possession of certain knowledge or techniques."
- *Practice orientation:* "The validity of these goals, even for a predominantly job-related scientific education, must be explicitly determined."
- *Learners' active acquisition:* Scientific training "must [involve] participation in this implementation, and thus the cognitive process, or at least replication, but never the mere adoption of existing results."
- *Active action:* "The postulate of the unity of research and learning corresponds to the [...] postulate of the unity of research and teaching."
- *Scope of application:* "Learning as research or inquiry-based learning is therefore not simply a didactic problem for previous universities but also a didactic problem for universities of applied sciences."

Practice-oriented, scholarly training in dynamic, active cognitive processes is thus valid not only for universities but also for universities of applied sciences. For example, in its founding years, the Brandenburg State Commission for Universities of Applied Sciences recommended

> building up sufficient capacities for applied research and development at universities of applied sciences [...]. Application-oriented research and development were the original tasks of universities of applied sciences. Fulfilling these tasks is important, on the one hand, in order for practice-oriented teaching to be constantly updated, since research and development at universities of applied sciences takes place in close dialogue and task-related cooperation with the professional world and is oriented towards current problems. At the same time, research and development can contribute to the intensification of creativity and the capacity for innovation, especially in the medium-sized companies in the region (BBLF 1993, pp. 18–19, translated).

In this sense, universities of applied sciences operate in a manner that is in the tradition of Wilhelm von Humboldt. Nevertheless, the right to award doctorates – the right demanded by Humboldt for universities – continues to be denied them. Universities of applied sciences therefore have no positions for doctoral candidates as academic teaching staff in their standard set-up and are dependent on third-party funded research projects for their research structure. The activities of research associates that are funded by third parties closely relate to the work packages defined in the research projects, as a rule, and are not associated with teaching activities. Maintaining the unity of research and teaching tends to be more voluntary here or is one of the responsibilities that falls to the university professors, who, as a general rule in Germany, receive no additional monetary incentive from the third-party funded research projects and face the problem of being overburdened with a very high teaching load of 18 semester hours per week (SWS) and usually enjoy only limited reductions in their hours for research projects.

34.2 Modern Instruction at Universities of Applied Sciences: Requirements for Instructors and Learners

Within this context, we must again raise the question of what exactly good teaching is, and the extent to which it is also geared towards occupational qualification and a focus on the students aligned with the Bologna reform and the acquisition of competencies (cf. Hannemann 2012). In 2000, the German Rectors' Conference (*Hochschulrektorenkonferenz*) found that a new quality initiative was needed in project-oriented teaching and forms of learning, problem-centered learning, variable forms of support, and competency-oriented forms of examination. New forms of instruction and learning therefore mean that learners must adapt to changing demands. Mandl and Reinmann-Rothmeier (1998, p. 198, translated) summarize the additional burden that modern teaching places on instructors and learners as follows:

- Situated learning on the basis of authentic problems: i.e. the starting point for learning processes is authentic problem situations that, owing to the realistic nature of their content and their relevance, motivate students to acquire new knowledge or new skills.
- Learning in multiple contexts: in order to prevent newly acquired knowledge or skills from remaining fixed on a particular situation, the same content is learned in several different contexts.
- Learning from multiple perspectives: in the learning context, the fact that it is possible to view individual content or problems from different perspectives, or that it is possible to explain them from various angles, is taken into account.
- Learning in a social context: [...] learning together and working with learners and experts within the context of situational problems are part of as many learning phases as possible.

Combined with modern media, the modern teaching and learning environment catering to different group strengths requires intensive and time-consuming preparation, which, as a rule, is carried out by the professors themselves at universities of applied sciences. A change in the roles of instructors and learners will also be a part of this change in higher education instruction. Learners should learn much more actively and in a more self-organized manner and should be able to solve problems in a variety of contexts. Instructors are therefore developing into *learning facilitators* and are experimenting with new didactic concepts and online learning materials in their (subject-related) teaching. This can only succeed if instructors receive practical help and support by means of an organizationally embedded didactic infrastructure. The prerequisite for this is their nationwide institutional involvement in the university of applied sciences, which creates space for the accompanying development of more far-reaching strategies. A *strategy for good teaching at universities of applied sciences* should be developed in a transparent and participatory way, providing concrete support measures with human and financial resources and addressing the question of the credibility of new methods in a manner that is motivating for instructors (Box 34.1).

Box 34.1: Third-Party Projects as an Opportunity for Universities of Applied Sciences
The project, entitled "InterKomp KMU 2.0," aimed to develop modular continuing education courses for small and medium-sized companies (SMEs) at the interface of engineering and culture on the subject of "international IT-based project and knowledge management in a multicultural environment." It was implemented as a joint project by TH Wildau and HWR Berlin and corporate partners from Berlin and Brandenburg (Scholl 2013) and funded by the Federal Ministry of Education and Research (BMBF). As a result, two training courses were developed by the project team of the TH Wildau and put online for free use by employees of very small, small, and medium-sized companies and trainers under Common License 3.0 for non-profits (InterKomp KMU 2.0, 2013). The online course, "Interkulturelles Arbeiten" ("Working interculturally"), also includes two role-playing games that were developed by students and converted into videos, each presenting a positive and a negative variant on the topic of intercultural collaboration in companies from Bulgaria and Germany. The student contribution was created as a project assignment

---

(continued)

Box 34.1: (continued)

in the course "Verwaltung und Recht" ("Administration and Law") on the subject of "Verwaltungsinformatik/Projektarbeit" ("administrative informatics / project work") in the winter semester of 2012/2013. This includes, among other things, the recognition of behavioral patterns and the backgrounds for such patterns. Examples are given for the individual problems of the users by way of support. Role play involves a freer, more relaxed engagement with relevant situations. In the case of genetic learning, the topic and timing were broadly specified, especially as co-workers from the actual project were available to provide voluntary (unpaid) help and advice to the project team, which consisted of three students. Challenges were also based on formal and organizational issues. For evaluation purposes, the learning scenarios were independently designed and filmed by the students; many problems and errors had to be dealt with independently, which is why a degree of inquiry-based learning was included.

Seventy-five percent of another research project, "TEDS@wildau," was funded by the Ministry of Science, Research, and Culture of the State of Brandenburg through the e-learning and e-knowledge program of the European Regional Development Fund (ERDF) and 25 percent was financed by the TH Wildau. The project is based on the idea of comprehensively involving user needs in the development of online information systems and learning platforms. In order to achieve this goal, the highly flexible analysis and survey system, referred to as the TEDS framework (cf. Scholl and Eisenberg 2011), was developed electronically as a product, "TEDS*MOODLE," and implemented as an activity in Moodle. It was made available to users (Scholl et al. 2014) in order to obtain sound evidence that could be used as a basis for improving the Moodle learning platform and its various virtual course "rooms." There were underlying questions about whether to standardize or differentiate the design based on target groups, and about the user experience or user expectations when dealing with Moodle. Students were first included in the 2013/2014 winter semester as part of their fifth semester (subject-related project work) and the first semester (subject-related empirical methods) while "TEDS*MOODLE" was still in development. As a result (Wiesner-Steiner et al. 2014; Scholl 2014; Scholl 2015), students have been actively involved in and experiencing the practical side of scientific work from the very first semester, motivated by their own choices.

34.3   Inquiry-Based and Genetic Learning Through Third-Party-Funded Projects

With regard to teaching and research, the BAK criticized the conditions prevailing at the time, which in many cases still pertain, in that many degree programs are structured in such a way that conducting research or participating in these programs only becomes possible after certain basic systematic knowledge has been acquired and certain courses in auxiliary disciplines have been completed (BAK 1970, p. 12). The BAK (1970, pp. 13–15) distinguished between three related but differentiated forms of university learning:

- "Inquiry-based learning as participation in the current research in the discipline or as the realization of potential research tasks, in some circumstances, beyond the previous framework, with all the disappointments, risks and hardships that are involved in research."
- "Genetic learning as a reenactment of important cognitive processes from the initial questions, through the difficult stages, to the result." The main way this differs from inquiry-based learning is that "from didactic points of view, the choice of problem, hypotheses, and methods is, to a certain extent, controlled by the instructor."
- Critical learning as "a course of study with specific research-oriented attitudes and behaviors that prompt an awareness of significant questions and problems in the discipline by means of special courses and experiences."

In my many years of teaching practice through real student projects based on third-party-funded projects, learning has primarily occurred to date as a mixture of inquiry-based, genetic, and critical learning. On the one hand, there is not enough time available for me to avoid intervening in the projects in a supervisory manner. In this respect, the situation has changed significantly over the course of the Bologna Process and as compared to the 1970s. On the other hand, most students at universities of applied sciences expect guidance as well as intensive support from instructors and express their displeasure when their expectations are not met. As the BAK (1970) explained, the advantages of genetic learning over a mere transfer of knowledge are obvious: motivation, problem awareness, skills, retention, and attitude. In contrast to pure inquiry-based learning, the drawbacks are that "the independence of students can unfold only within an arranged or simulated situation, while their maturity, frustration tolerance, and motivation are not radically put to the test" and "the psychological situation of the group is not optimal because of the difference in information on the one hand, and the difference in risk on the other, and the potential team leader again primarily plays the role of instructor." (BAK 1970, p. 25, translated). The actual student projects are very risky for an instructor.

34.4   Conclusion and Outlook

In summary, inquiry-based learning means *independent* project work with an unlimited, or at least a high risk of errors and detours, which is why the intensive, academic support of professors and lecturers as learning consultants or mentors is necessary: an individual with extensive teaching and research responsibilities can scarcely manage this. On the other hand, there were signs that were "much more distressing than encouraging" (BAK 1970), with regard both to the students – their indifference, unreliability, lack of consistency, and low demands – and to the academic tutors, who are regarded as indispensable for inquiry-based learning, but whose cooperation can only be secured through payment: additional challenges that still apply today.

Real third-party funded projects can be used as a starting point for independent student projects in order to reinforce the practical integration of students in research processes, scholarship, and knowledge management. Research or genetic learning can be carried out through student projects with real implications, but this presents a huge challenge in terms of effort and time for all involved, both learners and instructors. Inquiry-based learning and genetic learning both require the instructor to develop a clear didactic concept, organize the students into small groups, and provide multimedia materials, all in advance. The official subdivision of the students into small groups ties up additional capacity and often fails, owing to the curricular nature of a degree program. Instructors receive no credits for unofficial subdivisions.

The success story of the universities of applied sciences in Germany is qualified by the dilemma of their professors: if they take the demand for the unity of research and teaching seriously, then they need to be active and innovative in both areas at the same time. As a general rule, professors at universities of applied sciences only have access to non-professorial academic teaching staff and no academic support. Moreover, they are often restricted to a research team financed by third-party-funded projects that has no teaching function. Similarly, professional, outward-oriented, and internationally recognized research with prestigious scientific publications is mostly only possible through third-party funding. This is laborious and exhausting: national, EU-wide, or international project applications must be written, calculated, and submitted on time. Authorization is not guaranteed. In addition, the current funding rate for BMBF development programs, for example, is perhaps only 5 percent to a maximum of 15 percent. The projects approved after a month-long assessment (sometimes more than a year) are not easy to manage with what are usually scarce human resources. Voluntary support for ensuring the unity of research and teaching in the sense of exploratory or genetic learning currently involves self-exploitation in many cases. Moreover, the academic staff in third-party-funded projects regularly make use of the possibility of a cumulative dissertation – i.e. obtaining a doctoral degree by having pieces published in a variety of prestigious journals – and this is also often done outside paid working hours.

Challenges in the future will be determined by considering past experience: inquiry-based learning must be explicitly included in the module descriptions at the universities of applied sciences. Important requirements remain: there should be a significant reduction in the high teaching load at universities of applied sciences; consideration should be given to the idea of working in smaller groups; the time-consuming nature of inquiry-based learning should be recognized in the curriculum through sufficient semester hours per week (SWS) and ECTS, as well as the introduction of non-professorial academic teaching staff at universities of applied sciences. The integration of research and learning at the universities of applied sciences thus requires structural support from policymakers, which will involve extra funding, and from the universities of applied sciences themselves, which must develop a research infrastructure and culture. In addition, the right to award doctorates, which these institutions have hitherto been denied, would provide important impetus for ensuring future-oriented research and the unity of this research with teaching.

References

Brandenburgische Landeskommission für Fachhochschulen (BBLF) (ed.). (1993). *Fachhochschulen im Land Brandenburg. Empfehlungen* (2nd edn.). Brandenburger Schriften zu Wissenschaft und Forschung – vol. 2. Berlin: Verlag für Berlin-Brandenburg GmbH.

Bundesassistentenkonferenz (BAK) (1970). *Forschendes Lernen – Wissenschaftliches Prüfen: Schriften der BAK* (5th repr., new edn. 2009). Bielefeld: UniversitätsVerlagWebler.

Hannemann, K. (2012). Mit innovativer Lehre die beruflichen Herausforderungen von morgen meistern. In D. Lück-Schneider/D. Kirstein (eds.), *Gute Lehre und Forschung trotz schwieriger Rahmenbedingungen: Neue Strategien und Instrumente; Redebeiträge und Thesen des 23. Glienicker Gesprächs* (pp. 41–47). Beiträge aus dem Fachbereich Allgemeine Verwaltung (Contributions from the Department of General Administration) 14/2012. Berlin: Hochschule für Wirtschaft und Recht Berlin.

InterKomp KMU 2.0 (2013). InterKomp KMU 2.0. Retrieved 28 September 2014 from http://kmu-interkomp20.th-wildau.de/

Mandl, H./Reinmann-Rothmeier, G. (1998). Auf dem Weg zu einer neuen Kultur des Lehrens und Lernens. In G. Dörr/K. L. Jüngst (eds.), *Lernen mit Medien: Ergebnisse und Perspektiven zu medial vermittelten Lehr-Lernprozessen* (pp. 193–205). Weinheim: Juventa.

Scholl, H. J./Eisenberg, M. (2011). The TEDS framework for assessing information systems from a human actors' perspective: Extending and repurposing Taylor's Value-Added Model. *Journal of the American Society for Information Science and Technology* 64(4), pp. 789–804.

Scholl, M. (ed.). (2013). *Internationales IT-gestütztes Projekt- und Wissensmanagement im multikulturellen Umfeld: Abschlussbericht des BMBF-Projekts "InterKomp KMU 2.0"*. Aachen: Shaker.

Scholl, M. (2014). User Experience as a Personalized Evaluation of an Online Information System. In M. F. W. H. A. Janssen, F. Bannister, O. Glassey, H. J. Scholl, E. Tambouris, M. A. Wimmer/A. Macintosh (eds.), *Ebook: Electronic Government and Electronic Participation* (pp. 287–96). Amsterdam: IOS Press.

Scholl, M. (2015). An Implementation of User-Experience-Based Evaluation to Achieve Transparency in the Usage and Design of Information Artifacts. In T. X. Bui/R. H. Sprague

Jr. (eds.), *Proceedings of the 2015 48th Hawaii International Conference on System Sciences (HICSS)* (pp. 21–32). Kauai, Hawaii, USA: Conference Publishing Services (CPS).

Scholl, M./Ehrlich, E./Wiesner-Steiner, A./Edich, D. (2014). The Project TEDS@wildau. *47th Hawaii International Conference on System Science, Proceedings* (pp. 1935–45). Hawaii: IEEE.

Wiesner-Steiner, A./Scholl, M./Ehrlich, P. (2014). Prozesstransparenz, Nachvollziehbarkeit und nutzerorientierte Akzeptanzsicherung in (Verwaltungs-)Netzwerken. In E. Schweighofer, F. Kummer/W. Hötzendorfer (eds.), *Transparenz: Tagungsband des 17. Internationalen Rechtsinformatik Symposions (IRIS)* (pp. 171–78). Vienna: Österreichische Computer Gesellschaft & Erich Schweighofer.

Inquiry-Based Learning with Digital Media

35

Sandra Hofhues

35.1 Inquiry-Based Learning with Digital Media: More Questions Than Answers

How can academic teaching and learning be shaped in conformity with recent reforms in higher education and education policy? What role could digital media play in implementing research-oriented concepts? If you ask yourself questions like these, you will quickly find a wide range of existing concepts and approaches in institutions of higher learning and grapple with a vast number of scholarly and practice-oriented publications in Europe and the U.S. (Hillen and Landis 2014). The current challenges range from adequate spatial or technical infrastructure, e.g., the open accessibility of information and knowledge in libraries to the individual critical handling of technological developments, to name but a few. These challenges are more likely to arise due to a more open and largely problem-oriented form of teaching, and are not necessarily related to the use of digital media. How, for example, do students manage to pursue their own (research) questions during their studies and throughout their studies? Are there any new opportunities for implementing research-oriented teaching or inquiry-based learning through the use of digital media?

The present article therefore takes up the difficult task of systematizing the discussions in such a way that they are of scholarly and practical value. The use of digital media is without a doubt an essential development that has occurred in the last two decades, confronting higher education institutions with new and unprecedented challenges, regardless of whether they are engaged in inquiry-based learning and teaching or not. In the German-language discourse, two developments are central to an integrative understanding, the

S. Hofhues, Jun.-Prof. Dr. (✉)
Universität Köln, Institut für Allgemeine Didaktik und Schulforschung, Professur für Mediendidaktik/Medienpädagogik, Köln, Germany
e-mail: sandra.hofhues@uni-koeln.de

© The Author(s) 2019
H. A. Mieg (ed.), *Inquiry-Based Learning – Undergraduate Research*,
https://doi.org/10.1007/978-3-030-14223-0_35

latter being more the focus of this text: To begin with, federal and educational developmental programs succeeded in politically placing inquiry-based learning on the agenda again (e.g., Huber 2014; Reinmann 2015b) and in systematically (re)implementing it in institutions of higher learning. Secondly, many of the ideas and concepts being pursued aim at the parallel use of media, which is why there is an increasing conceptual merging of inquiry-based learning and technology-enhanced learning (TEL), understood as inquiry-based learning using digital media. At all stages of the (empirical) research process, digital media therefore serve the purpose of helping to achieve the learning objectives and in developing problem-solving strategies or extensive scientific skills, in addition to specialist knowledge. While tools are often initially introduced by faculty, it is likely that students will come back to these tools on their own as their knowledge and experience increase, or that faculty will make other, more complex tools available. What appears to be a logical consequence of the practical justification is slowly becoming interconnected in the related scholarly communities: thus the discourses on inquiry-based learning at the university are mainly conducted in academic teaching and learning, organized in Germany by the German Society for Academic Teaching and Learning (Deutsche Gesellschaft für Hochschuldidaktik). Questions as to the *appropriate* use of media tend to instead focus on representatives of information technology or technology-enhanced learning, which are usually established in the Society for Information Technology (Gesellschaft für Informatik, e-learning specialist group) or in the Society for Media in Science (Gesellschaft für Medien in der Wissenschaft, GMW).

35.2 Appropriate Media Use: Views on Technology-Enhanced Learning

In a TEL view, media are understood to be digital tools that support teaching and learning. These may be digital resources that are provided for learning, but they may also help improve communication and collaboration in courses (cf. Hillen and Landis 2014). Within specific subject cultures, as witnessed in the social sciences, digital media also support the collection and evaluation of data, or are the subject of theoretical engagement (e.g. Dürnberger 2014, p. 248 et seq.). Thus, almost every subject culture would be allowed to develop its own media usage strategy. In TEL, however, despite the everyday practices of its researchers, the departmental media strategy did not place value on assessing either the amount of media used or whether it was even used. Instead, the importance of media in attaining these practices is considered to be based on the learning objective of the course. Accordingly, the "education problem" (Kerres 2012, p. 276) will first be clarified before the use of media is specified. Thus, the planning of the course is somewhat decoupled from the respective technological development (Schulmeister 2007, p. 393). Before the *actual* use of media can be clarified, the learning objectives of a course must be determined. Modules and curricula provide a basic orientation for the context of higher education. The personal attitude of the instructors is also crucial in determining how learning ultimately can *and* should be achieved using media.

An important insight concerns the use of media by students themselves: Today's instructors must assume that in addition to the media offerings formally planned for the course, additional tools will be used by the students. These are used to allow students to organize themselves, to share and/or collaborate (e.g. self-initiated student groups on Facebook, instant messenger services such as WhatsApp, or pictures on Instagram). Such *modified, highly individual usage habits* can be found in all current media usage studies and can be determined independently of the respective subject cultures. What is difficult and what must be accepted is the following: It can be difficult to plan a course with them, because they are informal in nature (Hofhues 2016).

The organization within which the courses are offered has an indirect impact on the way media are used. Thus most universities and higher education institutions in the German-speaking world rely on classroom teaching, i.e. on the regular, personal transfer of knowledge on-site. The courses should, at best, be *enriched* with digital media. Such courses are referred to as "blended learning" (see Box 35.1) because they combine learning in the classroom and learning online. At the same time, along with distance-learning, online or open universities, there are also other types of higher education institutions that interpret higher education instruction differently, and sometimes more "medially" for specific target groups. It is likely that digital media will cover the entire spectrum of the transfer of knowledge, from communication of knowledge to collaboration and shared reflection.

Box 35.1: Blended Learning

One keyword repeatedly used in the context of technology-enhanced learning is "blended learning." The literal meaning of the word is "mixed" learning: In blended learning, classroom teaching – i.e. teaching components that are offered on-site at the educational institution – is mixed with those parts of the teaching that take place outside of class. For the sake of simplicity, it is common to differentiate by percentage which teaching content is presented in active class attendance, and which is presented online, e.g. a typical teaching format might involve completing tasks online, but first preparing and discussion the tasks during a face-to-face lesson. The online portion in such a blended learning format should amount to approximately 10–20%. If the "silver bullet" of inquiry-based learning as proposed by Huber (2009, 2014) is implemented and supported by a digital journal (e-portfolio), the online portion could increase to 50% or more. Learning would take place entirely online when both the communication of the contents and the processing of tasks, (peer) feedback and exams etc. are conducted online, as would occur at online universities based in the United States or as is the case in Massive Open Online Courses (MOOCs).

If knowledge acquisition outside of class attendance is to be promoted, it is currently likely that a learning management system (LMS) will be used. Ultimately, an LMS is a digital platform that serves to organize courses, and is also used as an information resource for instructors. For example, PDFs and links can be posted or other learning materials made available. An LMS could also be used to support the social exchange between students and instructors or to facilitate the collaboration of peers in forums or groups. This would then happen in an online classroom setting, fully excluding the public. Instructors could just as easily use openly accessible media if, for example, the scientific community is to be included in the course as providers of feedback. Social networks such as Facebook, blogs or communication services such as Twitter are used for such purposes. Individual or group reflections can also be triggered by means of digital media, e.g. with e-portfolios, which have taken up the portfolio method of collection and visualization of learning processes as a tool. The latter are mainly implemented for university-level degree programs that have a high practical portion, and where theory-practice transfer should be supported. These include not only dual degree programs, but also teaching certification (for an overview, see Meyer et al. 2011; Miller and Volk 2013). What all examples have in common is that the tools used ultimately refer to the learning objectives pursued in the courses. It is only with the inclusion of the learning objectives (see above) that it becomes possible to plan the use of media precisely for the purposes pursued (provision of resources, peer feedback, etc.).

35.3   Technology-Enhanced Learning in Higher Education Institutions: A Design Triangle

From one point of view, Reinmann (2015a) states that instructional design *should* constantly include media. On the one hand, this has always happened, for example by using blackboards or projectors. On the other, this view is new because the integration of digital media in the 2000s in particular has suggested special treatment. It is therefore best to use a design triangle for the concrete planning of the course and to ask the following against the background of the respective learning objectives:

- To what extent does the use of media serve to *impart* teaching content?
- To what extent does it support the *empowerment* of students – in other words, how much do they enjoy participating in class and how motivated is this participation?
- And how can students be *supervised* with/via digital media?

It is a widespread fallacy that media use per se would involve students more in their learning processes in the sense of the often described *shift from teaching to learning*, or that it would even enable inquiry-based learning. Recent developments in virtual identities, mobile applications (apps) or response systems (mobile audience or classroom response systems, better known as clickers) in teaching tend to follow simple attestations and thus a model of *drill and practice*. The crux of the matter: media-based tests or click-ers are very popular in subjects related to the natural sciences because they help to test specialist knowledge with appropriate brevity, and because they *supposedly* break up fron-tally organized (mass) courses with smaller interactions. In this context, Mayrberger (2012) would speak of a pseudo-participation of students in their learning processes. It is therefore all the more important to use a research orientation as a general setting for teach-ing, which ultimately provides both students and instructors with the framework within which they *can* learn, teach and become researchers.

35.4 The Relation of Inquiry-Based Learning and Digital Media: Digital Turns in Academic Teaching and Learning

How can inquiry-based learning be realized? What added value does the potential use of media generate? Examples of the implementation of inquiry-based learning in practice are as varied as those known for the use of media for study and teaching (see above). In the widely adopted writings of Huber (2009) and Wildt (2013), references are made to learn-ing throughout the first degree course ("student lifecycle"), questions are raised about the transition from school to college, and from college to work, or ambiguity in terms of the student lifecycle in terms of the use or (public) presentation of student research results among colleagues is discussed.

When it comes to students *pursuing their research questions themselves*, it is likely that digital media can (or do) serve all of the purposes outlined above. These are needed at vari-ous stages of the research process in order to specify research questions, to process these questions and, ultimately, to answer them. If inquiry-based learning is understood not as an individual, but as a shared cognitive process and interpreted collaboratively, digital media often function as communication device for (substantive) collaboration and the creation of teamwork, for the interaction between learners and instructors, and for the interaction between peers. In addition, media can become its own research domain and students can create related research questions that become possible only with the advent of digital media (e.g. research via the Internet) or methodically (e.g. big data). They also offer insights into "research workshops" ("Werkstätten des Forschens", Anastasiadis 2015, p. 260) away from physical classrooms (e.g. virtual laboratories, cf. Vogel and Woitsch 2013). If more receptive learning in the sense of an *engagement with research results* is addressed, it is clear that, according to this perspective, digital media are primar-ily needed as an information resource and, if necessary, are used to evaluate the informa-tion (for example via comment functions). The boundaries between receptive and productive inquiry-based learning are already fluid in these examples, however: Commenting or mutual, media- or technology-based questioning of content is stimulating, and both could be precursors for own research questions, which in turn are also recorded with media (e.g. in wikis). Other tools that are typical for the subject can also be used

(SPSS in social sciences, for example). This applies when data is repeatedly evaluated for practice purposes, and an exchange occurs.

Especially in the case of inquiry-based learning, it is no longer clear whether the use of media merely supports research-oriented teaching, or simply facilitates "research *as learning*" (Dürnberger 2014, p. 254, emphasis in original). What was once merely technical media would, from this perspective, become more of a space for communication, action and even experience (Hofhues et al. 2014). Accordingly, in the future, it would be possible to ask more about the possibilities of student appropriation of *their* (educational) spaces *for* research, and less about whether and with what digital media research is being conducted. The fact that digital media are part of these educational spaces is already a matter of course. At the same time, however, any (learning) locations with their specific infrastructure would become relevant, and these would be taken over by students in research practices.

35.5 Inquiry-Based Learning with Digital Media: Conclusions and (Basic) Conditions

It is probably the different traditions in higher education and technology-enhanced learning (TEL) that continue to make TEL and inquiry-based learning almost exclusively separate in institutions of higher education. It certainly pays to bring design approaches together conceptually, especially if one understands this overview as an attempt to integrate media into academic teaching and learning. The article primarily clarifies the premises under which digital media are generally important in teaching and learning. The TEL perspective was changed in favor of a higher education perspective, and it was assumed that different ways of using digital media are created depending on the type of game of inquiry-based learning. *But what are the challenges if inquiry-based learning and media-based learning actually combine two forms of learning?*

As striking as it may sound, the first answer to the last open question is just this simple: If one wishes to implement inquiry-based learning and media-based learning at the same time, it is important that two *challenging concepts* be planned and implemented in tandem. Dürnberger (2014, p. 261) points out with regard to inquiry-based learning with digital media that the simultaneity of technology-enhanced and research-based concepts can also overwhelm students. Taken in isolation, each of these forms of learning already places high demands on learners, who could also express themselves with frustration (ibid.). It can hardly be denied that instructors as well as students are called upon to combine two forms of learning: inquiry-based learning with TEL. It is more important for instructors and students to deal explicitly with uncertainties, vagueness, boundaries or disruptions to teaching and learning, and to make these an educational opportunity for both students and instructors. Also, the *educational spaces* that result from the interplay of the forms of learning are both diverse and stimulating, as well as fragile and uncertain in their outcomes (cf. Murtonen et al. 2017): Conceptually, inquiry-based learning always brings with it the possibility of non-success (failure), without having addressed or even dealt with specific challenges of using or dealing with digital media. Instructors and peers who help "[to] teach and [to] learn the adventure of research" within the learning process thereby become all the more important (Anastasiadis 2015). Like TEL, inquiry-based learning therefore relies on mutual commitment and responsibility.

A research orientation should therefore also be regarded as a *university-wide strategy* related to academic study and teaching, which is relevant for any media use of universities and institutions of higher learning. This would counteract skeptics, for example, who sometimes suspect an end unto itself behind the use of media, and who do not see its service to research (Oelkers 2015, p. 78). *Consistently* research-oriented study programs would focus on (time) periods for student research that are often not provided for in current curricula (Hofhues et al. 2014).

References

Anastasiadis, M. (2015). Abenteuer Forschung lehren und Lernen. In R. Egger/ C. Wustmann/A. Karber (Hrsg.), *Forschungsgeleitete Lehre in einem Massenstudium* (S. 257–276). Wiesbaden: Springer.

Dürnberger, H. (2014). *Forschendes Lernen unter Einsatz digitaler Medien beim Verfassen der Bachelorarbeit – Potenziale für die Schlüsselkompetenzentwicklung* [Dissertationsschrift]. Augsburg: Universität Augsburg.

Hillen, S. A./Landis, M. (2014). Two Perspectives on E-Learning Design: A Synopsis of a U. S. and a European Analysis. *IRRODL – The International Review of Research in Open and Distance Learning. 4*(15), 199–225.

Hofhues, S. (2016). Informelles Lernen mit digitalen Medien in der Hochschule. In M. Rohs (Hrsg.), *Handbuch Informelles Lernen* (S. 529–546). Heidelberg: Springer VS.

Hofhues, S./Reinmann, G./Schiefner-Rohs, M. (2014). Lernen und Medienhandeln im Format der Forschung. In O. Zawacki-Richter/D. Kergel/N. Kleinefeld/P. Muckel/J. Stöter/K. Brinkmann (Hrsg.), *Teaching Trends 14. Offen für neue Wege: Digitale Medien in der Hochschule* (S. 19–36). Münster: Waxmann.

Huber, L. (2009). Warum Forschendes Lernen nötig und möglich ist. In L. Huber/J. Hellmer/F. Schneider (Hrsg.), *Forschendes Lernen im Studium. Aktuelle Konzepte und Erfahrungen* (S. 9–35). Bielefeld: UniversitätsVerlagWebler.

Huber, L. (2014). Forschungsbasiertes, Forschungsorientiertes, Forschendes Lernen: Alles dasselbe? Ein Plädoyer für eine Verständigung über Begriffe und Unterscheidungen im Feld forschungsnahen Lehrens und Lernens. *Das Hochschulwesen, 1+2*, 32–39.

Kerres, M. (2012). *Mediendidaktik. Konzeption und Entwicklung mediengestützter Lernangebote. 3.* Auflage. München: Oldenbourg.

Mayrberger, K. (2012). Partizipatives Lernen mit dem Social Web gestalten: Zum Widerspruch einer »verordneten Partizipation«. *Medienpädagogik.* 21. Retrieved 05 August 2015 from http://www.medienpaed.com/Documents/medienpaed/21/mayrberger1201.pdf

Meyer, T./Mayrberger, K./Münte-Goussar, S./Schwalbe, C. (Hrsg.). (2011). *Kontrolle und Selbstkontrolle. Zur Ambivalenz von E-Portfolios in Bildungsprozessen.* Reihe Medienbildung und Gesellschaft (Band 19). Wiesbaden: VS.

Miller, D./Volk, B. (Hrsg.). (2013). *E-Portfolio an der Schnittstelle von Studium und Beruf.* Reihe Medien in der Wissenschaft (Band 63) (S. 105–132). Münster: Waxmann.

Murtonen, M./Gruber, H./Lehtinena, E. (2017). The return of behaviourist epistemology: A review of learning outcomes studies. *Educational Research Review*, *22*, 114–128. https://doi.org/10.1016/j.edurev.2017.08.001

Oelkers, J. (2015). Digitale Medien und die Entwicklung der akademischen Lehre. In D. Miller (Hrsg.), *Gerüstet fürs Studium. Lernstrategien und digitale Medien* (S. 67–78). Bern: h.e.p.

Reinmann, G. (2015a). *Studientext Didaktisches Design*. Hamburg: Universität Hamburg.

Reinmann, G. (2015b). Forschungs- und Berufsorientierung in der Lehre aus hochschuldidaktischer Sicht. In P. Tremp (Hrsg.), *Forschungsorientierung und Berufsbezug im Studium* (Blickpunkt Hochschuldidaktik) (S. 41–61). Bielefeld: Bertelsmann.

Schulmeister, R. (2007). *Grundlagen hypermedialer Lernsysteme. Theorie – Didaktik – Design*. München: Oldenbourg.

Vogel, B./Woitsch, A. (2013). *Orte des Selbststudiums*. HIS Forum Hochschule 7/2013. Hannover: HIS-Hochschul-Informations-System GmbH. Retrieved 05 August 2015 from http://www.dzhw.eu/pdf/pub_fh/fh-201307.pdf

Wildt, J. (2013). Entwicklung und Potenzial der Hochschuldidaktik. In M. Heiner/J. Wildt (Hrsg.), *Professionalisierung der Lehre. Perspektiven formeller und informeller Entwicklung von Lehrkompetenz im Kontext der Hochschulbildung* (S. 27–57). Bielefeld: Bertelsmann.

Inquiry-Based Learning and Heterogeneity 36

Ayla Satilmis

In the course of educational expansion, not only has the total number of students increased, but also their composition has changed: In quantitative terms, more and more people are gaining access to higher education – currently 46% of people born in a given year, as compared to just 5% in the mid-1950s. In terms of socio-structural dimensions, it is possible to say that today, more than ever, people from non-academic families are studying, as are people who already have professional experience and/or have no conventional university entrance qualification. In addition, students are more likely to be gainfully employed or have children or other care responsibilities. A health impairment is likewise no longer a barrier to study in and of itself. In short: Within a relatively short period of time, there has been a profound change in the higher education landscape, with the keyword "heterogeneity" pointing to the fact that the life contexts and educational biographies of students are currently more diverse than was previously the case.

The German Science Council (Wissenschaftsrat) has made reference to the changes and, in its 2008 recommendations on improving the quality of teaching and studying, pointed out that "the diverse requirements of a heterogeneously assembled student body [should] be better taken into account" (Wissenschaftsrat 2008, p. 53, translated). And in 2015, that same Council stressed: The "high numbers and the resulting increased heterogeneity among the students are fundamentally confronting the higher education system with new challenges regarding the organization, design and orientation of the courses offered" (Wissenschaftsrat 2015, p. 14, translated). The German Rectors' Conference (Hochschulrektorenkonferenz) has also addressed the issues of diversity and permeability within the context of the project "nexus – Concepts and Good Practice for Academic

A. Satilmis (✉)
Universität Bremen, Fachbereich Kulturwissenschaften, Projekt "enter science",
Bremen, Germany
e-mail: satilmis@uni-bremen.de

© The Author(s) 2019
H. A. Mieg (ed.), *Inquiry-Based Learning – Undergraduate Research*,
https://doi.org/10.1007/978-3-030-14223-0_36

Education," and has confirmed its relevance in the field of science (HRK 2013). Against this background, the question explored below will be: to what extent is inquiry-based learning suitable for heterogeneity-sensitive and inequality-relevant teaching-learning concept that fulfills the current requirements for the design of teaching?

36.1   Study-Relevant Dimensions of Heterogeneity

Although the question of heterogeneity in school and educational policy debates has been on the agenda since the late 1960s, especially in connection with opportunities (inequality), it has only attracted attention in higher education policy since the turn of the millennium (cf. Webler 2013). The current university-based debate on heterogeneity focuses in particular on changes in the student body and largely ignores the question of the diversity of young academics or the diversity of instructors, despite the fact that these aspects are at least as important in terms of scholarship and higher education policy. It is also striking that the topic of heterogeneity in higher education is treated "primarily in a *performance-related* and *problematizing* manner" (Wild and Esdar 2014, p. 22, translated; emphasis in original) and tends to be cast as negative. On top of that, the recognition of heterogeneity in university discourse often refers to social or ancestral attributions, and accentuates differences between students, for example those with a migrant background or without, from academic families or educational distance, etc.

As a rule, those who do not belong to the student majority due to their social background, or who do not correspond to the expectations of normalcy in academic life in terms of socio-cultural resources are usually marked as heterogeneous. In doing so, it is possible to find more heterogeneous dimensions that are relevant to the course of study and, in principle, address all students. A distinction can be made between at least three dimensions that outline study-relevant heterogeneity (Fig. 36.1):

- On the one hand, it is students' life situations and contexts as *structural* factors that influence student life and highlight opportunities in a course of study. These include (educational) biographical and basic socio-economic conditions that shape the course of studies and influence how the study requirements can be met, for example.
- On the other hand, study-relevant heterogeneity represents diversity of learning types with regard to *action or competence-related* aspects. These include learning experiences, as well as the way of acquiring knowledge, self-organization and problem-solving as cognitive skills.
- Moreover, there are *personality-related* dimensions of study-relevant heterogeneity, which are expressed in the choice of topic and the nature of the problem description, for example. Methodical preferences and the chosen subject combination are also included herewith.

Here, the paradigmatic dimensions of heterogeneity are of course not distinct. Sometimes they mesh, but they do not require one another. Taken in isolation, they are not

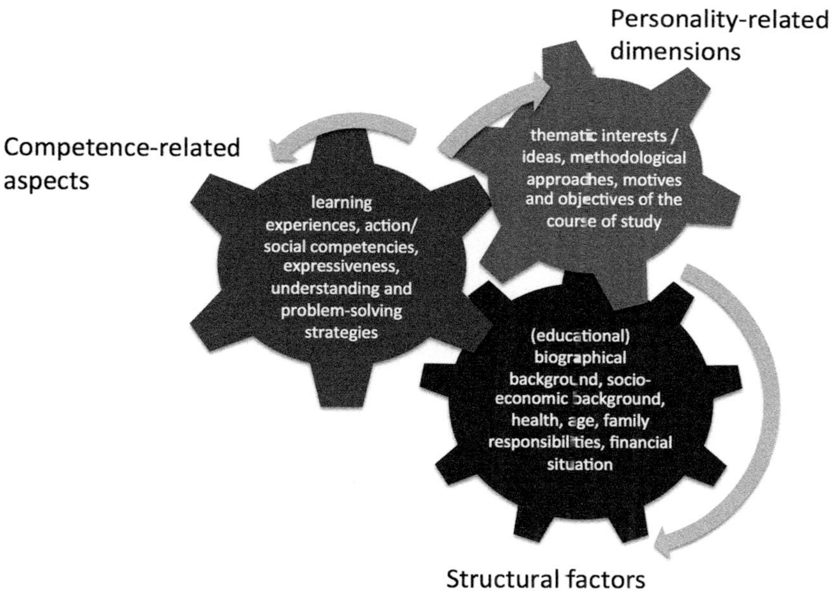

Fig. 36.1 Study-relevant dimensions of heterogeneity. (Source: author's representation)

very meaningful in terms of their impact on whether a course of study is successful. It is only in the overview of different study-relevant dimensions of heterogeneity and in the reconciliation with the requirements of the university and the relevant discipline that points of reference can be identified that favor or impede progress in the course of studies. Finally, the outlined categories of difference point to an immense variance in student profiles that teachers encounter in practice, and which they should recognize when designing teaching programs.

36.2   Convergence Between Inquiry-Based Learning and Heterogeneity

The expert report for a heterogeneity-oriented teaching-learning culture, recently drafted on behalf of the German Rector's Conference (Hochschulrektorenkonferenz), points to the enormous effort required from various institutions, and also emphasizes that higher education policy negotiations are necessary "with regard to understanding quality, heterogeneity and (distributive justice)" (Wild and Esdar 2014, p. 79, translated). This report concretely refers to inquiry-based learning and states that "these forms of indirect instruction place high demands on the [...] competence of instructors" (ibid., p. 50). As is further argued with regard to the students, action-oriented teaching-learning settings are "only effective [...] if learners had the necessary (technical, scientific-propaedeutic, cooperative, self-regulatory, etc.) abilities." Instructors who refer to inquiry-based learning are not considered "activators" in the report, but are explicitly considered "facilitators" in the sense of learning accompaniment (ibid., p. 48), although inquiry-based learning is commonly considered an empowering teaching method. On the other hand, good, heterogeneous teaching requires "strong structure, clear leadership, a cognitive framework and many short-term aids" (ibid., p. 84). In this respect, it could be concluded from the expert opinion that the open format of inquiry-based learning is not suitable for a heterogeneous body of students.

In contrast, we intend to subsequently show why inquiry-based learning is a tried and tested heterogeneity-sensitive teaching-learning concept, which, as an extremely student-oriented format, is able to conceptually and constructively address the diversity of students, and also addresses inequality-relevant dimensions within the university context. Formulated as a thesis: *Inquiry-based learning accounts for (1), includes (2) and fosters (3) heterogeneity* (see Fig. 36.2).

36.2.1 Inquiry-Based Learning Accounts for Heterogeneity

Provided that differences and inequalities within students are perceived and recognized, inquiry-based learning conceptually accommodates diversity in students' starting situations and interests. This is because inquiry-based learning takes heterogeneity into consideration by offering creative space and addressing various learning and skills development processes that are based on the skills and needs of the students. It is characterized by teaching-learning settings that aim to involve as many students as possible in a process of (relatively self-guided) learning and research. Despite the students' varying resources, learning styles, motivations and skills, inquiry-based learning offers them options to

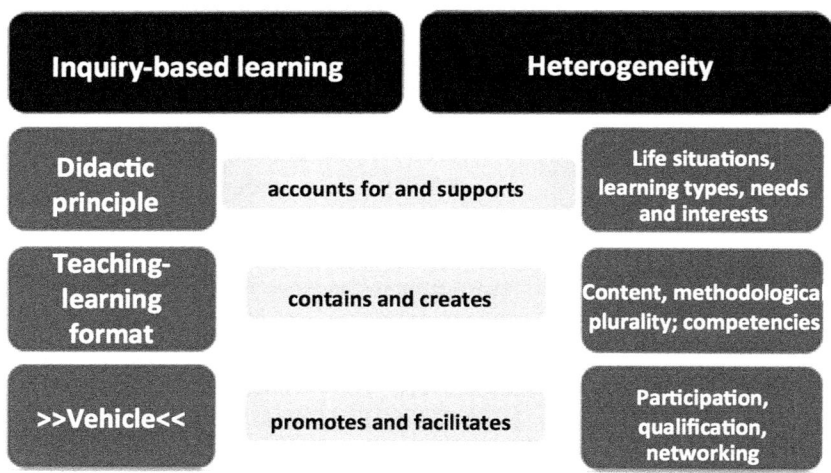

Fig. 36.2 Interplay of inquiry-based learning and heterogeneity. (Source: author's representation)

engage with their respective potential and resources, and supports them in developing their knowledge and abilities.

Although it is difficult to sufficiently take into account individual situations or problems, especially in large courses, inquiry-based learning as a didactic principle essentially allows and requires a student-oriented attitude. After all, good teaching is also characterized by flexible (not to be equated with individualized!) teaching-learning arrangements. The openness of the concept offers many possibilities for variation in practice, as long as the instructors themselves are open to this and provide a helping orientation framework (cf. Huber 2009). Nevertheless, and this should not be ignored here, the openness of the format simultaneously poses a difficulty, and requires both didactic and social design competencies on the part of the instructors. In order to facilitate multi-layered and lively learning, it is necessary to clarify any issues regarding fit, for example in terms of time resources for the teaching-learning process, but it is also necessary to clarify learning objectives and examination arrangements with the students at an early stage. This is not only important and profitable for the students, but also for the instructors: In this way, they gain insights into the unequal (initial) conditions of the students and structural imbalances that can be fed back into the upcoming learning activities and interwoven as a reflective practice in the teaching-learning process.

36.2.2 Inquiry-Based Learning Includes Heterogeneity

Just as inquiry-based learning considers and supports heterogeneous preconditions, interests or competencies, diversity is conversely relevant for inquiry-based learning: This is because the concept is based on the heterogeneity of science and research, and thus on the diversity of disciplines, methods and theories. "Epistemic diversity in research – the diversity of themes, objects, problems and approaches to problem solving" (Gläser 2014, p. 163, translated) is to some extent constitutive for inquiry-based learning. The diversity of forms and elements characteristic of the idea and practice of inquiry-based learning involves and generates a variety of perspectives and methods. As a teaching-learning approach, it is therefore predestined for interdisciplinary work and is suitable for mixed subject and competence teams, which thus open up synergies and advance the pluralization of knowledge. In addition, the forms of learning, research questions and approaches are characterized by the different ideas and problem descriptions of the students, i.e. their heterogeneity is an integral part of this concept.

In the case of inquiry-based learning, the interaction between instructors and learners differs of other teaching-learning formats primarily in the fact that processes of knowledge generation are designed to be as cooperative as possible (Special) knowledge is not taught to the students head-on and hierarchically as certainties or completed knowledge; instead, the participants embark together on a process of exploration and knowledge production. And if the subject area permits, diversity or heterogeneity can also be the subject of teaching and research (see Kaufmann, in this volume).

As knowledge and research practice that is newly constituted again and again (both in terms of topics and personnel), inquiry-based learning benefits from the diversity of students and their approaches to content and methodology. And moreover: inquiry-based learning takes into consideration diverse levels of knowledge and coping patterns, thus building on heterogeneity. However, this is associated with the challenge of getting involved in the research teaching-learning process (also as an instructor), of reflecting on practical routines, and of not excluding, ex ante, innovative but poorly tested approaches.

36.2.3 Inquiry-Based Learning Fosters Heterogeneity

So far, little attention has been paid to the fact that inquiry-based learning can also promote (institutional) heterogeneity and contribute to the diversification of academic life. This aspect is important because the higher education system at all levels is characterized by a high degree of social selection: Institutional mechanisms of exclusion are not only in play in terms of access to and completing a course of study, but social disadvantages are also brought to bear in the area of young researchers; overall, the chances of participation in the academic system are unevenly distributed (for example, Wolter 2011; Heitzmann and Klein 2012). Inquiry-based learning addresses these difficulties by encouraging and prompting *all* students to take part in research activities.

Detached from implicit notions of normality and competence expectations, exploratory learning grants equal opportunity to all students and assumes responsibility for taking on the knowledge generation process. In so doing, the research activities selected by the students can be carried out autonomously or "docked" onto existing research networks. Through active participation and the implementation of a small subproject within a larger research network, students can be professionally and socially involved and networked with the "scientific community." They can deal with subject-specific topics and methods, practice project management and thus (continue to) gain qualifications – all in a manner that is separate from the pressure to succeed. In this respect, inquiry-based learning can be regarded as a mode that supports students in their entry into research practice and the research community, thus expanding their opportunities to participate in the field of science. Inquiry-based learning can be used to bridge the gap between students and scientists or research facilities that foster the diversity of subject-related and academic identity processes of students. On the other hand, this contact allows the research facilities to generate up-and-coming scientists, and they gain insights into students' needs and issues (in detail, Satilmis 2013; Kaufmann and Satilmis 2015). All in all, this opens up opportunities to look at structural inequalities without hypostasizing them.

36.2.4 Interim Summary

Taking stock, it can be said that inquiry-based learning is a (didactic) path that accommodates and benefits from the heterogeneity of the students. At the same time, heterogeneity is conceptually important for inquiry-based learning, because the teaching-learning concept is based on multiperspectivity. Following on from the thesis formulated at the outset, which emphasizes the added value of inquiry-based learning in dealing with heterogeneity, it is now possible to add the following: *Heterogeneity provides a fertile basis for inquiry-based learning.*

Within the context of heterogeneity, one important aspect of inquiry-based learning lies in the fact that "non-traditional" students do not experience any deficient attributions in this teaching-learning approach, and that unconventional perspectives of cooperative scientific practice are also given space in which to develop. Finally, the idea of inquiry-based learning refers to an understanding of education that embraces the notion of social equality and "[includes] the obligation to create the social conditions to ensure the participation of all citizens" (Euler 2005, p. 257, translated). Inquiry-based learning allows students and scientists to approach one another reciprocally on research projects and, in particular, can reduce research-related inhibition on the part of students. In this way, prospects open up for the further development of learners and instructors, but also of the institution. In this respect, the teaching-learning format is understood as a "vehicle" for opening up the university socially.

36.3   Outlook: "e n t e r s c i e n c e" – Pluralization of Science Practice by Means of Inquiry-Based Learning

Overall, inquiry-based learning offers variegated starting points for a pluralization of scientific practice. How diversity in teaching and learning is driven forward and opening up academic life can be supported will subsequently be outlined on the basis of measures implemented at the University of Bremen.

At the University of Bremen, inquiry-based learning is understood to be a central profile trait and follows on from a long tradition of project-based studies (the "Bremen model") (cf. Kaufmann & Schelhowe, in this volume). In addition to the claim of a close link between teaching and research, it relies on a conscious commitment to heterogeneity. The pilot measure, "e n t e r s c i e n c e," which has been developing and implementing heterogeneity- and inequality-sensitive teaching-learning courses at the University of Bremen since 2011, must be situated within this context. As an interdisciplinary project, it operates at the interface of teaching, research and the promotion of young researchers in order to increase the participation chances of structurally disadvantaged students in academic life (cf. Satilmis 2013 and 2015).

The intersectional project strategically relies on the inquiry-based learning approach to achieve "scientific bonding" effects and contribute to the reflective extension of the science system. According to the core idea, the mechanisms of "scientific bonding" are effective when students familiarize themselves with academic life from an internal perspective, participate in research networks and experience "empowerment." In addition to transdisciplinary knowledge and methodological skills, these are general competencies in the sense of key qualifications, which are developed in "e n t e r s c i e n c e" and combined with a (self-)reflective practice. On the basis of self-guided learning, students are to gradually be able to grow into the research community, see the conditions and try things out. Finally, social and professional involvement in academic life increases the motivation to study and learn, and experiences of self-efficacy grow (Satilmis 2015). Basically, the quality of academic studies and the prospects for the successful completion thereof improve with early academic participation and support (cf., Merkt 2012, Kreft and Leichsenring 2012, p. 146 et seq.). This may be an explanation for the degree to which the "e n t e r s c i e n c e" courses resonate with students, which is attended by a strong interest on the part of instructors and researchers in the ideas and potential that students bring with them.

Although only a teaching-learning format, the concept of inquiry-based learning radiates far beyond the field of study and teaching: whether as a principle of student orientation, as a method of engagement with diversity, as a tool in dealing with heterogeneity or as a way for institutional pluralization, the added value that inquiry-based learning provides for lively and subject-related teaching, as well as for the equitable further development of the university, is enormous. This is because inquiry-based learning activates mechanisms of participation in science and research and can be excellently combined with university policy strategies for heterogeneous recruitment of junior researchers, but above all, inquiry-based learning in combination with heterogeneity addresses key topics of the education and higher education policy agenda in the sense of transforming institutions of higher learning.

References

Euler, D. (2005). Forschendes Lernen. In S. Spoun/W. Wunderlich (Hrsg.), *Studienziel Persönlichkeit. Beiträge zum Bildungsauftrag der Universität heute.* (S. 253–272). Frankfurt/New York: Campus

Gläser, J. (2014). Die epistemische Diversität der Forschung als theoretisches und politisches Problem. In R. Krempkow/P. Pohlenz/N. Huber (Hrsg.), *Diversity Management und Diversität in der Wissenschaft* (S. 163–184). Bielefeld: UniversitätsverlagWebler.

Heitzmann, D./Klein, U. (2012). Zugangsbarrieren und Exklusionsmechanismen an deutschen Hochschulen. In Dies. (Hrsg.), *Hochschule und Diversity. Theoretische Zugänge und empirische Bestandsaufnahme* (S. 11–45). Weinheim/Basel: Beltz Juventa.

HRK (Hrsg.). (2013). *Chancen erkennen – Vielfalt gestalten. Konzepte und gute Praxis für Diversität und Durchlässigkeit. Bonn.* Retrieved 15 March 2015 from http://www.hrk-nexus.de/fileadmin/redaktion/hrk-nexus/07-Downloads/07-02-Publikationen/nexus-Broschuere-Diversitaet.pdf

Huber, L. (2009). Warum Forschendes Lernen nötig und möglich ist. In L. Huber/J. Hellmer/F. Schneider (Hrsg.), *Forschendes Lernen im Studium* (S. 9–35). Bielefeld: UniversitätsverlagWebler.

Kaufmann, M. E./Satilmis, A. (2015). In-Between Disciplines. Forschendes Lernen als Frame für die Gestaltung transkultureller und -disziplinärer Lernräume. In H. Schelhowe/M. Schaumburg

/J. Jasper (Hrsg.), *Teaching is Touching the Future. Academic Teaching within and across disciplines* (S. 349–352). Bielefeld: UniversitätsverlagWebler.

Kreft, A./Leichsenring, H. (2012). Studienrelevante Diversität in der Lehre. In U. Klein/ D. Heitzmann (Hrsg.), *Hochschule und Diversity. Theoretische Zugänge und empirische Bestandsaufnahme* (S. 145–163). Weinheim/Basel: Beltz Juventa.

Merkt, M. (2012). Wer bestimmt den Studienerfolg? Die Perspektive der Studierenden als Gestaltungskriterium für Studienqualität und Lehrinnovation. In BMBF (Hrsg.), *Tagungsband Bildungsforschung 2020 – Herausforderungen und Perspektiven* (S. 212–222). Berlin: Bundesministerium für Bildung und Forschung.

Satilmis, A. (2013). Forschen im Studium mit enter science! Ein Projekt für Studierende mit Migrationshintergrund. In L. Huber/M. Kröger/H. Schelhowe (Hrsg.), *Forschendes Lernen als Profilmerkmal einer Universität. Beispiele aus der Universität Bremen* (S. 165–177). Bielefeld: UniversitätsverlagWebler.

Satilmis, A. (2015). Lernen und Forschen im Zeichen von Partizipation und Empowerment: enter science. In M. E. Kaufmann/K. Ghaffarizad/F. Hoffmann/F. Suckut (Hrsg.), *Diversity @ Uni Bremen: exzellent und chancengerecht?! Dokumentation* (S. 35–37). Bremen: Universität Bremen.

Webler, W. (2013). Umgang mit steigender Heterogenität bei Studierenden. In F. Gützkow/G. Quaißer (Hrsg.), *Hochschule gestalten – Denkanstöße zum Spannungsfeld von Unterschieden und Ungleichheit* (S. 119–148). Bielefeld: UniversitätsverlagWebler.

Wild, E./Esdar, W. (2014). *Eine heterogenitätsorientierte Lehr–/Lernkultur für eine Hochschule der Zukunft. Fachgutachen im Auftrag des Projekts nexus der Hochschulrektorenkonferenz.* Retrieved 15 March 2015 from http://www.hrk-nexus.de/fileadmin/redaktion/hrk-nexus/07-Downloads/07-02-Publikationen/Fachgutachten_Heterogenitaet.pdf

Wissenschaftsrat (2008). *Empfehlungen zur Qualitätsverbesserung von Lehre und Studium, 04.07.2008, Drs. 8639-08.* Retrieved 15 March 2015 from http://www.wissenschaftsrat.de/download/archiv/8639-08.pdf

Wissenschaftsrat (2015). *Arbeitsprogramm Januar – Juli 2015, Berlin 30.01.2015, Drs. 4430-15.* Retrieved 15 March 2015 from http://www.wissenschaftsrat.de/download/archiv/Arbeitsprogramm.pdf

Wolter, A. (2011). *Hochschulzugang und soziale Ungleichheit in Deutschland.* In Dossier Öffnung der Hochschule – Chancengleichheit, Diversität, Integration, hrsg. v. Heinrich-Böll-Stiftung. Retrieved 15 March 2015 from https://heimatkunde.boell.de/2011/02/18/hochschulzugang-und-soziale-ungleichheit-deutschland

Prospects for the Economy and Society?
The Issue of Employability and the
Implementation of Inquiry-Based Learning

37

Karsten Speck and Wilfried Schubarth

In this article, we intend to examine the contribution that inquiry-based learning makes to the economy and society based on the report by Schubarth and Speck (2013). We will examine (a) stakeholder interests in the economy, higher education and society, (b) the importance of inquiry-based learning in higher education policy and (c) the implementation of appropriate research and practical offers in institutions of higher learning.

37.1 Participant Interests in Higher Education Policy and Economy/Society

Over the course of the Bologna Process, the term "employability" has become increasingly central to the harmonization of European university education and the common university framework. An important milestone for the further development of the higher education system was the 1999 Bologna Declaration, which called for the introduction of comparable qualifications in Europe, and which justified the need for the employability of European citizens and the international competitiveness of the European higher education system (Bologna-Declaration 1999, p. 3). The German version of the Bologna-declaration (Bologna-Erklärung 1999) refers to "promoting the mobility and labor-market qualification of its citizens" and emphasizes the need for comparable degrees in order to "qualify

K. Speck, Prof. Dr. (✉)
Carl von Ossietzky Universität Oldenburg, Fakultät Bildungs- und Sozialwissenschaften, Institut für Pädagogik, Forschungsmethoden in den Erziehungs- und Bildungswissenschaften, Oldenburg, Germany
e-mail: karsten.speck@uni-oldenburg.de

W. Schubarth, Prof. Dr.
Universität Potsdam, Department Bildungswissenschaften, Professur für Erziehungs- und Sozialisationstheorien, Potsdam, Germany
e-mail: wilschub@uni-potsdam.de

© The Author(s) 2019
H. A. Mieg (ed.), *Inquiry-Based Learning – Undergraduate Research*,
https://doi.org/10.1007/978-3-030-14223-0_37

393

the labor market relevant qualifications of European citizens as well as the international competitiveness of the European higher education system to promote it" (Bologna-Erklärung 1999, p. 2 et seq., translated).

In its 1999 decision on the "Akkreditierung von Studiengängen mit den Abschlüssen Bachelor und Master" ("Accreditation of degree programs with the bachelor's and master's degrees"), the *German Accreditation Council*, which is responsible for quality assurance in the course of studies and in teaching in Germany by means of an accreditation of degree programs, formulated numerous minimum standards for the accreditation of degree programs (Akkreditierungsrat 1999). The requirements were a practical application or practical relevance of the course of study, as well as the employability or professional qualification of the university graduates. Accreditation procedures should "help to increase student mobility and improve international recognition of degrees" (ibid., p. 1). The accreditation agencies should take into consideration the "educational function of the degree program, and the likelihood that the degree can be completed within the projected number of terms, in particular in terms of the employability of the graduates and foreseeable developments in possible professional fields" (ibid., p. 2, translated).

The *German Science Council* (Wissenschaftsrat), which advises the German federal government and state governments, has been regularly and extensively engaged in recent years with (a) the employability of graduates and (b) the relationship between university education and the labor market. In 1999, for example, the German Science Council called for a stronger "discussion by institution of higher learning about problems in development, imparting of knowledge and preservation of employability" (Wissenschaftsrat 1999, p. 5). In 2000, the German Science Council defined three basic goals of academic study: "intellectual development through scholarship, scholarly based employability and the personal development of students" (Wissenschaftsrat 2000, p. 21). In the recommendations on the relationship between a university education and the labor market, the German Science Council assumes that the institutions of higher learning can contribute to the future safeguarding of the potential of skilled workers by "encouraging students to acquire skills-relevant competencies" and promote a broad university education (Wissenschaftsrat 2015, p. 9, translated).

The *German Rector's Conference* (Hochschulrektorenkonferenz, HRK) has dealt with the relationship between academic education and the labor market in many statements. It calls, inter alia, for (a) the further development of study contents with a view to better employability and a stronger integration of interdisciplinary and profession-related competencies in the study (HRK 2005), (b) institutions of higher learning to embrace socializing, action-oriented and character-forming functions, and to promote professional qualification among graduates by imparting key competencies and integrating vocational-field-oriented internships (HRK 2008); and (c) sensitivity on the part of institutions of higher learning for labor market/practice requirements and non-academic or interdisciplinary key qualifications, as well as an implementation of the labor marketability/employability expected by the study reform (HRK 2009).

The *Federal Society of the German Employer Associations* (BDA) has been involved in university policy for many years and criticizes the lack of practical training. The BDA advocates stronger practice orientation in degree programs (e.g. through internships, project-based and problem-based learning) and labor market-related degree programs (BDA 2014, p. 1). In the interest of employability, in a joint memorandum, the BDA, the HRK and the Federation of German Industry (BDI) have called on the institutions of higher learning to: (a) prepare students for a professional occupation in addition to social participation; (b) to apply technical content and methods in the degree programs, (c) to relate the study contents to fields of practice and, at the same time, to impart interdisciplinary and key competencies, (d) to support the development of scientific and labor market-relevant competencies during the course of studies and (e) to impart professional, methodological, social and personal competencies within the degree programs (BDA/HRK/BDI 2008, p. 6 et seq.).

The *German Chamber of Commerce and Industry* (DIHK) has already interviewed several companies about university graduates. The current survey reveals that, above all, companies expect graduates to exhibit a capacity for teamwork (B.A.: 72%; M.A.: 57%), the ability to work independently/self-manage (B.A.: 68%; M.A.: 66%) as well as an ability to analyze and make decisions (B.A.: 67%; M.A.: 68%) (DIHK 2015, pp. 10 and 17). The companies express the expectation (among others) that study material will be more application-oriented and that internships will be more integrated within degree programs (DIHK 2015, pp. 9 and 15). In a 2012 statement, the Chief Human Resource Officers at Leading German Companies also criticized the lack of practice orientation and practical relevance in university study. They advocated for greater practical relevance, longer practice phases of at least 3 months, and the integration of internships into curricula (Personalvorstände führender deutscher Unternehmen, 2012). At the same time, they emphasize the importance of interdisciplinary competencies: "Companies primarily hire well-educated individuals and not formal degrees" (ibid., p. 3, translated).

37.2 The Significance of Inquiry-Based Learning in Higher Education Policy

Parallel to the Bologna Process, inquiry-based learning has gained increased significance at institutions of higher learning, in publications and at conferences (Reiber 2007; Journal Hochschuldidaktik 2009; Ramm et al. 2014). Crucial for this are likely the demands for a professional qualification (B.A.) or a research-oriented degree (M.A.), the increasing research orientation and a third-party orientation in the institutions of higher learning, the limits of traditional teaching in the face of changing learning styles and the lack of compulsory attendance of students, as well as promoting relevant projects through the Teaching Quality Pact.

Compared to employability, inquiry-based learning has thus far only been afforded marginal importance in statements on university policy from the political arena, scientific organizations and employers. In addition to the handouts and conferences of the HRK, the German Science Council (Wissenschaftsrat) in particular has positioned itself repeatedly and in an interdisciplinary manner as being for inquiry-based learning in recent years:

- In 2006, the German Science Council (Wissenschaftsrat) emphasized the special importance of inquiry-based learning for later employment: University education can qualify someone to perform a qualified activity "if, in addition to imparting a constantly renewed canon of knowledge, it aims primarily at proficiency, developing questions independently, dealing systematically with problems, obtaining knowledge in a methodological manner and critically reflecting on fundamental questions" (Wissenschaftsrat 2006, p. 64, translated).
- In a 2008 recommendation, the Science Council noted that insufficient consideration had been given to inquiry-based learning during the reform processes and in teaching and study programs: "The implementation of this approach requires the additional and hitherto unfamiliar measures of counseling, guidance and structuring, but also a new, more binding relationship required between teachers and learners. [...] Teaching and study courses often do not focus on inquiry-based learning to the necessary extent" (Wissenschaftsrat 2008, p. 23, translated).
- In the current recommendations on the relationship between university education and the labor market (2015), the German Science Council (Wissenschaftsrat) points out that, more and more, institutions of higher learning are trying to increase the relevance of their study programs for the labor market (e.g. by means of innovative teaching and learning formats such as inquiry-based learning). Institutions of higher learning have been prompted to further expand inquiry-based learning (Wissenschaftsrat 2015, p. 14). In inquiry-based learning, the German Science Council recognizes "a promising approach that can foster the development of labor market relevant competencies that are relevant for the labor market, especially if it orients itself to practice-relevant issues, and at the same time picks up on the idea of 'education through scholarship'" (ibid., p. 12, translated).

37.3   Implementation of Employability and Inquiry-Based Learning

Finally, the question arises as to what the promotion of employability and the implementation of inquiry-based learning in Germany actually looks like. Due to the focus on other questions, the student survey provides no clear answers; however, it does provide empirical evidence. For example, in the survey, students were asked about practice-relevant and research-related courses offered within their degree programs (Ramm et al. 2014, p. 262 et seq., last updated: 2012/2013 winter semester):

Courses with a Practical Orientation According to the survey, practical relevance is offered less frequently at universities and more frequently at universities of applied sciences. For example, from a student's point of view, practical lectures (19% of universities vs. 34% of universities of applied sciences), courses on practicing practical activities (16% of universities vs. 23% of universities of applied sciences) and practice-oriented projects (13% of universities vs. 28% of universities of applied sciences) are offered to differing degrees in the degree programs. In view of the strong desire for practical relevance in the course of studies, however, a relatively large number of students are not informed about practical offers or deny that such offers exist in their degree programs. The practical relevance and vocational preparation are assessed very differently by the students at universities and universities of applied sciences: At the universities, 21% of students perceive a close practical relevance and 12% a good job preparation in their field of study. All the same, at the universities of applied sciences at least, 59% of students confirm a close practical relevance and 35% confirm good job preparation in their field of study.

Research-Related Courses At the universities, only 11% of students indicate that there are many courses dealing with teaching/learning research or (research-related) project seminars. 32% of students confirm there are few, and 17% confirm there are no courses dealing with teaching/learning research or project seminars. At any rate, 40% of the students do not know whether there are such courses at the universities. The situation is similar at the universities of applied sciences: 12% of students state that there are many courses dealing with teaching/learning research or (research-related) project seminars. 32% of students indicate there are few, and 21% indicate there are no courses dealing with teaching/learning research or project seminars. 35% of students at universities of applied sciences are not informed about whether there are such courses in their degree program. The findings also show: At the beginning of the course of study, there is less research relevance and significantly more students are uninformed about corresponding offers. At the universities, 31% of students attest that their field of study has a strong research orientation in the teaching; at the universities of applied sciences, this is a little less, at 22%. In addition, it has been noticeable that there has been a distinct increase in the research orientation at universities and universities of applied sciences in recent years.

37.4 Summary

It has been shown that the employability of graduates, and a practical and labor-market-relevant education oriented towards such employability, are given a high priority in many statements from higher education policy, scientific organizations and employers. It is also undisputed that, in addition to a practical and labor-market-relevant education in the interests of the economy, institutions of higher learning must also provide a basic academic, technical university education and interdisciplinary personal development (citizenship). Thus, a comprehensive university assignment aims at teaching or acquiring (1) an academic, technical university education, (2) a practical and labor market relevant (education) and (3) interdisciplinary personal development.

In principle, inquiry-based learning offers the opportunity to contribute to this comprehensive university mission. So far, however, inquiry-based learning is more of a marginal topic in higher education policy. The German Science Council, which, in addition to the German Rector's Conference, has dealt more intensively with the topic, considers inquiry-based learning to be a particularly suitable teaching and learning format for fostering labor market-relevant competencies and "education through scholarship" (*Bildung durch Wissenschaft*, e.g. independent development of questions, systematic engagement with problems, obtaining knowledge in a methodological manner, critically reflecting on fundamental questions), since students are actively involved here and an exemplary scientific cognitive process is reproduced. In summary, inquiry-based learning can (still) be established as a problem of meaning in university politics, a problem of theory, a problem of legitimacy and a problem of implementation in Germany (Box 37.1).

Box 37.1: Effects of Inquiry-Based Learning. Discussions on Practice-Relevant Transfer Competencies, Spring/Summer 2015 (Andrea Augsten)

The question is whether those proficiencies, which are promoted through inquiry-based learning in a course of study, are already noticeable in corporate practice. Below are excerpts from four interviews.

Moritz Gekeler worked as a futurologist at Daimler AG, as a lecturer and program manager at the HPI School of Design Thinking and as a design strategist at the SAP Design and Co-Innovation Center. At present, he heads the consulting firm DOLABORATE GmbH.

Angela Haas is a human-centered design expert at Swisscom AG and works on the interface between design and management. She is interested in design thinking in business management, among other things.

Ruth Lassalle is a senior consultant at HRpepper Management Consultants and teaches at Basel University. As a psychologist, she has many years of experience in change and development projects as well as in the field of personnel diagnostics and development.

Andrea Schröter has been the head of HR at Leifheit AG (Nassau/Lahn) since the end of 2012. As a lawyer, she has previously worked for the BASF Group and most recently as director of Global Human Resources at Tridonic GmbH & Co KG (Dornbirn/Austria).

What kind of people do you tend to hire?

Andrea Schröter: For me it is crucial to hire thinking people, regardless of whether this is scientific thinking, philosophical thinking, or both. It is crucial that newcomers to the profession form their opinions independently and freely. We need to get away from an anticipatory obedience and retain independent thinking people, and the autonomy and cognitive freedom in the mind of inquiry-based learning is very good for doing so.

Ruth Lasalle: The handling of complexity and analytical thinking is indispensable in the innovation environment. Career beginners in particular need a high tolerance for dealing with uncertainties and the ability to adapt to an organization and its

(continued)

Box 37.1 (continued)

culture. This can be associated with an intrinsically motivated, questioning attitude. Overall, however, it is questionable whether this ability is promoted solely through inquiry-based learning. In my view, getting to know different contexts and situations is especially important in order to be able to take different perspectives.

Moritz Gekeler: People with excellent expertise and, at the same time, an inquisitive gaze beyond the boundaries of their own discipline; that's exactly what we are looking for. Designing futures requires skills in possibility spaces, dealing with fuzzy goals, and an empathic capacity for communication in order to overcome the boundaries of terminology and personal assumptions.

Angela Haas: The chemistry has to be right. Applicants must be able to think in context and apply facts, insights and behaviors to other areas. This transfer is crucial and it gets noticed!

How important is it to be proficient in communication and teamwork? Does it help to have conducted research yourself?

Angela Haas: It always requires that ability and desire interact with one another. This fundamental idea shapes collaboration in multidisciplinary teams as the basis for innovation. Something new comes out when designers combine their proficiencies with other disciplines; here, designers are often more affine. Within the context of design and research, I see parallels: Both are looking for something new. This can offer added value, especially in interdisciplinary collaboration.

Moritz Gekeler: There are some parallels, but there are differences between scientists and designers: Scientists form hypotheses and try to substantiate or prove them. Designers, on the other hand, constantly design new hypotheses in the design process and design iteratively. If they have this freedom, they use it more intensively than pure scientists, because they want to cut to the chase more.

Ruth Lasalle: In my experience almost every applicant describes themselves as a particularly good team player. That is why it is important to check this in selection situations. Selection procedures which include interviews with situational questions as well as simulations such as role-plays have proven to be successful. For goal-oriented communication, the ability to bring things to the point, as well as developing a sense of what information my counterpart needs, is very important.

Andrea Schröter: We are currently actively working on setting up and integrating teams in which employees from different areas can work together. We want to transform our existing, functional organization into a flexible, drifting structure with project-based teams, at least in part in order to stay competitive. For our young people, this is no problem at all, but with older people, it is necessary to deliberately overstep the boundaries of the department. Career starters do not defend their "territory," but instead see their task, find it exciting, and actively approach people whose proficiencies they need for that task, whether in the company cafeteria or in the parking lot. Inquiry-based learning offers the opportunity to train your own signature (individuality and self-determination).

References

Akkreditierungsrat (1999). Akkreditierung von Akkreditierungsagenturen und Akkreditierung von Studiengängen mit den Abschlüssen Bachelor/Bakkalaureus und Master/Magister – Mindeststandards und Kriterien. Retrieved 29 November 2015 from http://ids.hof.uni-halle.de/documents/t564.htm

Bologna-Declaration (1999). *The Bologna Declaration. Joint declaration of the European ministers of Education.* Retrieved 29 November 2015 from http://www.ond.vlaanderen.be/hogeronderwijs/bologna/documents/mdc/bologna_declaration1.pdf

Bologna-Erklärung (1999). *Der Europäische Hochschulraum. Gemeinsame Erklärung der Europäischen Bildungsminister.* Retrieved 29 November 2015 from http://portal.tugraz.at/portal/page/portal/Files/International/files/formulare_broschueren/Bologna_Erklaerung.pdf

Bundesvereinigung der Deutschen Arbeitgeberverbände (BDA) (2014). *kompakt. Hochschulpolitik.* Retrieved 29 November 2015 from http://www.arbeitgeber.de/www%5Carbeitgeber.nsf/res/kompakt-Hochschulpolitik.pdf/$file/kompakt-Hochschulpolitik.pdf

Bundesvereinigung der Deutschen Arbeitgeberverbände/Bundesverband der Deutschen Industrie & Hochschulrektorenkonferenz (BDA/BDI/HRK) (2008). *Bildung schafft Zukunft. Beschäftigungsfähigkeit von Hochschulabsolventen stärken. Für eine bessere Arbeitsmarktrelevanz des Hochschulstudiums.* Berlin. Retrieved 29 November 2015 from http://www.arbeitgeber.de/www%5Carbeitgeber.nsf/res/72374EDE418466EBC125755A004AC403/$file/Beschaeftigungsfaehigkeit_Hochschulabsolventen.pdf

Deutscher Industrie- und Handelskammertag (DIHK) (2015). *Kompetent und praxisnah – Erwartungen der Wirtschaft an Hochschulabsolventen. Ergebnisse einer DIHK Online-Unternehmensbefragung.* Berlin/Brüssel. Retrieved 29 November 2015 from http://www.dihk.de/ressourcen/downloads/dihk-umfrage-hochschulabsolventen-2015.pdf/at_download/file?mdate=1433751323077

Hochschulrektorenkonferenz (HRK) (2005). *Empfehlung zur Sicherung der Qualität von Studium und Lehre in Bachelor- und Masterstudiengängen.* Retrieved 29 November 2015 from www.hrk.de/uploads/tx_szconvention/Beschluss_Kapazitaeten.pdf

Hochschulrektorenkonferenz (HRK) (2008). *Bologna-Reader III. FAQs – Häufig gestellte Fragen zum Bologna-Prozess an deutschen Hochschulen. Bologna-Zentrum. Beiträge zur Hochschulpolitik 8/2008.* Bonn Retrieved 29 November 2015 from http://hrk.de/fileadmin/redaktion/hrk/02-Dokumente/02-10-Publikationsdatenbank/Beitr-2008-08_BolognaReader_III_FAQs.pdf

Hochschulrektorenkonferenz (HRK) (2009). *Neue Anforderungen an die Lehre in Bachelor- und Master-Studiengängen. Jahrestagung des HRK Bologna-Zentrums.* Beiträge zur Hochschulpolitik 1/2009. Retrieved 29 November 2015 from http://www.hrk-bologna.de/bologna/de/download/dateien/5._Aufl._final.pdf

Journal Hochschuldidaktik (2009). *Forschendes lernen: Perspektiven eines Konzepts. 20 (2).*

Personalvorstände führender deutscher Unternehmen (2012). *Bologna@Germany 2012. 5. Erklärung der Personalvorstände führender deutscher Unternehmen.* Retrieved 29 November 2015 from http://www.arbeitgeber.de/www/arbeitgeber.nsf/res/Bologna@Germany2012.pdf/$file/Bologna@Germany2012.pdf

Ramm, M./Multrus, F./Bargel, T./Schmidt, M. (2014). *Studiensituation und studentische Orientierungen. 12.Studierendensurvey an Universitäten und Fachhochschulen.* Berlin: BMBF-Eigendruck.

Reiber, K. (2007). Grundlegung: Forschendes Lernen als Leitprinzip zeitgemäßer *Hochschulbildung.* Tübinger Beiträge zur Hochschuldidaktik, 1(3). Retrieved 29 November 2015 from http://tobias-lib.uni-tuebingen.de/volltexte/2007/2924/

Schubarth, W./Speck, K. (2013). *Employability und Praxisbezüge im wissenschaftlichen Studium. HRK-Fachgutachten* (ausgearbeitet für die HRK, unter Mitarbeit von Juliane Ulbricht, Ines Dudziak und Brigitta Zylla). Retrieved 29 November 2015 from http://www.hrk-nexus.de/fileadmin/redaktion/hrk-nexus/07-Downloads/07-02-Publikationen/Fachgutachten_Employability.pdf

Wissenschaftsrat (1999). *Stellungnahme zum Verhältnis von Hochschulausbildung und Beschäftigungssystem.* Retrieved 29 November 2015 from http://www.wissenschaftsrat.de/download/archiv/4099-99.pdf

Wissenschaftsrat (2000). *Empfehlungen zur Einführung neuer Studienstrukturen und -abschlüsse (Bakkalaureus/Bachelor – Magister/Master) in Deutschland.* Retrieved 29 November 2015 from http://www.wissenschaftsrat.de/download/archiv/4418-00.pdf

Wissenschaftsrat (2006). *Empfehlungen zur künftigen Rolle der Universitäten im Wissenschaftssystem.* Retrieved 29 November 2015 from *www.wissenschaftsrat.de/download/archiv/7067-06.pdf*

Wissenschaftsrat (2008). *Empfehlungen zur Qualitätsverbesserung von Lehre und Studium.* Retrieved 29 November 2015 from http://www.wissenschaftsrat.de/download/archiv/8639-08.pdf

Wissenschaftsrat (2015). *Empfehlungen zum Verhältnis von Hochschulbildung und Arbeitsmarkt.* Retrieved 29 November 2015 from www.wissenschaftsrat.de/download/archiv/4925-15.pdf

List of Authors

Ahrenholtz, Ingrid, Dr., Carl von Ossietzky Universität Oldenburg, Fakultät für Mathematik und Naturwissenschaften

Albrecht, Luise, Dipl.-Ing., M.Sc., architect, lecturer, Universität Wien

Ambos, Elizabeth L., PhD, US-Council on Undergraduate Research

Augsten, Andrea, PhD Candidate & Design Researcher, University of Wuppertal

Bartkus, Kenneth, PhD, professor, Jon M. Huntsman School of Business, Utah State University

Bartl, Diemut, product design specialist, Dark Horse GmbH, Berlin

Bernhardt, Tobias, MA, Jade Hochschule, Fachbereich Bauwesen Geoinformation Gesundheitstechnologie

Beyrow, Matthias, Prof., Fachhochschule Potsdam, Fachbereich Design

Bihrer, Andreas, Prof. Dr., Christian-Albrechts-Universität zu Kiel, Historisches Seminar, Professur für Geschichte des frühen und hohen Mittelalters sowie für Historische Grundwissenschaften

Bippus, Elke, Prof. Dr., ZHdK Zurich University of the Arts, ith Institute for Critical Theory

Blum, Martin, Prof. Dr. Ph.D., University of Hohenheim, Institute of Zoology, Project director "Humboldt reloaded – research experience right from the start"

Broemel, Roland, Prof. Dr., Goethe-Universität Frankfurt, Fachbereich Rechtswissenschaft, Professor für Öffentliches Recht

Bruhn, Stephan, Dr., Christian-Albrechts-Universität zu Kiel, Historisches Seminar, Professur für Geschichte des frühen und hohen Mittelalters sowie für Historische Grundwissenschaften

Buur, Jacob, Prof., University of Southern Denmark, SDU Design Research, Research Director

Dannemann, Anna, M.Sc., Technische Universität Chemnitz, Fakultät für Human- und Sozialwissenschaften, Institut für Angewandte Bewegungswissenschaften

© The Author(s) 2019
H. A. Mieg (ed.), *Inquiry-Based Learning – Undergraduate Research*,
https://doi.org/10.1007/978-3-030-14223-0

Dehlfing, Anne, MA PH, Universität Bremen, Fachbereich Human- und Gesundheitswissenschaften, Institut für Public Health und Pflegeforschung, Abteilung
Versorgungsforschung

Deicke, Wolfgang, Humboldt-Universität zu Berlin, bologna.lab

Fichten, Wolfgang, Prof. Dr., Carl von Ossietzky Universität Oldenburg – Leiter der
Forschungswerkstatt Schule und LehrerInnenbildung im Didaktischen Zentrum

Fleischer, Jörg, apl. Prof. Dr. Ph.D., Martin Luther University Halle-Wittenberg, Institute
of Biology/Zoology, coordinator "Humboldt reloaded – research experience right from
the start"

Fritz, Fiona, Christian-Albrechts-Universität zu Kiel, Historisches Seminar, Professur für
Geschichte des frühen und hohen Mittelalters sowie für Historische Grundwissenschaften

Gaspar Mallol, Monica, Lic.Phil, ZHdK Zürcher Hochschule der Künste, ith Institut für
Theorie

Gerstenberg, Julia, University of Hohenheim, Project coordination "Humboldt reloaded –
research experience right from the start"

Gess, Christopher, Humboldt-Universität zu Berlin, bologna.lab

Godau, Marion, Prof., Fachhochschule Potsdam, Fachbereich Design

Heidmann, Frank, Prof. Dr., Fachhochschule Potsdam, Fachbereich Design

Hobohm, Hans-Christoph, Prof. Dr., University of Applied Sciences Potsdam, Department
of Information Sciences, Professor for Library and Information Science

Hofhues, Sandra, Jun.-Prof. Dr., Universität zu Köln, Humanwissenschaftliche Fakultät,
Professur für Mediendidaktik/Medienpädagogik

Huber, Ludwig, Prof. em. Dr. Dr. h. c., Universität Bielefeld, Fakultät für
Erziehungswissenschaft

Jungmann, Thorsten, Prof. Dr.-Ing., Fachhochschule Bielefeld, Fachbereich Ingenieurwissenschaften und Mathematik, Professur für Ingenieurwissenschaftliche
Grundlagen und Technikdidaktik

Kaufmann, Margrit E., Dr., Universität Bremen, Wissenschaftliche Expertin für Diversity
der Universitätsleitung und Fachbereich Kulturwissenschaften

Lahn, Ulrike, Dipl. Soz., Fachhochschule Dortmund, Fachbereich Angewandte
Sozialwissenschaften

Langer, Constanze, Prof., Fachhochschule Potsdam, Fachbereich Design

Langemeyer, Ines, Prof. Dr., Karlsruher Institut für Technologie, Institut für Berufspädagogik und Allgemeine Pädagogik/House of Competence, Professur für
Lehr-Lernforschung

Lehmann, Judith, lecturer, Universidad de Buenos Aires, Facultad de Filosofia y Letras;
Universität der Künste Berlin

Maiwald, Christian, Dr. rer. nat., Technische Universität Chemnitz, Fakultät für Human-
und Sozialwissenschaften, Institut für Angewandte Bewegungswissenschaften

Marquard, Markus, Zentrum für Allgemeine Wissenschaftliche Weiterbildung (ZAWiW)
der Universität Ulm

Matthé, Sabine, Carl von Ossietzky Universität Oldenburg, Fakultät für Mathematik und Naturwissenschaften

Matthey, Josefine, Dipl.-Kommunikationswirtin, Projektmanagerin und Synchronsprecherin, Berlin

Meyer, Esther, M.Sc., Leuphana University Lüneburg, Center for Global Sustainability and Cultural Transformation and Methodology Center

Michel, Antje, Prof. Dr., Potsdam University of Applied Sciences, Department of Information Sciences, Professor of Information Didactics & Knowledge Transfer

Mieg, Harald A., Prof. Dr., honorary professor, Humboldt-Universität zu Berlin, Georg-Simmel Center for Metropolitan Studies, director of the national research project on inquiry-based learning in German universities ("ForschenLernen," 2014–2018)

Mozygemba, Kati, Dr., Universität Bremen, Fachbereich Human- und Gesundheitswissenschaften, Institut für Public Health und Pflegeforschung, Abteilung Versorgungsforschung

Müller-Christ, Georg, Prof. Dr., Universität Bremen, Fachbereich Wirtschaftswissenschaft, Fachgebiet Nachhaltiges Management

Muthorst, Olaf, Prof. Dr. iur., Freie Universität Berlin, Fachbereich Rechtswissenschaft

Passon, Jacqueline, Dr., Albert-Ludwigs-Universität Freiburg, Fakultät für Umwelt und Natürliche Ressourcen, Physische Geographie

Pasternack, Peer, Prof. Dr., Martin-Luther-Universität Halle-Wittenberg, Direktor des Instituts für Hochschulforschung an der Universität Halle-Wittenberg (HoF)

Poll, Christian, Dr. Ph.D., University of Hohenheim, Institute of Soil Science and Land Evaluation, coordinator "Humboldt reloaded – research experience right from the start"

Prytula, Michael, Prof. Dr.-Ing., Fachhochschule Potsdam, Institut für angewandte Forschung Urbane Zukunft

Reiber, Karin, Prof. Dr., Hochschule Esslingen, Professur für Erziehungswissenschaft/Didaktik

Reinmann, Gabi, Prof. Dr., Universität Hamburg, Hamburger Zentrum für Universitäres Lehren und Lernen (HUL)

Reis, Oliver, Dr. Dr., Universität Paderborn, Institut für Katholische Theologie, Professur für Religionspädagogik mit dem Schwerpunkt der Inklusion

Riehl, Felix, M.Sc., Technische Universität Chemnitz, Fakultät für Human- und Sozialwissenschaften, Institut für Angewandte Bewegungswissenschaften

Rubel, Katrin, M.A., HWR Berlin School of Economics and Law

Ruf, Andrea, PD Dr., Universität Vechta, Geschäftsführung Fakultät II – Natur- und Sozialwissenschaften

Satilmis, Ayla, Universität Bremen, Fachbereich Kulturwissenschaften, Projekt "enter science"

Schäfer, Thorsten, Prof. Dr. med., Universität Bochum, Medizinische Fakultät, Studiendekan der Medizinischen Fakultät

Schäfer, Ingolf, Dr., Universität Bremen, Fachbereich Mathematik/Informatik

Schelhowe, Heidi, Prof. Dr., Universität Bremen, Technologie-Zentrum Informatik und Informationstechnik

Schlesinger, Johannes, Dr., Geschäftsführer svGeosolutions GmbH, Freiburg

Schliemann, Oliver, Dr., Universität Bielefeld, Abteilung Philosophie

Schmidt-Wenzel, Alexandra, Prof. Dr., Fachhochschule Potsdam, Fachbereich Sozial- und Bildungswissenschaften, Professur für Soziale Arbeit mit dem Schwerpunkt Pädagogik der Lebensalter

Scholl, Margit, Prof. Dr. rer. nat., Technische Hochschule Wildau, Fachbereich Wirtschaft, Informatik, Recht, Professur für Wirtschafts- und Verwaltungsinformatik

Schröder, Tobias, Prof. Dr. Dipl.-Psych., Fachhochschule Potsdam, Institut für angewandte Forschung Urbane Zukunft

Schubarth, Wilfried, Prof. Dr., Universität Potsdam, Department Bildungswissenschaften, Professur für Erziehungs- und Sozialisationstheorien

Selje-Aßmann, Natascha, Dr. Ph.D., University of Hohenheim, Institute of Agricultural Sciences in the Tropics, coordinator "Humboldt reloaded – research experience right from the start"

Speck, Karsten, Prof. Dr., Carl von Ossietzky Universität Oldenburg, Fakultät Bildungs- und Sozialwissenschaften, Institut für Pädagogik, Forschungsmethoden in den Erziehungs- und Bildungswissenschaften

Spies, Anke, Prof. Dr., Carl von Ossietzky Universität Oldenburg, Fakultät Bildungs- und Sozialwissenschaften, Institut für Pädagogik, Professur für Erziehungswissenschaft

Tisler, Matthias Konrad, Dr. Ph.D., University of Hohenheim, Institute of Zoology, coordinator "Humboldt reloaded – research experience right from the start"

Vilsmaier, Ulli, Apl. Prof. Dr., Leuphana University of Lüneburg, Methodology Center and Institute for Ethics and Transdisciplinary Sustainability Research, Interrim Professorship 'Transdisciplinary Methods'

Wessels, Insa, Humboldt-Universität zu Berlin, bologna.lab

Wettach, Reto, Prof., Fachhochschule Potsdam, Fachbereich Design

Wiemer, Matthias, Georg-August-Universität Göttingen, Leitung Hochschuldidaktik

Wulf, Carmen, Dr., Dipl.-Psych., Carl von Ossietzky Universität Oldenburg, Institut für Pädagogik, Fachgruppe Forschungsmethoden in den Erziehungs- und Bildungswissenschaften

Zetzsche, Robert, Dipl.-Soziologe, Technische Universität Chemnitz, Fakultät für Human- und Sozialwissenschaften, Institut für Angewandte Bewegungswissenschaften

Printed by Printforce, the Netherlands